372

VIGILANCE AND RESTRAINT IN THE COMMON LAW OF JUDICIAL REVIEW

The mediation of the balance between vigilance and restraint is a fundamental feature of judicial review of administrative action in the Anglo-Commonwealth. This balance is realised through the modulation of the depth of scrutiny when reviewing the decisions of ministers, public bodies and officials. While variability is ubiquitous, it takes different shapes and forms. Dean R. Knight explores the main shapes and forms employed in judicial review in England, Canada, Australia and New Zealand over the last fifty years. Four schemata are drawn from the case law and taken back to conceptual foundations, exposing their commonality and differences. Each approach is evaluated. This detailed methodology provides a sound basis for decisions and debates about how variability should be brought to individual cases and will be of great value to legal scholars, judges and practitioners interested in judicial review.

DEAN R. KNIGHT is Senior Lecturer in the Faculty of Law and Co-Director of the New Zealand Centre for Public Law at Victoria University of Wellington. His scholarly interests include a wide range of topics in constitutional and administrative law, including judicial review and local democracy.

CAMBRIDGE STUDIES IN CONSTITUTIONAL LAW

The aim of this series is to produce leading monographs in constitutional law. All areas of constitutional law and public law fall within the ambit of the series, including human rights and civil liberties law, administrative law, as well as constitutional theory and the history of constitutional law. A wide variety of scholarly approaches is encouraged, with the governing criterion being simply that the work is of interest to an international audience. Thus, works concerned with only one jurisdiction will be included in the series as appropriate, while, at the same time, the series will include works which are explicitly comparative or theoretical – or both. The series editor likewise welcomes proposals that work at the intersection of constitutional and international law, or that seek to bridge the gaps between civil law systems, the US, and the common law jurisdictions of the Commonwealth.

Series Editors

David Dyzenhaus, *Professor of Law and Philosophy, University of Toronto, Canada*

Editorial Advisory Board

VIGILANCE AND RESTRAINT IN THE COMMON LAW OF JUDICIAL REVIEW

DEAN R. KNIGHT

Victoria University of Wellington

CAMBRIDGE
UNIVERSITY PRESS

University Printing House, Cambridge CB2 8BS, United Kingdom

One Liberty Plaza, 20th Floor, New York, NY 10006, USA

477 Williamstown Road, Port Melbourne, VIC 3207, Australia

314–321, 3rd Floor, Plot 3, Splendor Forum, Jasola District Centre, New Delhi – 110025, India

79 Anson Road, #06-04/06, Singapore 079906

Cambridge University Press is part of the University of Cambridge.

It furthers the University's mission by disseminating knowledge in the pursuit of
education, learning, and research at the highest international levels of excellence.

www.cambridge.org
Information on this title: www.cambridge.org/9781107190245
DOI: 10.1017/9781108100007

First published 2017

Printed in the United Kingdom by Clays, St Ives plc

A catalogue record for this publication is available from the British Library.

Library of Congress Cataloging-in-Publication Data

Names: Knight, Dean R. (Dean Robert), author.
Title: Vigilance and restraint in the common law of judicial review / Dean R.
    Knight.
Description: New York : Cambridge University Press, 2018. | Series: Cambridge
    studies in constitutional law ; 19 | Includes bibliographical references
    and index.
Identifiers: LCCN 2017058817 | ISBN 9781107190245 (hardback)
Subjects: LCSH: Judicial review. | Common law.
Classification: LCC K3175 .K65 2018 | DDC 347/.012—dc23 LC record available
    at https://lccn.loc.gov/2017058817

ISBN 978-1-107-19024-5 Hardback

for aleni

CONTENTS

CASES

A *v.* Secretary of State for the Home Department [2004] QB 335
A *v.* Secretary of State for the Home Department [2005] 2 AC 68
Adlam *v.* Stratford Racing Club Inc [2007] NZAR 543
Air Nelson Ltd *v.* Minister of Transport [2007] NZAR 266
Air Nelson Ltd *v.* Minister of Transport [2008] NZAR 139
Air New Zealand Ltd *v.* Wellington International Airport Ltd [2009] NZAR 138
Ala *v.* Secretary of State for the Home Department [2003] All ER (D) 283
Alberta (Information and Privacy Commissioner) *v.* Alberta Teachers' Association [2011]
  3 SCR 654
Andary *v.* Minister of Immigration and Multicultural Affairs [2003] FCAFC 211
Anisminic Ltd *v.* Foreign Compensation Commission [1969] 2 AC 147
Ashby *v.* Minister of Immigration [1981] 1 NZLR 222
Associated Provincial Picture Houses Ltd *v.* Wednesbury Corporation [1948] 1 KB 223
Attorney-General *v.* Problem Gambling Foundation of New Zealand [2017] 2 NZLR 470
Attorney-General (NSW) *v.* Quin (1990) 170 CLR 1
Attorney-General *v.* De Keyser's Royal Hotel Ltd [1920] AC 508
Attorney-General *v.* Steelfort Engineering Co Ltd (1999) 1 NZCC 61,030
Austin, Nichols & Co Inc *v.* Stichting Lodestar [2008] 2 NZLR 141
Australian Broadcasting Tribunal *v.* Bond (1990) 170 CLR 321
B *v.* Commissioner of Inland Revenue [2004] 2 NZLR 86
Baker *v.* Canada (Minister of Citizenship and Immigration) [1999] 2 SCR 817
Bank Mellat *v.* Her Majesty's Treasury (No 2) [2014] 1 AC 700
Bato Star Fishing Ltd *v.* Chief Director of Marine Coastal Management (2004) 4 SA 490
Belfast City Council *v.* Miss Behavin' Ltd [2007] 1 WLR 1420
BNZ Investments Ltd *v.* Commissioner of Inland Revenue (2007) 23 NZTC 21
Boddington *v.* British Transport Police [1999] 2 AC 143
Brierley Investments Ltd *v.* Bouzaid [1993] 3 NZLR 655
Bromley London Borough Council *v.* Greater London Council [1983] AC 768
Brown *v.* Stott [2003] 1 AC 681
Bruce *v.* Cole (1998) 45 NSWLR 163
Bulk Gas Users Group Ltd *v.* Attorney-General [1983] NZLR 129
Burmah Oil Company (Burma Trading) Ltd *v.* Lord Advocate [1965] AC 75
Canada (Attorney-General) *v.* Canadian Human Rights Commission [2013] FCA 75

ACKNOWLEDGEMENTS

This book started its life as a thesis completed at the London School of Economics and Political Science. I am indebted to those who helped and provided support during the completion of the thesis and this subsequent book.

I am very grateful to Tom Poole and Martin Loughlin for their rich scholarly advice and guidance during my time writing the thesis at the London School of Economics. I also valued the collegial support from my doctoral cohort – Aleks Bojovic, Megan Pearson, Sally-Anne Way, Sinead Agnew and Yaniv Roznai. I acknowledge the helpful feedback from David Dyzenhaus and Richard Rawlings during the examination process, as well as the comments from three anonymous referees during the commissioning phase of this book.

Numerous others provided inspiration, feedback and advice: thanks to Mark Bennett, Eddie Clark, Shaunnagh Dorsett, Ned Djordevic, Conor Gearty, Claudia Geiringer, Mark Hickford, Sasha Holden, Julie McCandless, Geoff McLay, Nicole Moreham, Linda Mulcahy, Nicole Roughan, Rick Snell, Chris Thomas, Rayner Thwaites, Grégoire Webber and Hanna Wilberg, along with others at Victoria University of Wellington and the London School of Economics.

Thanks to Luke Archer, William Hayter, Alex Ladyman, Conrad Reyners and Joel Rowan for research and other assistance. Thanks also to Hamish Clayton and Heather Palomino for their copy-editing of the thesis and manuscript respectively. I am grateful to Finola O'Sullivan, David Morris and others at Cambridge University Press who shepherded this book through the production process.

I greatly appreciated the support of my family, including my father and late mother, particularly while I was completing the thesis abroad. I am especially indebted to my partner, Alan, who shared the many ups-and-downs of this journey; I have been blessed by his love and support, for which I am deeply grateful.

Mike Taggart, who encouraged me on this path, spoke about administrative law as 'the space where the state (and its emanations) and the citizen/subject/rights-bearing individual come into contact – and sometimes clash – and the maintenance of a relatively free and democratic society depends on the fair and orderly resolution of disputes.' Urging us to map the growth of administrative law theory and doctrine, he continued: 'Understanding the ideas that have shaped those encounters enables us to better shape our future.'

To all those who have supported me during this modest attempt at some cartography, I am very grateful. Kia ora, fa'afetai lava, thank you.

Wellington,
July 2017

1

Introduction

1.1 Vigilance and Restraint:
the Variation of the Depth of Scrutiny

One of the key features of the system of judicial review is the variation of the depth of scrutiny by the supervising court when examining administrative decisions. The circumstances of different cases lead to different emphases being drawn between the competing notions of judicial vigilance and restraint.[1] But the *manner* in which this balance is mediated and the depth of scrutiny is modulated differs across time and across jurisdictions. This book examines the methodologies used to vary the depth of scrutiny in English and other Anglo-Commonwealth (Australia, New Zealand and Canada) systems of judicial review over the last 50 years or so.[2]

In this book I identify four schemata which are employed to organise the modulation of the depth of scrutiny:

(a) *scope of review*, based on an array of formalistic categories which determine whether judicial intervention is permissible;[3]
(b) *grounds of review*, based on a simplified and generalised set of grounds of intervention;[4]
(c) *intensity of review*, based on explicit calibration of the depth of scrutiny taking into account a series of constitutional, institutional and functional factors;[5] and

---

[1] For the adopted language of 'vigilance' and 'restraint', see Michael Fordham, 'Surveying the Grounds' in Peter Leyland and Terry Woods (eds.), *Administrative Law Facing the Future* (Blackstone, 1997) and Michael Fordham, *Judicial Review Handbook* (6th edn, Hart Publishing, 2012), [P14].
[2] See text to n. 60 for extended discussion of the territorial scope of this book, along with an explanation of the jurisdictional descriptors used.
[3] See Chapter 2.
[4] See Chapter 3.
[5] See Chapter 4.

(d) *contextual review*, based on an unstructured (and sometimes instinctive) overall judgement about whether to intervene according to the
circumstances of the case.[6]

These four schemata – loosely drawn from the language and structure
of Professor Stanley de Smith's acclaimed judicial review textbook as
it changed over its seven editions – provide structure for the study. For
each of the schemata, doctrinal, theoretical and normative dimensions are
examined.

The *doctrinal* dimension demonstrates that modulation of the depth of
scrutiny is ubiquitous in the Anglo-Commonwealth family of common
law jurisdictions.[7] The manner in which it manifests itself, however, is
not constant or uniform; I identify the different ways the variation of the
depth of scrutiny has been organised and given effect – distilling the four
schemata described above. De Smith's textbook on judicial review is used
to frame this doctrinal study; as well as employing the language seen in
the textbook over time to mark the different methodologies, the doctrinal
study echoes the subject-matter, comparative approach and life-time of de
Smith's textbook.

When identifying the different schemata, I describe the basic character of the different approaches and identify where these approaches are,
or have been, deployed. While each method can be seen in a number of
jurisdictions at different times, some associations of varying strength are
identified. Australia remains strongly committed to the formalistic scope
of review approach that was historically applied in English administrative
law. English law today still founds itself on a grounds of review approach,
but there is some pressure towards the more circumstantial approaches of
intensity of review and contextual review particularly when human rights
are engaged. Grounds of review also have strong currency in New Zealand,
but the preference for methodological simplicity means contextual review
also finds strong favour. Canada has long rejected approaches based on
doctrinal categories or grounds and the modulation of the depth of scrutiny assumes a central role. However, the way in which the deferential forms
of review have been expressed, in contradiction to correctness review, has
varied between variegated forms of reasonableness (intensity of review) or
a simplified, umbrella form of reasonableness where the depth of scrutiny
implicitly floats according to the circumstances (contextual review).

---

[6] See Chapter 5.
[7] See further Section 1.2.

The *conceptual* dimension turns to the conceptual foundation and justification for each schemata.[8] Doctrinal diversity is matched by conceptual diversity: scholars support different approaches to the mediation of the balance between vigilance and restraint. Through the lens of the debate on the constitutional underpinnings of judicial review, I draw out the relationship between the manner in which the depth of review is modulated and the constitutional dynamics of judicial review generally, that is, whether the work of judges on judicial review is mandated by reference to legislative intent (the ultra vires school) or independently by the common law (the common law school). By seeking to associate a number of scholars with the different schemata I have identified, I seek to illuminate the conceptual basis of the schemata by inquiring into the scholars' attitudes about the relationship between the administration, legislature and the courts.

A number of general points are evident. The scope of review approach is favoured by formalists, who tend to support ultra vires as the constitutional justification of judicial review. They emphasise a strong linkage between judicial methodology and legislative mandate, and seek to minimise judicial discretion. Those supporting the grounds of review schema tend to be aligned with the common law school. They demonstrate more faith in the judicial role and are more open to normative argument by judges. However, they show a preference for substantive values to be translated into the architecture of judicial review doctrine, rather than deployed without structure or constraint. The intensity of review schema garners support from some in the ultra vires school. In a concession to the problems associated with the line-drawing of categorical approaches, a more open-textured approach based on the balancing of competing factors is supported. The overarching emphasis on legislative intent remains but, rather than effected indirectly through doctrinal proxies, it assumes a key role in the explicit calibration of the depth of review. Contextual review is anathema to those from the ultra vires school; it only finds support from some in the common law school or from those who seek to stand outside the ultra vires–common law contest. The centrality of judicial discretion to the contextual review method means those supporting it promote a rarefied role for judges within the constitutional order.

Thus, the different schools of thought on the constitutional underpinnings debate do not map neatly onto the different schemata for modulation

---

[8] See further Section 1.3.

of the depth of scrutiny. But some conceptual patterns relating to the nature of institutional relationships within the administrative system can be identified.

Finally, the *normative* dimension evaluates the efficacy and virtue of each schema, assessing their strengths and weaknesses as mechanisms for mediating the balance between vigilance and restraint.[9] I employ Fuller's principles of legality/efficacy to guide this normative enquiry: generality, accessibility, prospectivity, clarity, stability, non-contradiction, non-impossibility, and congruence (with hortatory versatility added too). These principles are a useful means to interrogate the nature of power possessed by the courts in the supervisory jurisdiction and to assess the virtue of the different ways they modulate that power, through the variation of the depth of scrutiny.

While the principles are not intended to operate as a summative checklist to determine an ideal-type schema, a number of more general conclusions are drawn. The scope of review schema tends to harness a two-track style. While ostensibly delivering the rule-structure encouraged by Fuller, closer analysis reveals latent judicial discretion and strong potential for doctrinal manipulation. Thus, its performance against most criteria is weaker than is apparent, particularly due to a lack of congruence between the expression and application of the rules and an overall lack of clarity and coherence. At the other end of the spectrum, contextual review's rejection of doctrinal structure in favour of judicial judgement and instinct means it performs poorly against most criteria. The grounds and intensity of review schemata both perform admirably against Fuller's virtues, although emphasising different qualities. The distinction between the two turns on the extent to which calibration of the depth of review takes place directly, through a judgement based on enumerated conceptual factors, or indirectly, through the animation of doctrinal categories and vacillation between them. Notably, the doctrine–discretion dynamic is manifested differently. None performs perfectly, given the various trade-offs involved. However, the analysis allows us to recognise the strengths and weaknesses of the different schemata when deliberating on appropriate forms of mediating the balance between vigilance and restraint.

In the sections that follow I outline my general approach in expanded detail. I explain more fully each of the analytical dimensions – doctrinal, conceptual and normative – and justify the methodology I adopt for each.

---

[9] See further Section 1.4.

1.2   Doctrinal Manifestation: Organisational Schemata and Trends

Variability has been an ever-present feature of judicial review method. While it may seem elementary, my study of the last half century or so seeks to put that proposition beyond doubt. The inherent variability of the supervisory jurisdiction is sometimes lost sight of, as administrative law discourse reacts adversely to particular doctrinal manifestations of variability.

Deference: 'That's a dreadful word', says New Zealand's Chief Justice.[10]

Anxious scrutiny: '[J]udges devise catch-phrases devoid of legal meaning', a judge of the UK's Supreme Court complains, 'in order to describe concepts which they are unwilling or unable to define.'[11]

Variegated standards of unreasonableness: An experience 'marked by ebbs and flows of deference, confounding tests and new words for old problems', cautions Canadian Supreme Court judges, 'but no solutions that provide real guidance for litigants, counsel, administrative decision makers or judicial review judges.'[12]

Jurisdictional and non-jurisdictional error: '[T]he old insistence upon preserving the chimerical distinction between jurisdictional and non-jurisdictional error of law might be interred, without tears', encourages an Australian High Court judge.[13]

These remarks, all from judges drawn from final appellate courts in the Anglo-Commonwealth, provide some insight into the strength of feeling exhibited towards some of the doctrines which have played key roles in modulating the depth of scrutiny in judicial review. A similar set of pejorative comments from scholars, lawyers and bureaucrats could readily be recited. The animated discourse about these doctrines, along with uncomplimentary views about the labels ascribed to them, suggest the modulation of the depth of review in judicial review remains controversial.

The first part of the chapters that follow is devoted to a close study of the key doctrines in judicial review across the Anglo-Commonwealth over the last half-century. As well as demonstrating that variability is commonplace, the purpose is to elicit how the variation of the depth of

---

[10] *Ye v. Minister of Immigration* (NZSC, transcript, 21–23 April 2009, SC53/2008) 179 (Elias CJ).

[11] Lord Sumption, 'Anxious Scrutiny' (ALBA annual lecture, London, November 2014) 1.

[12] *Dunsmuir v. New Brunswick* [2008] 1 SCR 190 (Bastarache and LeBel JJ) [1].

[13] *Re Minister for Immigration and Multicultural Affairs; ex parte Miah* (2000) 179 ALR 238, [212] (Kirby J).

scrutiny has been differently expressed and the schematic nature of the methodologies associated with that variation. The trends over time are captured, as mentioned earlier, by an analysis of the language, structure and organising principles in de Smith's distinguished textbook, *Judicial Review of Administrative Action*.[14] De Smith's textbook, while not assuming any exalted function in judicial review, provides a series of cues about the nature of the system of judicial review it expounds. It is a convenient entry-point for the examination of Anglo-Commonwealth judicial review doctrine because it adopts a similar style and set of parameters to my study in this book (points I explain in more detail shortly).

Over its seven editions, de Smith's textbook contains a subtle linguistic change in the way in which the supervisory jurisdiction is explained and its principles organised. This study draws out the key shifts as they relate to the modulation of the depth of scrutiny. Most notably, the nomenclature adopted to denominate much of the nature and circumstances of judicial intervention has changed over time: from 'scope of review' to 'grounds of review' to – perhaps, at least formatively – 'intensity of review'. Hinted at, but not yet prominently recognised, is a form of 'contextual review'.

The change in nomenclature, I argue, is not merely linguistic. The evolution in the denomination of judicial intervention speaks to change in the underlying style of review. The organisational transition – from scope to grounds to intensity, along with some limited recognition of context – points to a move away from legal formalism and categorical approaches towards more open-textured and explicitly circumstantial approaches. The linguistic developments are, I suggest, helpful to mark out the different judicial review methodologies and schemata employed over time and throughout the Anglo-Commonwealth, at least in general terms. The various schemata represent different ways to organise and execute the supervisory task. And, importantly, different ways to mediate the balance between restraint and vigilance. Each schema provides distinct ways to modulate the depth of scrutiny to take account of context and the limitations of judicial supervision.

Some care needs to be taken in relation to the definition of these schemata, however. They are constructed in order to capture the dominant methodologies operating in systems of judicial review at different times and in different places. Thus, I construct these schemata recognising a

---

[14] De Smith, *Judicial Review of Administrative Action* (1st edn–7th edn, Stevens/Sweet & Maxwell, 1959–2013). The textbook is referred to as 'de Smith', along with the appropriate edition number.

number of limitations in the way they sketch the doctrine they describe. First, they are necessarily generalised précis, limited in the extent to which they can capture the vast and nuanced doctrines existing at any point in time. But the value lies in capturing the essence and emphasis of the different approaches. Secondly, there is some overlap between the given schema and instances where underlying doctrines could plausibly be categorised under multiple schemata. Judgements have been required in a number of situations; I have tried to address the doctrine under the schema which is most emblematic of the underlying methodology and explained my basis for doing so. Thirdly, in some cases, behind the prevalent methodology, some elements of the other approaches may also be seen. This might arise due to a degree of doctrinal diversity within the jurisdiction. Alternatively, in some cases, courts may employ a blend of styles; for example, it is possible that a more formalised scope of review style might be adopted for preliminary matters such as amenability to review, while the heart of the supervision is conducted with a grounds or intensity of review style. Or, for example, in a jurisdiction principally employing a grounds of review approach, aspects of intensity of review or contextual review may appear in a subsidiary way, within particular grounds of review. However, this diversity or blending does not compromise the analysis. A project with these parameters necessarily has a meta-level focus. The key concern is the dominant style and the nature of the methods that are foregrounded in the judicial analysis; inevitably, the schemata are not watertight compartments. The distinctive aspects are captured in my study; outlying instances do not undermine the definition of the emblematic judicial style.

The organisational framework for the doctrinal study, and ultimately the book as a whole, is drawn, as mentioned, from de Smith's textbook. The parameters of the study – subject-matter, timeframe and comparative focus – are cast relatively broadly, echoing the parameters of de Smith's textbook and taking into account the meta-perspective adopted. Below, I rationalise the reliance on de Smith's work and justify the parameters employed for the doctrinal study. In doing so, I explain how my treatment engages with existing scholarship and how this book makes an original contribution.

Organisational Framework: De Smith's Textbook on Judicial Review

The employment of de Smith to frame and organise the doctrinal study is useful in a schematic project of this kind. Judges are situated actors, called on to focus on individual cases. Under the common law style of reasoning, they rarely address the architecture of the system of judicial review or turn their attention to the overarching schema.[15] As Galligan explains, the courts 'rarely make efforts to draw out the generalised features of their decisions' or 'attempt to construct a pattern of interlocking rules'; instead, 'each decision is largely a fresh exercise of discretion according to the variables of the situation'.[16] Administrative law textbook writers therefore have an important and palpable structuring and organising role. Taggart recognised the value of studying textbooks in order to chart an intellectual history of a discipline: 'textbooks [allow] us to draw textual and contextual pictures, and to identify significant events and changing concepts'.[17] Further, the assistance of a textbook makes this project possible. While I pay close attention to an extensive corpus of case law across the jurisdictions, the identification and tracing of general schematic trends sometimes requires a degree of approximation that can only be filled by reference to secondary, not primary, sources. It is simply not feasible otherwise. Indeed, the cataloguing project undertaken by de Smith represented a doctorate in its own right. Hence, reliance on secondary sources is, in some cases, essential to generate schemata, in order that the theoretical and normative dimensions of the schema can also be examined.

De Smith's textbook is, in particular, especially suitable for this task. Its *lifespan*, definition of *subject-matter*, *comparative focus*, *style* of exposition and overall *standing* mean it provides a convenient foundation for the doctrinal study.

First, the *lifespan* of de Smith's textbook is just over a half-century, with seven editions published between 1959 and 2013. Although the authorship, structure and organisational language changed over that period, de Smith's original style was retained throughout. The original edition was a published version of a PhD thesis completed at the London School of Economics and Political Science in 1959.[18] De Smith completed one further edition while occupying the Chair in Public Law at the LSE (1968) and another while holding the Downing Professorship of the Laws of

---

[15] Lord Diplock's seminal speech in *Council of Civil Service Unions* v. *Minister for the Civil Service* [1985] AC 374 (*CCSU*) and the Supreme Court of Canada's landmark decision in *Dunsmuir*, above n. 12, are two obvious exceptions.

[16] D.J. Galligan, 'Judicial Review and the Textbook Writers' (1982) 2 OJLS 257, 268.

[17] Michael Taggart, 'Prolegomenon to an Intellectual History of Administrative Law in the Twentieth Century' (2005) 43 Osgoode Hall LJ 223, 228.

[18] S.A. de Smith, *Judicial Review of Administrative Action: A Study in Case Law* (PhD thesis, London School of Economics and Political Science, 1959).

England at Cambridge University (1973).[19] After de Smith's death in 1974, the fourth edition was updated by John Evans (1980), an academic who went onto a distinguished career at Osgoode Hall Law School and later served on the Canadian Federal Court of Appeal.[20] The first four editions of de Smith's text are very similar in character, continuing de Smith's original structure and style throughout.

The fifth edition of de Smith's text (1995) was subject to substantial restructuring and rewriting.[21] Most obviously, the text was rewritten under new guardianship: Lord Woolf and Professor Jowell took over as authors.[22] The production of the fifth edition also followed a vigorous period of change within English judicial review.[23] No longer was judicial review, as de Smith famously described it, 'sporadic and peripheral';[24] instead, Woolf and Jowell argued that 'the effect of judicial review on the practical exercise of power has now become constant and central'.[25] Regardless of the restructuring and rewriting of the text, Woolf and Jowell attempted to remain faithful to de Smith's original style.[26] De Smith's method of crystallising a line of cases into a series of propositions remained, as did the commitment to a broad corpus of case law (both historic and international, particularly from the Commonwealth).[27]

The sixth edition of the text (2007) was published over a decade after the fifth edition.[28] It contained some significant changes, driven by changes within the system of judicial review.[29] The emblematic change was the revision of the title of the text, with 'Judicial Review' standing solitary without its former 'of Administrative Action' counterpart; this recognised a slightly broader focus also incorporating judicial review of legislation in

---

[19] 'Professor S.A. de Smith' (1974) 33 CLJ 177 (obituary) and 'Professor S.A. de Smith' (1974) 37 MLR 241 (obituary).

[20] 'The Honourable John Maxwell Evans': www.justice.gc.ca.

[21] De Smith (5th edn), vii.

[22] *Ibid.* Woolf and Jowell were assisted in the 5th edition by Andrew le Sueur.

[23] *Ibid.*, specifically noting the dramatic change. In the subsequent edition, Woolf, Jowell and le Sueur described the 1980s and early 1990s as involving a large increase in applications, increased 'sophistication' in grounds and judicial reasoning, and 'burgeoning academic literature': de Smith (6th edn), v.

[24] De Smith (5th edn), vii.

[25] *Ibid.*

[26] *Ibid.*, vii–viii.

[27] *Ibid.*, viii.

[28] De Smith (6th edn), v. A supplement was published 1998: de Smith (5th edn, suppl.).

[29] *Ibid.*, v–vi.

some situations.[30] There was also a minor change to the panel of authors, with Andrew Le Sueur joining Woolf and Jowell as a joint author.[31] The seventh, and current, edition (2013) was published six years after the sixth.[32] The final edition follows the same format and style as the sixth, largely enlarging aspects of the commentary and references.

Secondly, the definition of the parameters of the textbook – its *subject* and *comparative* focus – is consistent with the general focus of this book. De Smith's focus was conveyed by the original title: 'Judicial Review of Administrative Action' (while the title of recent editions has been truncated, the principal focus on the role of judges in the traditional administrative law domain remains). This focus on supervision of administrative decision-making, broadly defined, is echoed in this book.[33] The textbook is principally focused on English administrative law but also draws on Commonwealth case law. De Smith explained in the original edition: 'On some ... matters we shall be able to find strong persuasive authority in the decisions of courts in Commonwealth countries'.[34] This practice continued through the editions which followed.[35] The current authors record their continuing commitment to 'refer to the experience of other jurisdictions ... without any pretence at creating a work of comparative law'.[36] This comparative focus coincides with the comparative brief of this study and my concern with the judicial methodology within a broader common law of judicial review.

Thirdly, the textbook's *style of exposition* was analytical and almost scientific in character. 'It is about "the law" and touches only occasionally on the prophets.'[37] De Smith was generally content to catalogue and describe the law as it was. 'By gathering in the cases so assiduously,' Harlow remarks, 'in some sense [he] petrified the law, preserving it, like amber,

---

[30] *Ibid.*, vii. The authors preferred the term 'public functions'. The rise of human rights and impact of European Community law led to primary legislation being brought into the province of judicial review and thus ambit of the text expanded slightly.

[31] Catherine Donnelly joined the 6th edition as an assistant editor.

[32] De Smith (7th edn). Catherine Donnelly and Ivan Hare joined the editorial panel. A further supplement was published in 2009: de Smith (6th edn, suppl.).

[33] See text to n. 46.

[34] De Smith (1st edn), 25.

[35] In later editions, this non-English case law was grouped under the heading 'Comparative Perspectives', with Canada, New Zealand, and Australia featuring prominently.

[36] De Smith (7th edn), vi.

[37] J.A.G. Griffith (1960) 18 CLJ 228 (book review), 229.

with all its impurities.'[38] His views were incisive but subdued; as Williams observed, 'de Smith did not offer criticism in strident tones; he accepted the law as it stood and his criticisms and comments ... are gently integrated into the discussions'.[39] That tradition continued throughout the first four editions, including the edition edited by Evans. The passing of the editorship to Woolf and Jowell in the fifth edition and significant restructuring perhaps signalled a more normative turn. However, the hallmarks of de Smith's style continue to dominate. Indeed, in the seventh edition, the editors avowed their ongoing commitment to 'meticulous coverage of the case law' and 'elucidation of principle' that made the textbook distinctive.[40] This tradition makes it more suitable for a doctrinal study than some of the other long-serving textbooks in the field, such as the administrative law textbooks written by Wade and Craig.[41] For example, Craig tends to adopt a more normative style and emphasis. Wade's textbook, while assuming similar standing to de Smith's, tends to more heavily reflect the predilections of the original (and successor) author(s) and lacks the analytical elegance of de Smith.[42]

Finally, the textbook has particular *standing*: it is one of the most distinguished textbooks on judicial review in the Anglo-Commonwealth.[43]

---

[38] Carol Harlow, 'Politics and Principles' (1981) 44 MLR 113, 115. See also Galligan, above n. 16, 268 ('a book for someone who wants to know what the law is'); Louis L. Jaffe (1961) 74 Harv LR 636 (book review), 636.

[39] D.G.T. Williams (1974) 33 CLJ 324 (book review), 325.

[40] De Smith (7th edn), vi.

[41] William Wade and Christopher Forsyth, *Administrative Law* (1st edn–11th edn, Oxford University Press 1961–2014); P.P. Craig, *Administrative Law* (1st edn–8th edn, Sweet & Maxwell, 1983–2016).

[42] See e.g. Galligan, above n. 16; Martin Loughlin, 'The Pathways of Public Law Scholarship' in G.P. Wilson (ed.), *Frontiers of Legal Scholarship* (Wiley, 1995), 163, 169 fn. 31.

[43] O. Hood Phillips (1960) 23 MLR 458 (book review) ('indispensable'; 'may already be described as a standard textbook on the subject'); Griffith, above n. 37 ('comprehensive scholarship'; '[n]o comparable book on this aspect of English law exists'; 'immeasurably the best book on its subject or any part of it'); Jaffe, above n. 38 ('accepted in England as first-rate and definitive'; 'admirable instrument'); G. Ganz (1969) 32 MLR 116 (book review) ('could not be bettered'; the textbook's 'depth of analysis, breadth of scholarship, unfailing accuracy and fluency of style are beyond praise'); D.G.T. Williams (1974) 33 CLJ 324 (book review) ('unquestionably one of the great legal works of the twentieth century'); Harlow, above n. 38 ('classic text'; 'admirably thorough'; 'work of immense scholarship'; 'paramount position as the standard work of reference for scholars'); Galligan, above n. 16 (together with Wade's textbook, 'the dominant influences on the development of administrative law in modern Britain'); Cosmo Graham (1995) 3 EPL 150 (book review) ('it is the best, most authoritative, book on judicial review in England'); Patrick Birkinshaw (2009) 15 EPL 279 (book review) ('priceless value and inestimable importance'); Sir John Laws [1996] JR 49

De Smith's 'work in administrative law', one of his obituaries noted, 'has been of seminal significance in the development of the principles of judicial review by courts throughout the Commonwealth'.[44] Indeed, the textbook is famous for being the first substantial text with a focus on the judicial review of administrative action and is often accorded the tribute of legitimising the field of study.[45]

Subject-matter: Judicial Review
of Administrative Action

This doctrinal study, and book generally, explores the mediation of vigilance and restraint through the variation of the depth of scrutiny across the full ambit of judicial review of administrative action. It covers the judicial supervision of decisions of ministers, officials, public bodies and others subject to judicial review and not just in particular sectors of administrative law.[46] As noted above, this ambit echoes the coverage of de Smith's textbook.

A number of caveats to this broad approach: first, I acknowledge that judicial review is only one feature of administrative law and not necessarily the most prevalent mechanism for addressing grievances against the administration.[47] However, judicial review still has a pre-eminent status within administrative law; its formal role garners particular attention, especially in administrative law scholarship. Further, judicial review has a hortatory function, where the principles generated in the system resonate through the balance of the administrative law sphere.[48]

(book review) ('enormously scholarly'; 'text of major importance'; 'truly excellent quality'); Fordham, *Judicial Review Handbook*, above n. 1, [11.2.3] (one of the 'leading textbook commentaries').

[44] 'Professor S.A. de Smith', above n. 19.

[45] Griffith, above n. 37; Hood Phillips, above n. 43; Harlow, above n. 38.

[46] Compare e.g. Jaime Arancibia, *Judicial Review of Commercial Regulation* (Oxford University Press, 2011); Piers von Berg (ed.), *Criminal Judicial Review* (Hart Publishing, 2014); Richard Moules, *Environmental Judicial Review* (Hart Publishing, 2011).

[47] For justification of a similar approach, see de Smith (7th edn), 8. De Smith famously described judicial review as 'inevitably sporadic and peripheral' (de Smith (1st edn), 3). More recent editions cast the effect of judicial review in more significant terms: (de Smith (5th edn), vii, 19 (its influence is now 'constant and central'; 'caution is now needed before relegating judicial review to a minor role'); de Smith (6th edn), 4 and (7th edn), 8 ('principles developed through judicial review have become central to all of public administration')). See discussions in Graham, above n. 43, 151 and Michael Taggart, '"Australian Exceptionalism" in Judicial Review' (2008) 36 FLR 1, 3 fn. 11.

[48] See text to n. 116.

Secondly, the focus on judicial review means judicial supervision of administrative action through statutory appeals is not directly covered. While there may be some convergence between the two forms of supervision, I have adopted a traditional approach by distinguishing between the two and only focusing on judicial review.[49] Further, in the case of the appellate jurisdiction, the review methodology and mediation of vigilance and restraint is conditioned more heavily by statutory injunctions, which distinguishes it somewhat from the judicial review jurisdiction.

Thirdly, as mentioned earlier, the doctrinal study focuses on cases which are emblematic of a general style or method. Inevitably, that means the cases discussed are often – but not always – decisions of final appellate courts. While there may be subtle methodological variations at different hierarchical levels within each jurisdiction, it is beyond the scope of this work to interrogate any of those nuances, except in obvious cases.

Finally, my treatment of judicial review aims to be comprehensive and to engage with the overarching methodology and organisation of judicial review as it relates to the modulation of the depth of scrutiny. This contrasts with other scholarship which addresses these issues in confined areas of administrative law and judicial review.[50] Notably, my examination addresses questions of variable intensity in both rights and non-rights cases. It is not restricted to the domain of human rights adjudication, where 'deference' has become fashionable and subjected to much analysis and discussion.[51] A broader focus is important. On the one hand,

---

[49]   The extent on convergence between the appeal and review method varies across the Anglo-Commonwealth: see e.g. *Re J* [2006] 1 AC 80 and *E* v. *Secretary of State for the Home Office* [2004] QB 1044 (Eng.); *Austin Nichols & Co* v. *Stiching Lodestar* [2008] 2 NZLR 141 (NZ); *Dr Q* v. *College of Physicians and Surgeons of British Columbia* [2003] 1 SCR 226 (Can.); *Minister for Immigration and Ethnic Affairs* v. *Pochi* (1980) 44 FLR 41 (Aus.).

[50]   Daly's examination of deference is narrower than it first appears (Paul Daly, *A Theory of Deference in Administrative Law* (Cambridge University Press, 2012)). First, his study is restricted to deference in the exercise of statutory powers and excludes non-statutory, executive and prerogative powers; secondly, it is only attentive to formal and explicit judicial recognition of deference. In contrast to my study, therefore, it omits areas where the modulation of intensity is rife and underplays the extent of deference found in Anglo-Australasian jurisdictions. Arancibia only addresses deference and the modulation of the depth of scrutiny in particular contexts, in his case, commercial regulation (Arancibia, above n. 46).

[51]   See e.g. Jeffrey Jowell, 'Judicial Deference' [2003] PL 592; Jeffrey Jowell, 'Judicial Deference and Human Rights' in Paul Craig and Richard Rawlings (eds.), *Law and Administration in Europe* (Oxford University Press, 2003), 73; Alison Young, 'In Defence of Due Deference' (2009) 72 MLR 554; Murray Hunt, 'Sovereignty's Blight' in Nicholas Bamforth and Peter Leyland (eds.), *Public Law in a Multi-layered Constitution* (Hart Publishing, 2003);

some solidarity can be seen between the role of deference in the human rights domain and its more traditional administrative law partner (judicial review of 'public wrongs', as it has been described);[52] modulation of the depth of scrutiny is common to both and is often informed by similar conceptual drivers. On the other hand, the notion of deference is, in my view, a particularised and specialised form of modulation of depth of scrutiny. Despite its prominence, deference in the human rights context arises in a subordinate fashion, in the context of whether administrative (and sometimes legislative) action is legally compliant with human rights instruments. In other words, it arises in the context of a particular ground of review or aspect of legality. This specialised and myopic focus means deference scholarship tends to miss the broader and schematic aspects of the modulation of the depth of judicial scrutiny. That said, the methodology and style adopted in human rights cases are explored in a general sense, to the extent that they are evident in different schemata.

Because I am not drawn into a specialised account of deference in human rights cases, I remain agnostic on the 'bifurcation' debate that others have framed within administrative law; that is, the question of whether different methodologies are required in human rights and non-human rights cases.[53] My broader focus means this question becomes less

---

Richard Clayton, 'Judicial Deference and Democratic Dialogue' [2004] PL 33; Aileen Kavanagh, *Constitutional Review under the UK Human Rights Act* (Cambridge University Press, 2009); Aileen Kavanagh, 'Deference or Defiance?' in Grant Huscroft (ed.), *Expounding the Constitution* (Cambridge University Press, 2008), 346; Lord Steyn, 'Deference: A Tangled Story' [2005] PL 346; T.R.S. Allan, 'Human Rights and Judicial Review' [2006] CLJ 671; Aileen Kavanagh, 'Judicial Restraint in the Pursuit of Justice' (2010) UTLJ 23; Richard A. Edwards, 'Judicial Deference under the Human Rights Act' (2002) 65 MLR 859; Tom Hickman, *Public Law after the Human Rights Act* (Hart Publishing, 2010); Alan D.P. Brady, *Proportionality and Deference under the UK Human Rights Act* (Cambridge University Press, 2012); Ian Leigh, 'The Standard of Judicial Review after the Human Rights Act' in Helen Fenwick and Gavin Phillipson (eds.), *Judicial Reasoning under the UK Human Rights Act* (Cambridge University Press, 2007); Julian Rivers, 'Proportionality and Variable Intensity of Review' (2006) 65 CLJ 174; Mark Elliott, 'The Human Rights Act 1998 and the Standard of Substantive Review' (2001) 60 CLJ 301; Gavin Phillipson, 'Deference, Discretion, and Democracy in the Human Rights Act Era' (2007) 60 CLP 40; David Dyzenhaus, 'Proportionality and Defence in a Culture of Justification' in Grant Huscroft, Bradley W. Miller and Grégoire Webber (eds.), *Proportionality and the Rule of Law* (Cambridge University Press, 2014), 234.

52 Michael Taggart, 'Proportionality, Deference, *Wednesbury*' [2008] NZ Law Rev 424, 448. See also *R (Dixon) v. Somerset City Council* [1998] Env LR 111, 112 (judicial review 'is about wrongs – that is to say misuses of public power').

53 See e.g. Taggart, 'Proportionality', above n. 52, 477 (for bifurcation); Murray Hunt, 'Against Bifurcation' in David Dyzenhaus, Murray Hunt and Grant Huscroft (eds.),

important and questions of bifurcation are subsumed within it. Notions of 'deference' – whether explicitly calibrated or accommodated in a more unstructured fashion – feature in the schematic analysis. This assumes, therefore, that bifurcation is unnecessary and the modulation of the depth of scrutiny to take account of the human rights dimension is possible under all the different schemata. But I leave open the question of whether differentiated methodologies might be justified because of the engagement of human rights. That question is secondary to the principal and higher-order focus on the efficacy and virtue of the methodology themselves. I return to this point in more detail, following the examination of the different schemata.[54]

Timeframe: Last Half Century and More

The timeframe adopted for the doctrinal study opens with the publication of de Smith's textbook on judicial review in 1959 and continues to the present day.[55] This coincides with the lifespan of de Smith's textbook and reflects the generations in which English-style judicial review matured into a recognised and distinct discipline. The timeframe also captures great periods of change in (especially English) judicial review, variously characterised as including a 'revitalisation' period where courts tended to adopt a more assertive role (1960s and 1970s),[56] the 'systematisation' of judicial review doctrine (particularly notable in the mid-1980s),[57] a human rights 'revolution' (especially in the latter part of the twentieth century and

---

A Simple Common Lawyer (Hart Publishing, 2009), 99 (against bifurcation, with unifying doctrine of deference); Paul Craig, 'Proportionality, Rationality and Review' [2010] NZ Law Rev 265 (against bifurcation, with unifying doctrine of proportionality); Dyzenhaus, 'Proportionality and Deference', above n. 51 (against bifurcation).

[54] See Section 6.4 in the final chapter.

[55] For accounts of earlier periods, see W.A. Robson, 'Administrative Law in England, 1919–1948' in Lord Campion and others (eds.), *British Government Since 1918* (George Allen and Unwin, 1956), 85; W.A. Robson, 'Administrative Law' in Morris Ginsberg (ed.), *Law and Opinion in England in the 20th Century* (Stevens & Sons, 1959), 193; Sir Stephen Sedley, 'The Sound of Silence' (1994) 110 LQR 270; Jeffrey Jowell, 'Administrative Law' in Vernon Bogdanor (ed.), *The British Constitution in the Twentieth Century* (Oxford University Press, 2003), 373; Philip Murray, 'Process, Substance and the History of Error of Law Review' in John Bell and others, *Public Law Adjudication in Common Law Systems* (Bloomsbury, 2016), 87.

[56] See e.g. Jeffrey Jowell, 'Administrative Law', above n. 55, 373; Carol Harlow, 'A Special Relationship?' in Ian Loveland (ed.), *A Special Relationship?* (Oxford University Press, 1995), 79.

[57] See e.g. Sian Elias, 'Administrative Law for Living People' (2009) CLJ 47.

beyond),[58] and the 'multi-streaming' of judicial review as transnational, state and sub-state systems are all blended into administrative law cases.[59]

The schematic focus and attention to dominant methodologies, in part through the lens of a secondary source, means the historical parameters are not exact or rigid. In some cases, it draws in cases from earlier in time; however, the relevance of these lies in framing a particular style or methodology from a particular generation in Anglo-Commonwealth judicial review.

The ultimate ambition of the book is more contemporary, addressing the normative question of how the courts should modulate the depth of scrutiny in judicial review nowadays. Thus, it is not my intention to construct a comprehensive historiography of Anglo-Commonwealth judicial review over its lifetime. Beyond identifying general trends over time, the main purpose of the historical aspects of the study is to generate schemata and methodologies to analyse. Greater emphasis is therefore placed on more recent developments over the lifetime of the study (particularly in the contest between grounds of review and intensity of review – two schemata which sometimes overlap and have some parallel manifestation).

Comparative Focus: Anglo-Commonwealth

As explained above, this book is situated within Anglo-Commonwealth administrative law jurisprudence; it draws on English, Australian, New Zealand and Canadian approaches to the modulation of the depth of scrutiny and related scholarship.[60] The comparative focus on these jurisdictions is adopted for a number of reasons.

---

[58] See e.g. Michael Taggart, 'Reinventing Administrative Law' in Nicholas Bamforth and Peter Leyland (eds.), *Public Law in a Multi-Layered Constitution* (Hart Publishing, 2003), 311; Hickman, *Public Law*, above n. 51.

[59] Richard Rawlings, 'Modelling Judicial Review' (2008) 61 CLP 95.

[60] For the purposes of simplicity, I use the terms 'England' and 'English' to capture the system of judicial review in England and Wales. See generally Richard Ireland, 'Law in Wales' in Peter Cane and Joanne Conaghan (eds.), *The New Oxford Companion to Law* (Oxford University Press, 2008), 1231; Timothy Jones and Jane Williams, 'Wales as a Jurisdiction' [2004] PL 78. The distinct jurisdictions of Scotland and Northern Ireland are not addressed. Scotland's system of judicial review has, amongst other things, different origins, different procedural rules and different jurisdictional ambit. Judicial review in Northern Ireland is similarly distinctive. See generally Lord Clyde and Denis Edwards, *Judicial Review* (W. Green, 2000); Gordon Anthony, *Judicial Review in Northern Ireland* (2nd edn, Hart Publishing, 2008); de Smith (7th edn), 8. For the purposes of consistency, I also use the description of English courts to capture the Appellate Committee of House of Lords and UK Supreme Court when adjudicating on English appeals and other matters which are relevant to the English system, such as cases brought under the Human Rights Act 1998. I first came

First, these jurisdictions share a strong common law heritage, espe-cially in administrative law.[61] A common law tradition and commitment is evident and they are often described as being members of a 'common law family'.[62] These Commonwealth jurisdictions have been characterised as having 'a significant degree of doctrinal and institutional similarity, overlying a substratum of considerable cultural difference'.[63] These shared origins are especially strong in relation to administrative law, as was noted by de Smith in his first edition.[64] That historical anchor remains, even as the jurisdictions adopt indigenous approaches: '[W]hile doctrine now is diver-sifying', Saunders says, 'it is doing so from a common base'.[65] Secondly, in the latter decades, the adoption of human rights instruments – in Canada, England, New Zealand and in some state jurisdictions in Australia – has profoundly influenced administrative law in these jurisdictions.[66] This has brought renewed comparative interest, particularly in the nature and form of devices moderating the extent of judicial scrutiny in human rights adjudication.[67] Thirdly, there continues to be a reciprocity of interest in evolution and developments amongst these Anglo-Commonwealth juris-dictions. The sharing of ideas and doctrines – 'legal transplants',[68] as it has

---

across the 'Anglo-Commonwealth' label in Taggart's work: see e.g. Taggart, 'Prolegomenon', above n. 17. While the term is not beyond criticism, it is increasingly employed by scholars and there is a lack of suitable alternative descriptors.

[61] Cheryl Saunders, 'Constitution as a Catalyst' (2012) 10 NZJPIL 143, 147.

[62] Cheryl Saunders, 'Apples, Oranges and Comparative Administrative Law' [2006] AJ 423, 427; Susan Rose-Ackerman and Peter L. Lindseth, 'Comparative Administrative Law' (2010) 28 Windsor YB Access Just 435, 444. See also Lord Cooke on the strength of the common law tradition and the mutual influence of English and other Commonwealth case law: *The Turning Points of the Common Law* (Sweet & Maxwell, 1997), 2; see also 'The Road Ahead For the Common Law' (2004) 53 ICLQ 273, 273.

[63] Saunders, 'Comparative Administrative Law', above n. 62, 427.

[64] De Smith (1st edn), 25 (Commonwealth countries generally applied 'the same funda-mental body of principles'). See also Saunders, 'Catalyst', above n. 61, 147 ('Until some-where towards the end of the 1960s, administrative law doctrine, such as it was, was much the same across Commonwealth countries.'); Philip A. Joseph, 'The Contribution of the Court of Appeal to Commonwealth Administrative Law' in Rick Bigwood, *The Permanent New Zealand Court of Appeal* (Hart Publishing, 2009), 41, 41.

[65] Saunders, 'Catalyst', above n. 61, 146.

[66] See generally Stephen Gardbaum, *The New Commonwealth Model of Constitutionalism* (Cambridge University Press, 2013).

[67] In this context, the variation is usually described in terms of the role of 'deference' in human rights adjudication: see Section 4.2.3.

[68] Alan Watson, *Legal Transplants* (University of Georgia Press, 1974) and *Comparative Law* (2nd edn, Vandeplas, 2008). See also J.W.F. Allison, 'Transplantation and Cross Fertilisation in European Public Law' in Jack Beatson and Takis Tridimas (eds.), *New Directions in European Public Law* (Hart Publishing, 1998).

been described – is 'largely uncontentious'.[69] Comparative analysis and cross-fertilisation is evident in the judicial process,[70] as well as in the scholarly community.[71] Finally, the Anglo-Commonwealth ambit is consistent with de Smith's treatment in his distinguished textbook.[72]

While there is a strong comparative practice in public law in the Anglo-Commonwealth, this book adds a distinctive contribution to the question of the modulation of the depth of scrutiny in these common law jurisdictions. Canadian law features prominently in comparative public law scholarship. However, much of the comparative focus is restricted to deference in human rights adjudication and there is less attention to the more general modulation of the depth of scrutiny in the traditional administrative law domain.[73] My study aims to more strongly connect the Canadian approach and experience in the broader context of traditional administrative law throughout the Anglo-Commonwealth. The system of

[69] Saunders, 'Comparative Administrative Law', above n. 62, 426.

[70] Taggart, 'Exceptionalism', above n. 47, 2; Saunders, 'Comparative Administrative Law', above n. 62, 426; Joseph, 'Commonwealth Administrative Law', above n. 64, 49 (role of Privy Council in facilitating 'ongoing transnational conversations' and move from an English-centred monologue to more diverse dialogue).

[71] For a discussion of the connections and interactions, see e.g. Michael Taggart, 'The Tub of Public Law' in David Dyzenhaus (ed.), *The Unity of Public Law* (Hart Publishing, 2004), 455; Taggart, 'Prolegomenon', above n. 17, 233; Thomas Poole, 'Between the Devil and the Deep Blue Sea' in Linda Pearson, Carol Harlow and Michael Taggart (eds.), *Administrative Law in a Changing State* (Hart Publishing, 2008), 15; Hugh Corder, 'Comparing Administrative Justice across the Commonwealth [2006] AJ 1; Saunders, 'Comparative Administrative Law', above n. 62. For some notable examples of the comparative work, see Michael Taggart, 'Outside Canadian Administrative Law' (1996) 46 UTLJ 649; David Dyzenhaus, Murray Hunt and Michael Taggart, 'The Principle of Legality in Administrative Law' (2001) 1 OUCLJ 5; David Dyzenhaus (ed.), *The Unity of Public Law* (Hart Publishing, 2004); David Mullan, 'Judicial Review of the Executive' (2010) 8 NZJPIL 1; (2010) NZ Law Rev, pt 2 ('Proportionality, Deference, *Wednesbury*' (special issue)); (2006) AJ ('Comparative Administrative Justice' (special issue)); P.P. Craig, 'Judicial Review of Questions of Law' in S. Rose-Ackerman and P. Lindseth (eds.), *Comparative Administrative Law* (Edward Elgar, 2011). Also notable are the numerous festschrifts honouring key scholars within the Anglo-Commonwealth: see e.g. Grant Huscroft and Michael Taggart (eds.), *Inside and Outside Canadian Administrative Law* (University of Toronto Press, 2006) (Mullan, Canada); Linda Pearson, Carol Harlow and Michael Taggart (eds.), *Administrative Law in a Changing State* (Hart Publishing, 2008) (Aronson, Australia); Dyzenhaus, Hunt and Huscroft (eds.), *A Simple Common Lawyer*, above n. 53 (Taggart, New Zealand).

[72] See text to n. 34.

[73] See e.g. the literature at n. 51 above. Notable exceptions include Daly, above n. 50, and Mullan ('Deference: Is it Useful Outside Canada?' (2006) AJ 42). Daly's study contains a number of limitations which I have noted earlier, above n. 50, and Mullan's work is modest and limited in scope. See also David Mullan, 'Proportionality' (2010) NZ Law Rev 233 (whether English and New Zealand style proportionality should be adopted in Canada).

judicial review in Australia is also underexplored in this context, again in contrast to its place in Anglo-Commonwealth comparative public law. Much of the comparative work focuses on isolating Australian judicial review and highlighting only its difference.[74] There seems to be an aversion to Australia's commitment to legal formalism and a rush to condemn its failure to keep pace with the 'progressive' path elsewhere in the Anglo-Commonwealth. However, my approach is more benevolent and seeks to locate the Australian approach and methodology within a broader frame. In particular, I aim to align the current Australian experience with the scope of review approach also seen in English administrative law and explain how variation of the depth of scrutiny is still achieved, albeit more covertly.

My restriction to Anglo-Commonwealth jurisdictions means I do not address administrative law systems such as the United States or those in continental Europe. While deference doctrine is apparent in these jurisdictions too (and has been subjected to much study),[75] they lack the same English law anchor and traditions found in the jurisdictions I study. To a certain degree, too, Canadian law has absorbed aspects of the United States law, ensuring the emphatic North American style of deference on some questions of law is reflected in my doctrinal examination.[76] European law – both Community law and Convention rights – has undoubtedly profoundly influenced English law.[77] Where it has directly affected the method or style of domestic law, this is acknowledged; however, it is not feasible to separately address the original jurisprudence. The definition of jurisdictions in my doctrinal study aims to find a logistical balance between commonality and difference, in order to be able to undertake a meaningful normative assessment.

Against that backdrop, I note some limitations of this comparative treatment. First, I acknowledge the limitations of a comparative study of public law questions, when these questions are ultimately rooted in each

---

[74] See, especially, Taggart, 'Exceptionalism', above n. 47.

[75] See e.g. *Chevron USA Inc v. Natural Resources Defense Council* 467 US 837 (1984); Gary Lawson and Stephen Kam, 'Making Law Out of Nothing at All' (2013) 65 Admin LR 1; Daly, above n. 50, 17 (US); P.P. Craig, *EU Administrative Law* (2nd edn, Oxford University Press, 2012); 'Judicial Review, Intensity and Deference in EU Law' in Dyzenhaus, *Unity of Public Law*, above n. 71, 335 (EU).

[76] Taggart, 'Tub', above n. 71, 472; Michael Taggart, 'Outside Canadian Administrative Law' (1996) 46 UTLJ 649, 650.

[77] See e.g. Allison, above n. 68; Carol Harlow, 'Export, Import: The Ebb and Flow of English Public Law' [2000] PL 240; Hickman, *Public Law*, above n. 51.

jurisdiction's social and political history and settings.[78] As mentioned above, I am not attempting to explain or justify the different approaches by reference to each jurisdiction's legal and political culture, history or infrastructure. It is not the main purpose of this book to account for the particularised origins of the development; rather, the focus is on distilling different approaches, explaining their conceptual foundations, and evaluating their efficacy and virtue. Secondly, I do not claim that these jurisdictions necessarily exhibit a common or unified jurisprudence, as some others have argued.[79] In order to validate such a claim, a much more comprehensive and systemic study is required – something that is beyond the scope of this book. My concern is solely the manner by which variability is manifest, whether shared or distinct.

The familial similarity and collegial interest means these Anglo-Commonwealth jurisdictions represent a suitable group for the present study. While sharing some commonalities, they manifest doctrinal differences: each jurisdiction presents different approaches – and, in some cases, different approaches over time – to the mediation of vigilance and restraint. This provides a rich domain for studying the modulation of the depth of scrutiny, allowing the identification and explanations of those doctrinal differences, as well as tracing conceptual patterns and language. There is a natural but slight bias towards English judicial review: English law has been a lynchpin of the common law style and it is the principal focus of de Smith's textbook. The comparative analysis aims to thoroughly engage with the methodologies for mediating vigilance and restraint throughout all these Anglo-Commonwealth jurisdictions, but inevitably English law represents the anchor-stone of the analysis. Finally, the order for addressing each jurisdiction within the different schemata reflects, to some degree, the dominance of the different methodologies within the jurisdictions.

1.3   Conceptual Underpinnings: Constitutional Foundations and Methodology

The conceptual dimension turns to the scholarly accounts of judicial review and their relationship with the schemata and models of variable intensity identified in the doctrinal dimension. The aim is to draw out the

---

[78] Taggart, 'Tub', above n. 71, 461; Saunders, 'Comparative Administrative Law', above n. 62; Rose-Ackerman and Lindseth, above n. 62, 436.

[79] David Dyzenhaus, '*Baker:* Unity of Public Law' in Dyzenhaus, *Unity of Public Law*, above n. 71; Dyzenhaus, Hunt and Taggart, 'The Principle of Legality', above n. 71.

various conceptual foundations of each schema, by reference to the work of a number of different scholars who have championed different models or whose scholarship is predicated on them. Particular attention is paid to the contribution of the different scholars to debates about the purpose or foundations of judicial review and their attitudes towards the methodology administrative law requires.

The purpose of this dimension is twofold. First, the analysis seeks to expose and explain the conceptual assumptions that underpin the different models, building on doctrinal analysis. Secondly, the analysis seeks to connect the doctrinal landscape about the modulation of the depth of scrutiny with the scholarly debates that run through administrative law.

The debate about the conceptual underpinnings of judicial review provides useful material from which to interrogate the differing accounts of the modulation of the depth of scrutiny in judicial review. The debate is about the underlying *source* of the authority for the courts to engage in judicial review and, consequently, the source of the values and principles which fashion the *content* of judicial review, particularly the grounds and remedies of judicial review. In general terms, the debate divides into two different schools. First, there are those who contend that the system of judicial review must refer back to, and always reflect, the legislative intent of Parliament (the ultra vires school). Secondly, there are others who contend that the courts' supervisory jurisdiction on judicial review is inherent, not delegated to the courts by Parliament, and the principles and grounds applied in judicial review are developed by the courts under the rubric of the common law. As well as these two main schools, there are some scholars who argue that this basic dichotomy is flawed.

The positions adopted by the leading scholars are explored under the same taxonomy applied to the doctrinal study. That is, the scholars are grouped according to whether they exhibit a preference for the scope of review, grounds of review, intensity of review, or contextual review schemata. As with the doctrinal study, there are some overlaps. While I have been able to align each of the scholars (except for one) with one particular schema, the scholarship of some display multiple tendencies. For example, Craig's scholarship is generally predicated on a framework of grounds of review, but he is also attentive to explicit variation of intensity. Similarly, Aronson's scholarship is located within a scope of review paradigm but aspects of a grounds of review approach occasionally appear. However, a dominant orientation is usually obvious. As for the doctrinal study, a degree of judgement has been required when aligning the scholars with the different schemata. The only exception has been Hickman, where this type of parsing has not been possible, and his different orientations feature under the rubric of two different schemata.[80]

Within this basic grouping there are some concentrations analogous to the conceptual underpinnings debate. For example, those favouring an ultra vires justification of judicial review tend to exhibit a preference for formalism seen in the scope of review schema. On the other hand, those emphasising the common law school and the deployment of value-based adjudication in judicial review generally group towards the contextual review end of the spectrum. However, there is not necessarily a simple correlation between the position on the conceptual underpinnings debate and the position adopted on the modulation of the depth of scrutiny. The conceptual underpinnings debate can be read as collapsing into near con-sensus, at least when viewed from an instrumental perspective; that is, the schools generally agree on the nature of the *doctrinal content* of judi-cial review but differ on the *label* to be attached to the origin of this con-tent. Furthermore, the debates are not perfect proxies for questions about modulation. For example, proponents of some schemata rationalise the methodology by reference to different conceptual schools. The usefulness of exploring the conceptual underpinnings debate comes from the insight it provides into different scholars' positions on the nature of judicial adju-dication and judicial review, along with the theory of government that underpins their scholarship. In other words, it is a fruitful way to capture their perspectives on the inter-relationship between the legislature, judici-ary and administration.

As well as exploring the scholars' different positions on the conceptual underpinnings debate, I also build in their direct contribution to the debate on the modulation of the depth of scrutiny and the different normative frameworks they promote to organise a judicial review. What schemata does their scholarship generally support? Attention is also paid to the appropriate drivers for the modulation of the depth of scrutiny. Although the principal question being explored in this book is the manner by which the depth of review is modulated, this question does require an apprecia-tion of the types of factors which should be influential in this process. On this question there is more agreement between many of the scholars. To differing degrees, scholars draw out factors such as institutional autonomy, relative expertise, magnitude of the decision (including whether human

---

[80] See Section 3.3.3 and Section 5.3.3.

rights are impugned), and the availability of other mechanisms through which to hold the administration to account.

The scholars I discuss are, of course, only representative of the conceptual debates. The ones selected are those who are emblematic of the different positions, within the schemata and jurisdictions being examined.[81] I have generally favoured those who have presented a normative model for modulating the depth of scrutiny or have otherwise made their preferences clear. In addition, the extent to which the different scholars have taken a position on these questions varies. In some cases, particularly on the conceptual underpinnings debate, some scholars have not directly engaged in the debate. In these cases, I have sought to identify the likely position they adopt based on their writing generally.

1.4   Normative Assessment: Principles of Efficacy and Virtue

The normative dimension, building on the doctrinal study and conceptual discussion, assesses the respective merits of each schema. As mentioned at the outset, I employ Fuller's principles of legality or efficacy as a tool to examine the virtue of the different approaches.[82] Fuller identified eight criteria. First, laws ought to be *general*, in the sense that there must be rules of some kind. Secondly, laws ought to be promulgated and *publicly accessible*. Thirdly, laws should be *prospective*. Fourthly, laws should be *clear*. Fifthly, laws should be *non-contradictory*. Sixthly, laws should *not require the impossible*. Seventhly, laws should be *relatively stable*. Finally, there should be *congruence between law and official action* applying that law. To that I have added one further criterion, *hortatory versatility*, to recognise also the wider function of judicial review in administrative law.

These criteria are used to focus the normative assessment in the following chapters. Shortly, I introduce the criteria adopted, explain the gist of

---

[81] The authors of de Smith's textbook are not included, in part because their attitudes are generally evident in the doctrinal study. Jowell is the one author who has most directly engaged with depth of scrutiny and deference; his position echoes Hunt's (see Section 4.3.3). Dawn Oliver, one of the key catalysts of the constitutional underpinnings debate, is also not included because variability of the depth of review in administrative law has not been a key feature of her scholarship. I regret the absence of female voices here.

[82] Lon L. Fuller, *The Morality of Law* (Yale University Press, 1964). See generally Colleen Murphy, 'Lon Fuller and the Moral Value of the Rule of Law' (2005) 25 Law & Phil 239; Jeremy Waldron, 'Why Law – Efficacy, Freedom, or Fidelity?' (1994) 13 Law & Phil 259; Martin Loughlin, *Foundations of Public Law* (Oxford University Press, 2010), 333–5; David Dyzenhaus, 'Process and Substance as Aspects of the Public Law Form' (2015) 74 Camb LJ 284.

Fuller's concern in relation to each, along with the particular issues each criterion raises in the particular context. Before doing so, I explain the purpose of adopting Fuller's criteria for this analysis.

The various schemata modulating the depth of scrutiny exhibit both commonality and individuality. On the one hand, all the schemata enable significant *variability* in the supervisory task. On the other hand, the *manner* in which this variability is expressed by each schema differs. Isolating the former allows us to focus the normative assessment on the efficacy of the latter; the principal concern is with the *means* by which the depth of scrutiny is modulated, not the *fact* of modulation per se. The assumption that judicial review is variable in nature – corroborated in the doctrinal study and not seriously contended otherwise by scholars in the conceptual debates – allows us to turn our attention to the way the modulation takes place.[83]

How, then, do we assess the merits of the *means* of modulation? Some measure is needed to guide the assessment. It is insufficient merely to assert that one means is, for example, more 'robust' than others, without dissecting why that is so.[84] One perspective, and the one I employ here, is to treat the schemata as rule-regimes which regulate the exercise of power and discretion of judges in the supervisory jurisdiction. In other words, judicial review of administrative decision-making is not merely the judicial *supervision* of the application of rules by the administration but also involves the *creation and deployment* of rules about the exercise of judicial power. Judges are agents of public power too.

Viewed in this way, we can then draw on rule of law scholarship addressing the appropriateness and efficacy of rule-regimes in order to assess the merits of the different schemata. Fuller's principles of legality are well regarded as a set of standards for examining rule-based systems for their value and virtue. His criteria have been echoed by a number of others writing on the rule of law.[85] There has been some debate about their

---

[83] For others squarely recognising the ubiquity of variability in judicial review, see e.g. Taggart, 'Proportionality', above n. 76, 150; D.G.T. Williams, 'Justiciability and the Control of Discretionary Power' in Michael Taggart (ed.), *The Province of Administrative Law* (Hart Publishing, 1997), 103, 106; Philip A. Joseph, 'Exploratory Questions in Administrative Law' (2012) 25 NZULR 75, 75.

[84] See e.g. Daly, above n. 50. Daly makes this claim a number of times speaking to his normative preference for 'doctrinal', not 'epistemic', deference; however, the orientation of his project is more towards the drivers of deference, rather than the means by which it is manifest.

[85] See e.g. Joseph Raz, 'The Rule of Law and its Virtue' (1977) 93 LQR 195; Tom Bingham, *The Rule of Law* (Penguin, 2011).

jurisprudential quality (expressions of morality or otherwise) but this characterisation is not important for present purposes.[86] Their value lies in the expression of these qualities as standards against which to evaluate rules and regimes.

My goal here is relatively modest; the focus is on the efficacy of the modulation of the depth of scrutiny, as one way to assess the normative value of the schemata. It assumes the judicial methodology in the supervisory jurisdiction has a rule-based character, which therefore justifies a rule of law style of analysis. Some points about the selection of this Fullerian perspective for evaluating the schemata now follow.

First, some may argue the achievement of administrative justice, through whatever means, is the most important measure of the normative value of each schema. However, my normative assessment does not prejudge that evaluation. Rather, my assessment assumes that the ubiquity of variability throughout the different schemata supports the goals of administrative justice. The fact the supervisory jurisdiction is a check or review function does not prevent scrutiny of its internal morality and how it explicates methodological rules. I am not unconcerned with the delivery of administrative justice (however that is to be defined), but I say that the achievement of that ultimate objective is left open by the different schemata because of the inherent variability of, and discretion that imbues, them all. My normative analysis does draw out the extent and nature of discretion within the rule-regimes, and may speak, at least briefly, to whether the ability to achieve those objectives is loosely or tightly encumbered. But this is of only limited salience because the overriding conclusion is that all the different schemata enable variability, such that the goals of administrative justice can be achieved.

Secondly, some may object to the rule of law evaluation, suggesting it unduly skews the analysis in favour of those schemata with explicit rules and against those largely founded in discretion and judgement. I acknowledge that inevitably this Fullerian approach is more critical of regimes operating without rules or with little rule structure. This, in itself, is an important observation when exploring the virtues of different judicial methods,

---

[86] Fuller's original claim was that these qualities of law have 'moral virtue' (Fuller, *Morality of Law*, above n. 82, 53, 204). Others – particularly Raz – doubted this and argued the criteria were more instrumental in nature (Raz, above n. 85, 226). It has been argued that they stand more as 'functional or prudential criteria', in that the 'serious failure to comply with these criteria would make it impossible to subject human conduct to rules, thereby rendering the rule system ineffective' (Loughlin, *Foundations*, above n. 82, 334).

although my analysis is more nuanced than that basic conclusion. Those
rejecting a Fullerian approach would need to demonstrate that limitless
judicial discretion is essential for the delivery of administrative justice.
Yet, as explained above and demonstrated throughout the study, the variability necessary to deliver administrative justice is present in each schema.
In other words, the demands of administrative justice do not dictate judicial rulelessness over doctrinal structure and expectations of methodical
reasoning. Thus, I argue the Fullerian approach remains a useful one for
assessing the manner in which power – here, judicial power – is exercised.
It is fair, I think, to subject judicial method to scrutiny based on standard
expectations about the deployment of power. Indeed, it would be ironic –
and, in my view, indefensible – to argue that the fact that judicial review
mandates the courts to enforce the rule of law (against the administration
in favour of the citizen) justifies rule of law disregarding behaviour by the
courts themselves.

Thirdly, the mode of analysis has some sympathy with the debate about
the rules versus standards and their respective characteristics.[87] That is, the
Fullerian criteria provide lines of enquiry to explore the quality of regulating (judicial) power in certain ways; to some degree, the qualitative assessment echoes points in normative debates about the virtue of regulating
(citizen) action through legal rules or standards (or principles). However,
while I acknowledge some synergy between the normative frameworks,
it is not my intention to contribute directly to the rules versus standards
debate. Rather, the Fullerian criteria provides a basis for discussing the
relative strengths and weaknesses of each schema.

I return now to the criteria themselves, briefly explaining the nature
of Fuller's concern in relation to each and how each fits in the present
context of assessing methodologies in the supervisory jurisdiction. In
the normative assessment that follows in each chapter, I elaborate on
aspects of Fuller's articulation of these criteria, where further explanation is needed. As will be apparent, the criteria tend to overlap at times
and sometimes converge. Further, it is important to note that these criteria are aspirational in character; even Fuller did not characterise them

---

[87] See e.g. Pierre J. Schlag, 'Rules and Standards' (1985) 33 UCLA L Rev 379; Louis Kaplow,
'Rules Versus Standards: An Economic Analysis' (1992) 42 Duke LJ 557; Eric A. Posner,
'Standards, Rules, and Social Norms' (1997) 211 Harvard Journal of Law & Public Policy
101; Ronald Dworkin, *Taking Rights Seriously* (Harvard University Press, 1977); Cass R.
Sunstein, 'Problems with Rules' (1995) 83 Calif L Rev 953; Timothy Endicott, 'Are There
Any Rules?' (2001) 5 Legal Ethics 199.

as absolute duties.[88] They are useful, though, in exposing lines of analysis. Inevitably there are trade-offs that must be made between the different criteria when evaluating schemata for normative purposes. The criteria are intended to help guide that assessment and to illuminate the trade-offs that are involved.

Fuller's explanation of *generality* focuses on the need for rules. A preference is expressed for 'general declarations' of rules, over other forms of commanding compliance.[89] The faithful application of previously declared rules – combining the idea of generality with congruence – is seen to be an essential feature of social ordering through law; a functioning legal order demands 'the existence of a relatively stable reciprocity of expectations between lawgiver and subject'.[90] Fuller recognises the preference for rules is only aspirational; he speaks of a 'struggle' between 'broad freedom of action' and declared general rules.[91] This recognises an important trade-off when assessing generality – between flexibility and responsiveness on the one hand, and consistency and predictability on the other.[92] The normative analysis under this criterion therefore focuses on the role rules play within each schema and the balance drawn between rule and discretion.

The virtue of *public accessibility* has a number of aspects. First, from an instrumental perspective, openness helps expose the legal regime and power exercised to scrutiny and critique.[93] Secondly, the promulgation of publicly accessible rules is an essential ingredient to understanding a legal regime (viz. clarity) and being able to predict the outcome of cases.[94] Thirdly, public promulgation has a non-instrumental aspect in the way it enhances the legitimacy and 'basic integrity' of the legal regime.[95] Rule-making and rule-application are both undertaken by the courts when exercising their supervisory jurisdiction and are inevitably intertwined; furthermore, judicial discretion assumes a powerful role. Thus it is also necessary under this criterion to be attentive to transparency in the

---

[88] Fuller, *Morality of Law*, above n. 82, 43. The only one he marks out as essential is promulgation (public accessibility of law to those affected).

[89] *Ibid.*, 210.

[90] *Ibid.*, 209.

[91] *Ibid.*, 213.

[92] On equality and consistency, see *ibid.*, 211. See also John Rawls, *A Theory of Justice* (Belknap, 1971); Karen Steyn, 'Consistency' (1997) 2 JR 22; Jeffrey Jowell, 'Is Equality a Constitutional Principle?' (1994) 47 CLR 1.

[93] Fuller, *Morality of Law*, above n. 82, 51.

[94] *Ibid.*, 50. See further text to n. 102.

[95] Fuller, *Morality of Law*, above n. 82, 212, 214 and 222.

judicial reasoning process. Fuller highlighted the importance of reason-giving as an aspect of accessibility (and clarity); it is properly taken for granted, he says, that the courts 'must explain and justify their decisions, [and] that they must demonstrate that the rules they apply are "grounded in principle".[96] This criterion therefore values the public articulation of principles or rules governing the courts' supervisory jurisdiction, along with the reasoned elaboration of the basis on which those principles or rules are applied in particular cases. This is consistent with the 'culture of justification' which the courts tend to expect of administrative decision-makers nowadays.[97]

A retroactive law is, in Fuller's account, a 'monstrosity' – objectionable in terms of both morality and efficacy – and thus *prospectivity* is seen as an important virtue.[98] However, Fuller was also prepared to admit that, in the context of a system of generally prospective laws, laws with retroactive effect may in some circumstances be tolerable.[99] Notably, he acknowledged that judicial adjudication of disputes inevitably has some retroactive effect, so deeper analysis is required to parse and condemn any retroactivity.[100] In the present context, with a focus on regime design, retrospectivity in the pure sense does not arise; however, the nature of any retrospective effect arising from the application of the rules can be assessed.[101] Again, the virtues of clarity, legal certainty and predictability have been acknowledged by the courts in the context of administrative decision-making.[102]

---

[96] Lon L. Fuller, *Anatomy of Law* (Greenwood Press, 1976), 91. See also John Rawls, *The Law of Peoples* (Harvard University Press, 2001); Jon Elster, 'Deliberation and Constitution Making' in Jon Elster (ed.), *Deliberative Democracy* (Cambridge University Press, 1998), 97, 111 ('the civilizing force of hypocrisy'); Francisco J. Urbina, 'A Critique of Proportionality' (2012) 57 Am J Juris 49, drawing on Mattias Kumm, 'The Idea of Socratic Contestation and the Right to Justification' (2010) 4 Law and Ethics of Human Rights 147 (by demanding justification, 'Socratic contestation … increase[s] rationality').

[97] Etienne Mureinik, 'A Bridge to Where?' (1994) 10 SAJHR 31; David Dyzenhaus, 'Law as Justification' (1998) 14 SAJHR 11; Taggart, 'Proportionality', above n. 76, 461. On reason-giving, see generally P.P. Craig, 'The Common Law, Reasons and Administrative Justice' [1994] CLJ 282; Andrew le Sueur, 'Legal Duties to Give Reasons' (1999) 52 CLP 150; Mark Elliott, 'Has the Common Law Duty to Give Reasons Come of Age Yet?' [2011] PL 56.

[98] Fuller, *Morality of Law*, above n. 82, 53.

[99] *Ibid.*, 53.

[100] *Ibid.*, 56. See also Fuller, *Anatomy of Law*, above n. 96, 100.

[101] Fuller, *Anatomy of Law*, above n. 96, 101.

[102] See e.g. the treatment of legitimate expectations (*R (Coughlan)* v. *North and East Devon Health Authority* [2001] QB 213 and *R (Preston)* v. *Inland Revenue Commissioners* [1985] AC 835) and vagueness (*Black Clawson Ltd* v. *Papierwerke Attorney-General* [1975] AC 591 and *R* v. *Misra* [2005] 1 Cr App R 328). See generally Robert Thomas, *Legitimate Expectations and Proportionality in Administrative Law* (Hart Publishing, 2000);

Clarity is described by Fuller as 'one of the most essential ingredients of legality'.[103] This criterion condemns vagueness and obscurity in legal rules.[104] Much of the underlying rationale for this principle is legal certainty. Laws should be clear in meaning so that they are capable of being obeyed and in order that people can live their lives conscious of the legal consequences which may flow from their actions.[105] Thus, this principle factors in concerns about predictability within the legal regime. Fuller is also concerned that lack of clarity – regimes that are vague, indefinite and favour governmental discretion – may 'rob' the regimes of their legitimacy.[106] In the particular context of judicial review schemata, this criterion addresses how clearly the principles governing the deployment of the courts' supervisory jurisdiction are expressed, whether they are understandable, and whether they unduly rely on standards that are vague or indeterminate.

Stability, in the sense employed by Fuller, requires that laws not change too frequently.[107] The objection, like for retrospective rules, is that instability makes the law unpredictable and difficult to comply with. Hence, there is a degree of overlap between this criterion and the criteria looking at clarity, prospectivity and non-impossibility; they all address the predictability of laws and the ability to comply with laws. As the different legal regimes and methodologies have been isolated, the focus under this criterion is the treatment of change and evolution *within* each schema, rather than changes from one schema to another.

The focus of *non-contradiction and coherence* is the schematic unity of the system and the extent to which it is bound together by principle.[108]

Soren Schønberg, *Legitimate Expectations in Administrative Law* (Oxford University Press, 2000); Timothy A.O. Endicott, *Vagueness in Law* (Oxford University Press, 2001).

[103] Fuller, *Morality of Law*, above n. 82, 63.

[104] *Ibid.*, 63, 212 and 213.

[105] *Ibid.*, 209 and 212. See also Friedrich von Hayek, *The Road to Serfdom* (University of Chicago Press, 1944); Joseph Raz, *The Authority of Law* (Claredon, 1979); Jeremy Waldron, *The Law* (Routledge, 1990); Max Weber, *Economy and Society* (University of California Press, 1978) ('legal guaranty'); Jürgen Habermas, *Between Facts and Norms* (MIT Press, 1996).

[106] Fuller, *Morality of Law*, above n. 82, 212.

[107] *Ibid.*, 79.

[108] See also Ronald Dworkin, *Law's Empire* (Harvard University Press, 1988), 134, 167 ('integrity') and Neil MacCormick, *Rhetoric and The Rule of Law* (Oxford University Press, 2005), 189 and 193 ('normative coherence' is a 'commonly accepted criterion' of the soundness of judicial rulings; legal norms should be 'rationally related as a set, instrumentally or intrinsically, to the realization of some common value or values' or as 'fulfilling some more or less clearly articulated common principle or principles').

Coherence contrasts law as a seamless web with law as a patchwork quilt. Although consistent treatment contributes to coherence, coherence raises broader questions about the meta-architecture of a schema, that is, its organising theory or manner in which it is systematised. The focus extends to matters such as its comprehensiveness, connectedness, and internal unity.[109] Fuller commends coherence, not just in rule-making but in rule-application too. This he describes as a 'problem of system', where the 'rules applied to the decision of individual controversies cannot simply be isolated exercises of judicial wisdom'; even when deployed, they must maintain 'some systematic interrelationship' and 'display some coherent internal structure'.[110] Coherence and non-contradiction are enhanced by 'principles that transcend their immediate application' and 'bind the elements of law into a coherent system of thought'.[111]

In Fuller's original account, *non-impossibility* is focused on the (in)ability to achieve compliance with rules. In other words, concern is expressed about standards set by rules that cannot be achieved. While this principle has virtue, its concern does not directly arise in this context because the rules and methodology deployed by judges are self-created and judges are unlikely to fashion totally unachievable rules to regulate their own behaviour. However, the gist of this principle is the *practicality* of compliance. Indeed, Fuller also expresses this principle in terms of the 'possib[ility] of execution';[112] further he acknowledges that 'no hard and fast line' could be drawn and the virtue was more a question of degree.[113] In this context, this principle therefore speaks more squarely to the practicality of the different schemata. In particular, this criterion looks at their effect on the litigation and supervision process.[114] It is attentive to any procedural consequences and how the schemata might affect advocacy and deliberation in judicial review hearings and decisions.

Congruence insists that official action is faithful to declared rules.[115] This criterion seeks to bind the other criteria with a focus on operation and

---

[109]   Ken Kress, 'Coherence and Formalism' (1993) 16 Harv J L & Pub Policy 639.

[110]   Fuller, *Anatomy of Law*, above n. 96, 94.

[111]   *Ibid.*, 94.

[112]   Fuller, *Morality of Law*, above n. 82, 208.

[113]   *Ibid.*, 79.

[114]   The practical analysis is based on logical deductions about the effect of different schema on procedure, advocacy, and deliberation. It is not feasible in the context of this book to undertake empirical work to further test these assumptions.

[115]   Fuller, *Morality of Law*, above n. 82, 81.

implementation. Fuller is quick to rebut the idea that the merger of law-maker and law-applier, as is the case here, necessarily brings congruence. First, the nature of the judicial hierarchy means congruence may still be impaired because the making of law by judges is always subject to higher court (dis)approval. Secondly, there remains room for dissonance between the declaration and application of law, even by the same actor.[116] In the context of evaluating the different judicial review schemata, this principle allows us to examine the fidelity between the rule and regime expressed by judges and applied by judges. This aspiration for congruence, fidelity and candour is based on the same impulse that has driven the courts to develop similar expectations of administrative decision-makers. The courts expect administrators to faithfully apply the law. This principle expects the same of the judges.

The final criterion – *hortatory versatility* – is not found in Fuller's account but is an important dimension of judicial review. While judicial review's immediate role is the policing of administrative legality, it also has an important collateral role in articulating and elaborating the principles of good administration that ministers, public bodies and officials ought to honour. These principles of good administration have currency both within and beyond the system of judicial review itself – described by Harlow and Rawlings as its 'hortatory function'.[117] While my predominant concern in this book is the system of judicial review itself, the utility of the principles of review beyond the system and in administrative law generally should not be ignored when evaluating different schema.

---

[116] *Ibid.*, 82 ('the tune called may be quite undanceable by anyone, including the tune-caller'). King echoes this concern, when he worries about the gap between 'what judges say and do': Jeff King, 'Proportionality' [2010] NZ L Rev 327, 334. Craig makes a similar point, arguing that the 'courts have an obligation to say what they do and do what they say': *UK, EU and Global Administrative Law* (Cambridge University Press, 2015), 257.

[117] Carol Harlow and Richard Rawlings, *Law and Administration* (3rd edn, Cambridge University Press, 2009), 669. Harlow and Rawlings say the goal of the hortatory or edu-cative function is 'ultimately the internalising by administrators of legal values' (at 728). The establishment of general principles for the proper exercise of discretion helps promote good decision-making on a prophylactic basis ('fire-watching') rather than merely addressing deficiencies after the fact ('fire-fighting') (*ibid.*, 728). See also David Feldman, 'Judicial Review' (1988) 66 Pub Admin 21 (role of law in *structuring*, not just *directing* and *limiting*, discretion); Simon Halliday, *Judicial Review and Compliance with Administrative Law* (Hart Publishing, 2004), 15 (judicial review's messaging role and the way general principles influence bureaucratic values and decision-making); Marc Hartogh and Simon Halliday, *Judicial Review and Bureaucratic Impact* (Cambridge University Press, 2004).

1.5   Summary

This book interrogates the different approaches employed, in schematic terms, to modulate the depth of scrutiny in judicial review, in order to identify their virtue when judged in terms of the efficacy of the rule-systems and methodologies. Of the four schemata – scope, grounds, intensity, context – the grounds and intensity of review approaches are strongest. In the chapters that follow, each schema is examined, drawing out its doctrinal manifestation, conceptual underpinnings and normative value.

2

Scope of Review

2.1 Introduction

The scope of review schema exhibits the characteristics of legal formalism. The depth of scrutiny is modulated indirectly, by the classification of a decision or function into a category which determines whether the decision or function is capable of being reviewable or not. Multifarious, often complexly drawn, categories are the main feature of the doctrinal landscape. The language of jurisdiction is particularly prominent, as is a (purportedly) sharp distinction between legality and merits. The approach dominates Australian administrative law today, but was also the prevailing style of English judicial review at the opening point of this study when de Smith penned his first edition. This style of judicial method continued, I argue, throughout the period of reinvigoration of judicial review in the 1960 and 1970s; even though the categories were often recast to enable more intensive review, the formalistic categorical approach still assumed importance until a more generalised and systematised approach was adopted in the mid-1980s.

The scope of review approach is generally synonymous with a strong ultra vires conception of judicial review and steadfast commitment to formalist – not value-laden – legal method and finds only limited support in the scholarship. From a normative perspective, this schema performs poorly against the principles of efficacy, largely due to its complexity and a lack of congruence between rule-expression and rule-application. While rules dominate the schema, they are open to manipulation and tend to assume a ritualistic role, expressing conclusions based on more normative – but latent – judicial assessment of whether to intervene or not.

2.2 Doctrinal Manifestation

The scope of review label is drawn from the early editions of de Smith's textbook, where it was associated with a complex and formalistic style of legal method. After tracing its recognition in de Smith's textbook, I describe its operation in modern Australian law, before returning to its historical deployment in English law.

2.2.1   De Smith Derivation

'Scope of review' is employed frequently by de Smith through the first four editions to showcase the analysis of the circumstances of judicial intervention. While lucid in exposition, de Smith did not incorporate an explicit organising device for the analysis; the striking feature of the book is the vast morass of case law it incorporates. As Harlow notes: 'Its framework is the traditional framework of remedies and its emphasis is the caselaw emphasis of the common lawyer.'[1] Vires and jurisdiction are loose themes that are evident throughout the text, but the language of scope of review is a significant feature.

De Smith's introductory exposition was dotted with references to 'scope of review'. '[S]cope of review ... may vary' according to the form of the proceeding;[2] no uniformity 'characterises the scope of review';[3] 'scope of judicial review often depends upon' the classification of the impugned function.[4] Scope of review was a phrase used as an analogue for the circumstances in which judicial relief was available. The phrase also appeared in the scene-setting chapter where de Smith undertook an in-depth study of the classification of functions (as 'legislative, administrative (or executive), judicial or ministerial').[5] 'The scope of judicial review of administrative action ...', de Smith said, 'frequently depend[s] upon the classification of a particular statutory function.'[6] However, his critical eye recognised that generating definitions of each was 'exceedingly difficult' and that the judicial approach adopted was 'riddled with ambiguities', a point discussed further later.[7]

---

[1] Carol Harlow, 'Politics and Principles' (1981) 44 MLR 114, 115.
[2] De Smith (1st edn), 15; (2nd edn), 22; (3rd edn), 22; (4th edn), 27.
[3] De Smith (1st edn), 15; (2nd edn), 22; (3rd edn), 22; (4th edn), 27.
[4] De Smith (1st edn), 17; (2nd edn), 25; (3rd edn), 26; (4th edn), 29.
[5] De Smith (1st edn–4th edn), ch. 2.
[6] De Smith (1st edn), 29; (2nd edn), 54.
[7] De Smith (1st edn), 29; (2nd edn), 54. He observes that 'where a definition formulated by the courts for a particular purpose has appeared to them to be unserviceable for a different purpose, they have shown no hesitation in disregarding it and adopting another definition'.

Elsewhere throughout the text, the phrase 'scope of review' operated as a common label for exposition of the circumstances in which administrative action could be impugned by judicial review. The heart of de Smith's examination was undertaken under the part heading 'Principles and Scope of Judicial Review'.[8] The scope of review was explored in two different contexts: review of 'vires, jurisdiction, law and fact',[9] and 'discretionary power'.[10] The former was characterised by an account of various distinctions which determined whether a matter was reviewable or not, in particular, distinctions between: (a) law, fact and discretion;[11] (b) ministerial, legislative, executive, and judicial functions;[12] and (c) jurisdictional and non-jurisdictional matters.[13] The combinations of various classifications were explained as affecting the scope of review, a number of which are instanced and explained shortly.[14] At this stage, the critical points are that, first, scope of review language was adopted to convey whether or not impugned decisions or actions were reviewable, and, secondly, reviewability was determined by classification into different categories.

The chapter which addressed the review of discretionary power also employed the language of scope of review.[15] Scope of review of discretionary power was said to be 'conditioned by a variety of factors', including statutory wording and purpose, subject-matter, character of the relevant authority, form of proceedings,[16] materials available to the reviewing court, and, ultimately, 'whether a court is of the opinion that judicial intervention would be in the public interest'.[17] Here, the scope of review

---

[8] De Smith (1st edn), 54; (2nd edn), 81; (3rd edn), 79; (4th edn), 91. Scope of review is not specifically mentioned in the chapters dealing with natural justice.

[9] De Smith (1st edn–4th edn), ch. 3.

[10] De Smith (1st edn–4th edn), ch. 6.

[11] De Smith (1st edn), 60–1 (law and fact vs discretion) and 83–92 (law and fact); (2nd edn), 89–90 and 113–26; (3rd edn), 84–5 and 111–22; (4th edn), 96–7 and 126–41.

[12] De Smith (1st edn), 61–5; (2nd edn), 90–4; (3rd edn), 92–4; (4th edn), 106–8.

[13] De Smith (1st edn), 65–83; (2nd edn), 94–113; (3rd edn), 94–110; (4th edn), 108–26.

[14] See Section 2.2.3.

[15] De Smith (1st edn–4th edn), ch. 6.

[16] De Smith (1st edn), 169–70; (2nd edn), 267–9; (3rd edn), 249–51; (4th edn), 281–3. A particular contradistinction is made between review under the prerogative writs and statutory appeals.

[17] De Smith (1st edn), 169; (2nd edn), 267; (3rd edn), 249; (4th edn), 281.

was explained in terms of a series of principles governing the exercise of discretionary power:[18]

> In general, a discretion must be exercised only by the authority to which it is committed. The authority must genuinely address itself to the matter before it: it must not act under the dictation of another body or disable itself from exercising a discretion in each individual case. In the purported exercise of its discretion it must not do what it has been forbidden to do, nor must it do what it has not been authorised to do. It must act in good faith, must have regard to all relevant considerations ... must not seek to promote purposes alien to the spirit of the legislation that gives it power to act, and must not act arbitrarily or capriciously.

The scope of review language continued to be employed throughout the analysis of the unreasonable exercise of power.[19] De Smith's analysis separated questions of reasonableness, where reasonableness was specified in the empowering legislation, and those situations where it was not. Against a general backdrop of a judicial reluctance to allow free-standing challenges on the basis of unreasonableness, de Smith's account was characterised by the identification of a series of formal distinctions conditioning whether review was more likely or not. In particular, he addressed distinctions based on the form of the proceedings (unlikely for declaratory, prohibitory and mandatory orders and most unlikely for certiorari); form of the discretion (available where reasonableness enjoined in statute but unlikely for a wide, unqualified discretion); nature of the decision-maker (less likely for ministerial decisions than for judicial decisions or decisions of licensing bodies like local authorities); and type of decision (for legislative decisions, likely in relation to by-laws but unlikely in relation to statutory instruments made by ministers).

'Scope of review' was, in summary, a significant feature of the language of the early editions, reflecting the formalistic and categorical nature of judicial review at the time. The supervisory jurisdiction was characterised by classification of decisions and errors into different categories: some reviewable, others not. The concept of modulation of depth of review was not expressed explicitly. However, the discussion of the regime was frequently characterised by unstable definitions and porous boundaries;

---

[18] De Smith (1st edn), 172; (2nd edn), 271; (3rd edn), 252; (4th edn), 285. The text was equivocal on whether or not these grounds of invalidity were examples only or whether they were 'heads of invalidity' in their own right, but de Smith noted that the latter approach would tend to enlarge the scope of review: de Smith (1st edn), 189; (2nd edn), 302; (3rd edn), 282; (4th edn), 323.

[19] De Smith (1st edn), 214–21; (2nd edn), 330–7; (3rd edn), 303–11; (4th edn), 346–54.

the corollary – often expressed explicitly – was that this left the decision whether or not to intervene able to be manipulated by judges.

From the fifth edition onwards, scope of review, and associated features of this strongly formalist and categorical approach, were downplayed and consigned to more minor roles within the text.[20] The language of 'scope of review' was refined and heavily circumscribed. The phrase was adopted as the headline for the part of the text addressing 'questions relating to the jurisdiction of the court to be seised of a matter to which an application for judicial review',[21] namely, standing,[22] and the bodies against whom judicial review may be brought.[23] Also assigned to this part, somewhat awkwardly, was a significantly abridged version of the previous chapter on vires and jurisdiction, blended with the previous chapter on the statutory restriction of review.[24] Woolf and Jowell acknowledged that the 'reduced significance' of jurisdictional error necessitated this dramatic pruning;[25] 'the concept of jurisdictional error is no longer the organising concept of judicial review', they said.[26] This is seen particularly in the relegation of the former chapter on the classification of functions that served as an entry-point for de Smith's analysis. No longer meriting placement with the main body of analysis in the fifth and sixth editions, an abridged version was reproduced as an appendix instead.[27]

2.2.2   Australia: Abstract Formalism

Australian administrative law today bears the hallmarks of the scope of review schema seen in de Smith's textbook in the early editions. It continues to echo the abstract formalism that was once replete – but has since dissipated – in English administrative law.[28]

---

[20] See e.g. de Smith (5th edn), 299 (nature of review under statutory appeal rights).
[21] De Smith (5th edn), ix.
[22] De Smith (5th edn), ch. 2.
[23] De Smith (5th edn), ch. 3.
[24] De Smith (5th edn), ch. 5.
[25] De Smith (5th edn), ix.
[26] De Smith (5th edn), 97.
[27] De Smith (5th edn–7th edn), app ('Classification of Functions'). Despite its demotion, the authors suggested the topic may still be of some 'analytical and historic interest' (de Smith (5th edn), ix).
[28] The term 'abstract formalism' is borrowed from Thomas Poole, 'Between the Devil and the Deep Blue Sea' in Linda Pearson, Carol Harlow and Michael Taggart (eds.), *Administrative Law in a Changing State* (Hart Publishing, 2008), 15, 42. England's historic experience is addressed below: Section 2.2.3.

Prerogative writs and a remedial focus provide the foundation of much of the system of judicial review in Australia.[29] However, a number of legislative and institutional features also contribute to its peculiarity and somewhat disjointed nature.[30] Federalism provides plural administrative law systems, but tied together by a unified common law under the guardianship of the High Court of Australia.[31] The authority to engage in judicial review is attributed to a number of different sources: constitution, statute and common law.[32] The procedure and grounds of judicial review are partly codified.[33] On a non-comprehensive basis, the Administrative

---

[29] For a brief sketch of the general path of Australian administrative law, relative to English developments, see Peter Cane, 'The Making of Australian Administrative law' (2003) 23 Aust Bar Rev 114. See also Stephen Gageler, 'Impact of Migration Law on the Development of Australian Administrative Law' (2010) 17 AJ Admin L 92.

[30] See generally Cheryl Saunders, 'Constitution as a Catalyst' (2012) 10 NZJPIL 143, 153–7; Peter Cane and Leighton McDonald, *Principles of Administrative Law* (Oxford University Press, 2008), 34.

[31] While the federal system enables, strictly speaking, different systems of administrative law, the fact that the High Court is mandated as a final court of appeal for state and federal judicial systems means there is a universal common law, with the High Court operating as guardian: see *Kirk* v. *Industrial Court of New South Wales* (2010) 239 CLR 531, [99].

[32] The High Court obtains its mandate to engage in judicial review from s. 75(v) of the Constitution, with 'original' (viz. inherent) jurisdiction in relation to the prerogative writs (except for certiorari, which is only available as an ancillary remedy). The Federal Court does not have inherent jurisdiction and acquired its jurisdiction under the Judiciary Act 1903 (mirroring the High Court's mandate under s. 75(v) of the Constitution, and developing by reference to the common law) and ADJR. In addition, the Federal Court has (quite limited) jurisdiction to review immigration decisions under the Migration Act 1958 with such decisions otherwise being excluded from review under the ADJR by a privative clause. State courts acquired their jurisdiction from the common law (as modified by statutory codification), although the High Court recently indicated aspects of state judicial review also have a constitutional dimension (*Kirk*, above n. 31), [55]). See generally Peter Cane and Leighton McDonald, *Principles of Administrative Law* (2nd edn, Oxford University Press, 2012), ch. 3; Mark Aronson and Matthew Groves, *Judicial Review of Administrative Action* (5th edn, Thomson Reuters, 2013), 7.

[33] The Administrative Decisions (Judicial Review) Act 1977 (ADJR Act) codifies the procedure and grounds for review of most decisions of Commonwealth bodies. Some states (ACT, Qld, Tas.) also have similar codified regimes addressing procedure and grounds of review; other state courts retain the common law procedure and grounds. The codified grounds in the ADJR Act are generally taken to reflect, with some exceptions, the common law grounds: see *Kioa* v. *West* (1985) 159 CLR 550, 576 and Cane and McDonald, *Principles of Administrative Law* (Oxford University Press, 2008), 111. See generally Cheryl Saunders, 'Constitution, Codes, and Administrative Law' in Christopher Forsyth and others (eds.), *Effective Judicial Review* (Oxford University Press, 2010), 61; Saunders, 'Catalyst', above n. 30; Timothy H. Jones, 'Judicial Review and Codification' (2006) 20 LS 517; Mark Aronson, 'Is the ADJR Act Hampering the Development of Australian Administrative Law?' (2004) 15 PLR 202.

Decisions (Judicial Review) Act 1977 (Cth) provides a codified regime for the review of federal administrative decisions made under statute. Some, but not all, states have similar partial codified regimes.

Doctrine is strongly focused on matters jurisdictional, with this classification generally dictating whether matters are subject to review or not. This is underscored by a strong commitment to the legality–merits dichotomy. The factors combine to inhibit the reach of reasonableness and other substantive review. These doctrinal features, together with the fastidious manner in which they are applied, have led to Australian administrative law being described as 'exceptional' amongst its Anglo-Commonwealth brethren.[34]

Centrality of Jurisdictional Error

Jurisdictional error is the centrepiece of Australian administrative law.[35] In general terms, jurisdictional errors are reviewable; non-jurisdictional errors are not, unless they appear 'on the record' (narrowly conceived). This is, in part, driven by the fragmented nature of the regime; some remedies are only available for jurisdictional errors. In particular, jurisdictional error must be established for the writs of prohibition and mandamus; however, certiorari is not so limited.

First, while jurisdictional error has been prevalent in Australia for some time, the emblematic case entrenching its dominant role is *Craig*.[36] The prosecution in a criminal trial sought to review the decision of the District Court judge to stay the trial until the defendant was granted legal aid,

---

[34] Cane, 'Australian Administrative Law', above n. 29, 133 (the removal of Australia from 'the mainstream of developments in the rest of the common-law world'); Michael Taggart, '"Australian Exceptionalism" in Judicial Review' (2008) 36 FLR 1; Anthony Mason, 'Mike Taggart and Australian Exceptionalism' in David Dyzenhaus, Murray Hunt and Grant Huscroft (eds.), *A Simple Common Lawyer* (Hart Publishing, 2009), 179; Mark Aronson, 'Process, Quality and Variable Standards' in Dyzenhaus, Hunt and Huscroft (eds.), *A Simple Common Lawyer*, 5; Alan Freckelton, 'The Concept of Deference in Judicial Review of Administrative Decisions in Australia – Part 1' (2013) 73 AIAL Forum 52.

[35] Cane and McDonald, above n. 30, 111; Saunders, 'Catalyst', above n. 30, 148; Mark Aronson, 'Jurisdictional Error without the Tears' in Matthew Groves and H.P. Lee (eds.), *Australian Administrative Law* (Cambridge University Press, 2007), 330, 330; Taggart, 'Exceptionalism', above n. 34, 8; J.K. Kirk, 'The Concept of Jurisdictional Error' in Neil Williams (ed.), *Key Issues in Judicial Review* (Federation, 2014), 11; Aaron Moss, 'Tiptoeing Through the Tripwires' (2016) 44 Feb LR 467. For the pedigree of the term 'jurisdictional error' in Australia, see Gageler, 'Migration Law', above n. 29, 95.

[36] *Craig v. South Australia* (1995) 184 CLR 163. For earlier background see e.g. *Public Service Association of South Australia v. Federated Clerks' Union of Australia* (1991) 173 CLR 132; Aronson and Groves, above n. 32, 13–19; John Gilmour, '*Kirk*: Newton's Apple Fell' (2011) 34 Aust Bar Rev 155.

arguing that the judge had misunderstood the law governing the trial of defendants in the absence of legal aid. In doing so, the High Court rejected the claim for certiorari on the basis that if there was any legal error, it was neither jurisdictional nor apparent on the face of the record. Notably, it also firmly reinforced the primacy of jurisdictional error in Australia.

The Court identified the different categories of error which are treated as jurisdictional.[37] Jurisdictional error arises when an inferior court 'mistakenly asserts or denies the existence of jurisdiction or if it misapprehends or disregards the nature or limits of its functions or powers in a case where it correctly recognises that jurisdiction does exist'; when it 'makes an order or decision ... which is based upon a mistaken assumption or denial of jurisdiction or a misconception or disregard of the nature or limits of jurisdiction'; or when it 'purports to act wholly or partly outside the general area of its jurisdiction in the sense of entertaining a matter or making a decision or order of a kind which wholly or partly lies outside the theoretical limits of its functions and powers'.[38] The Court went on also to catalogue 'less obvious' instances of jurisdictional error where the inferior court 'while acting wholly within the general area of its jurisdiction ... [does] something which it lacks authority to do'.[39] This includes acting in circumstances where factual pre-conditions expressed in the statute are not satisfied, disregarding relevant considerations, taking into account irrelevant considerations or misconstruing the empowering statute or other instrument. The Court's explanation of each category was long, convoluted and imbued with the language of authority and jurisdiction.

The Court also recorded the types of errors made by administrative tribunals and other decision-makers that are treated as jurisdictional:[40]

> If such an administrative tribunal falls into an error of law which causes it to identify a wrong issue, to ask itself a wrong question, to ignore relevant material, to rely on irrelevant material or, at least in some circumstances, to make an erroneous finding or to reach a mistaken conclusion, and the tribunal's exercise or purported exercise of power is thereby affected, it exceeds its authority or powers. Such an error of law is jurisdictional error which will invalidate any order or decision of the tribunal which reflects it.

Notably, the categories of jurisdictional errors for administrative tribunals and other decision-makers were cast more broadly. It is presumed that any

---

[37] (1995) 184 CLR 163, [11]–[12].
[38] Ibid. For an attempt at a simplified, but still lengthy, summary, see Aronson, 'Jurisdictional Error', above n. 35, 335.
[39] Craig, above n. 36, [11]–[12].
[40] Ibid., [14].

error of law made on the part of a tribunal or other decision-maker is a jurisdictional error, whereas in the case of inferior courts it is presumed non-jurisdictional.[41] A breach of the rules of natural justice was also subsequently declared to be a jurisdictional error.[42]

More recently, the High Court in *Kirk* returned to the definition of jurisdictional error, in a case quashing the decision of an inferior court for jurisdictional error.[43] It maintained the centrality of jurisdictional errors and reiterated the procedural, institutional and constitutional factors which led to Australia's retention of jurisdictional error.[44] These factors 'point to the continued need for, and utility of, the distinction between jurisdictional and non-jurisdictional error in the Australian constitutional context'.[45] Referring to the enumerated categories, the High Court said: 'It is neither necessary, nor possible, to attempt to mark the metes and bounds of jurisdictional error'.[46] It refuted the notion that the categories of jurisdictional error in *Craig* provide 'a rigid taxonomy of jurisdictional error'; they were merely examples of such an error.[47] Despite that, it ruled that the two errors alleged in *Kirk* (misconstruction of the breadth of a criminal offence and non-compliance with a fundamental rule of criminal procedure regarding the giving of evidence by an accused) did fall within the exemplar categories of jurisdictional error.[48] Further, in the course of its reflection on *Craig*, it doubted the strength of the distinction between inferior courts and other tribunals or decision-makers in a formal sense; this suggests that the broader and narrower conceptions of jurisdictional error depend more on the nature and function of the decision-making body, rather than formal description.[49]

Secondly, the parsing of fact-finding in jurisdictional terms is well illustrated by the *Enfield* case.[50] The case concerned whether a proposed

---

[41] The distinction was cast as a presumption, implicitly rebuttable, although the strength of the presumptions have been debated: Aronson and Groves, above n. 32, 221. However, see the softening of this distinction in *Kirk* below (text to n. 49).

[42] *Re Refugee Review Tribunal, ex parte Aala* (2000) 204 CLR 82.

[43] *Kirk* v. *Industrial Court of New South Wales* (2010) 239 CLR 531, above n. 31.

[44] *Ibid.*, [66]–[70].

[45] *Ibid.*, [100].

[46] *Ibid.*, [71].

[47] *Ibid.*, [73].

[48] *Ibid.*, [74] and [76].

[49] *Ibid.*, [70]. See Cane and McDonald, above n. 30, 151 and John Basten, 'The Supervisory Jurisdiction of the Supreme Court' (2011) 85 ALJ 273, 293.

[50] *City of Enfield* v. *Development Assessment Commission* (2000) 199 CLR 135. See Margaret Allars, 'Chevron in Australia' (2002) 54 Admin LR 569; Freckelton, 'Deference – Part 1', above n. 34. See also *M70/2011* v. *Minister for Immigration and Citizenship* [2011] HCA 32, [57].

development was a 'special industry' (in this case, principally whether the waste management development generated offensive odours or not). This statutory precondition affected the extent of public notification and consequential determination of the planning application. The Development Assessment Commission determined it was not a special industry but on review the Supreme Court of South Australia disagreed and declared the consent ultra vires. On appeal, the Full Court quashed the Supreme Court's ruling, saying that the judge ought to have deferred to the judgement of the Commission and, in the absence of 'obvious and clear' departure from planning rules, should have avoided descending into merits review.[51] However, the High Court strongly rebuked any attempt to incorporate notions of deference into the review task and overturned the Full Court. Whether or not the proposed development was a special industry was a jurisdictional fact and therefore a question for the reviewing court to 'determine independently for itself'.[52] This different treatment of jurisdictional and non-jurisdictional facts was, the Court said, 'the product not of any doctrine of "deference", but of basic principles of administrative law respecting the exercise of discretionary powers'.[53] In other words, it was animated by the distinction between legality and merits.[54] So, while fact-finding relating to a jurisdictional issue is characterised as raising questions of legality and subjected to de novo review,[55] fact-finding relating to a non-jurisdictional issue is characterised as forming part of the merits and is not subjected to extremely deferential review.[56] Again, as with errors of law, the crux is therefore the determination of whether the precondition is jurisdictional or not.

One further dimension applies to jurisdictional facts. The Australian courts have adopted a different approach to review in relation to a particular class of jurisdictional facts. Where the statutory precondition has a subjective character (such as if the decision-maker is 'satisfied' or

---

[51] *Enfield*, above n. 50, [24].

[52] *Ibid.*, [48]. The Court said, though, that in the course of independently determining whether the factual condition existed, judges may in appropriate cases give weight to the factual determinations of the original decision-maker ([45]). This sits uncomfortably with the notion of de novo review. For criticism see Cane and McDonald, above n. 30, 157.

[53] *Enfield*, above n. 50, [44]. See also *Minister for Immigration and Multicultural Affairs* v. *Eshetu* (1999) 197 CLR 611, 640.

[54] *Enfield*, above n. 50, [44], endorsing *Attorney-General (NSW)* v. *Quin* (1990) 170 CLR 1; *R (NSW Plumbers & Gasfitters Employees' Union)* v. *Alley* (1981) 153 CLR 37; *Minister for Aboriginal Affairs* v. *Peko-Wallsend Ltd* (1986) 162 CLR 24. See Aronson, 'Jurisdictional Error', above n. 35, fn. 92 for doubts about the determinacy of the term 'merits'.

[55] This is subject to the subjective/objective gloss below: see text to n. 57.

[56] *Enfield*, above n. 50, [44], endorsing *Waterford* v. *The Commonwealth* (1987) 163 CLR 54.

'believes'), the courts have still treated the existence of state of mind as a jurisdictional fact but have not engaged in the same de novo review adopted for objective jurisdictional facts.[57] Instead, the courts are entitled to test the rationality and logic of the finding.[58]

Legality–Merits Dichotomy

'To judges the law; to others the merits.'[59] A strong dichotomy between legality and merits is also evident in Australian administrative law. The remarks of Brennan J in *Quin* are frequently repeated:[60] '[T]he merits of administrative action, to the extent that they can be distinguished from legality, are for the repository of the relevant power and, subject to political control, for the repository alone.' The impact of this distinction on the scope of review is explained by Saunders:[61]

> Australian doctrine limits the appropriate scope of judicial review by drawing a sharp distinction between questions of lawfulness on the one hand and questions of merit on the other, understood to encompass considerations of policy, fact and the exercise of discretion within lawful parameters.

The term 'merits' is admittedly somewhat circular; it has been described as 'that diminishing field left after permissible judicial review'.[62]

Most significantly, the legality–merits distinction reinforces the role of jurisdictional error, seeking to legitimate intervention under the guise of jurisdictional error. However, it also had the effect of significantly quelling the development of other substantive grounds of review of the kind seen in other Anglo-Commonwealth jurisdictions. Doctrines which potentially adopt more intensive review of the merits, such as variegated forms of unreasonableness, proportionality and legitimate expectation, have been roundly rejected by the Australian courts. The strict approach to the separation has, Cane and McDonald argue, emphasised 'the importance of leaving *some* latitude for administrators to get this "wrong"' and 'the wariness of Australian judges about enforcing so-called "substantive" versions

---

[57] Cane and McDonald, above n. 30, 157–62.
[58] *Minister for Immigration and Citizenship* v. *SZMDS* (2010) CLR 611, 625 and 643. See text to n. 69. Cane and McDonald suggest the precise nature of the basis of review is still in a state of flux; Cane and McDonald, above n. 30, 157.
[59] Gageler, 'Migration Law', above n. 29, 104.
[60] *Quin*, above n. 54, 36.
[61] Saunders, 'Catalyst', above n. 30, 148.
[62] *Greyhound Racing Authority (NSW)* v. *Bragg* [2003] NSWCA 388, adopted in Cane and McDonald, above n. 30, 42.

of the "rule of law", which explicitly invite judges to make value judgements on the fairness of outcomes'.[63]

The old-fashioned (highly deferential and residual) *Wednesbury*
formulation of unreasonableness dominates Australian jurisprudence;
the courts have generally resisted moves elsewhere to fashion variable
forms of unreasonableness.[64] 'Australian judicial review doctrine is indeed
exceptionalist,' Aronson says, 'particularly in its failure so far to have coun-
tenanced any relaxation in the strictness of unreasonableness review'.[65]
The commitment to *Wednesbury* can be seen in *Peko-Wallsend Ltd*.[66] As
well as endorsing *Wednesbury*'s test, Mason J echoed its deferential formulation, in a passage which has been frequently cited:[67]

> The limited role of a court reviewing the exercise of an administrative dis-
> cretion must constantly be borne in mind. It is not the function of the court
> to substitute its own decision for that of the administrator by exercising a
> discretion which the legislature has vested in the administrator. Its role is
> to set limits on the exercise of that discretion, and a decision made within
> those boundaries cannot be impugned.

The belief that the reach of the *Wednesbury* test was 'extremely confined'
was later reiterated by Brennan J in *Quin*.[68] *Wednesbury*'s deferential
approach has also been mimicked in a companion test of 'serious irrationality or illogicality', applied in relation to jurisdictional facts that have a
subjective character.[69]

---

[63] Cane and McDonald, above n. 30, 42.
[64] See generally Geoffrey Airo-Farulla, 'Rationality and Judicial Review of Administrative
 Action' (2002) MULR 543; Aronson and Groves, above n. 32, ch. 5; Cane and McDonald,
 above n. 30, 167–76.
[65] Aronson, 'Variable Standards', above n. 34, 32.
[66] *Peko-Wallsend*, above n. 54.
[67] (1986) 162 CLR 24, 40. See also *Chan* v. *Minister for Immigration and Ethnic Affairs* (1989)
 169 CLR 379; *Kruger* v. *The Commonwealth* (1997) 190 CLR 1; *Eshetu*, above n. 53. For earlier endorsement, see *Parramatta City Council* v. *Pestell* (1972) 128 CLR 305. See generally
 Airo-Faulla, 'Rationality', above n. 64, 559.
[68] *Quin*, above n. 54.
[69] *Re Minister for Immigration and Multicultural Affairs; ex parte Applicant S20/2002* (2003)
 198 ALR 59; *Minister for Immigration and Multicultural and Indigenous Affairs* v. *SGLB*
 (2004) 207 ALR 12 and *SZMDS*, above n. 58. McHugh and Gummow JJ in *S20/2002* characterised *Wednesbury* unreasonableness as only applying to review of statutory discretion;
 the 'newly-blessed close relation' of serious irrationality, applying to fact-finding, therefore
 enabled the Court to circumvent a privative clause preventing review for unreasonableness:
 see Aronson and Groves, above n. 32, 256. Aronson has doubted whether the different tests
 actually pose different standards: 'Variable Standards', above n. 34, 11.

The High Court's recent decision in *Minister for Immigration and Citizenship* v. *Li* suggests, perhaps, some weakening in this stringent approach to reasonableness review.[70] Without disavowing *Wednesbury* or its endorsement in a line of Australian cases, the High Court said the standard should not always be equated with 'an irrational, if not bizarre, decision'; the standard takes its colour from the (legislative) context.[71] This hints at a more contextual approach to the reasonableness threshold, although the methodology for determining it – and particularly the role of statutory construction in this – was not developed.[72]

Particularly notable in the Australian context is the absence of any variegated, intermediate, or sliding scale of unreasonableness, particularly when fundamental human rights are impugned.[73] Other than continuing to entrench reasonableness or irrationality equivalent to *Wednesbury*'s high standard, the High Court has not been called on to directly engage with similar developments in other jurisdictions; however, the Federal Court has expressly repelled attempts to seed variable standards of unreasonableness.[74] As Aronson and Groves record bluntly: '"Anxious scrutiny" is not part of Australia's judicial review language.'[75] Proportionality has also failed to gain any traction in traditional administrative law cases.[76]

---

[70] (2013) 249 CLR 332.

[71] *Ibid.*, 67–8 (Hayne, Kiefel and Bell JJ) ('The legal standard of reasonableness must be the standard indicated by the true construction of the statute'). However, French CJ and Gagelar J found no need to depart from the traditionally stringent *Wednesbury* formulation ([30], [113]).

[72] See Leighton McDonald, 'Rethinking Unreasonableness Review' (2014) 25 PLR 117, 132 suggesting the reference to context is an 'awkward fit with Australia's broader judicial review jurisprudence' and thus '*Wednesbury* may continue to be applied as a default position – at least in most cases'.

[73] Taggart, 'Exceptionalism', above n. 34, 12; Mason, above n. 34, 183; Alan Freckleton, 'The Concept of Deference in Judicial Review of Administrative Decisions in Australia – Part 2' (2013) 73 AIAL Forum 48, 52.

[74] See e.g. *SZADC* v. *Minister for Immigration and Multicultural and Indigenous Affairs* [2003] FCA 1497; *SHJB* v. *Minister for Immigration and Multicultural and Indigenous Affairs* (2003) 134 FCR 43. See Aronson, 'Variable Standards', above n. 34, 19, fn. 63.

[75] Aronson and Groves, above n. 32, 367.

[76] Although it was once mentioned as a possible candidate for a basis for review (*Australian Broadcasting Tribunal* v. *Bond* (1990) 170 CLR 321, 367) it has been rejected as a ground or basis for review (see e.g. *Cunliffe* v. *Commonwealth (Migration Agents case)* (1994) 182 CLR 272, 178; *Bruce* v. *Cole* (1998) 45 NSWLR 163, 185; *Andary* v. *Minister of Immigration and Multicultural Affairs* [2003] FCAFC 211). Proportionality does, however, feature in human rights adjudication in states with human rights instruments: see e.g. *Momcilovic* v. *The Queen* (2011) 280 ALR 221. See generally Janina Boughey, 'The Reasonableness of Proportionality in the Australian Administrative Law Context' (2015) 43 Fed L Rev 59.

While it is occasionally mentioned in passing, Saunders notes '[t]here are no signs of its adoption in the administrative law context'.[77] Similarly, the principle of substantive legitimate expectations has not gained any purchase.[78]

Finally, the legal and judicial culture appears to entrench the formal, categorical and ritualistic approach. The dominant judicial sensibility in Australia has been described as 'esoteric and abstract formalism' or 'devotion to legalism'.[79] In other words:[80]

> [A] highly technical approach to problems; the employment of formal, conceptual and logical analysis, often related to literalism and sometimes originalism; a belief that law is an inductive science of principles drawn from the cases, rather than the application of broad, overarching principles to particular disputes; a downplaying of the role of principle, policy, values and justice in adjudication; and in extreme forms a denial of judicial law-making.

A number of factors are cited as reasons for this legalistic judicial psyche, the centrality of jurisdictional error and the potent legality–merits demarcation: the strong commitment to the separation of powers, fortified by its constitutional entrenchment;[81] the disjointed and fragmented regimes;[82] partial, but perhaps unfruitful, codification;[83] the existence of a non-specialist merits review tribunal (the Administrative Appeals Tribunal) with co-extensive jurisdiction, coupled with a desire to preserve its different mandate in relation to merits review.[84] Others have suggested

---

[77] Saunders, 'Catalyst', above n. 30, 148, fn. 26.

[78] *Quin*, above n. 54; *Minister for Immigration, Local Government and Ethnic Affairs v. Kurtovic* (1990) 21 FCR 193; *Re Minister for Immigration and Multicultural Affairs; ex parte Lam* (2003) 214 CLR 1. See Matthew Groves, 'Treaties and Legitimate Expectations' [2010] JR 323 for an explanation of why the initial promise provided in *Minister for Immigration and Ethnic Affairs v. Teoh* (1995) 183 CLR 273 was not realised.

[79] Poole, 'Deep Blue Sea', above n. 28, 42 and Taggart, 'Exceptionalism', above n. 34, 7 respectively. See also Owen Dixon, 'Upon Taking the Oath of Office as Chief Justice' in Owen Dixon, *Jesting Pilate* (Law Book Co, 1965) 245, 247 ('strict and complete legalism'). For a spirited defence of aspects of the formalistic culture, see Aronson, 'Variable Standards', above n. 34.

[80] Taggart, 'Exceptionalism', above n. 34, 7. See also Poole, 'Deep Blue Sea', above n. 28, 25.

[81] See e.g. *Lam*, above n. 78, [76]. See generally Cane and McDonald, above n. 30, 42; 'Catalyst', above n. 30. Compare Mason, above n. 34, 182 ('limiting review to jurisdictional errors does not rest on the Constitution; its stance rests on the common law').

[82] See text to n. 30 above.

[83] Cane, 'Australian Administrative Law', above n. 29, 133. See also n. 33 above.

[84] Peter Cane, 'Merits Review and Judicial Review' (2000) 28 Fed L Rev 213; Peter Cane, *Administrative Tribunals and Adjudication* (Hart Publishing, 2009); Saunders, 'Catalyst', above n. 30, 157.

the commitment to legal formalism is more cultural; that is, it is embedded in the psyche of leading law schools and state bars and has been the *raison d'être* of a number of senior, influential judges.[85]

2.2.3   England: (Historic) Classic Model

At the time de Smith first compiled his work on judicial review, formalistic and deferential supervision was the dominant approach in judicial review in England (and was echoed throughout the Anglo-Commonwealth jurisdictions).[86] The judicial method had a technical and formalistic character where the courts' ability to intervene was conditioned according to rigid categories of analysis. This style of legal reasoning is described by Harlow as the 'classic model' of judicial review.[87] Judicial review doctrine was rigid and circumspect. 'The grounds for review were restricted', Harlow explains, 'and a strict interpretation of the doctrine of precedent inhibited rapid changes of direction'.[88] Critical distinctions – Harlow instances distinctions between rights and privileges, and between judicial and administrative acts – were central to whether a decision was reviewable.

While judicial restraint characterised the early and middle parts of the twentieth century,[89] the supervisory jurisdiction began to be reinvigorated

---

[85] Taggart, 'Exceptionalism', above n. 34, 7.

[86] Sian Elias, 'Righting Administrative Law' in Dyzenhaus, Hunt and Huscroft, above n. 34, 57 (NZ); Philip A. Joseph, 'The Contribution of the Court of Appeal to Commonwealth Administrative Law' in Rick Bigwood (ed.), *The Permanent New Zealand Court of Appeal* (Hart Publishing, 2009), 41 (NZ); Michael Taggart, 'The New Zealandness of New Zealand Public Law' (2004) PLR 81 (NZ); P.W. Hogg, 'The Supreme Court of Canada and Administrative Law, 1949–1971' (1973) 11 Osgoode LJ 187 (Can.); Audrey Macklin, 'Standard of Review' in Colleen Flood and Lorne Sossin (eds.), *Administrative Law in Context* (2nd edn, Emond Montgomery, 2012), 279 (Can.); Michael Taggart, 'Prolegomenon to an Intellectual History of Administrative Law in the Twentieth Century' (2005) 43 Osgoode Hall LJ 224 (Can.); Cane and McDonald, above n. 30, 15 (Aus.).

[87] Carol Harlow, 'A Special Relationship?' in Ian Loveland (ed.), *A Special Relationship?* (Oxford University Press, 1995), 79, 83. See also Michael Taggart, 'Reinventing Administrative Law' in Nicholas Bamforth and Peter Leyland (eds.), *Public Law in a Multi-Layered Constitution* (Hart Publishing, 2003), 311, 312. See also Richard Rawlings, 'Modelling Judicial Review' (2008) 61 CLP 95, 98.

[88] Harlow, 'A Special Relationship?', above n. 87, 83. Other features identified by Harlow include the absence of a strong distinction between public and private law; the insistence on injury to interests to justify reviewability; a system which was markedly remedial in nature and orientation.

[89] *Ibid.*, 83; Michael Taggart, 'Proportionality, Deference, *Wednesbury*' [2008] NZLR 424, 429; Rodney Austin, 'Administrative Law's Reaction to the Changing Concepts of Public Service' in Peter Leyland and Terry Woods (eds.), *Administrative Law Facing the Future* (Blackstone, 1997), 30.

in the 1960s, with a 'trilogy of great cases' – *Ridge* v. *Baldwin, Anisminic* and *Padfield* – marking a transition into what has been described as 'a new activist era'.[90] However, the approach marked by scope of review continued to dominate. Depth of review continued to be determined by a process of doctrinal classification. The judicial reinvigoration enlarged the ambit of some of the categories which were subjected to judicial scrutiny and made some particular distinctions obsolete. But it did not repudiate the essential style of legal analysis: depth of scrutiny – expressed in binary terms – continued to be set indirectly through a process of categorisation.

For present purposes, it is sufficient to identify a number of threads which help illustrate the character of legal analysis involved:

(a) the pre-eminence of the concept of jurisdiction;
(b) a strong distinction between law, fact and discretion (including deferential review in relation to the latter);
(c) functional dichotomies (particularly distinctions between matters judicial and administrative).[91]

The focus I have adopted here is on classifications addressing matters that nowadays are addressed under grounds or intensity of review. As Harlow notes, the classic model adopted numerous other classifications affecting, for example, the entitlement to seek particular writs or relief and other procedural matters. While these other distinctions augment the categorical and formalistic character of the legal reasoning under the scope of review model, the focus adopted enables the methodological changes to be more readily identified.

Jurisdiction

The concept of jurisdiction was deeply imbedded in the scope of review methodology. Jurisdiction was a key dividing line for determining whether administrative matters were reviewable or not. As noted earlier, the later

---

[90] Harlow, 'A Special Relationship?', above n. 87, 84 and 87. See also William Wade and Christopher Forsyth, *Administrative Law* (11th edn, Oxford University Press, 2014), 12 and Carol Harlow and Richard Rawlings, *Law and Administration* (3rd edn, Cambridge University Press, 2009), 100–2. Two major 'territorial claims' – the royal prerogative and decisions subject to privative clauses – were also settled in favour of the courts, 'effectively opening all issues of administrative law to legal scrutiny': Stephen Sedley, 'Foreword' in Leyland and Woods, above n. 89, xi.

[91] For a recent account of these historic dichotomies, see Philip A. Joseph, 'False Dichotomies in Administrative Law' [2016] NZ Law Rev 127.

editions of de Smith suggested that jurisdictional error might have been the 'organising principle' of these editions.[92]

The development of judicial review in terms of jurisdiction is traced by de Smith back to the seventeenth century.[93] From a historic perspective, the case of *Terry* v. *Huntington* is commonly cited as one of the earliest instances of jurisdiction dictating the reviewability of a matter.[94] Hale CB drew a distinction between jurisdictional and non-jurisdictional errors, when ruling that commissioners of excise had unlawfully levied duty on 'low wines' when their authority only related to 'strong wines':[95]

> [T]he matter here is not within their jurisdiction, which is a stinted, limited jurisdiction; and that implies a negative, viz that they shall not proceed at all in other cases. But if they should commit a mistake in a thing that were within their power, that would not be examinable here.

A similar distinction was drawn in relation to review of inferior courts by certiorari, although the courts also asserted the power to quash errors on the face of the record.[96]

The distinction continued into the first part of the twentieth century.[97] For example, in *R* v. *Nat Bell Liquors Ltd*, the Privy Council rebuked a Canadian superior court for overreaching the jurisdictional boundary when reviewing by way of certiorari a conviction for liquor possession:[98]

> [The superior Court's] jurisdiction is to see that the inferior Court has not exceeded its own, and for that very reason it is bound not to interfere in what has been done within that jurisdiction for in so doing it would itself, in turn, transgress the limits within which its own jurisdiction of supervision, not of review, is confined.

Likewise, Lord Denning in *R (Shaw)* v. *Northumberland Compensation Appeal Tribunal* said:[99]

> No one has ever doubted that the Court of King's Bench can intervene to prevent a statutory tribunal from exceeding the jurisdiction which Parliament has conferred on it; but it is quite another thing to say that the

---

[92] De Smith (5th edn), 97.
[93] De Smith (1st edn), 65.
[94] (1668) Hard 480, 145 ER 557. See de Smith (1st edn), 65 and Wade and Forsyth, above n. 90, 208, fn. 10. See also P.P. Craig, *Administrative Law* (8th edn, Sweet & Maxwell, 2016) [16-019].
[95] *Terry* v. *Huntington*, above n. 94, 483.
[96] De Smith (1st edn), 65. See e.g. *Walsall Overseers* v. *London & North Western Railway Co* (1878) 4 App Cas 30.
[97] Craig, *Administrative Law*, above n. 94, [16-021].
[98] [1922] 2 AC 128, 156.
[99] [1952] 1 KB 338, 346.

> King's Bench can intervene when a tribunal makes a mistake of law. A tri-
> bunal may often decide a point of law wrongly whilst keeping well within
> its jurisdiction.

While recognising this jurisdictional demarcation, Lord Denning is attributed with reviving the 'face of the record' gloss,[100] the exception allowing a
reviewing court to quash by certiorari 'any determination by the tribunal
which, on the face of it, offends against the law'.[101] Again, the power to
intervene is cast in categorical terms, with the consequence that the matter
is either subjected to correctness style review or it is treated as being a matter for the decision-maker and not subjected to review.

The distinction between jurisdictional and non-jurisdictional errors
of *law* was famously extinguished as a result of *Anisminic Ltd* v. *Foreign
Compensation Commission*.[102] The House of Lords undermined the previous distinction by effectively ruling that all errors of law made by an administrative body or official were capable of being treated as jurisdictional, in
a rather contorted effort to circumvent a privative clause which otherwise
would have applied. While this significantly broadened the scope of matters subjected to review, it did not amount to the abandonment of the categorical method synonymous with the scope of review model. First, all
errors of law were treated as being jurisdictional and subject to review. In
that sense, jurisdiction continued to be a key feature, but its definition was
extended and more matters were therefore exposed to review. A formalist approach still remained, but it was powered by an 'activist', rather than
'inactivist', orientation.[103] The change was significant in terms of the way
that it heralded a more vigilant supervisory jurisdiction, but the categorical

---

[100] Craig, *Administrative Law*, above n. 94, [16-034]. While the doctrine was historically significant, it oddly fell from prominence in the first half of the twentieth century.

[101] Although the scope of the 'record' been debated, Denning LJ then said it included 'at least
the document which initiates the proceedings, the pleadings, if any, and the adjudication,
but not the evidence, nor the reasons, unless the tribunal chooses to incorporate them'
(*Shaw*, above n. 99, 131).

[102] [1969] 2 AC 147. The effect of the ruling took some time to realise: Lord Diplock,
'Administrative Law' (1974) 33 CLJ 233 (distinction 'obsolete'); *Racal Communications*
[1981] AC 374 ('for practical purposes abolished'); *O'Reilly* v. *Mackman* [1983] 2 AC 278
(English public law now liberated from 'drawing esoteric distinctions'). See also *Pearlman*
v. *Harrow School Governors* [1979] QB 56 (Denning LJ). See Craig, *Administrative Law*,
above n. 94, [16-021]; William Wade, 'Constitutional and Administrative Aspects of the
Anisminic Case' (1969) 85 LQR 211; Ivan Hare, 'The Separation of Powers and Judicial
Review for Error of Law' in Christopher Forsyth and Ivan Hare (eds.), *The Golden Metwand
and the Crooked Cord* (Oxford University Press, 2008), 113.

[103] For the identification of different strategies in terms such as this, see Martin Loughlin,
'Procedural Fairness' (1978) 28 UTLJ 215, 220.

methodology remained. Secondly, review of factual errors still continued to be parsed according to their jurisdictional character.[104]

Law–Fact–Discretion

Under a scope of review approach, whether matters were subjected to review depended on their classification as a matter of law, fact or discretion, and usually in combination with the jurisdictional overlay. As mentioned earlier, distinctions between law, fact and discretion were prominent in de Smith's account of the scope of review.[105] While recognising the doctrinal significance of these distinctions, de Smith also displayed some scepticism about the robustness of the distinctions drawn between law, fact and discretion, and thus the potential judicial manipulation of the scope of review.[106]

The line-drawing had two complementary purposes. First, it demarcated those matters which the courts were prepared to review, and review on a strict basis. Secondly, the line-drawing had an allocative aspect, signalling that certain matters remained the responsibility of the original decision-maker. The former has been addressed in the previous section. The latter is the residual area of freedom – the 'four corners' of discretion – into which the courts would not enter.[107] Based on a formalist conception of the separation of powers, the courts regarded it as improper to interfere in the executive's policy-making function within this sphere.[108] A number of examples illustrate the effect of the nature of the matter on the style of review applied by the courts.

First, the doctrine now known as *Wednesbury* unreasonableness operated to regulate the law–discretion divide.[109] For matters of discretion or other matters falling outside the rubric of jurisdiction, Lord Greene stated the test for intervention in very deferential terms: 'if a decision on a competent matter is so unreasonable that no reasonable authority could ever

---

[104] Wade and Forsyth, above n. 90, 208, 217 and 227. See also text to n. 59.

[105] De Smith (1st edn), 60–1 (law and fact vs discretion) and 83–92 (law and fact).

[106] See e.g. de Smith (1st edn), 60–1.

[107] Taggart, 'Proportionality', above n. 89, 430.

[108] Harlow, 'A Special Relationship?', above n. 87, 85. See also Harlow and Rawlings, above n. 90, 95.

[109] *Associated Provincial Picture Houses Ltd* v. *Wednesbury Corporation* [1948] 1 KB 223. It is trite to say the principle had been exercised well before *Wednesbury* itself, but it became high authority for the principle: see John Laws, '*Wednesbury*' in Christopher Forsyth and Ivan Hare (eds.), *The Golden Metwand and the Crooked Cord* (Claredon, 1998), 185 and T.R. Hickman, 'The Reasonableness Principle' (2004) 63 CLJ 166.

have come to it, then the courts can interfere'.[110] Warning against judicial intervention, the well-known effect of this test was to immunise the merits from review except in the most egregious cases.[111] The *Wednesbury* case, Taggart argues, exemplifies the classic model of judicial review sketched by Harlow.[112] The rigid and constrained approach 'purported to keep the judges' noses out of the tent of politics'.[113] The *Wednesbury* test survives today, but its role is clouded nowadays by competing doctrines, attempts at re-definition, and new concepts (discussed in later chapters).[114]

Secondly, the seminal case of *Padfield* also highlights the distinction that was historically taken between law and discretion, as well as the way the scope of review could be changed by redrawing the categories of intervention.[115] The case focused on the grant of power to a minister to determine ('if the Minister in any case so directs') whether a complaint about the operation of a price-fixing regime should be directed to a committee of investigation. The referral of the complaint would have set off a chain of consequences that would have been politically unpalatable for the Minister, so he declined to refer it.

When this refusal to refer was subjected to review, the traditional approach was elaborated by Lord Morris in dissent. 'The Minister was given an executive discretion', said Lord Morris.[116] Citing *Wednesbury*, 'it is no part of the duty of any court to act as a Court of Appeal from his decision or to express any opinion as to whether it was wise or unwise'.[117] Similar sentiments were expressed by Lord Diplock, speaking for the majority of the Court of Appeal below. The matter was a policy decision and, subject to the Minister's accountability to Parliament, 'it is for him and no one else to decide to what extent he should exercise his limited powers of control'.[118]

---

[110] The term 'unreasonableness' is used in two different ways in the case: as a synonym for various other bases for intervention such as relevancy and bad faith, and in the pure unreasonableness sense quoted. The latter formulation is the one that has generally endured. See generally Craig, *Administrative Law*, above n. 94, [19-002]; Paul Craig, 'Unreasonableness and Proportionality in UK Law' in Evelyn Ellis (ed.), *The Principle of Proportionality in the Laws of Europe* (Hart Publishing, 1999), 85, 94; Harlow and Rawlings, above n. 90, 43; Taggart, 'Proportionality', above n. 89, 427.

[111] A rare exception from before *Wednesbury's* time was *Roberts* v. *Hopwoods* [1925] AC 578.

[112] Taggart, 'Reinventing', above n. 87, 312.

[113] *Ibid.*, 313.

[114] See Section 3.2.

[115] *Padfield* v. *Minister of Agriculture, Fisheries and Food* [1968] AC 997.

[116] *Ibid.*, 1040.

[117] *Ibid.*

[118] *Ibid.*, 1012.

But the majority of the House of Lords treated the question as raising a legal question, not framing an area of discretion which could not be scrutinised. Rejecting a literal approach to statutory interpretation, Lord Reid employed a purposive construction, noting that 'Parliament must have conferred the discretion with the intention that it should be used to promote the policy and objects of the Act'.[119] And the question of whether the Minister's motives not to refer the complaint 'thwarted' or 'ran counter to' the policy and objects of the Act was a legal matter for the courts to determine (in this case, concluding they did). The matter was reframed as a matter of law, not discretion, thereby changing the scope of review that applied.

Thirdly, the much maligned decision in *Liversidge* v. *Anderson* during the Second World War was based on a judicial view that the statutory precondition 'reasonable cause to believe' signalled a zone of executive discretion.[120] Therefore the basis of the Secretary of State's grounds for believing that a person was 'of hostile origins or associations' was not capable of being reviewed by the courts. Viscount Maugham said:[121]

> [T]his is so clearly a matter for executive discretion and nothing else that I cannot myself believe that those responsible for the Order in Council could have contemplated for a moment the possibility of the action of the Secretary of State being subject to the discussion, criticism and control of a judge in a court of law.

Lord Atkin's famous dissent in the case was based on a different conception of the nature of the precondition, preferring to treat it as a matter which touched on jurisdiction and law:[122]

> If its meaning is the subject of dispute as to legal rights, then ordinarily the reasonableness of the cause, and even the existence of any cause is in our law to be determined by the judge and not by the tribunal of fact if the functions deciding law and fact are divided.

De Smith suggested that in cases such of this, the 'scope of review is conditioned by practical realities'; he questioned the majority's characterisation of the power as subjective and discretionary, and doubted that such classification would be repeated except in extraordinary circumstances.[123]

---

[119]   *Ibid.*, 1030.
[120]   [1942] AC 206.
[121]   *Ibid.*, 220. The only constraint remaining was that the decision-maker needed to act in good faith.
[122]   *Ibid.*, 228.
[123]   De Smith (1st edn), 216 and 241.

Ultimately, years later, Lord Atkin's dissenting view was to prevail; the majority restrained classification was treated as an aberration and eventually condemned by the House of Lords in *Rossminster*.[124] In any event, the point presently important is how dichotomies underscored the judicial views: notions of discretion versus law were in play and dictated whether or not the matter was subjected to review. The majority treated the requirement as posing a question of administrative discretion in relation to which judicial restraint applied; Lord Atkin, in the minority, preferred to read it as a legal issue, in relation to which assessment of compliance was capable of being determined by the courts.

Functional Dichotomies

The formalistic scope of review model placed significant weight on the nature of the power being exercised to determine the applicable scope of review. Doctrines often treated legislative, judicial, and executive/administrative functions differently, varying the extent to which different functions were exposed to judicial scrutiny. As de Smith said, the classification of these functions was 'of particular importance'.[125]

A number of other examples help demonstrate the role functional dichotomies took under the scope of review approach. First, different treatment of inferior courts and administrative tribunals or officials has already been alluded to in the context of jurisdictional errors of law.[126] For a period following *Anisminic*, it was uncertain whether the collapse of the distinction between jurisdictional and non-jurisdictional errors of law was also applicable to inferior courts as well as administrative tribunals and officials.[127]

Secondly, one of most notable functional dichotomies of part of this era – until it was re-framed in *Ridge* v. *Baldwin* – was the proposition that procedural fairness only applied to decision-makers exercising 'judicial', rather than 'administrative', functions.[128] Although, strictly speaking, this

---

[124] *R (Rossminster)* v. *Inland Revenue Commissioners* [1980] AC 952, 1011. In *Ridge* v. *Baldwin* [1964] AC 40, Lord Atkin referred to *Liversidge* as a 'very peculiar' decision and the Privy Council adopted an approach consistent with Lord Atkin's dissenting approach in *Nakkuda Ali* v. *Jayaatne* [1951] AC 66.

[125] De Smith (1st edn), 17. The judicial–administrative distinction was particularly acute in its interaction with remedial and procedural matters, e.g. judicial acts could only be challenged in some writs and not others.

[126] See text to n. 92 above.

[127] See Craig, *Administrative Law*, above n. 94, [16-024]. See particularly *Racal Communications*, above n. 102.

[128] Mark Elliott, *Beatson, Matthews and Elliott's Administrative Law* (4th edn, Oxford University Press, 2011), 348; H.W.R. Wade, 'The Twilight of Natural Justice' (1951)

addressed the nature of obligations imposed on the administration by the courts, rather than directly addressing the nature of judicial scrutiny that applied to compliance with those obligations, the doctrine still mimics the latter.

Thus, for instance, the House of Lords in *Local Government Board* v. *Arlidge* took the view that the adjudicative model of natural justice was not applicable to the Board's administrative decision-making in relation to house closure orders, warning that '[j]udicial methods may, in many points of administration, be entirely unsuitable, and produce delays, expense, and public and private injury'.[129] Similarly, in *Franklin* v. *Minister of Town and Country Planning*, the House also held the procedural standards modelled on the judicial process (bias, in this case) were inapplicable to bodies required to act in a purely administrative fashion.[130] During this period, Loughlin explains, 'the courts adopted a formal classificatory approach to implying procedural safeguards', based on the judicial–administrative dichotomy.[131]

Again, during the reinvigoration of judicial review in 1960s, the House of Lords resiled from this restrictive approach in the landmark *Ridge* v. *Baldwin* decision.[132] Lord Reid adopted a broader conception of natural justice or fairness, disapproving its restriction to those bodies required to act judicially; instead, its applicability should turn on the nature of the power and effect on the individual.[133]

Thirdly, some classes of administrative acts and decisions (classes that were 'perhaps more extensive than in most foreign systems') were said to be unreviewable because of their subject-matter.[134] For example, for a

---

67 LQR 103. A broader view of natural justice, based on effect, was adopted in the nineteenth century: see e.g. *Cooper* v. *Board of Works for Wandsworth District* (1863) 143 ER 414. See a return to this approach in *Ridge* v. *Baldwin*, above n. 124, and text to n. 132.

[129] [1915] AC 120. See also *Board of Education* v. *Rice* [1911] AC 179 where the House of Lords, while recognising the flexibility of the principles of natural justice, also recognised that administrative bodies were entitled to establish their own procedures, discussed in Loughlin, above n. 103, 218.

[130] *Franklin* v. *Minister of Town and Country Planning* [1948] AC 87. See also *Nakkuda Ali*, above n. 124.

[131] Loughlin, above n. 103, 219.

[132] *Ridge* v. *Baldwin*, above n. 124. See also *Re HK (Infant)* [1967] 2 QB 617 for clear rejection of the process of categorisation to determine whether natural justice or fairness applied. Compare *Pearlberg* v. *Varty* [1972] 1 WLR 534.

[133] Elements of a categorical approach remained. See e.g. the mention of 'well-known classes of cases' where natural justice routinely applied in *Durayappah* v. *Fernando* [1967] 2 AC 337, 349.

[134] De Smith (1st edn), 17.

significant period, the royal prerogative was treated differently than other exercises of power; when the source of administrative power was monarchical, its exercise was treated as being immune from review, thus continuing a categorical approach based on institutional character.[135]

Finally, in relation to the review of subordinate legislation, a distinction was drawn based on the character of the law-making body. The scope of review depended on whether the subordinate legislation was made by a minister or sub-national body. While bylaws or regulations made by both were reviewable for jurisdictional questions, unreasonableness review was permitted only in relation to local authority bylaws, not regulations or other subordinate instruments made by ministers.[136]

2.2.4   Conclusion

Categorical formalism prevails under scope of review. This approach dominated English law before it was systematised in the mid-1980s and continues today in Australia. It is a method grounded in categorical distinctions – such as law–fact–policy, process–substance, judicial–administrative–legislative, jurisdictional and non-jurisdictional. This, as Dyzenhaus explains, is the method of formalism:[137]

> Formalism is formal in that it requires judges to operate with categories and distinctions that determine results without the judges having to deploy substantive arguments that underpin the categories and distinctions.

That is the essence of the judicial style under the scope of review method.

---

[135] De Smith (1st edn), 188. The courts were only prepared to enquire into whether the particular prerogative existed, but would not look at the manner in which it was, or should have been, exercised: Ian Loveland, *Constitutional Law, Administrative Law and Human Rights* (5th edn, Oxford University Press, 2009), 102 ('limited review'). See e.g. *Attorney-General v. De Keyser's Royal Hotel Ltd* [1920] AC 508; *China Navigation Co Ltd v. Attorney-General* [1932] 2 KB 197 (prerogative established and not reviewable); *Burmah Oil Company (Burma Trading) Ltd v. Lord Advocate* [1965] AC 75 (prerogative power not established). See generally Paul Jackson, 'The Royal Prerogative' (1964) 6 MLR 709. For subsequent and incremental circumscription of the non-justiciability of the prerogative, see e.g. *R (Lain) v. Criminal Injuries Compensation Board* [1967] 2 QB 864; *Council of Civil Service Unions v. Minister for the Civil Service* [1985] AC 374; *R (Bentley) v. Secretary of State for the Home Office* [1994] QB 349; *R (Fire Brigades Union) v. Secretary of State for the Home Office* [1995] 2 AC 513; *R (Abbasi) v. Secretary of State for Foreign and Commonwealth Affairs* [2002] EWCA Civ 1598.

[136] Compare *Kruse v. Johnson* [1898] 2 QB 91 (local authority bylaw) and *Sparks v. Edward Ash Ltd* [1943] KB 223. See also *Taylor v. Brighton Corporation* [1947] KB 736.

[137] David Dyzenhaus, 'Constituting the Rule of Law' (2002) 27 Queens LJ 445, 450.

2.3 Conceptual Foundations

I turn now to the theoretical basis for this style of methodology and schema. It is rare nowadays to find continuing commitment to the scope of review model. Categorical formalism has largely gone out of fashion. Notable exceptions include Christopher Forsyth's defence of formalism in administrative law, and the work of Australian scholars, such as Aronson, who seek to rationalise the continuing application of abstract formalism in that jurisdiction.

The formalism of scope of review shares its ethos with the ultra vires or legislative intent school. The definition of the role of the judiciary is cast in technical terms, giving effect to the will of Parliament. While conceding some need for the judiciary to fashion principles of judicial review, the cues are said to be found in the product of (the sovereign) Parliament, not by resort to independent substantive values. The constitutional order is kept stable through the maintenance of a separation of powers based on law-making, law-applying, law-interpreting models of the legislature, administration and judiciary respectively.

2.3.1 Christopher Forsyth: Passionate Formalism and Ultra Vires

Forsyth is stringent in his defence of formalism.[138] He continues to echo the Diceyan sentiments of his former colleague and co-author, Sir William Wade.[139] He explains the formalist's approach in terms of permissible and impermissible sources of law.[140] Answers to administrative law questions are to be found, he says, in legislation and judicial decisions and should not be based on substantive reasoning. Statutes are to be applied based on their face, based on text, without reference to background motivations and so forth. The system of precedent is the 'great engine of certainty in the legal system' and the identification of *ratio decidendi* continues to be 'a meaningful endeavour'.[141] In contrast, substantive reasoning based on moral, economic, political, institutional

---

[138] Christopher Forsyth, 'Showing the Fly the Way Out of the Flybottle' (2007) 66 CLJ 325.
[139] From the 7th edition on, they penned the famous administrative law textbook together (Wade and Forsyth, above n. 90) until Wade's death in 2004; Forsyth continues to author the textbook today.
[140] Forsyth, 'Flybottle', above n. 138, 328.
[141] *Ibid.*, 329.

or other social considerations is 'simply irrelevant'.[142] This formal reasoning, he argues, is a 'virtue'; it is ingrained in the English common
law method, it buttresses (a formal conception of) the rule of law, and it
promotes certainty.[143] He criticises those who argue judicial discretion
should subsume these 'stark categories'.[144] Categories serve to 'structure
and constrain the judicial role'; judges are subject to law and the law must
continue to be their master.[145]

Hand-in-hand with Forsyth's spirited defence of formalism comes
his commitment to the ultra vires or legislative intent theory of judicial
review (albeit, in the end, modified from its original direct legislative
intent formulation).[146] Forsyth argues that those who doubt the ultra vires
justification of judicial review undermine 'the proper balance of powers
between the elected and non-elected parts of the constitution'.[147] Ultra
vires proponents and judges who apply it fulfil the legislature's intention
and are 'guardians' of the constitutional order; naysayers who challenge
the intention of Parliament are 'subverters' of this order.[148] While he
acknowledges that principles and grounds of judicial review are judicial
creations, he links the *authority* to do so back to the presumed or implied
intention of the legislature. '[T]he legislature is taken to have granted
an *imprimatur* to the judges to develop the law in the particular area'.[149]
His reliance on the implied or general intent of the legislature avoids the
insurmountable defect of the traditional ultra vires or specific legislative
intent theory, namely that it is impossible to characterise judicial intervention as the delegated enforcement of boundaries set by the legislature
when the legislature does not concern itself with or legislate the detailed
principles of judicial review that are applied by the courts. Despite the
modified ultra vires theory admitting that the responsibility for articulating the principles of good administration lies with the courts, Forsyth

---

[142] *Ibid.*, 328.
[143] *Ibid.*, 347.
[144] *Ibid.*, 339. His comments here are in relation to the question of remedies – distinction
between void, voidable, nullity, and so forth – but are equally applicable elsewhere.
[145] Forsyth, 'The Metaphysics of Nullity' in Forsyth and Hare, above n. 102, 141.
[146] Forsyth edited the collection of essays drawn from the famed symposium at which this
debate was vigorously debated: Christopher Forsyth, *Judicial Review and the Constitution*
(Hart Publishing, 2000). See also his own contribution, 'Of Fig Leaves and Fairy Tales' in
Judicial Review and the Constitution, 29. See also Christopher Forsyth and Mark Elliott,
'The Legitimacy of Judicial Review' [2003] PL 286.
[147] Forsyth, 'Fig Leaves', above n. 146, 137.
[148] *Ibid.*, 137.
[149] *Ibid.*, 135.

(subsequently) fortifies the connection back to legislative intent.[150] He argues, writing with Mark Elliott, that when fashioning these principles, the courts 'rely frequently and closely upon an analysis of the relevant statute'.[151] So, it need not be merely assumed that the legislature intends power should be exercised in accordance with the rule of law as elaborated by judges. The limits can instead be justified as a matter of inference: 'judges determine the boundaries of the decision-makers' power by inferences drawn from the relevant statute', usually without 'reliance upon the common law or any other extra-statutory source of law'.[152] The primacy of the ultra vires doctrine follows in Forsyth's view: 'the courts' one and only task is to determine whether the administrative action in question is intra vires or ultra vires'.[153]

Ultra vires therefore continues to be the ultimate organising principle for Forsyth and his position in the debate on the constitutional underpinnings directly manifests itself in his favoured operational schema for judicial review. His take on the systemisation of judicial review grounds and principles is overlaid with an ultra vires gloss.[154] For example, Forsyth commends as 'orthodox' Lord Browne-Wilkinson's tripartite recital of the grounds of review but emphasises that if any of the grounds are made out the decision-maker is 'acting ultra vires his powers and therefore unlawfully'.[155] And these heads of judicial review come not from the common law; rather 'the existence and development of the heads of review … involves the application of general principles of good administration through an explicitly constitutional mode of statutory construction'.[156] In Forsyth's world, everything must be linked back to the legislature and statute.

Forsyth therefore promotes legal reasoning that is attentive to the form, not substance, of administrative decisions and circumstances; in doing so, he seeks to defend the role of strict categories in administrative law.

---

[150] Forsyth and Elliott, above n. 146, 299–306.
[151] Ibid., 303.
[152] Ibid., 303, 306.
[153] Ibid., 306.
[154] The distinction between the scope of review and grounds of review schemata is more a combination of the degree of tightness and overall attitude, as both employ categorical approaches. See text to 311.
[155] Forsyth, 'Fig Leaves', above n. 146, 123.
[156] Forsyth and Elliott, above n. 146, 307.

2.3.2   Mark Aronson: (Reluctant) Bottom-up Formalism

Aronson's native jurisdiction is dominated by abstract formalism and he appears content, perhaps a little reluctantly, to work within that paradigm. In particular, he is anxious to deflect condemnatory claims of formalism and sees formalistic schema as still being capable of addressing the issues arising in a modern administrative state, just like other schemata.[157]

First and foremost, Aronson, like Forsyth, objects to formalism's negative connotations. He suggests the central accusations from its critics are a lack of style and lack of transparency in the judicial reasoning process, neither of which he regards as particularly problematic. Instead he treats the accusations of formalism as a claim that Australian law 'should be more directly normative or principles-based'.[158] On this point, he appears somewhat ambivalent, a point discussed below.

Secondly, in terms of the debate on the constitutional foundations of judicial review, Aronson has not signalled a definitive position. In his text, he characterises it – perhaps pejoratively – as a 'British debate'.[159] His account of the debate indicates he has little interest in engaging with it and he suggests it has little to offer in Australia, particularly with its different constitutional setting. Instead, the theoretical debate in Australia is drawn as a contest between 'bottom-up' and 'top-down':[160] that is, whether the grounds of judicial review are to be developed by reference to overarching or abstract principles (top-down) or whether a more incremental and conservative approach should be adopted (bottom-up). While not strident about a bottom-up approach – grounded in the tight application of precedent and incremental development – Aronson seems comfortable working within that framework. Aronson suggests judicial review probably needs a bit of both.[161] Sceptical about abstract legal principles being applied in their own right, he also suggests the development of rule-based legal reasoning is enhanced if coordinated by principles and values.[162]

---

[157] Aronson, 'Variable Standards', above n. 34.
[158] *Ibid.*, 24.
[159] Aronson and Groves, above n. 32, 119 and 122. The ultra vires debate is not prominent in Australia; for rare mention, see Stephen Gageler, 'The Underpinnings of Judicial Review of Administrative Action' (2000) 28 Fed LR 303, 311 (identifying some alignment between the ultra vires theory and the conceptual approach typically employed in Australia).
[160] See n. 212 below.
[161] Aronson, 'Variable Standards', above n. 34, 22.
[162] *Ibid.*, 26.

Thirdly, the key dichotomy employed by Aronson, in terms of an organising schema, is between *process* and *quality*.[163] A formal, categorical distinction – resonant of the scope of review schema – reigns. He treats process grounds – grounds like error of law, relevancy, non-satisfaction of preconditions and so forth – as being equivalent to matters of jurisdiction. When viewed abstractly these grounds, he argues, 'mark out the limits of or boundaries to an administrative decision-maker's powers (almost in a spatial sense), and ... dictate the procedures to be observed'.[164] In his view, these grounds do not raise any questions about the legitimacy of judicial review because their application 'usually does not turn on ... the degree to which (if at all) the court's view of the process requirements differs from the decision-maker's view'.[165] There are typically right answers to these questions and the courts are entitled to express their view on these matters; any margin or latitude arises only indirectly, he argues. The corollary is that the *balance* – the quality of a decision or its merits – is not so straightforward and second-guessing such balance is generally to be avoided by the courts. This is the binary approach which has dominated Aronson's home jurisdiction.

Aronson is not dogmatic about the demarcation but he is wary of the consequences of engaging in qualitative review. 'Judicial review "shifts gears" when it engages in qualitative review'.[166] For instance, he argues that qualitative review entails a greater evidentiary corpus and more work on the part of judges. One senses that Aronson may entertain greater deployment of qualitative grounds, albeit on a cautious and reserved basis. He wonders if this would be preferable to the current practice of covertly stretching process grounds in order to address qualitative concerns – an admission of the manipulability of this formalist schema. And he worries that the strict adherence to the process–quality distinction in order to avoid adverse consequence of judicial discretion on the part of the supervisory court leaves administrative discretion too unconstrained, at least as it relates to the merits. Addressing uncertainty in one creates uncertainty in the other.[167]

Although he hints at being open to more qualitative review, including in the context of reasonableness review, he stops short of recommending

---

[163] *Ibid.*, 7.
[164] *Ibid.*, 9.
[165] *Ibid.*, 9.
[166] *Ibid.*, 32.
[167] *Ibid.*, 28.

explicit doctrinal variability. On the matter of the modulation of the depth of review, Aronson comes across as agnostic on the question of whether the legal principles and grounds should be explicitly variable.[168] He records the fact that Australia, unlike its Anglo-Commonwealth siblings, has not deployed variable grounds and is content to identify the Australian resistance to such a move.[169] For him, reasonableness is inevitably 'variable in its application ... [e]ven if the standard were to remain the same'.[170] More important, he suggests, is the question of whether the standard should be more 'demanding' in cases where human rights are engaged (on which he expresses no view):[171] seeds, perhaps, of some interest in escaping the confines of the bottom-up or scope of review approach.

2.3.3   Conclusion

Those who exhibit support for scope of review schema tend to have a formalist orientation. Forsyth actively promotes a commitment to the formalist agenda; Aronson comes across more as a passive participant. Framed in terms of King's models of judicial restraint, this is the domain of the formalist institutionalists.[172] Judicial restraint manifests itself through formal but abstract distinctions based on the formalist separation of power between legislatures, the executive and the courts. Judicial restraint is governed by allocative distinctions between law and politics, principle and policy, justiciable and non-justiciable, and so forth.[173]

Much of this is consistent with the position adopted on the constitutional underpinnings of judicial review. Forsyth has been one of the main protagonists behind the ultra vires or legislative intent theory. Aronson identifies a divide in Australian jurisprudence between 'top-downers' and 'bottom-uppers', which has some analogue to the ultra vires debate, and

---

[168] On this point, Aronson's position is drawn from his response to Taggart's criticism of Australia's exceptionalism and challenge for greater variability: *ibid.*, responding to Taggart, 'Exceptionalism', above n. 34.

[169] Aronson, 'Variable Standards', above n. 34, 7. He notes that, although the courts have acknowledged that unreasonableness and irrationality are matters of degree, this does not operate as variation of intensity 'according to the gravity [or] the context' as seen in other jurisdictions (at 19).

[170] *Ibid.*, 32.

[171] *Ibid.*

[172] Jeff King, 'Institutional Approaches to Judicial Restraint' (2008) 28 OJLS 409, 414.

[173] *Ibid.*

seems (mostly) content to continue to work with the incremental and subordinate judicial role presented by the latter.

Thus, we can think about scope of review being based in a formal vision of the separation of powers, where the judicial role is drawn narrowly and confined to distinct realms. The colour of judicial review is drawn from parliamentary intent, rather than values divined by judges. And this manifests a strong commitment to a formalistic style of judging: black-letter law, strong precedent, conservative incrementalism, certainty and stability – with little open admission that judges can readily manipulate doctrine and undercut those features.

2.4   Normative Assessment

The scope of review schema is characterised by its formal and categorical approach to the modulation of the depth of scrutiny, based on a suite of complex rules. The method is synonymous, particularly in Australia, with an abstract and technical judicial mentality. On the one hand, its embrace of general rules means it performs well in terms of many of the principles of efficacy. On the other hand, it still enables variability and judicial discretion, but does so indirectly and latently. Its reliance on categorical proxies to determine the depth of review and corresponding propensity for manipulation means the veneer of rules cloaks significant judicial discretion. Thus, the performance of the schema – when viewed more closely and critically – is less favourable.

Generality

The scope of review methodology is heavily doctrinal and grounded in categorisation, as the earlier doctrinal study demonstrates. On its face, therefore, it is the most rule-bound and least flexible schema and thus satisfies the expectations of generality. However, the latent judicial discretion and potential for manipulation significantly diminishes the role of rules and consequently the generality of the schema.

In formal terms, the rigid categories and formal boundaries of the scope of review methodology aim to emphasise consistency and order, at the expense of adaptability and flexibility. The attention to form seeks to avoid normative, value-based considerations. The English experience with this style of supervision was marked by distinctions between law, fact and discretion, between the character of the power under review, and distinctions between error within jurisdiction and errors going to jurisdiction. These distinctions, when drawn in combination, affected whether a power was open to challenge or not. The distinctions employed were multifarious and complex. In Australia today, jurisdictional error manifests an all-important boundary for the scope of review.[174] In general terms, matters jurisdictional are subject to close judicial scrutiny; matters not are not (with only a few exceptions). Similarly, the legality–merits dichotomy assumes a prominent role. Supervision is dependent on a process of 'very fine line-drawing'.[175] It is this process of classification or allocation to different classes which dictates the depth of scrutiny (even though the language of depth of scrutiny and intensity is not employed).[176]

Under a scope of review method, *law* stands at the centre of the deliberative task, with categories structuring and constraining the judicial role.[177] The scope of review schema presents itself as deductive and mechanical. This style of reasoning and adjudication, with formal categorisation at its core, is grounded in the notion of rules; it is based around a settled catalogue of categories operating as a blue-print of the depth of judicial scrutiny. The rules generally adopt a binary approach to the depth of scrutiny and, although typically equated with judicial restraint, are agnostic as to the depth of review.

The predominant question under a scope of review approach is whether a matter is capable of being reviewed by the courts. The depth of judicial scrutiny is generally binary, in the sense of the issue being exposed to review or not, and is conditioned by the nature of the decision, decision-maker and so forth. The judicial approach commended by the schema has a mechanical flavour: identification of the applicable categories; classification of impugned decision into those categories; resultant conclusion about whether the decision is subjected to review or not; in the case of those decisions exposed to review, evaluation of whether the decision was adequate. The categories delineate whether review of certain matters is permissible, thereby effectively dictating whether or not the supervising

---

174 While Australian administrative law manifests a scope of review mentality, the phraseology of grounds of review is still found in the Australian system, particularly in the codified regimes which sought to shift the focus from remedies to grounds. However, the grounds do not have the same generalised and monolithic nature as seen in other jurisdictions, are overshadowed by the concepts of jurisdiction and legality–merits, and have a much more technical and minutial expression. See Cane and McDonald, above n. 30, 111 ('key question is whether an error which gives rise to a particular ground of review can be classified as a jurisdictional error'); de Smith (7th edn), 234. See Section 3.2.4.

175 Aronson, 'Jurisdictional Error', above n. 35, 333.

176 Cane and McDonald, above n. 30, 155.

177 Forsyth, 'Metaphysics', above n. 145, 145.

court should intervene or not.[178] There is an absence of any intermediate options or a range of possibilities. This is especially notable in Australia, where the prevalent depths of review are a form of correctness review or a very deferential opposite, with no middle ground or sliding scale of intensity occupying the space between the two extremes. Any residual variability or methodological nuance is subordinate to the dominant question of whether a matter is reviewable or not.

Although this restrained and exclusionary approach gives an impression of judicial conservatism and restraint, the categorical style of legal reasoning is more agnostic to the depth of review. It can be deployed to dictate restrained judicial supervision; it can also be deployed to dictate more vigilant judicial supervision. Categorical formalism still endured after the reinvigoration of judicial review, even though the definition of the categories was re-drawn to mandate more intensive review. As Poole observes, 'methodological formalism does not necessarily equate to conservative outcomes'.[179] He rightly points to Australia's rejection of deference in Enfield and the more intensive review that then followed – something normally associated with the embrace of a doctrinal deference. A similar point is made by Cane, who notes the irony that the expansion in the concept of jurisdiction has actually led to increased judicial control over the merits.[180]

Thus, on its face, the scope of review schema scores well in terms of generality. Although the catalogue is multifarious and complex, in theory, the schema enables those affected and the administration to determine the courts' expected approach to the review of particular decisions.

Despite being deeply rooted in formal distinctions and rhetoric, categorical complexity enables variability and judicial discretion – albeit on an indirect and latent basis. The rule-based nature of the scope of review schema is therefore undermined and the generality of the regime significantly compromised. Modulation of the depth of scrutiny is not explicit. The judicial ability to vary the depth of review occurs indirectly, based on the complexities of the categorisation task. The definitions that characterised the doctrinal approach are often unstable and the distinctions

---

[178] Here, the high threshold set by Wednesbury is generally equated with the inability to review the decision.

[179] Poole, 'Deep Blue Sea', above n. 28, 29.

[180] Cane, 'Merits Review', above n. 84, 221. See also Allars, above n. 50, 570; Mark Aronson, 'The Resurgence of Jurisdictional Facts' (2001) 12 PLR 17; Taggart, 'Exceptionalism', above n. 34, 9; Cane and McDonald, above n. 30, 150.

porous. This brings with it the latent ability to modulate the depth of review through manipulation of the classification task.

Similarly, while the strict approach to jurisdictional error in Australia purports to leave no room for any latitude, Aronson observes that this may still be achieved indirectly: 'There is considerable debate, for example, as to whether ... a factual prerequisite is jurisdictional or non-jurisdictional'.[181] Although there is strong hostility to the language of deference,[182] the notion of deference is still central to the judicial methodology. Rather than being embraced overtly, it is fashioned by line-drawing based on jurisdictional error, which as a consequence leaves autonomous space for decision-makers. The ubiquitous 'legality/merits' dichotomy also has judicial restraint or deference at its core.[183] This approach to judicial restraint has been described as 'exclusionary deference' (in contradistinction to 'standard of review' deference); in other words, deference arises by the exclusion of certain decisions from review.[184] The combination of abstract and imprecise criteria combined with the need for judicial judgement means the jurisdictional error methodology is undoubtedly 'manipulable'.[185] Cane and McDonald say the 'legality/merits distinction is flexible enough for judges to pay considerable deference to decision-makers'.[186] More pointedly, Taggart argues forcefully that the jurisdictional error label 'can mask the degree of judicial discretion involved and obscure the reasons for intervening or not in a particular case'.[187]

The schema is unable to suppress normative considerations; these considerations remain covert and the methodology is cloaked with fictional formal discourse and deliberations. These accusations are well rehearsed in the literature. As de Smith said in the first edition of his text: '[I]n many cases the truth of the matter is that the mode of classifying ... is determined by the scope of review that the courts deem to be desirable and practicable'

---

[181] Aronson, 'Variable Standards', above n. 34, 10. Aronson also highlights discretionary choices which similarly condition intervention (directory vs mandatory requirements; ability to withhold relief for delay): 'Jurisdictional Facts', above n. 180, 17.

[182] See particularly its rejection in *Enfield*, above n. 50. See also a highly critical extra-judicial perspective: K.M. Hayne, 'Deference' [2011] PL 75.

[183] Taggart adopts an analogy from Dworkin to describe this space: '[D]iscretion is the hole in the middle of the doughnut filled with policy and politics, and into which the courts will not enter.' See Taggart, 'Exceptionalism', above n. 34, 13, borrowing from Ronald Dworkin, *Taking Rights Seriously* (Harvard University Press, 1978), 31.

[184] Cane, 'Merits Review', above n. 84, 226.

[185] Basten, above n. 49, 287.

[186] Cane and McDonald, above n. 30, 42.

[187] Taggart, 'Exceptionalism', above n. 34, 8.

or 'is often nothing more than a rationalisation of a decision prompted by considerations of public policy'.[188] In a similar vein, Aronson has characterised Australia's jurisdictional error lodestar as 'conclusory'.[189] Others have described it as 'manipulable'[190] or 'flexible',[191] and suggested the doctrine 'masks' judicial discretion.[192] Poole, one of the stronger critics of the Australian jurisprudence, describes this abstract legalism as a 'parody' – a ritual that the participants acknowledge seeks to disguise the underlying normative assessment that occurs:[193] 'Judges revel in the opaque and obscurantist quality of their judgments. Law becomes ritual. And no-one is remotely convinced that any of it is apolitical.'[194]

Thus, the scope of review schema, in reality, disappoints in terms of generality. It is plagued by a two-track style. It is a formal, ruled-based system. But one that is prone to manipulation and dissonance in application.

Public Accessibility and Transparency

Seemingly grounded in legal methodology – detached and deductively logical – the schema appears to be relatively accessible and transparent. However, the potential for, and practice of, judicial manipulation of the formal categories and distinction means accessibility and transparency are undermined.[195]

We expect that the obligation to elaborate the basis for a decision improves the quality of a decision or outcome.[196] But if the reasoning required, as here, is restricted to formal categorisation, then the prophylactic aspects of open reasoning are not fully reached. The discourse of justification does not connect with the conceptual basis for review, risking lack of attention to conceptual considerations. The use of formal categories and distinctions to give effect, by proxy, to conceptual values has dangers though. As Dyzenhaus points out, the categories and distinctions are

---

[188]   De Smith (1st edn), 50, 51.
[189]   Aronson, 'Jurisdictional Error', above n. 35, 330.
[190]   Basten, above n. 49, 287.
[191]   Cane and McDonald, above n. 30, 42.
[192]   Taggart, 'Exceptionalism', above n. 34, 8.
[193]   Poole, 'Deep Blue Sea', above n. 28, 33.
[194]   *Ibid.*
[195]   For the realist deconstruction of formalist legal reasoning see Felix S. Cohen, 'Transcendental Nonsense and the Functionalist Approach' (1935) 35 Colum L Rev 809.
[196]   Lon L. Fuller, *Anatomy of Law* (Greenwood Press, 1976), 91.

slated to operate in a 'detached' manner, however, 'they are capable of determining results that contradict the very arguments for these categories and distinctions'.[197]

Indirect and categorical legal reasoning is less problematic where the conceptual and normative basis for review align with established legal categories. However, where the normative force for vigilance or restraint does not match the depth of scrutiny that a particular category implicitly delivers there is an incentive to manipulate the classification process. As the distinctions framing the categories are often able to be overcome with relative ease, this encourages dissonance and leads to lack of congruence in application. Scope of review has a particularly poor record of ensuring alignment between the conceptual and the doctrinal.

It may be argued that when judges approach individual cases, they do so against the backdrop of received wisdom on these conceptual dimensions. That is, the categories serve as shorthand responses for this broader suite of conceptual factors and it can be assumed that the doctrinal response in an individual case can be read together with its generic conceptual underpinnings. However, this is still unsatisfactory. The nature of doctrinal argumentation and reasoning can easily overshadow the conceptual and instrumental basis for review. There is no guarantee that connections between the doctrinal and conceptual will be made; it can only be hoped that conceptual underpinnings will be inculcated into the deliberative process. Moreover, while affected people may be able to fill in the gaps and interpret the doctrinal approach in the light of the conceptual underpinnings, the partial approach undermines the deliberative value of transparency and reasoning.

Prospectivity

Scope of review, as with all the schema, is prospective in operation, given it is generally based on doctrinal rules promulgated in advance. However, the extent of (covert) judicial discretion and lack of congruence means there is some potential for the regime to have some retrospective effect as the content of rules are not controlling. The lack of predictability and clarity undermines legal certainty and adds some concern about prospectivity.

Clarity

The scope of review approach performs poorly in terms of clarity. The dominance of abstract legalism and complex classification tasks contribute to a lack of guidance, consistency and understandability.

---

[197] Dyzenhaus, 'Rule of Law', above n. 137, 450.

The language associated with this schema is typically dominated by abstract legal concepts, such as jurisdiction, nullity, ultra vires, and so forth. It also involves a complex classification based on various combinations of the nature of alleged error, the nature of the decision-maker, the nature of the statutory power in question and, in some cases, the nature of the remedy sought. The process of categorisation is not straightforward. It cannot, as Spigelman observes, be reduced to a 'single test or theory or logical process'.[198] The account from the judiciary is that this is principally a process of statutory interpretation.[199] Notably, the determination turns on the nature and form of the decision, not its effect. As Brennan J in *Quin* said: '[T]he scope of judicial review must be defined not in terms of the protection of individual interests but in terms of the extent of power and the legality of its exercise.'[200]

Its opacity is frequently acknowledged though. For example, jurisdictional error has been described by judges as a 'slippery term'.[201] Kirby J lamented that the distinction in contemporary Australian law was 'uncertain' and 'often extremely difficult to find'.[202] Despite the acknowledgment of this complexity and uncertainty, the High Court has remained trenchant about its utility. For example, Hayne J in *Aala* said 'difficulty of drawing a bright line' should not 'obscure the difference that is illustrated by considering clear cases of each species of error'.[203] Similarly, Glesson CJ said the difference between legality and merits 'is not always clear-cut'; but so too, he said, is the difference between night and day: '[t]wilight does not invalidate the distinction'.[204] Regardless, the central doctrinal tests under the scope of review approach are undoubtedly complex and uncertain. Moreover, the methodology inevitably incorporates normative dimensions, despite its appearance otherwise. As mentioned earlier, jurisdictional error tends to operate as a conclusory label, when other – often undisclosed – errors are identified.[205]

---

[198] J.J. Spigelman, 'The Centrality of Jurisdictional Error' (2010) 21 PLR 77.
[199] See e.g. *Project Blue Sky Inc v. Australian Broadcasting Authority* (1998) 194 CLR 355, 389.
[200] *Quin*, above n. 54, 35.
[201] *Minister for Immigration and Multicultural and Indigenous Affairs v. B* (2004) 219 CLR 365, [106].
[202] *Re Minister for Immigration and Multicultural Affairs; ex parte Miah* (2000) 179 ALR 238, [211] (Kirby J).
[203] *Aala*, above n. 42, [162].
[204] Murray Gleeson, 'Judicial Legitimacy' (2000) 20 Aust Bar Rev 4, 11.
[205] Aronson, 'Jurisdictional Error', above n. 35, 333.

The language of scope of review is hollow and inaccessible, even for those conversant in law. Moreover, this jargon disguises the basis for intervention and seeks to cloak the task in law-like 'detached' language, in order to improve its legitimacy. But these terms convey little to participants or affected people about the expectations the law places on decision-makers or the approach the courts adopt when policing them.

Stability

The scope of review schema is generally stable but is not immune from evolution and change. Rather than evolution being expressly contemplated by the regime, doctrinal change has generally taken the form of recasting or reformulating existing categories.

The redefinition of matters of jurisdiction in England following *Anisminic* is a notable example, along with other cases such as *Padfield* and *Ridge* v. *Baldwin*, which signalled a more vigilant era on the part of the courts. On my account, though, the more vigilant turn did not involve the repudiation of the underlying methodology. A scope of review schema continued to be employed, where the depth of review was determined indirectly through a process of classification. The key difference was that casting the boundaries provided scope for intensive judicial scrutiny.[206] This was, in Loughlin's language, a shift from 'inactive formalism' to 'active formalism'.[207]

Similarly in Australia, the concept of jurisdictional error has been recast over time. The shape of the doctrinal categories has adapted over time as the judicial philosophy about what matters should be subjected to review has changed. A number of aspects have expanded or contracted over time: for example, jurisdictional error used to be more narrowly defined in relation to inferior courts, scope for jurisdictional factual error has expanded, and the face of the record exception for non-jurisdictional errors has enlarged.[208] Indeed, some of these developments are essentially activist in nature, as they have been used to deflect attempts by the legislature to restrict the reach of judicial review over some matters.[209]

For present purposes, these evolutionary type of changes tend to be generational and relatively benign. They do not present the volatile instability that is of particular concern under the rubric of instability, as identified by Fuller.

---

[206] See text to nn. 102, 115, 132 above.
[207] Loughlin, above n. 103, 221.
[208] Cane and McDonald, above n. 30, 151.
[209] *Ibid.*, 150.

On a more micro level, though, the openness of the scheme to judi-cial manipulation does challenge the ideal of stability. The covert ability of judges to vary the depth of review through classification process means that, in effect, outcomes are more fluid than the formal regime admits. Thus, overall, the schema can present a degree of instability, due to the latent judicial discretion involved.

Non-contradiction and Coherence

The scope of review approach is characterised by its doctrinal morass and the lack of any organising theory. Multifarious categories implicitly deter-mine the depth of scrutiny but the distinctions often overlap and intersect. No schematic harmony is evident. Conclusory labels such as jurisdic-tional error or ultra vires merely signal judicial intervention, rather than providing shape for the underlying doctrine. The covert role of discretion and dissonance between the potential formal and tacit judicial method-ologies exacerbates the lack of doctrinal coherence. De Smith lamented that 'no uniformity characterises the scope of review' in English law and said this necessitated the articulation of the circumstances of judicial intervention 'either in minute detail or at a high level of generality'.[210] It was, as Gageler described, 'just a mass of case law', without any organising theory.[211] Similarly, Australian judges display a preference for 'bottom-up', rather than 'top-down', legal reasoning.[212] Gageler captures the distinction as follows:[213]

> In 'top down' reasoning the judge or legal analyst adopts a theory about an area of law. The theory is then used to organise and explain the cases; to marginalise some and to canonise others. In 'bottom up' reasoning the judge or legal analyst starts with the mass of cases or the legislative text and moves only so far as necessary to resolve the case at hand.

Rather than adopting 'an open-textured, common-law approach to admin-istrative law', Cane speaks of Australian judges deploying 'a more technical

---

[210]   De Smith (1st edn), 15.
[211]   Gageler, 'Underpinnings', above n. 159, 304 ('notable milestones but there was no administrative law equivalent of *Donoghue* v. *Stevenson*').
[212]   *Ibid.*, drawing on Richard A. Posner, 'Legal Reasoning from the Top Down and From the Bottom Up' (1992) U Chicago LR 433; Keith Mason, 'What is Wrong with Top-Down Legal Reasoning' (2004) 78 ALJ 574; Taggart, 'Exceptionalism', above n. 34, 7 fn. 37; Aronson, 'Variable Standards', above n. 34, 22. This 'bottom-up' preference also helps explain the different role played by grounds of review in Australia (where they are technical and subordinate) and elsewhere (where they are generalised and monolithic).
[213]   Gageler, 'Underpinnings', above n. 159, 303.

style of reasoning focused on statutory interpretation'.[214] The centrality of jurisdictional error also discloses a 'preference to work within existing historic or doctrinal categories'.[215] It emphasises the Australian aversion to overarching and generalised principles and preference for incremental doctrinal development based on previous cases and categories.[216]

Coherence requires a degree of doctrinal unity and harmony, a feature generally lacking under the scope of review approach.

Non-impossibility and Practicality

On its face, the scope of review schema also presents itself well in terms of practicality. The maintenance of a strong distinction between law on the one hand, and fact and policy on the other, makes the litigation process relatively straightforward. Its less intrusive style and focus on law means the evidential corpus required is modest. Questions of law can be resolved without resort to extensive evidence. Highly deferential approaches to fact-finding, substance, and the quality of the decision mean little evidence or context is required. Intervention on such matters is only justified when it is manifest or readily apparent from the decision itself, avoiding the need for close forensic examination. This focus colours the style of advocacy required. The categorisation focus foreshortens the style of argumentation. The language and logic of law is encouraged, rather than more normative and value-laden debate. To this extent, it is convenient and expedient.

The potential for covert judicial discretion and manipulation in order to achieve normative outcomes places a significant gloss on this, however. The true motives and basis for intervention are not readily transparent and makes the focus of cases unpredictable. This makes it risky for litigation to presume the case will only be decided on formal terms and based on the restricted set of material mandated by the simplified form of procedure.

Congruence and Candour

This schema is particularly prone to judicial manipulation, as is evident from much of this analysis. For example, many of the rules have a

---

[214] Cane, 'Australian Administrative Law', above n. 29, 133. Cane attributes this, in part, to the ADJR Act.

[215] Taggart, 'Exceptionalism', above n. 34, 9.

[216] Aronson identifies an increasing preference on the part of the High Court to 'fine tune' existing principles rather than reshaping general ones: Aronson, 'Variable Standards', above n. 34, 22.

conclusory character. And the key distinctions are porous and depend on judicial judgement. The judicial process of classification is often contrived – with tacit sanction – in order to ameliorate the shortcomings of a framework constructed on strict categories and bright line distinctions.[217] Thus, there is discord between rule-expression and rule-application and a lack of candour is exhibited.

Hortatory Versatility

The absence of clarity means the schema is ill-suited as a hortatory device. It is difficult to detect from it a series of norms which can readily be utilised beyond judicial review in any collateral or educative role. The catalogue of situations where the courts will intervene or not is too technical – and, at times, too inconsistent – to provide instructive messaging for the bureaucracy. Moreover, the emphasis on matters jurisdictional, as seen especially in Australia, as a generalised overarching principle is too abstract and conclusory to have meaningful educative or structuring value. It is barely sustainable for those operating with knowledge and expertise within the system; it is, inevitably, a mystery for those outside it. As Harlow and Rawlings note, vires-based explanations of judicial review tend to emphasise the directing and limiting functions of judicial review, rather than the hortatory or educative aspects.[218]

2.5   Conclusion

The language of scope of review was noticeable in the first four editions of de Smith's text, recognising the then dominance of categorical formalism in English law. That style of review continues to this day in Australia, where jurisdiction operates as the lodestar of the judicial method. Those scholars supporting it generally profess a conservative vision for judicial review: influenced heavily by the distinction between law and merits, and anxious to ensure the courts honour and give effect to signals from the legislature.

From a normative perspective, the virtues of the scope of review schema are off-set by its two-track nature: that is, where the overt and covert are intertwined. Ostensibly, the formality of the method and emphasis on general rules provides value in terms of the efficacy of the scheme, particularly

---

[217] Sian Elias, 'Righting Administrative Law' in Dyzenhaus, Hunt and Huscroft, above n. 34, 71.
[218] Harlow and Rawlings, above n. 90, 728.

in terms of generality, prospectivity, stability and practicality. But the complexity of the promulgated rules means clarity and coherence suffer, and the schema fails therefore to exhibit hortatory versatility. The virtue of the rule-based system is undone by the failure of the rules to capture and express the underlying normative principles of administrative justice and good governance, leaving open, and perhaps condoning, the covert influence of judges' normative instincts.

3

Grounds of Review

3.1 Introduction

The grounds of review schema is based, as the label suggests, on a few generalised 'grounds' or 'heads' of review. The most famous formulation is the tripartite statement of illegality, procedural impropriety and irrationality, with the potential for further grounds to be added.[1] The grounds are designed to capture, in systematic and simplified form, the circumstances in which the courts are prepared to intervene. This continues the indirect and categorical approach to the determination of the depth of scrutiny but with a different emphasis. The depth of review is captured by a few grounds, more generalised and expressed with a degree of abstraction. But, as with the scope of review approach, classification – in this case, based on which ground is engaged – dominates the mediation of the balance between vigilance and restraint. In some cases the grounds manifest a depth of scrutiny which is strict; in others it is deferential.

The grounds of review schema was adopted as the organisational framework for much of de Smith's text from the fifth edition onwards. Since Lord Diplock's seminal speech in *Council of Civil Service Unions (CCSU)*,[2] a grounds of review approach continues to be the prevailing method in England and New Zealand. In contrast, grounds do not occupy such a preeminent role in Canada and Australia, although grounds expressed in this style are not unknown.

The abstracted approach to the expression of the circumstances of intervention finds support amongst some from the common law school. The judge-created grounds express a series of generalised norms about how public power ought to be exercised; a number of scholars champion the articulation of common law values in this generalised way, without the need to (torturously, they say) link the basis of intervention back to

---

[1] See Section 3.2.2.
[2] [1985] AC 374.

legislative intent and notions of vires. Notions of legality, rationality and justice, drawn from the common law, provide sufficient foundation.

The guidance provided by generalised grounds exhibits a degree of rule-structure, which means the approach measures up well against Fuller's principles of efficacy. The systemisation of the circumstances of intervention into simplified form aids clarity, practicality, coherence and congruence in application. However, pressures to evolve additional grounds of review, in order to express more nuanced degrees of scrutiny, undercut these virtues to some extent. The indirectness by which the depth of review is calibrated – both in relation to the traditional and emergent grounds – also places a gloss on the performance of the schema.

3.2   Doctrinal Manifestation

The 'grounds of review' label, while not unique, is drawn particularly from the fifth and later editions of de Smith's textbook, following Lord Diplock's tripartite expression of grounds in *CCSU*. After tracing the language and role in de Smith's textbook, I explain the currency of grounds in the English and New Zealand systems of judicial review. I also briefly explain how any limited appearance of grounds in Australian and Canadian law is overshadowed by other techniques.

3.2.1   De Smith Derivation

The framework of grounds of review became prominent in the fifth edition of de Smith following a major reorganisation of the text. The language of scope of review was replaced with 'grounds of review'. Lord Diplock's tripartite statement of grounds of review from *CCSU* is adopted as its organising principle for much of the fifth and sixth editions.[3] The grounds of review identified by Lord Diplock were conscripted as chapter headings in the heart of de Smith's text.[4]

Initially, the new authors referred to the language of grounds of review somewhat equivocally; Woolf and Jowell said the part of the text in the

---

[3] Five chapters were devoted to 'procedural fairness' (chs. 8–12) and one each to 'illegality' (ch. 7) and the 'unreasonable exercise of power' (ch. 13). For a contemporaneous endorsement of this reorganisation, see Cosmo Graham (1995) 3 EPL 149 (book review).

[4] The suitability of the grounds of review for 'chapter headings' had been noted some years before by Lord Donaldson: see de Smith (5th edn), 294, citing Lord Donaldson in *R (Brind) v. Secretary of State for the Home Department* [1991] 1 AC 696, 722.

fifth edition elaborating the circumstances in which judicial intervention may arise 'deals with what are loosely called the "grounds" of review'.[5] Any tentativeness about the language was not matched by the pervasiveness of their deployment though. Lord Diplock's grounds of review were said to provide 'a useful structure to help delineate the bounds of the unlawful decision'.[6] And the seven chapters in the part entitled 'Grounds of Review' that followed adopted Lord Diplock's structure and formulation, with only minor modifications to the language. They pointed to the growing mainstreaming of this tripartite schema, a decade after its genesis in *CCSU*, to justify its adoption: 'This classification has been generally adopted in practice and usefully provides three distinct ways in which decisions may fall short of lawful standards'.[7] This tripartite structure found favour in other texts and treatise on judicial review,[8] and it has been suggested that the tripartite grounds are '[u]sually cited as the basis of the modern doctrine of judicial review'.[9] Woolf and Jowell cautioned, however, against interpreting the framework too rigidly. 'Adopting this classification does not mechanically assign any particular administrative offence to any one of the categories', they said.[10] Overlap and classification under multiple grounds were acknowledged. It was also conceded that the judicial dicta acknowledging the grounds were not exhaustive.[11]

Lord Diplock's grounds of review were entrenched in the sixth edition, with them continuing as the organisational backbone of the text, without any of the earlier tentativeness about their currency.[12] The caveat that the grounds were 'by no means ... self-contained' continued, and the possibility of the emergence of other grounds – then particularly, 'abuse of power' – was noted.[13] Some chapters in the sixth edition were, however,

---

[5] De Smith (5th edn), ix.

[6] *Ibid.*, ix and 293, adopting the grounds from *CCSU*, above n. 2, 410. See text to n. 21.

[7] De Smith (5th edn), 293. Woolf and Jowell said they started revising the textbook five years after *CCSU* was decided, even though the edition was not published until 1995: de Smith (5th edn), viii.

[8] See nn. 34 and 35.

[9] Carol Harlow and Richard Rawlings, *Law and Administration* (3rd edn, Cambridge University Press, 2009), 10.

[10] De Smith (5th edn), 294.

[11] *Ibid.*, 294. The authors pointed to Lord Scarman's caveat in *R (Nottinghamshire City Council) v. Secretary of State for the Environment* [1986] AC 240, 249 ('valuable, and already "classical", but certainly not exhaustive'). Lord Diplock's speech itself also left the door open for the development of other grounds: *CCSU*, above n. 2, 410.

[12] De Smith (6th edn), vii; (7th edn), viii.

[13] De Smith (6th edn), vii; (7th edn), viii.

recast to reflect contemporary developments. Most notably, the chapter entitled 'The Unreasonable Exercise of Power' was anointed with a much broader label, 'Substantive Review and Justification' – thereby encompassing irrational, unreasonable and disproportionate decisions.[14] The authors expressed surprise about the extent of developments under this ground, but boldly asserted:[15]

> Substantive review is now fully recognised, prompted in particular by the more intense scrutiny that has been accorded to cases where human rights (or 'constitutional rights' as they are now explicitly called) are engaged, and where the concept of proportionality is applied.

The consolidation of commentary on legitimate expectations, blending legitimate expectations either triggering procedural fairness or protecting substantive outcomes, saw some departure from Lord Diplock's tripartite schema. The authors were vague about whether this change was a consequence of the recognition of legitimate expectation as a self-standing ground of review or was adopted merely for pragmatic purposes; they hinted at both.[16] Proportionality was also marked out for extensive treatment, but again its potential status as a ground of review in its own right was left open. Proportionality, in the sense of both 'a test of fair balance' and 'a structured test of justifiability',[17] was addressed under the more general rubric of substantive review and justification.[18] The authors identified the established, but circumscribed, role for proportionality when reviewing directly effective European Community law and human rights adjudication under the Human Rights Act 1998;[19] the unresolved question of whether it should be mandated as a ground of review (either in addition to, or in substitution for, the unreasonableness ground) was also highlighted.[20] The treatment of these emergent grounds was, we will see, consistent with the evolutionary aspects of the grounds of review schema.

---

[14] De Smith (6th edn), ch. 11.
[15] De Smith (6th edn), ix; (7th edn), ix.
[16] De Smith (6th edn), ix; (7th edn), ix. They noted they had previously discussed substantive legitimate expectations in the context of unreasonable decisions, 'where it was then just emerging as a substantive ground'.
[17] De Smith (6th edn), 543, 585 and 586; (7th edn), 588, 629 and 630.
[18] See text to n. 100.
[19] De Smith (6th edn), 584; (7th edn), 627.
[20] De Smith (6th edn), 585; (7th edn), 628. Particular reference was made to Dyson LJ's dicta in *R (Association of British Civilian Internees)* v. *Secretary of State for Defence* [2003] QB 1397 ([33]–[35]) questioning whether *Wednesbury* should be given its burial rights.

3.2.2   *England: Lord Diplock's CCSU grounds*

As mentioned, the grounds of review schema became the dominant organising framework in English judicial review since Lord Diplock's speech in *CCSU*:[21]

> [O]ne can conveniently classify under three heads the grounds upon which administrative action is subject to control by judicial review. The first ground I would call 'illegality', the second 'irrationality' and the third 'procedural impropriety'.

Lord Diplock had been instrumental in the development of, as he put it, 'a comprehensive system of administrative law'.[22] His tripartite statement of the grounds of judicial review – 'illegality', 'procedural impropriety', and 'irrationality' – represented an important move in the systemisation of judicial review. Lord Diplock also acknowledged his tripartite statement should not fetter the development of further grounds on 'a case by case basis' (a point returned to in detail later).[23] Somewhat overshadowed by Lord Diplock's speech, Lord Roskill also echoed the tripartite formulation of grounds in *CCSU*;[24] he endorsed the 'new nomenclature' adopted by Lord Diplock, noting that the 'words ... have the great advantage of making clear the differences between each ground'.[25]

Lord Diplock's statement of grounds has since assumed a certain cachet in administrative law, although there is nothing special about it being cast in tripartite form. As Forsyth notes, the threefold formula 'immediately went canonical'.[26] The grounds were endorsed and adopted as a doctrinal framework in numerous cases, including at the highest level in *Brind*,[27]

---

[21] *CCSU*, above n. 2, 410. See also the modulation of heightened scrutiny, light touch review and doctrinal deference in England (Section 4.2.3), along with instances of contextual review and non-doctrinal deference (Section 5.2.4).

[22] *R (National Federation of Self Employed and Small Businesses Ltd)* v. *Inland Revenue Commissioners* [1982] AC 617, 641. Indeed, Lord Diplock described these developments as 'the great achievement' of the English courts in his judicial lifetime. For an account of his influence, see Lord Woolf, 'The Role of the English Judiciary in Developing Public Law' (1986) 27 Wm & Mary L Rev 669.

[23] *CCSU*, above n. 2, 410.

[24] *Ibid.*, 414 ('three separate grounds': 'error of law', 'exercises a power in so unreasonable a manner that the exercise becomes open to review upon what are called, in lawyers' shorthand, *Wednesbury* principles', 'acted contrary to [the] principles of natural justice').

[25] *Ibid.*

[26] Christopher F. Forsyth, '*Council of Civil Service Unions* v. *Minister for Civil Service* (1985)' in Peter Cane and Joanne Conaghan (eds.), *The New Oxford Companion to Law* (Oxford University Press, 2008), 245.

[27] *Brind*, above n. 4, 722, 750.

Wheeler,[28] *Boddington*,[29] and *Nottinghamshire City Council*.[30] Years after their exposition, Fordham argues the threefold classification appears 'largely intact' (despite other significant change in public law) and 'remains the most helpful outline', even if some 'trendier' labels have continued to emerge.[31] Many English administrative law texts also adopt or endorse the authoritative nature of the statement. De Smith's text was reorganised around these grounds of review, as outlined earlier. Harlow and Rawlings contend the tripartite statement is '[u]sually cited as the basis of the modern doctrine of judicial review'.[32] Wade and Forsyth included the famous passage from the speech in a separate appendix, acknowledging the frequent reference throughout their text to Lord Diplock's 'exposition of the principles of judicial review'.[33] Similar acknowledgement of the special status of the statement is found in a number of other academic textbooks.[34] In addition, the grounds permeate academic and practice texts and guides, with the tripartite grounds adopted as a framework for analysing the basis on which judges will impugn decisions of public bodies and officials.[35]

While Lord Diplock's tripartite statement is generally regarded as the leading expression of the grounds of review, it is by no means the only one. Other English judges have also sought to summarise the grounds of review, sometimes expressing them with slightly different variants. For example, Lord Templeman in *Preston* identified the grounds of review as

---

[28] *Wheeler* v. *Leicester City Council* [1985] AC 1054, 1078.

[29] *Boddington* v. *British Transport Police* [1999] 2 AC 143, 152.

[30] *R (Nottinghamshire City Council)* v. *Secretary of State for the Environment* [1986] AC 240, 249 ('valuable, and already "classical"').

[31] Michael Fordham, 'Surveying the Grounds' in Peter Leyland and Terry Woods (eds.), *Administrative Law Facing the Future* (Oxford University Press, 1997), 184, 185 (notably, 'want of due process' for procedural impropriety and 'abuse of power' for irrationality).

[32] Harlow and Rawlings, above n. 9, 107.

[33] William Wade and Christopher Forsyth, *Administrative Law* (11th edn, Oxford University Press, 2014), 824.

[34] See e.g. John Alder, *Constitutional and Administrative Law* (6th edn, Palgrave, 2007), 379 ('I shall organise the grounds of judicial review on the basis of Lord Diplock's classification in *CCSU*'); A.W. Bradley and K.D. Ewing, *Constitutional and Administrative Law* (14th edn, Pearson, 2007), 727; Jeffrey Jowell, 'The Rule of Law and its Underlying Values' in Jeffrey Jowell and Dawn Oliver (eds.), *The Changing Constitution* (6th edn, Oxford University Press, 2007), 5, 226 ('We have followed the well-known division of grounds of review enunciated by Lord Diplock in the *GCHQ* case').

[35] See e.g. Michael Fordham, *Judicial Review Handbook* (6th edn, Hart Publishing, 2012), [P45] ('unlawfulness', 'unreasonableness', 'unfairness'); Treasury Solicitor, *The Judge Over Your Shoulder* (4th edn, 2006), [2.5]; *Halsbury's Laws of England*, 'Administrative Law', [1238] and 'Judicial Review' [602]; Lord Neuberger and others, *Civil Court Practice 2009 (the Green Book)* (LexisNexis, 2009–), [CPR 54.1[3A]].

when a decision-maker 'exceeds its powers, commits an error of law, commits a breach of natural justice, reaches a decision which no reasonable tribunal could have reached, or abuses its powers'.[36] More recently, Lord Bingham in *Corner House Research* expressed the grounds of review in more positive terms.[37]

Occasionally, some judges have also sought to articulate a singular overarching principle of judicial review, in combination with the identification of particular instances of intervention analogous with Lord Diplock's grounds of review. For example, Lord Brightman in *Puhlhofer* articulated a single ground of 'abuse of power', but explained its constituent elements in similar terms to Lord Diplock: 'bad faith, a mistake in construing the limits of the power, a procedural irregularity, or unreasonableness in the *Wednesbury* sense – unreasonableness verging on an absurdity'.[38]

Alternative judicial expression of the grounds does not take away from the general scheme of categorical grounds of review. Variation in how the grounds are expressed is not always material. As explained earlier, the case-by-case nature and instrumentalism of the common law means judges are rarely called on to address the overarching doctrinal schema of judicial review.[39] Their focus is usually on one or two particular grounds of review, not their universal expression. Any comprehensive statement of the grounds of review is often dictum, made in passing. Certainly, none of the alternative expressions purport to represent the systemisation of the discipline that coloured Lord Diplock's exposition.

While marginal differences do not undercut the role of grounds of review as a schematic framework, deviations within the framework itself may be significant in themselves. They may be the realisation of the evolutionary dimension of the grounds of review framework, including lexical changes which signal substantive changes to the grounds themselves.[40] The extent to which the grounds of review have evolved beyond the traditional

---

[36]   *R (Preston)* v. *Inland Revenue Commissioners* [1985] AC 835, 862.

[37]   *R (Corner House Research)* v. *Director of Serious Fraud Office* [2009] 1 AC 756, [32].

[38]   *R (Puhlhofer)* v. *Hillingdon London Borough Council* [1986] AC 484, 518. See also *Nottinghamshire*, above n. 30, 250 ('abuse of power'); *R (Bancoult)* v. *Secretary of State for Foreign and Commonwealth Affairs (No 2)* [2008] QB 365 (Sedley LJ) [60]– [61] ('abuse of power'). See T.R.S. Allan, 'The Constitutional Foundations of Judicial Review' (2002) 61 CLJ 87, 113–15. For further discussion of a singular abuse of power standard, see Section 5.2.

[39]   See Section 1.2 above.

[40]   Andrew le Sueur, Javan Herberg and Rosalind English, *Principles of Public Law* (2nd edn, Cavendish, 1999), 226.

three grounds is addressed in detail later. For present purposes, the important point is that none of the evolutionary developments has seriously repugned the framework of the established grounds.

Similarly, the schematic approaches of textbooks are not uniform, even when organising their analysis around grounds of review. 'Unfortunately, there is no general agreement on how to classify the grounds of review and textbooks take different approaches', Le Sueur laments.[41] '[T]he same material is divided up in quite different ways, with different chapter headings and subheadings.'[42] As identified, it is quite common to adopt Lord Diplock's tripartite statement; however, a range of other approaches are also adopted. For example, Craig's substantive analysis of judicial review is crafted around a series of chapters, the topics of which emulate an expanded set of grounds of review.[43] Wade and Forsyth commend Lord Diplock's statement of grounds, but diffuse the circumstances of judicial intervention throughout the text; again, though shades of the tripartite grounds are evident.[44] While some variation is evident amongst textbook writers and commentators, this does not unduly undermine the nature of grounds of review as a doctrinal framework. As Le Sueur notes, to some degree, differences may be 'merely terminological and organisational'.[45] The grounds of review are amalgamations of various bases of intervention; the alternative expressions are typically disaggregated versions of the tripartite grounds.

Turning to the operation of the schema and its mediation of vigilance and restraint, the depth of scrutiny is modulated in four different ways:

(a) selection of the applicable grounds of review, through a process of *classification*, from the potentially overlapping tripartite grounds;
(b) *evolution*, through the recognition of alternative grounds of review manifesting different degrees of intensity;
(c) *reformulation* of the traditional grounds (albeit such efforts have been largely unsuccessful); and
(d) *circumscription* of the ordinarily available grounds of review.

Classification

First, the grounds of review tend to overlap, potentially allowing errors to be classified under multiple grounds. Indeed, many judges, including the

---

[41] *Ibid.*, 226.
[42] *Ibid.*, 226.
[43] P.P. Craig, *Administrative Law* (8th edn, Sweet & Maxwell, 2016), chs. 12–23.
[44] Wade and Forsyth, above n. 33, chs. 7–14.
[45] Le Sueur, Herberg and English, above n. 40, 226.

architects of the tripartite grounds, have warned about approaching the threefold division too clinically.[46] As will be shown, though, the distinctions on which these grounds are based tend to break down.[47] This style of modulation is best illustrated by reference to some of the key dichotomies in judicial review: law versus fact and law versus discretion.

Turning first to the dichotomy between *law and fact*. Under the grounds of review schema, an alleged error may be classified as one of law or fact, enabling different depth of review.[48] If the error is one of law, then the court can express its own view on whether the decision is correct; if it is a factual error, the deferential *Wednesbury* standard of unreasonableness would ordinarily apply. The commentary in de Smith reflects this unstable division between law and fact. As in earlier editions, Woolf and Jowell spend some time addressing the boundary between law and fact, which, they repeat, 'is not always easy to perceive'.[49] While noting that the courts generally leave the assessment of fact to the primary decision-maker, Woolf and Jowell note that factual error 'can just as easily be absorbed into a traditional legal ground of review'.[50] Other commentators are similarly sceptical, doubting whether there is a sound analytical approach to the distinction and suggesting that pragmatic considerations must be in play. For example, Williams explained that the use of the terms 'law' and 'fact' in this context are 'simply flexible concepts that can be used to contain or conceal more pragmatic reasoning'.[51] Even more manipulable is the classification of a question as a mixed question of law and fact. This conjugated label has been described as 'one of the baffling gadgets in the judicial toolbox'.[52] It allows vigilant *or* restrained review, depending on judicial preference.

---

[46] See e.g. *Boddington*, above n. 29, 152, 170 (the grounds 'are not water tight compartments'; 'different grounds of review "run into one another"'); *Wheeler*, above n. 28, 1078 ('nor are they mutually exclusive'). See also *R (Oladenhinde) v. Secretary of State for the Home Department* [1991] 1 AC 254, 280.

[47] Michael Taggart, 'Administrative Law' [2006] NZ Law Rev 75, 83.

[48] Timothy Endicott, 'Questions of Law' (1998) 114 LQR 292; Paul Craig, 'Judicial Review, Appeal and Factual Error' [2004] PL 788; Rebecca Williams, 'When is an Error not an Error?' [2007] PL 793; H.W.R. Wade, 'Anglo-American Administrative Law' (1966) 82 LQR 226.

[49] De Smith (5th edn), 277, 277–89.

[50] De Smith (5th edn), 288; (6th edn), 562–9.

[51] Williams, above n. 48, 798. See also Endicott, above n. 48, 320 ('must be pursuing some sort of inarticulate pragmatic approach, which leads to the all sorts of inconsistency because its motivating principles are silent and undeveloped'); Craig, 'Factual Error', above n. 48, 788.

[52] Endicott, above n. 48, 301.

Two particular examples illustrate this type of modulation of intensity, in the context of the law–fact dichotomy. The first, illustrated by the *Puhlhofer* case, demonstrates the difficulty in determining whether a particular administrative finding is based on any (mis-)understanding of law or factual judgement.[53] In *Puhlhofer*, the entitlement to government housing assistance depended on being homeless, that is, whether the couple had 'no accommodation'. The local authority declined assistance because the couple were living temporarily in a bed and breakfast – without cooking or laundry facilities – and were therefore not homeless. But was the alleged error on the part of the local authority an error of law (the local authority misinterpreting the meaning of accommodation) or one of fact (the bed and breakfast was wrongly classified as accommodation)? Ultimately, the House of Lords ruled the critical determination was a factual one; thus intervention was only justified under the irrationality ground if the determination was manifestly unreasonable. But it was also plausible for the determination to be classified as a question of law, which would have entailed more vigilant review.[54] The uncertainty in classification leaves it open to the courts to deploy differing degrees of scrutiny, ostensibly on normative, not descriptive, reasons.

Secondly, factual findings not normally subject to close scrutiny under the irrationality ground may be treated as giving rise to an instance of illegality.[55] Sometimes justified under the 'jurisdictional or precedent fact' principle, if a factual finding is a statutory precondition to the exercise of power the courts sometimes (but not always) subject the factual circumstances or criteria to closer review, assessing whether, in their view, it is satisfied.[56] The reasoning goes as follows. Where the legislative framework dictates that the presence of a particular fact is a precondition to the exercise of a statutory power, certain administrative action is only permitted if a particular fact is established. Acting in the absence of the fact being established would be acting without any legal authority or jurisdiction, thereby justifying the greater scrutiny seen under the unlawfulness ground

---

[53] *R (Puhlhofer)* v. *Hillingdon London Borough Council* [1986] AC 484. See *Jones* v. *First Tier Tribunal (Rev 1)* [2013] 2 AC 48 (Lord Carnwath) for recent judicial acknowledgement of the fact that 'the division between law and fact ... is not purely objective' ([46]), adopting his extra-judicial comments that the classification need also take into account expediency and policy ('Tribunal Justice' [2009] PL 48, 63).

[54] Endicott, above n. 48, 298.

[55] Mark Elliott, *Beatson, Matthews and Elliott's Administrative Law* (4th edn, Oxford University Press, 2011), 61.

[56] See ch. 2, text to n. 104 for earlier treatment in the scope of review era.

of review. But, as will be shown, the syntactical nature of a precondition is not always determinative and the courts are still sometimes reluctant to apply an exacting eye to certain factual preconditions.

The exemplar case is *R (Khawaja)* v. *Secretary of State for the Home Department*, where immigrants successfully challenged moves to deport them.[57] The power to deport was conditional on a factual determination that the immigrants were 'illegal entrants'. Because the contested determination – that the immigrants were 'illegal entrants' – was a 'precedent or jurisdictional fact', the House of Lords was prepared to assess itself whether the factual precondition existed or not. This vigilant approach has not been replicated, however, where the factual precondition is slightly indeterminate or involves a degree of evaluation and judgement. While these factual preconditions present the same jurisdictional problems as more objective or determinate facts, the courts have shown greater reticence and reverted to supervising by the more deferential *Wednesbury* unreasonableness approach.[58] For example, in *South Yorkshire Transport*, the House of Lords declined to treat the factual determination of whether or not a transport company was operating in 'a substantial part of the United Kingdom', when that determination operated as a threshold for investigation by a fair trading commission.[59] Lord Mustill said a 'clear-cut approach' cannot be applied in every case of jurisdictional preconditions, especially where the relevant criterion is imprecise.[60] In such cases, the court can intervene 'if the decision is so aberrant that it cannot be classed as rational'.[61]

The flexible nature of this style of categorisation is therefore obvious. In some cases, statutory preconditions are treated as touching matters of law; in others, they are treated in the same way as ordinary fact-finding and only subjected to deferential review under the irrationality ground. The elastic nature of the classification problem is seen vividly in the recent case of *R (A)* v. *London Borough of Croydon*,[62] where the Supreme Court decided different elements within the same factual precondition should be subject to different degrees of scrutiny. The critical provision required a local authority to provide accommodation for any 'child in need within

---

[57] [1984] AC 74, overruling *R (Zamir)* v. *Secretary of State for the Home Department* [1980] AC 930. See also *R (Zerek)* v. *Fulham, Hammersmith and Kensington Rent Tribunal* [1951] 2 KB 1.

[58] Elliott, above n. 55, 77.

[59] *R (South Yorkshire Transport)* v. *Monopolies and Mergers Commission* [1993] 1 WLR 23.

[60] *Ibid.*, 32.

[61] *Ibid.*

[62] [2009] 1 WLR 2557.

their area'. The Supreme Court ruled that if there was a dispute about a local authority's factual finding about whether a person was actually a 'child' (based on doubts about official documents), it was for the courts on judicial review to 'determine where the truth lies on the evidence available', with 'no margin of discretion' applying.[63] However, this strict standard of scrutiny did not apply to the corresponding element 'in need', which would continue to be challengeable only on *Wednesbury* grounds.[64] The approach ultimately turned on the objective character of the term 'child', in contrast to the evaluative nature of the balance of the precondition.

This distinction between *law and discretion* also presents a subtle reclassification choice to judges. The intensity applied by the courts to legal questions is strict, in contrast to the deferential approach adopted to reviewing the exercise of discretion. Therefore, treating the influence of an external norm such as human rights as speaking to questions of legality – rather than as a factor which must be taken into account in the exercise of discretion – affects the depth of review applied. Both courses remain open to a supervising court under common law review, and the choice between both allows the significant modulation of the depth of review.

The best example of this is the *principle of legality*, which adopts a strict approach to compliance with human rights norms under the illegality ground.[65] The courts read down legal powers to avoid conflict with (so-called) 'fundamental' or 'constitutional' rights except where legislation necessarily authorises the rights being limited.[66] The judicial method

---

[63] *R (A)*, above n. 62, [46] and [54]. While the Court did not formally resolve whether the precondition amounted to a jurisdictional or precedent fact, Lady Hale made her views plain in her concluding obiter remark (at [32]): 'If ever there were a jurisdictional fact, it might be thought, this is it.'

[64] *Ibid.*, [26].

[65] See generally Fordham, *Judicial Review Handbook*, above n. 35, [35.1]; Michael Fordham and Thomas de la Mare, 'Anxious Scrutiny, the Principle of Legality and the Human Rights Act' [2001] JR 40; David Dyzenhaus, Murray Hunt and Michael Taggart, 'The Principle of Legality in Administrative Law' (2001) 1 OUCLJ 5, 20; Philip Sales, 'A Comparison of the Principle of Legality and Section 3 of the Human Rights Act 1998' [2009] LQR 598; Thomas Poole, 'Justice, Rights, and Judicial Humility' [2000] JR 106.

[66] These adjectives remain ambiguous. Hickman attributes the advent of the adjective 'fundamental' in relation to rights to *Morris* v. *Beardmore* [1981] AC 446, where Lord Scarman noted that the modifier was 'unfamiliar to common lawyers' due to the absence of written constitutional rights: Tom Hickman, *Public Law after the Human Rights Act* (Hart Publishing, 2010), 17. See also Laws LJ's remarks in *International Transport* that 'the common law has come to recognise and endorse the notion of constitutional or fundamental rights' (*International Transport Roth GmbH* v. *Secretary of State for the Home Department* [2003] QB 728, [71]).

applied is a strict one, in contrast to the soft-edged evaluation that would otherwise take place under the unreasonableness ground (under either the *Wednesbury* test or, arguably, any stricter formulation).[67] The application of the principle, under the guise of the legality ground rather than irrationality, produces 'high-intensity review'.[68] Indeed, the principle of legality is occasionally identified as a sibling to the principle of anxious scrutiny under the unreasonableness ground, because both have been deployed by judges to enable more intensive protection of human rights.[69]

Notable cases where this methodology was adopted include *R (Pierson) v. Secretary of State for the Home Department*[70] and *R (Simms) v. Secretary of State for the Home Department*.[71] In *Pierson*, a prisoner serving a life sentence had been told he would serve a tariff period of at least fifteen years in prison before being considered for parole but the Home Secretary subsequently raised the tariff period to twenty years. In ruling the Home Secretary's actions unlawful, two Lords referred to a general interpretative principle that general legislative wording should be read subject to human rights. Lord Browne-Wilkinson articulated the interpretative approach as a general principle:[72]

> A power conferred by Parliament in general terms is not to be taken to authorise the doing of acts by the donee of the power which adversely affect the legal rights of a citizen or the basic principles on which the law of the United Kingdom is based unless the statute conferring the power makes it clear that such was the intention of Parliament.

Describing it as a 'spirit of legality', Lord Steyn drew an analogy with the long-standing presumption that powers granted to public bodies and officials must be exercised consistently with the common law principle of procedural fairness.[73] The principle also gained support in *Simms*, when the House of Lords overturned a blanket ban on prisoners giving interviews to journalists. Lord Hoffmann said: 'In the absence of express language or necessary implication to the contrary, the courts ... presume that even the most general words were intended to be subject to the basic

---

[67] The nature of the deferential standard under the unreasonableness ground, including its variegated and stricter formulations, is discussed below: see Section 4.2.3.

[68] Fordham and de la Mare, above n. 65, 45.

[69] De Smith (6th edn), 242–7, 569–70, and 594–5 and Fordham and de la Mare, above n. 65.

[70] [1998] AC 539.

[71] [2000] 2 AC 115.

[72] *Pierson*, above n. 70, 573.

[73] *Ibid.*, 575.

rights of the individual.'[74] Lord Steyn echoed these sentiments, express-ing a 'presumption of general application operating as a constitutional principle' that if a 'fundamental or basic right' was at stake the provisions should where possible be interpreted consistently with those rights.[75]

The translation of the interplay between rights norms and other factors from discretion to law, gives rise to potential variability, enabling judges to deploy greater scrutiny if they consider the human rights dimensions or higher level norms justify it. The conditions under which this maxi-mum intensity can be deployed are not definitive. First, conflict with a 'fundamental human right' must be identified; however, as these human rights norms are by definition unenumerated, the set of recognised rights is pliable. Secondly, it must be established that it was not the express or implied legislative intent of Parliament to mandate restrictions on those rights when conferring the discretionary power. The threshold for reliance on the principle of legality is therefore versatile, giving the doctrine the character of variable intensity.

Evolution

When the grounds were encapsulated in their tripartite formulation, the door was also left open for other grounds of review to develop.[76] These emergent grounds present different depths of scrutiny – usually more vigi-lant intensity – to the traditional tripartite grounds. The recognition of potential development of other grounds of review brings other dimensions of variability to the judicial method. This variability is both immediate (where a ground has been recognised within the overall schema) and longer-term (where a ground is able to be explored as prospective ground). Moreover, the emergent grounds tend not to have the universal applica-tion of the traditional tripartite grounds; the narrower gateways to reliance on them adds another layer of classification, which further augments the variability associated with them.

Lord Diplock acknowledged further grounds may develop on 'a case by case basis', noting particularly the possibility that proportionality might be recognised as a ground of review.[77] The possibility that the suite of grounds might be enlarged was also noted in a number of cases that endorsed the tripartite formulation. While acknowledging the value of the tripartite

---

[74] *Simms*, above n. 71, 131.
[75] *Ibid.*, 130.
[76] *CCSU*, above n. 2, 410.
[77] *Ibid.*

statement, Lord Scarman in *Nottinghamshire* was quick to note that it was 'certainly not exhaustive analysis of the grounds upon which courts will embark on the judicial review'.[78] Similarly, Lord Roskill in *Wheeler* repeated the three grounds were not exhaustive and 'further grounds may hereafter require to';[79] subsequently in *Brind* he stressed that 'any such development would be likely to be on a case by case basis'.[80]

A number of additional or alternative grounds have been promoted; some grounds have achieved some recognition, although none seem to have yet achieved the same exalted status of the traditional tripartite grounds. The slightly opaque status of grounds of review make it difficult to definitively assess whether and when a basis for judicial intervention is sufficiently recognised so as to be regarded as a ground of review. First, as explained earlier, the focus on individual cases means judges are often agnostic to the overall schema of judicial review and may not herald such developments, beyond identifying an error as a justifiable basis for intervention.

Secondly, the overlapping and multi-dimensional nature of grounds of review mean their genesis is often interwoven with an existing ground of review. Potential grounds of review are sometimes adopted merely as touchstones which may indicate another ground of review has been established. For example, unjustified inconsistent treatment may be the reason why a court holds administrative action to be invalid under the unreasonableness ground.[81] Similarly, the failure to honour a legitimate expectation has sometimes been treated as giving rise to a breach of the unfairness or procedural impropriety grounds.[82] Indeed, Lord Diplock's seminal speech systemising the grounds of review noted that previously intervention for irrationality was justified by relying on 'an inferred though unidentifiable' error of law.[83]

Thirdly, the recognition of a new ground of review need not await the imprimatur of final appellate courts. The common law may develop within lower courts and become sufficiently imbedded – whether or not final appellate courts have had the opportunity or inclination to comment on

---

[78] *Nottinghamshire County Council* [1986] AC 240, 249.

[79] *Wheeler*, above n. 28, 1078.

[80] *Brind*, above n. 4, 750 (then rejecting proportionality as a ground of review).

[81] See e.g. *R (Middlebrook Mushrooms Ltd)* v. *Agricultural Wages Board of England and Wales* [2004] EWHC 1447.

[82] *R (Coughlan)* v. *North and East Devon Health Authority* [2001] QB 213, [57].

[83] *CCSU*, above n. 2, 410, attributing this 'ingenious explanation' to Viscount Radcliffe in *Edwards* v. *Bairstow* [1956] AC 14.

the development.[84] As a consequence, some emerging grounds are suspended in a sort of twilight zone. The looseness of *stare decisis* principle in judicial review and the large doses of discretion available to a reviewing judge means it is still possible for some emergent grounds to be adopted in occasional cases, even though the ground does not then, or subsequently, command widespread support.

A number of substantive grounds of review have been promoted and, in some cases, appear to have assumed new status as potential grounds of review, at least in some circumstances. As Rawlings remarks: 'Future historians will record that, in the shadow of the ECHR, the pace of development in the grounds for review quickened in the late 1980s and 1990s.'[85] The most prominent emergent grounds include substantive legitimate expectation, mistake of fact, and proportionality. A further set of other grounds have also been promoted, such as inconsistent treatment, substantive fairness, and the innominate ground, but have gained less traction.

Substantive protection of *legitimate expectations* was recognised in English law in the seminal *Coughlan* case in 2001 and is often regarded as a separate ground of review.[86] As noted earlier, the sixth edition of de Smith addresses legitimate expectations in a separate chapter; the authors implicitly treat substantive legitimate expectation as having the status of a self-standing ground of review, but are coy in making any formal pronouncement to that effect.[87]

---

[84] See e.g. discussion of *Coughlan* (text to n. 86) below, where the seminal decision about legitimate expectation as a ground of review was given by the Court of Appeal. Final appellate courts, of course, retain the power to disapprove of any developments. Further, developments which seek to *substitute* a new ground for a ground previously recognised by final appellate courts need approval at the highest level; see e.g. the Court of Appeal's hesitation to substitute proportionality for irrationality: *British Civilian Internees*, above n. 20, [33]–[35].

[85] Richard Rawlings, 'Modelling Judicial Review' (2008) 61 CLP 95, 105.

[86] *Coughlan*, above n. 82. This development was endorsed by the House of Lords in *R (Reprotech) v. East Sussex County Council* [2003] 1 WLR 348, [34] and the Privy Council in *Paponette v. Attorney-General of Trinidad and Tobago* [2012] 1 AC 1. The possibility that legitimate expectations might be afforded some substantive protection was foreshadowed particularly in *Preston* (n. 36) although the circumstances for protection were not made out in that case. Notably, Australian administrative law has resisted moves to recognise substantive legitimate expectation: see ch. 2, text to n. 78 above.

[87] See text to n. 16 above. Fordham also hedges on this point, adopting legitimate expectation (both procedural and substantive) as a ground of review and later adopting substantive legitimate expectation as '[o]ne species of substantive fairness': Fordham, *Judicial Review Handbook*, above n. 35, [41.1] and [54.2].

Substantive legitimate expectation mandates judicial intervention where an assurance or other action of the administration induces 'a legitimate expectation of a benefit which is substantive' and the frustration of such expectation 'is so unfair that to take a new and different course will amount to an abuse of power'.[88] While expressed as a general ground of review, the ground is only engaged in 'limited conditions'; '[n]o magic formula', de Smith's sixth edition notes, but a range of contextual factors which seek to balance the 'relative virtues and defects of certainty and flexibility'.[89]

Presented with an assurance or other conduct inducting an expectation, the courts must assess the ground(s) most applicable to the circumstances. The Court of Appeal in *Coughlan* identified three alternatives.[90] First, the court may determine that it is appropriate only to assess the relevance and weight under the illegality and irrationality grounds, to ensure the assurance has been taken into account and the weight given to it relative to other grounds is not unreasonable. Secondly, under the procedural impropriety ground, a requirement to consult before reneging on the assurance may be imposed. Finally, the court may afford the expectation some substantive protection and assess whether departing from it is unfair as to amount to an abuse of power. The Court conceded that the 'difficult task will be to decide into which category the decision should be allotted'.[91] Little guidance was given about criteria influencing this assessment, apart from noting that, in the particular case, the importance of the promise and fact it was made to only a few people were significant factors, along with the limited (financial only) consequences for the administration if it was required to honour the assurance.[92] This has been taken to require an assessment in other cases of the nature of the express or implied representation or promise, the legitimacy, in the circumstances, of relying on the representation or promise, and the absence of any public interest supporting the administrative change of position.[93]

---

[88] *Coughlan*, above n. 82, [57].

[89] De Smith (6th edn), 613. See also Elliott, *Administrative Law*, above n. 58, 199.

[90] *Coughlan*, above n. 82, [57].

[91] *Ibid.*, [57]. Laws LJ later suggested, obiter, that 'the first and third categories explained in *Coughlan* are not hermetically sealed' and should be viewed more as 'more or less intrusive quality of review'; *R (Begbie) v. Secretary of State for Education and Employment* [2000] 1 WLR 1115, 1129. Elliott tentatively echoes these sentiments: *Administrative Law*, above n. 58, 200.

[92] *Coughlan*, above n. 82, [60].

[93] De Smith (6th edn), 612–30. On the opaqueness of the standard see particularly *Begbie*, above n. 91; *R (Abdi & Nadarajah) v. Secretary of State for the Home Department* [2005] EWCA Civ 1363. See further Mark Elliott, 'Legitimate Expectations and the Search for Principle' [2006] JR 281.

If the expectation makes it through the gateway and is assessed to be worthy of substantive protection, then the administration's failure to honour that assurance or expectation is subjected to more intensive review than applied that under the traditional grounds of review, especially in relation to the assessment of weight under the irrationality ground of review.[94] The substantive protection path allows the courts 'to determine whether there is a sufficient overriding interest to justify a departure from what has been previously promised';[95] in contrast, the default 'conventional' or *Wednesbury* ground focuses solely on 'rationality and whether the public body has given proper weight to the implications of not fulfilling the promise'.[96] The mandate to assess whether the departure is justified has been equated to high-intensity or correctness review.[97]

Since its recognition, the ground continues to be successfully relied on intermittently.[98] In other instances, review based on the ground failed because the qualifying conditions were not made out or departing from the assurance was justified in the public interest.[99]

Proportionality is often marked out as a candidate for another ground of review.[100] Despite some strong proponents, it has failed to yet crystallise as a ground of universal application. However, it has been endorsed in particular spheres within administrative law; most obviously in the domain of human rights adjudication, but also in relation to the review of excessive penalties and sanctions and directly effective European Community law.

---

[94] De Smith (6th edn), 630, drawing on *Coughlan*, above n. 82. The authors initially suggest this amounts to correctness review; however, later they ponder, based on *Begbie*, whether the degree of scrutiny might be better treated as a 'sliding scale of review', depending on the particular circumstances: de Smith (6th edn), 631 and 632.

[95] *Coughlan*, above n. 82, [58].

[96] *Ibid.*, [58].

[97] Elliott, *Administrative Law*, above n. 58, 200; de Smith (6th edn), [12-047]. An analogy with the proportionality methodology has also been made: *Abdi*, above n. 93, [68].

[98] See e.g. *R (Bibi) v. London Borough of Newham* [2002] 1 WLR 237; *R (HSMP Forum (UK) Ltd) v. Secretary of State for the Home Department* [2008] EWHC 664 and [2009] EWHC 711.

[99] See e.g. *R (Bancoult) v. Secretary of State for Foreign and Commonwealth Affairs (No 2)* [2008] 3 WLR 955, [62] (absence of unambiguous promise); *R (Bhatt Murphy (a firm)) v. The Independent Assessor* [2008] EWCA Civ 755 (absence of clear assurance); *R (Thomson) v. Minister of State for Children* [2005] EWHC 1378 (assurance not clear; public interest justified change); *R (Bath) v. North Somerset Council* [2008] EWHC 630 (absence of unqualified assurance); *R (London Borough of Lewisham) v. Assessment and Qualifications Alliance* [2013] EWHC 211 (absence of clear statement or practice).

[100] *CCSU*, above n. 2, 410.

The nature of the deployment of proportionality within the schema of judicial review remains unclear, though. On one account, proportionality is a ground of review of limited application; an alternative account treats proportionality merely as an interpretative test or calculus to determine compliance with human rights instruments under the illegality ground of review. As with other emergent grounds, proportionality has the potential to mandate greater depth of review than the traditional irrationality ground allows, although this is not always the case necessarily, given the tractable nature of proportionality review.

The possibility that proportionality might be adopted as an additional ground was foreshadowed in *CCSU*. However, such a development was subsequently forestalled by the House of Lords in *Brind*, with judges then expressing concern that adoption of proportionality would amount to an inappropriate move towards merits review.[101] The question has since been left open. The Court of Appeal in *R (Association of British Civilian Internees)* v. *Secretary of State for Defence* suggested proportionality should be substituted for *Wednesbury* unreasonableness, but accepted that any such change could only be made by a court at the highest level.[102] While the possibility has been acknowledged, the House of Lords and Supreme Court have left the question open.[103] Debate continues about whether proportionality ought to supplant irrationality as the leading substantive ground of review. Craig continues to be one of the leading advocates for the embrace of proportionality as a universal ground.[104] Others have joined in his promotion of proportionality but on a more limited basis. For example, Taggart argued in favour of an enhanced role for proportionality for all cases addressing human rights (including rights beyond those recorded in statutory bills of rights), but also argued for the retention of reasonableness review for the remaining cases addressing 'public wrongs'.[105]

---

[101] *Brind*, above n. 4. See also *R (International Traders' Ferry Ltd)* v. *Chief Constable of Sussex* [1999] 2 AC 418.

[102] *British Civilian Internees*, above n. 20, [34]–[37].

[103] *Somerville* v. *Scottish Ministers* [2007] 1 WLR 2734, [55] (HL); *Kennedy* v. *Charity Commission* [2014] 2 WLR 808, [54] (SC); *Pham* v. *Secretary of State for the Home Department* [2015] 1 WLR 1591, [98] (SC; Lord Mance). For other tentative endorsement see *R (Alconbury Developments Ltd)* v. *Secretary of State for the Environment, Transport and the Regions* [2003] 2 AC 295, [51] (Lord Slynn); *R (Nolan)* v. *Manchester Metropolitan University* [1994] ELR 380 (Sedley LJ).

[104] Craig, *Administrative Law*, above n. 43, ch. 21.

[105] Michael Taggart, 'Proportionality, Deference, *Wednesbury*' [2008] NZ Law Rev 424. See also Jeff King, 'Proportionality' (2010) NZ Law Rev 327.

While not assuming status as a universal ground of review, the language of disproportionality has, however, still been relied on in (non-human rights) cases to quash disproportionate or excessive sanctions or penalties.[106] Lord Denning's remarks in *Hook* stating the courts can intervene if 'punishment is altogether excessive and out of proportion to the occasion' is often highlighted.[107] Following the systemisation of the grounds in *CCSU*, other judges have adopted similar language suggesting proportionality might be regarded as a ground of review in a particular set of circumstances.[108] However, the magnitude of disproportionality required for intervention is generally analogous to the threshold for intervention under the irrationality ground. The degree of coincidence suggests disproportionality may operate merely as an indicator of unreasonableness under the rubric of the established irrationality ground, rather than an independent ground in its own right.[109] In any event, the expression of a different basis of intervention may still allow judges to avoid the demands of the *Wednesbury* irrationality test and rely on disproportionality to modulate the supervisory intensity (albeit any difference may be marginal).

Further, a structured form of proportionality has been established as the dominant method of review under bills of right, such as the Human Rights Act 1998. Indeed, the adoption of the proportionality doctrine has been described as 'one of the most profound changes to judicial reasoning brought about by the [Human Rights Act]'.[110] Proportionality is not referred to in the Human Rights Act or European Convention; however, the English courts have, consistently with the approach in other jurisdictions, interpreted limitations clauses as involving a proportionality assessment.[111] The European Court of Human Rights ruled that the phrase

---

[106] See generally Michael Fordham, 'Common Law Proportionality' [2002] JR 110, [16]–[17] and Fordham, *Judicial Review Handbook*, above n. 35, [58.3].

[107] *R (Hook)* v. *Barnsley Metropolitan Borough Council* [1976] 1 WLR 1052. See also *R (Cinnamond)* v. *St Albans Crown Court* [1981] QB 480.

[108] See e.g. *Ghosh* v. *General Medical Council* [2001] 1 WLR 1915; *Dad* v. *General Dental Council* [2000] 1 WLR 1538; *R (X)* v. *London Borough of Newham* [1995] ELR 303; *R (Hall)* v. *Eastbourne Magistrates' Court* [1993] COD 140; *R (Adair)* v. *Truro Crown Court* [1997] COD 296.

[109] For examples of cases interweaving disproportionality and unreasonableness, see *R (Haddow)* v. *Thanet District Council* (1992) 157 JP 545; *R (A)* v. *Head Teacher of P School* [2002] ELR 244; *Dad* v. *General Dental Council* [2000] 1 WLR 1538; *Sanders* v. *Kingston (No 2)* [2006] LGR 111.

[110] Aileen Kavanagh, *Constitutional Review under the UK Human Rights Act* (Cambridge University Press, 2009), 233.

[111] Julian Rivers, 'Proportionality and Variable Intensity of Review' (2006) 65 CLJ 174, 174–82; Grégoire Webber, *The Negotiable Constitution* (Cambridge University Press, 2009), 59–65.

'necessary in a democratic society' in the European Convention requires the court to assess the proportionality of the rights-infringing measure.[112] A similarly styled test has been adopted under the Human Rights Act 1998, assessing whether the government objective is 'sufficiently important' to justify limiting rights, whether measures adopted are 'rationally connected' to that objective, whether the impairment of rights are 'no more than is necessary' to achieve that objective, and whether a 'fair balance' was struck.[113]

For present purposes, our interest in the deployment of this particular form of proportionality lies in its relationship with the traditional grounds of review. As outlined earlier, reliance on proportionality in the human rights domain can be explained in different ways. The first account is evolutionary. That is, the courts have modified the substantive grounds of review when human rights instruments such as the Human Rights Act 1998 are directly impugned. In other words, rather than subjecting decisions to scrutiny under the irrationality ground of review, the courts have endorsed, to a limited extent, proportionality as a ground to review the substance of a decision. Under this account, administrative law is effectively bifurcated and cases where human rights instruments are engaged are subjected to different principles of review. The second account addresses proportionality in the colours of (il)legality. The judicial enquiry is on the lawfulness of the actions of the administration, given the legislative decree

---

For the origins of the proportionality test, see generally Jeffrey Jowell, 'Proportionality' in Jeffrey Jowell and D. Oliver (eds.), *New Directions in Judicial Review* (Steven & Sons, 1988), 51, 52–9; Moshe Cohen-Eliya and Iddo Porat, 'American Balancing and German Proportionality'(2010) 8 ICON 263; Dieter Grimm, 'Proportionality in Canadian and German Constitutional Jurisprudence' (2007) 57 UTLJ 393; Taggart, 'Proportionality', above n. 105, 437; Thomas Poole, 'Proportionality in Perspective' [2010] NZ Law Rev 369.

[112] *Sunday Times* v. *United Kingdom* (1979) 2 EHHR 245.

[113] *De Freitas* v. *Permanent Secretary of Ministry of Agriculture, Fisheries, Lands and Housing* [1999] 1 AC 69, adopted by Lord Steyn in *R (Daly)* v. *Secretary of State for the Home Department* [2001] 2 AC 532. The three-part *de Freitas* test was augmented in *Huang* v. *Secretary of State for the Home Office* [2007] 2 AC 167 by the addition of the fourth 'fair balance' requirement. See also *Alconbury Developments*, above n. 103; *R (SB)* v. *Governors of Denbigh High School* [2007] 1 AC 100; *Belfast City Council* v. *Miss Behavin' Ltd* (2007) 1 WLR 581; *A* v. *Secretary of State for the Home Department* [2005] 2 AC 68, [30]; *Bank Mellat* v. *Her Majesty's Treasury (No 2)* [2014] 1 AC 700, [68]–[76]; *R (Nicklinson)* v. *Ministry of Justice* [2014] 3 WLR 200 [166]–[171], [348]. English courts have sometimes also deployed a proportionality analysis in relation to unqualified rights. See e.g. *R* v. *A (No 2)* [2002] 1 AC 45 and R *(Pretty)* v. *Director of Puplic Prosecutions* [2002] 1 AC 800; see generally Kavanagh, *Constitutional Review*, above n. 110, 257–67 and Ian Leigh, 'Taking Rights Proportionately' (2002) 47 PL 265, 283–4.

in section 6(1) of the Human Rights Act 1998 that it is 'unlawful for a public authority to act in a way which is incompatible with a Convention right'. Thus, proportionality is the interpretative method for assessing whether a statutory obligation has been violated, not a freshly endorsed substantive ground of review. In other words, whether or not, as a matter of law, interference with rights is incompatible is settled through the proportionality calculus (at least for those cases where limitation clauses apply).

This point has received limited attention. Much of the discussion about the place of proportionality identifies a contrast with the *Wednesbury* unreasonableness ground.[114] Indeed, Lord Steyn's endorsement of proportionality in *Daly* compared proportionality to the 'traditional grounds of review'.[115] Framing proportionality in this way – 'through the lens of administrative law', as Hickman put it – points to proportionality operating as a new ground of review.[116] Others characterise proportionality as an aspect of the illegality ground of review. For example, Leigh suggests 'a new form of over-arching *illegality* – in the sense that Lord Diplock used that term in [*CCSU*]' – is created.[117] In particular, the obligation to act compatibly with Convention rights enables legality review, noting that 'there is nothing which suggests that its sole effect is to modify the *Wednesbury* ground of review, as seems universally to be assumed'.[118] Craig similarly acknowledges that proportionality under the Human Rights Act operates as a legal 'test' but, at the same time, also tends to speak of proportionality as a new ground of review.[119] 'Section 6(1) creates a new statutory head of illegality for breach of a Convention right', Craig says. 'It is a free-standing ground of challenge.'[120] On the one hand, this is consistent with Leigh's illegality formulation. On the other hand, it also tends to mark a breach of Convention rights (along with the proportionality test implicitly involved) as an independent ground of review; this is reinforced by Craig's treatment

---

[114] See e.g. Kavanagh, above n. 110, 244 and 267; Elliott, *Administrative Law*, above n. 58, 289; de Smith (6th edn), 587.

[115] *Daly*, above n. 113, [27]–[28].

[116] Hickman, *Public Law*, above n. 66, 110.

[117] Leigh, above n. 113, 282.

[118] *Ibid.*, 282. Hickman adopts Leigh's analysis, suggesting proportionality is better viewed as forming part of the 'standard of legality', rather than being an alternative 'standard of review': Hickman, *Public Law*, above n. 66, 110.

[119] Craig, *Administrative Law*, above n. 43, [21-020]. Craig often refers to proportionality as a standard of review, but this seems to be used interchangeably for a ground of review.

[120] *Ibid.*, [20-017]. See also Paul Craig, 'Proportionality, Rationality and Review' [2010] NZ Law Rev 265, 293.

elsewhere of proportionality, where he analyses its status in tandem with the existing *Wednesbury* ground.[121]

In any event, this structured form of proportionality potentially mandates depth of review that is more intense compared to substantive review under the *Wednesbury* standard (regardless of whether deployed under the guise of illegality or as an alternative substantive ground). It has generally been understood and applied by judges as involving close scrutiny of the governmental action.[122] This point is often overstated because proportionality does not, in itself, dictate the depth of scrutiny and is better understood as a relational concept which relies on other factors to settle the depth of scrutiny that is applied. Indeed, it is increasingly acknowledged that proportionality inquiry necessarily operates in tandem with notions of deference or intensity.[123] The modulation implicit in proportionality therefore enables greater variability, over and above the evolutionary dimension. Further, the components of the proportionality review – particularly the touchstones of 'sufficiently', 'rationally', 'necessary', and 'fair balance' – provide ample room for judicial discretion.[124]

Mistake of fact has also received some recognition as a ground of general application, beyond the limited circumstances in which fact finding could traditionally be challenged.[125] In *E v. Secretary of State for the Home*

---

[121] Craig, *Administrative Law*, above n. 43, ch. 21.

[122] See *Daly*, above n. 113; *Denbigh High*, above n. 113; *A v. Secretary of State*, above n. 113; Jeffrey Jowell, 'Judicial Deference and Human Rights' in Paul Craig and Richard Rawlings (eds.), *Law and Administration in Europe* (Oxford University Press, 2003), 67, 79; Elliott, *Administrative Law*, above n. 55, 288. Compare Kavanagh, above n. 110, 243.

[123] See e.g. Murray Hunt, 'Against Bifurcation' in David Dyzenhaus, Murray Hunt and Grant Huscroft (eds.), *A Simple Common Lawyer* (Hart Publishing, 2009), 99, 111 ('complain[ing] that a decision is disproportionate, without more, would be like complaining that a decision is too big'); Rivers, above n. 111, 202–3. Craig, one of proportionality's key proponents, concedes this: Paul Craig, 'Unreasonableness and Proportionality in UK Law' in Evelyn Ellis (ed.), *The Principle of Proportionality in the Laws of Europe* (Hart Publishing, 1999), 85, 100 and 'Rationality', above n. 120, 287–92. See recent endorsement of this point in *Kennedy*, above n. 103, [54] and the emphasis of proportionality's flexibility and nuance in *Nicklinson*, above n. 113. See the recent judicial acknowledgement of this point in *Pham v. Secretary of State for the Home Secretary* [2015] 1 WLR 1591, [96] and [114].

[124] Thomas Poole, 'The Reformation of English Administrative Law' (2009) 68 CLJ 142, 146 ('plastic', can be applied 'almost infinitely forcefully or infinitely cautiously', can produce 'an area of discretionary judgement that can be massively broad or incredibly narrow'). See also Grégoire C.N. Webber 'Proportionality, Balancing, and the Cult of Constitutional Rights Scholarship' (2010) 23 CJLJ 179.

[125] Christopher Forsyth and Emma Dring, 'The Emergence of Material Error of Fact as a Ground for Judicial Review' in Christopher Forsyth and others (eds.), *Effective Judicial Review* (Oxford University Press, 2010), 245.

Department, the Court of Appeal recognised that 'a mistake of fact giving rise to unfairness is a separate head of challenge'.[126] The factual mistake must be 'established' (that is, shown 'by objective and uncontentious evidence'), must have played a 'material', albeit not decisive, part in the reasoning, and the claimant must not have been responsible for the error.[127] The linkage with fairness casts some doubt on its status as a free-standing ground of review; it is unclear whether the reference stands merely as a conclusion or whether the mistake is merely a touchstone within the broader rubric of unfairness.[128]

Finally, a range of *other possible substantive grounds* have been proposed as counterpoints to the *Wednesbury* unreasonableness ground, but their impact on judicial doctrines has been quite mixed. These include potential grounds like inequality or inconsistency,[129] substantive fairness,[130] and the so-called 'innominate' ground.[131] These grounds either have assumed a subsidiary role informing the assessment under other grounds or appear to have been overtaken by other developments (such as substantive protection of legitimate expectations and variegated forms of unreasonableness). While their impact on judicial review doctrines nowadays is therefore limited, dalliances with these alternative grounds speak to the judicial penchant for promoting alternative doctrinal grounds to circumvent *Wednesbury*'s deferential degree of scrutiny.

---

[126] [2004] QB 1044, [66]. The question arose in an appeal on a point of law, where the principles mimic judicial review principles. Although not yet addressed by the Supreme Court, other courts have followed the approach: see e.g. *R (Iran)* v. *Secretary of State for the Home Department* [2005] Imm AR 535, [95]; *MT (Algeria) Secretary of State for the Home Department* [2008] QB 533, [67].

[127] [2004] QB 1044, [63].

[128] Craig, *Administrative Law*, above n. 43, [17-017].

[129] There are some examples of inequality or inconsistency forming a basis for judicial intervention. It is doubtful, though, whether this has crystallised into a basis for intervention in its own right as a common law ground: *Matadeen* v. *Pointu* [1990] AC 98. Compare *R (Gurung)* v. *Minister of Defence* [2002] EWHC Admin 2463; *R (Urmaza)* v. *Secretary of State for the Home Department* [1996] COD 479. See Craig, *Administrative Law*, above n. 43, [23-002].

[130] The courts have, at times, explored the adoption of a ground which involves an enquiry, in the round, about the overall fairness of the case. For cases employing the language of substantive fairness, see e.g. *Pierson*, above n. 70; *R (Hindley)* v. *Secretary of State for the Home Office* [2000] QB 152 (CA), [2001] 1 AC 410 (HL); *R (Hamble (Offshore) Fisheries Ltd)* v. *Ministry of Agriculture, Fisheries and Food* [1995] 2 All ER 714. Nowadays the idea of substantive fairness has largely been overtaken by variegated and more intense forms of unreasonableness or more specific grounds such as substantive legitimate expectation. See generally Fordham, *Judicial Review Handbook*, above n. 35, [54.1].

[131] *R (Guinness plc)* v. *Panel on Take-overs and Mergers* [1990] 1 QB 146, 159–60. See discussion of contextual review: ch. 5; text to n. 53.

Reformulation

In addition to the development of novel or emerging grounds, there has been some attempt to recast the grounds of review in a way which would affect the depth of review. The most obvious example is the attempt to simplify the irrationality or unreasonableness ground. That is, rather than seeking to variegate unreasonableness into differing degrees, a number of judges and scholars promoted the idea that the deferential *Wednesbury* unreasonableness ground ought to be given unified and simplified expression.[132] These attempts can be viewed in different ways. On the one hand, they potentially represent a ground of unreasonableness which has a greater vigilance than is apparent under its original *Wednesbury* formulation. To this extent, these efforts can be explained as the revision of an existing ground of review, hence their mention at this point. On the other hand, they potentially signal a new – more contextual – style of review. Their emphasis on context and circumstance, teamed with the mandate of significant judicial discretion, tends towards a departure from the categorical approach which underlies the grounds of review schema. These developments are therefore discussed under contextual review later.[133]

Circumscription

Access to the traditional grounds of review may be circumscribed through the application of the principle of non-justiciability. In its strongest formulation, review may not be permitted at all – that is, none of the grounds of review are treated as being applicable.[134] In its softer formulation, the suite of grounds of review may be circumscribed or modified to take account of the context of particular cases. Harris has described these two different techniques as exhibiting 'primary' and 'secondary' non-justiciability respectively.[135] In doing so, greater weight is placed on judicial restraint and more deferential supervision results.

---

[132] See especially Lord Cooke's views, below n. 153, including comments in *International Traders' Ferry* and *Daly* while sitting as a member of the House of Lords.

[133] See Section 5.2.

[134] It is possible to frame non-justiciability in terms of explicit variable intensity; however, the courts have been slow to connect this methodology with other developments in variable intensity and usually deploy it as a stand-alone doctrine. For the identification of the linkages, see Taggart, 'Administrative Law', above n. 47, 84; Andrew Le Sueur, 'The Rise and Ruin of Unreasonableness?' [2005] JR 32. King goes further and suggests the justiciability principle has now been overtaken by the notion of deference: Jeff A. King, 'The Justiciability of Resource Allocation' (2007) 70 MLR 197, 198.

[135] B.V. Harris, 'Judicial Review, Justiciability and the Prerogative of Mercy' (2003) 62 CLJ 631.

The principle of primary non-justiciability is well recognised. The courts may decline to review a matter, as a preliminary or jurisdictional matter, on the basis that it is non-justiciable. It is perhaps most famously seen in the House of Lords in *CCSU* where their Lordships ruled, on the one hand, that the royal prerogative was not automatically non-justiciable but, on the other hand, that the national security issues raised by the application for review were not suitable for judicial determination.[136] The case is also notable for Lord Roskill's categorical list of certain types of decision that would be non-justiciable.[137] The categories of cases that are non-justiciable under English law have been whittled down over time.[138]

The principle of secondary non-justiciability – 'modified review', as Fordham puts it[139] – draws a stronger connection with the traditional grounds of review. The traditional grounds of review are modified, either substituting more deferential grounds of review or by disapplying particular grounds. A number of examples illustrate the circumscription or adaptation of the usual suite of grounds of review.

First, the basis for reviewing prosecutorial discretion is narrowly limited in England. Once entirely non-justiciable,[140] nowadays decisions to prosecute are reviewable only for dishonesty, bad faith and other exceptional circumstances – not the traditional *CCSU* grounds. Lord Steyn said in *Kebelene*, 'absent dishonesty or mala fides or an exceptional circumstance, the decision of the Director to consent to the prosecution ... is not amenable to judicial review'.[141] Secondly, English courts have adopted a similar circumscribed approach when reviewing commercial decisions.[142]

---

[136] *CCSU*, above n. 2, See also *Campaign for Nuclear Disarmament* v. *Prime Minister* [2002] EWHC 2777.

[137] *CCSU*, above n. 2, 418.

[138] See e.g. *Bancoult* v. *Secretary of State for Foreign and Commonwealth Affairs* [2008] 3 WLR 955; ch. 2, n. 135; Thomas Poole, 'Judicial Review at the Margins' (2010) 60 UTLJ 81. Compare *R (Gentle)* v. *The Prime Minister* [2008] 1 AC 1356.

[139] Fordham, *Judicial Review Handbook*, above n. 35, [P32]. Fordham also includes under this label the principle of anxious scrutiny and related developments. I have addressed the latter under the rubric of intensity of review (see Section 4.2), although it is plausible to conceive of the more intense expressions of unreasonableness as the articulation of alternate grounds of review.

[140] See e.g. *Gouriet* v. *Union of Post Office Workers* [1978] AC 435.

[141] *R (Kebelene)* v. *Director of Public Prosecutions* [2000] 2 AC 326. See also *Sharma* v. *Antoine* [2007] 1 WLR 780, [14].

[142] See e.g. *Mass Energy Ltd* v. *Birmingham City Council* [1994] Env LR 298; *Ealing Community Transport Ltd* v. *Council of the London Borough of Ealing* [1999] All ER (D) 953; *R (Cookson)* v. *Ministry of Defence* [2005] EWCA Civ 811; *R (Gamesa Energy UK Ltd)* v. *National Assembly for Wales* [2006] EWHC 2167; *Supportways Community Services Ltd* v.

Thirdly, the UK Supreme Court in *R (Cart)* v. *Upper Tribunal* recently adopted a form of secondary non-justiciability in relation to the judicial review of the Upper Tribunal's refusal to grant permission to appeal decisions of lower tribunals.[143] Presented with a specially developed tribunals system, with its own provision for appeal and review by appellate bodies comprised of superior court judges, the Supreme Court was reluctant to allow review on 'the full panoply of grounds', largely for reasons of comity and pragmatism.[144] Instead, the Court ruled that judicial review would only be allowed where the criteria for making a second-tier appeal from the Upper Tribunal to the Court of Appeal is made out (namely, if the matter raises an important point of principle or practice or there is some other compelling reason for the court to hear it).[145] This approach was seen to represent a half-way house between the usual grounds that would be available and an even narrower set of grounds proposed by the Court of Appeal below.[146]

Finally, the English courts have circumscribed the grounds available to review the decisions made within visitatorial jurisdiction. In *R (Page)* v. *Hull University Visitor*, for example, a majority of the House of Lords ruled that the long-standing exclusive jurisdiction of visitors on internal affairs of charitable or academic foundations meant that their decisions could not be impugned on the basis of the standard error of law ground.[147] Only errors falling outside their jurisdiction (in the narrow sense) were reviewable. However, review for breaches of other grounds such as procedural impropriety remained.

Before leaving the circumscription of the grounds of review, it is important to note the set of cases manifesting a 'super-*Wednesbury*' – that is, more deferential – form of unreasonableness could be conceived as circumscription of the grounds of review akin to the other instances

---

Hampshire County Council [2006] LGR 836. This is broadly consistent with Aranciba's account that a 'light touch' approach is generally adopted for the review of commercial decisions (although he does not draw a strong distinction between *Wednesbury* unreasonableness and modified review); Jaime Arancibia, *Judicial Review of Commercial Regulation* (Oxford University Press, 2011), 56. See also discussion in the New Zealand context (text to n. 206).

[143] [2012] 1 AC 663; *Eba* v. *Advocate General for Scotland* [2012] 1 AC 710 (companion case).

[144] *Cart*, above n. 143, [33].

[145] *Ibid.*, [104].

[146] *Cart* v. *Upper Tribunal* [2011] QB 120, [36], namely, restricted to pre-*Anisminic* excess of jurisdiction and the denial of fundamental justice.

[147] [1993] AC 682. See, similarly, *R (Calder & Persaud)* v. *Visitors to the Inns of Court* [1994] QB 1.

discussed.[148] However, I prefer to analyse these developments under the rubric of intensity of review because the theme of the different approach has been more strongly connected to the variegation of the unreasonableness ground.[149]

3.2.3   New Zealand: Lord Cooke's Simple Trio of Grounds

Judicial review in New Zealand also centres on a tripartite expression of grounds of review, although the prevailing nomenclature is a simplified version of Lord Diplock's recitation in *CCSU*.[150] Contemporaneous with the systemisation of the grounds in *CCSU*, Lord Cooke propounded a similar tripartite statement of grounds of review:[151]

> [T]he substantive principles of judicial review are simply that the decision-maker must act in accordance with law, fairly and reasonably.

The threefold classification mimics Lord Diplock's categorisation, although Lord Cooke observed that he expressed these principles in similar form some five years before *CCSU*.[152] The grounds articulated are similar in nature, except for their simplified language and expression as positive norms or standards to be complied with by administrators. While Lord Cooke contemplated a more aggressive simplification project for the underlying doctrine,[153] the simplified version of the grounds still map onto Lord Diplock's threefold set of principles and are generally regarded as mirroring the English principles.[154]

The extra-judicial statement of the grounds was subsequently confirmed in decisions which followed. Lord Cooke repeated his simple statement of

---

[148] *Nottinghamshire*, above n. 78, and *R (Hammersmith and Fulham London Borough Council)* v. *Secretary of State for the Environment* [1991] 1 AC 521.

[149] See Section 4.2.3.

[150] See also the rise of intensity of review in New Zealand (Section 4.2.4) and the simplified and instinctive forms of contextual review (Section 5.2.2).

[151] Robin Cooke, 'The Struggle for Simplicity in Administrative Law' in Michael Taggart (ed.), *Judicial Review of Administrative Action in the 1980s* (Oxford University Press, 1986), 1, 5.

[152] *Ibid.*, 6, referring to 'Third Thoughts on Administrative Law' [1979] NZ Recent Law 218, 225.

[153] In particular, Lord Cooke favoured a simplified and non-exaggerated standard of reasonableness: see e.g. Cooke, 'Simplicity', above n. 151, 15; 'The Road Ahead For the Common Law' (2004) 53 ICLQ 273, 285; *International Traders' Ferry*, above n. 101, 452; *Daly*, above n. 113, 549.

[154] Taylor notes some uncertainty arising from inconsistency in the use of 'unreasonableness', '*Wednesbury* unreasonableness', and 'irrationality': G.D.S. Taylor, *Judicial Review* (LexisNexis, 2010), 435. However, this was shared in the English expression of the grounds.

the grounds of review in *New Zealand Fishing Industry Association Inc* v. *Minister of Agriculture and Fisheries*, a case now frequently cited as authority for the threefold formulation.[155] The tripartite identification of the grounds of review have been repeated and endorsed in numerous other cases: Lord Cooke's simplified version,[156] Lord Diplock's formulation,[157] and analogous versions.[158] As an example, one High Court judge recently recorded that the recognised grounds of review 'remain firmly those stated by Lord Diplock in *CCSU*' and also 'are captured in Cooke J's wonderfully succinct statement in *New Zealand Fishing*'.[159] As with Lord Diplock's statement, cautionary comments about potential overlap and merger are also prominent.[160]

As in England, a number of judges have adopted similar but marginally different formulations of the grounds of review. For example, Keith J in *Peters* v. *Davison* adopted the language used by Lord Templeman to describe the grounds of review in *Preston*.[161] Similarly, Richardson J used the shorthand of 'familiar *Wednesbury* grounds' in *Mackenzie District Council* and *Woolworths* – grounds, though, which echo the tripartite formulations of Lord Diplock and Lord Cooke.[162] Chief Justice Elias recently spoke extra-judicially of overarching requirements of 'reasonableness,

---

[155] [1988] 1 NZLR 544, 552. See also *Minister of Energy* v. *Petrocorp Exploration Ltd* [1989] 1 NZLR 348, 352; *Jenssen* v. *Director-General of Agriculture and Fisheries* (CA313/91, 16.9.92), 3.

[156] See e.g. *Peters* v. *Davison* [1999] 2 NZLR 164, 208; *BNZ Investments Ltd* v. *Commissioner of Inland Revenue* (2007) 23 NZTC 21,078, [15]; *Osbourne* v. *Chief Executive of the Ministry of Social Development* [2010] 1 NZLR 559, [54]. See also Matthew Smith, *New Zealand Judicial Review Handbook* (2nd edn, Thomson Reuters, 2016), [4.1.2].

[157] See e.g. *University of Auckland* v. *International Education Appeal Authority (No 1)* [2010] NZAR 1, [35]; *Adlam* v. *Stratford Racing Club Inc* [2007] NZAR 543; *NZI Financial Corporation Ltd* v. *New Zealand Kiwifruit Authority* [1986] 1 NZLR 159, 172. See also Smith, above n. 156, [4.1.3].

[158] See e.g. *Pring* v. *Wanganui District Court* [1999] NZRMA 519, [7]; *Official Assignee* v. *Chief Executive of Ministry of Fisheries* [2002] 2 NZLR 222 [85]; *Brierley Investments Ltd* v. *Bouzaid* [1993] 3 NZLR 655, 660. See also Smith, above n. 156, [4.1.4] and [4.1.5].

[159] *Powerco* v. *Commerce Commission* (HC, CIV-2005-485-1066, 9.5.2006), [21]. The question arose in the context of whether proportionality was a recognised ground of review, which Wild J held it was not.

[160] See e.g. *New Zealand Fishing Industry*, above n. 155. See generally Smith, above n. 156, [4.2].

[161] *Peters* v. *Davison*, above n. 156, 180. See also *Miller* v. *Commissioner of Inland Revenue* [1995] 3 NZLR 664, 668.

[162] *Mackenzie District Council* v. *Electricity Corporation of New Zealand* [1992] 3 NZLR 41, 43; *Wellington City Council* v. *Woolworths New Zealand Ltd (No 2)* [1996] 2 NZLR 537, 545 (although expressed in a more disaggregated fashion).

fairness, [and] legality', to which she also added 'consistency, and equal treatment'.[163]

The tripartite expression of the grounds is also recognised as the prevailing orthodoxy in textbooks and practice guides. Joseph's leading textbook on constitutional and administrative law speaks of Lord Diplock's threefold formulation as the 'principal grounds of review', adopting each as chapter headings for his detailed exposition.[164] Taylor describes the tripartite classification as 'conventional' and 'the "firmly" recognised current description' of New Zealand's grounds of review.[165] However, recognising the expectation that the text would be organised under these grounds, Taylor mounts an extended defence of his alternative structure.[166] The tripartite statement is entrenched in a number of other practice guides and texts,[167] including Smith's handbook on judicial review.[168]

One recent attempt to recast the principles of judicial review in New Zealand deserves particular mention. In his separate reasons delivered in *Lab Tests*, Hammond J took the opportunity to reflect on the general shape of judicial review. He is critical of the established doctrinal grounds of review.[169] However, his alternative approach to judicial review – proposed tentatively – in many respects reprises the current threefold statement. At the outset, he identifies a tension between two schools of thought on judicial review. On the one hand, a 'traditional' or 'orthodox' camp which emphasises the role of supervisory courts ensuring that administrators

---

[163] Sian Elias, 'National Lecture on Administrative Law (AIAL conference, July 2013), 9.

[164] Philip A. Joseph, *Constitutional and Administrative Law* (4th edn, Brookers, 2014), 854, chs. 23, 24, 25.

[165] Taylor, above n. 154, [11.01], adopting the adverb from Wild J in *Powerco*, above n. 159, [21].

[166] Taylor, above n. 154, [11.01] and [11.02]. Taylor instead borrowed the framework adopted by Sir Kenneth Keith in his teaching: Who? How? What? Why?

[167] McGrath (ed.), *The Laws of New Zealand* (LexisNexis, 2004), 'Administrative Law', [6] ('Major grounds of review'); Crown Law Office, *A Judge Over Your Shoulder* (2005), [14] ('The grounds of challenge can be broadly divided into: illegality (acting outside the scope of the power; getting the law wrong); unfairness (sometimes referred to as procedural impropriety); unreasonableness.'); Geoffrey Palmer and Matthew Palmer, *Bridled Power* (4th edn, Oxford University Press, 2005), 292–5 (identifying illegality, breach of the rules of natural justice, irrationality or unreasonableness, along with legitimate expectations).

[168] Smith, above n. 156, [4.1], recognising the threefold summary formulations, but later also identifying twenty-six 'separate but overlapping' individual grounds of review.

[169] *Lab Tests Auckland Ltd* v. *Auckland District Health Board* [2009] 1 NZLR 776 (CA). Leave for appeal was, oddly, declined: (2009) 19 PRNZ 217 (SC) ('ultimately turns on its own facts' and no arguable question of public or general importance).

'remain within the powers granted to them by law';[170] on the other hand, a 'more modern' camp promotes more aggressive intervention to 'restrain the abuse of power and to secure good administration'.[171] He suggests this leads to confusion about the circumstances in which the courts will intervene:[172]

> [W]hen fundamental disputes about 'purpose' are leavened with confusion as to the principles on which courts will intervene (often called the "grounds for review"), the state of the law is rendered distinctly problematic.

Hammond J notes the judicial efforts to formulate 'a unified theory of judicial review', particularly Lord Cooke's threefold statement.[173] However, he dismisses this type of taxonomy because 'grand theorem approaches fail', he says, 'to drill down far enough to enable respectable advice to be given to parties who are supposed to abide by the law'.[174] Further, he points to the lack of an agreed schematic:[175]

> As far as the grounds of review are concerned, the difficulty stems partly from the lack of an agreed classification or taxonomy, accompanied by properly developed substantive principles as to when a court will intervene by way of judicial review, particularly in 'merits' cases.

Instead, Hammond J promotes a 'functional rather than doctrinal' approach to the grounds of review.[176] On this basis, he suggests the grounds of review be grouped according to procedural grounds of review ('the conduct of the decision maker and include procedural fairness requirements, fair hearing rules, and rules against bias'), the decision-maker's reasoning processes ('things like misappreciation of the law; unauthorised delegation; and the perennial problem of control of the exercise of a discretion'), and grounds relating to the decision itself, not the procedures adopted or reasoning process ('substantive grounds of review, even where a decision maker has assiduously followed all required procedures and has made no errors of reasoning').[177] Acknowledging confusion – fog of the 'pea souper' kind – in relation to substantive grounds of review, he latches onto the

---

[170] *Lab Tests* (CA), above n. 169, [363].

[171] *Ibid.*, [367].

[172] *Ibid.*, [370].

[173] *Ibid.*, [374].

[174] *Ibid.*, [378]. Notably, he dismissed 'spectrums of response' or 'deference' as 'quite unhelpful, and even unworkable' ([379]).

[175] *Ibid.*, [380].

[176] *Ibid.*, [381].

[177] *Ibid.*, [382]–[384].

concept of abuse of power and suggests substantive principles on which the merits of a decision can be challenged could be developed under this rubric. But he leaves the articulation of those principles for another day, noting only that proportionality and substantive fairness are two possibilities which have particular currency nowadays.[178]

While Hammond J appears to berate the traditional doctrinal approach to grounds of review and a tripartite formulation, his own formulation maintains a commitment to a grounds of review schematic. In many respects, his recital of the grounds of review in functional terms merely redraws the traditional grounds with a slightly different emphasis. His taxonomy simply recreates groups which mimic the chapter divisions of Lord Diplock and Lord Cooke, albeit with new chapter headings: procedural grounds rather than procedural impropriety/fairly; reasoning process grounds rather than illegality/in accordance with law; and substantive or abuse of power grounds rather than irrationality/reasonably. Subtle differences may lie in the allocation of some specific grounds (for example, it is unclear where Hammond J sees relevancy principles being located; whether as reasoning or substantive grounds). And he seems to anticipate that substantive grounds would have many threads, under a general rubric of abuse of power. But this, too, is consistent with the notion that the suite of grounds may be enlarged over time; the fact that the space most ripe for development relates to merits review is not seriously in question. In general terms, Hammond J's attempt to reinvent the principles of judicial review is large on rhetoric but short on substance. While he made a plea for 'better charts' to map judicial review principles and warned against 'simply exchanging one shibboleth for another', his own analysis risks doing exactly that.[179]

In summary, like its English parent, New Zealand's jurisprudence is generally structured around well-entrenched grounds of review, expressed in tripartite form. While other formulations have been promoted, a categorical approach to the intensity of review continues to dominate.

The modulation of the depth of scrutiny in New Zealand echoes the English experience, with classification, evolution, reformulation and circumscription being utilised to provide variability within the schema. Here, I focus on some particular instances of the style of variation which have particular resonance in the New Zealand context.

---

[178] *Ibid.*, [391]–[392].
[179] *Ibid.*, [378].

Classification

The judicial discretion as to the process of classification is acknowledged in New Zealand. As discussed above, there is a strong recognition of the overlapping character of the grounds and the consequential effect of classifying justiciable matters in each category.

An increasingly common technique in New Zealand is the reliance on the principle of legality which moves matters from the realm of discretion, where deferential grounds apply, into the realm of legality, where strict scrutiny is applied.[180] One particular instance of this – the development of the *presumption of consistency* in relation to the influence of international instruments on domestic administrative law – acutely demonstrates the particular significance of the classification technique in the distinction between law and discretion.[181] The depth of judicial review differs, depending on whether the challenge is mounted under the illegality ground (under the presumption of consistency, a doctrine which mimics the principle of legality) or the irrationality ground. The presumption of consistency requires any administrative power to be read consistently with international law obligations, except where the statutory matrix is otherwise inconsistent.[182] Framed in this way as a matter of law, this approach allows the courts to assess whether or not international law obligations have been correctly applied and effectively circumscribes the discretion available to any public body or official. In contrast, the relevancy approach treats the impact of international instruments as a matter of substance or discretion. As long as the administration has turned its mind to the relevant legal instruments, the weight given to those international law norms can only be impugned under the irrationality ground.[183]

Another example of the process of classification determining the depth of review is the approach to statutory preconditions. Following the English

---

[180] See e.g. *Cropp* v. *Judicial Committee* [2008] 3 NZLR 774, [26]; *Canterbury Regional Council* v. *Independent Fisheries Ltd* [2013] 2 NZLR 57, [140]; Claudia Geiringer 'The Principle of Legality and the Bill of Rights Act' (2008) 6 NZJPIL 59; Taggart, 'Proportionality', above n. 105, 431.

[181] See generally Claudia Geiringer, '*Tavita* and All That' (2004) 21 NZULR 66 and 'International Law through the Lens of *Zaoui*' (2006) 17 PLR 300. The presumption operates more strongly in New Zealand than in England: see Philip Sales and Joanne Clement, 'International Law in Domestic Courts' [2008] LQR 388, 393.

[182] *Puli'uvea* v. *Removal Review Authority* [1996] 3 NZLR 538; *Zaoui* v. *Attorney-General (No 2)* [2006] 1 NZLR 289; *Ye* v. *Minister of Immigration* [2010] 1 NZLR 104.

[183] See *Ashby* v. *Minister of Immigration* [1981] 1 NZLR 222; *Tavita* v. *Minister of Immigration* [1994] 2 NZLR 257. See also Geiringer, '*Tavita*', above n. 181.

approach to jurisdictional facts, the New Zealand courts scrutinise the presence of some – but not all – factual preconditions closely. For example, the courts have mandated close supervision of 'gate-keeper' fact-finding that a development proposal has no adverse environmental effects such that public participation can be dispensed with.[184] In contrast, a statutory precondition requiring a factual finding that it was desirable to protect shareholders and the public interest before placing a company into statutory administration was not treated as a jurisdictional fact and was only subjected to reasonableness review.[185]

Reformulation

Efforts to recast the grounds of review in order to modify their depth of scrutiny have been notable in New Zealand, particularly in relation to irrationality and reasonableness review.[186]

Evolution

Like England, some emergent grounds have crystallised, although their application remains narrow and restricted to particular circumstances.

The recognition of *substantive legitimate expectation* as a ground of review in New Zealand is somewhat unsettled.[187] While the ground has not received the same degree of approval as in England, there is some support (largely within the lower courts) for this ground. The Court of Appeal foreshadowed that intervention may be justified, under the more general rubric of abuse of power or unfairness, where the administration reneges on an assurance or promise.[188] A number of decisions in the High Court have also, in principle and in accordance with *Coughlan*, indicated that an expectation may be afforded substantive protection in some situations.[189]

---

184   *Discount Brands Ltd* v. *Westfield (New Zealand) Ltd* [2005] 2 NZLR 597.
185   *Hawkins* v. *Minister of Justice* [1991] 2 NZLR 530.
186   See particularly Lord Cooke's efforts (text to n. 153) and Thomas J in *Waitakere City Council* v. *Lovelock* [1997] 2 NZLR 385.
187   See generally Hanna Wilberg, 'Administrative Law' [2010] NZ Law Rev 177, 207 (position 'remains uncertain'; 'some support for some limited substantive effect') and Smith, above n. 156, [55.4] ('some support'; 'remains contentious as a review ground').
188   *Attorney-General* v. *Steelfort Engineering Co Ltd* (1999) 1 NZCC 61-030, relying on *Preston*, above n. 36. See also *New Zealand Māori Council* v. *Attorney-General (Broadcasting Assets)* [1994] 1 AC 466, 467 (PC).
189   See e.g. *Challis* v. *Destination Marlborough Trust Board Inc* [2003] 2 NZLR 107; *New Zealand Association for Migration and Investments Inc* v. *Attorney-General* [2006] NZAR 45; *Comptroller of Customs* v. *Terminals (New Zealand) Ltd* (2012) 2 NZCC 55-040.

Other courts have been more equivocal and, occasionally, hostile;[190] further, the courts have sometimes ruled that particular statutory schemes (notably, tax and revenue collection schemes) are incompatible with the substantive protection of expectations.[191] In any event, most cases fail on the facts at the first stage, failing to demonstrate a clear and unambiguous assurance deserving of protection.

The limited embrace of *proportionality* is mirrored in New Zealand. There has been reluctance to embrace proportionality as a universal ground of review, but the courts have been prepared to intervene to address (excessive) disproportionality in penalties and sanctions. For example, the Court of Appeal in *Institute of Chartered Accountants of New Zealand* v. *Bevan* recognised the courts may intervene to quash penalties which were excessive and disproportionate.[192] However, the Court was not prepared to enter 'the broader question, raised for instance by Lord Diplock as long ago as 1984, whether proportionality is a distinct head of review', Keith said. 'Rather, we limit ourselves to the penalty cases such as *Hook* and take comfort from commentary on proportionality which, while recording the controversy about its separate existence, singles out the penalty area as established.'[193]

In the human rights domain, the New Zealand courts have also endorsed proportionality, like their English counterparts, as the test to determine whether government action abridging rights is justified and therefore lawful. Proportionality has been used to assess whether government action amounts to 'reasonable limits ... demonstrably justified in a free and democratic society' under the general limitation provision in the New Zealand Bill of Rights Act 1990.[194] Just as the text of the NZ Bill of Rights

---

[190] See e.g. *GXL Royalties Ltd* v. *Minister of Energy* [2010] NZAR 658; *Air New Zealand Ltd* v. *Wellington International Airport Ltd* [2009] NZAR 138.

[191] *Bouzaid*, above n. 158; *Westpac Banking Corporation* v. *Commissioner of Inland Review* [2009] 2 NZLR 99.

[192] [2003] 1 NZLR 154, [53]. Other courts have characterised disproportionate treatment merely as a touchstone under the irrationality ground: *Isaac* v. *Minister of Consumer Affairs* [1990] 2 NZLR 606, 636; *University of Auckland* v. *International Education Appeal Authority (No 1)* [2010] NZAR 1.

[193] *Bevan*, above n. 192, [55]. See also *Powerco*, above n. 159, [14] (whether 'stand alone ground of review' remains 'unanswered') and *Wolf* v. *Minister of Immigration* [2004] NZAR 414 (taking a 'cautious approach' about its status but ruling that inapplicable to the particular case). See generally Jason Varuhas, '*Powerco* v. *Commerce Commission*' (2006) 4 NZJPIL 339 and 'Keeping Things in Proportion' (2006) 22 NZULR 300; Taggart, 'Proportionality', above n. 105.

[194] New Zealand Bill of Rights Act 1990, s. 5; *Hansen* v. *R* [2007] 3 NZLR 1; *Moonen* v. *Film and Literature Board of Review* [2000] 2 NZLR 9. See generally Paul Rishworth and others,

Act was drawn from the Canadian experience, so too was the associated proportionality calculus.[195]

The possibility of a free-standing *mistake of fact* ground of review was also floated in New Zealand by Lord Cooke in the 1980s in *Dagayanasi v. Minister of Immigration*, but he failed to secure the support of his then fellow judges for such a development.[196] He was prepared to rule that a ministerial decision to deport an overstayer was 'invalid on the ground of mistake [of fact] as well as on the ground of procedural unfairness' because it was based on an inaccurate conclusion in a medical report about the overstayer's unwell child to obtain adequate treatment overseas.[197] Subsequently, several other cases at appellate level have left the door open for its recognition but have not definitively ruled on its status.[198] Despite its tenuous acceptance amongst higher courts, this ground has been successfully relied on in a number of High Court decisions.[199] One other instance of intervention for factual error is notable. The Privy Council in *Erebus Royal Commission* ruled the decision-makers must base their decision 'upon evidence that has some probative value', but characterised any failure to do so as a breach of the natural justice ground.[200] (Again, this reiterates the role of classification and preconception of errors under different grounds in order to attract deeper scrutiny.)

The New Zealand Bill of Rights (Oxford University Press, 2003), 139. However, Geiringer observes that, in practice, the proportionality method has actually been deployed less frequently in administrative law cases than the widespread endorsement attests: Claudia Geiringer, 'Sources of Resistance to Proportionality Review of Administrative Power under the New Zealand Bill of Rights Act 1990' (2013) 11 NZJPIL 123.

195 Adopting the approach from *R v. Oakes* [1986] 1 SCR 103 under the Canadian Charter of Rights and Freedoms.

196 [1980] 2 NZLR 130. See also *New Zealand Fishing Industry*, above n. 155; Hanna Wilberg, 'Substantive Grounds of Review' (Legal Research Foundation conference, April 2011, Auckland) and 'Administrative Law' [2016] NZ Law Rev 571, 577.

197 *Daganayasi*, above n. 196, 149; Richmond P (132) and Richardson J (149) both expressly left the question open.

198 *Lewis v. Wilson & Horton Ltd* [2000] 3 NZLR 546, [92]; *Air Nelson Ltd v. Minister of Transport* [2008] NZAR 139, [52]–[55]; *Ririnui v. Landcorp Farming Ltd* [2016] 1 NZLR 1056 (speaking favourably about the development of a mistake of fact ground but ultimately not needing to resolve the question).

199 See e.g. *Taiaroa v. Minister of Justice* (CP 99/94, High Court, 4.10.1994); *Northern Inshore Fisheries Company Ltd v. Minister of Fisheries* (CP 235/01, High Court, 4.3.2002); *D v. M and Board of Trustees of Auckland Grammar School* [2003] NZAR 726; *Air Nelson Ltd v. Minister of Transport* [2007] NZAR 266. The ground as applied has similar criteria to those required in *E v. Secretary of State for the Home Department*, above n. 126.

200 [1983] NZLR 662, 671.

Other substantive grounds, such as unequal treatment,[201] substantive fairness,[202] and the innominate ground,[203] have had limited success, despite some strong efforts to have them recognised.

Circumscription

Circumscription of the grounds of review, under the guise of non-justiciability, is seen in New Zealand jurisprudence too. For example, non-justiciability, in its absolute sense, was deployed in the Court of Appeal's decision in *Curtis v. Minister of Defence*.[204] The Court avoided the question of the legality of the disbanding of the air strike force, reasoning that it was a political question which the government of the day should be held accountable for through political – not legal – processes. Partial non-justiciability is also evident in similar areas to those in England. Prosecutorial decisions are only subject to limited review.[205] Commercial decisions of quasi-public bodies are subjected to a circumscribed set of grounds; a particularly notable instance is *Mercury Energy* where the Privy Council, hearing an appeal from New Zealand, doubted that decisions of State-owned Enterprises were reviewable in the absence of 'fraud, corruption or bad faith'.[206]

3.2.4   Australia: Multifarious and Formalistic Grounds Only

As explained earlier, the Australian regime features grounds of review, both under common law review and within the (non-comprehensive) codified regimes.[207] In particular, the categories of jurisdictional error are sometimes described as grounds of review,[208] and the ADJR (Cth) and some other state legislation purport to codify lists of grounds of review.[209]

---

[201] *Pharmaceutical Management Agency Ltd v. Roussel Uclaf Australia Pty Ltd* [1998] NZAR 58; *Isaac v. Minister of Consumer Affairs* [1990] 2 NZLR 606; *Murphy v. Rodney District Council* [2004] 3 NZLR 421.

[202] See ch. 5 text to n. 18.

[203] See Section 5.2.2.

[204] [2002] 2 NZLR 744, [26]–[28].

[205] *Polynesian Spa Ltd v. Osborne* [2005] NZAR 408.

[206] *Mercury Energy Ltd v. Electricity Corporation of New Zealand* [1994] 2 NZLR 385, 391. See also *Lab Tests*, above n. 169; *Air New Zealand Ltd*, above n. 190; *Attorney-General v. Problem Gambling Foundation of New Zealand* [2017] 2 NZLR 470 and Wilberg, 'Administrative Law', above n. 187; cf. *Ririnui v. Landcorp Farming Ltd* [2016] 1 NZLR 1056.

[207] See Section 2.2.2 above.

[208] See e.g. Peter Cane and Leighton McDonald, *Principles of Administrative Law* (Oxford University Press, 2008), ch. 5.

[209] *Ibid.*, 115. Only half of the applications for review of federal action are brought under the ADJR.

These grounds are, however, more synonymous with the tight categorical approach employed under the scope of review model. First, they do
not operate as monolithic and generalised grounds of review like Lord
Diplock's *CCSU* tripartite grounds. The ADJR effectively sought to take
a ('largely formulaic') snap-shot of the common law grounds available at
the time of codification (1977) – well before Lord Diplock's systemisation of judicial review in *CCSU*.[210] Codification is multifarious, compris-
ing seventeen different grounds.[211] The grounds therefore have a 'bottom
up' character, reflecting the categorical bases on which the then common
law enabled review – rather than purporting to introduce 'top down' general principles.[212] This is consistent with their application. They have not
been applied benevolently; the argumentation about them and their scope
has been described as 'arcane and technical'.[213] Secondly, the common law
grounds – again, which are multifarious and reflective of old-fashioned
English categories – are not monolithic and are ultimately subordinated to
the more dominant jurisdictional error doctrine and the legality–merits
dichotomy. For present purposes, therefore, the Australian methodology
has been discussed under the rubric of 'scope of review'; the language of
grounds of review is used differently to other Anglo-Commonwealth jurisdictions and the grounds themselves have different content and character.

Before leaving the Australian jurisdiction, it needs to be noted that there
may be some appetite for the articulation of a series of top-down principles which have similar content to the grounds of review. Kirby J was a
well-known and outspoken critic of the rigid approach and lack of more
generalised principles seen in other jurisdictions.[214] More recently, French
CJ referred to general principles of administrative justice, echoing the
generalised grounds of review seen elsewhere, although acknowledging
they do not have direct purchase in Australian administrative law. In *Li*,
he described the concept of administrative justice as requiring compliance

---

[210] Mark Aronson, 'Is the ADJR Act Hampering the Development of Australian Administrative
Law?' (2005) 15 PLR 202, 203 and *Kioa* v. *West* (1985) 159 CLR 550, 576.

[211] Aronson, 'ADJR Act', above n. 210, 203 (noting, though, that the number depends on how
one counts them) and Matthew Groves, 'Should We Follow the Gospel of the ADJR Act?'
(2010) 34 MULR 736, 756; Timothy H. Jones, 'Judicial Review and Codification' (2006) 20
LS 517, 525.

[212] Aronson, 'ADJR Act', above n. 210.

[213] Jones, 'Codification', above n. 211, 535. See also Groves, 'ADJR Act', above n. 211; de Smith
(7th edn), 234. Compare Cane and McDonald, above n. 208, 115.

[214] See e.g. *Re Minister for Immigration and Multicultural Affairs, ex parte S20/2002* (2003) 198
ALR 59, [150]–[170].

with the 'criteria of lawfulness, fairness and rationality'.[215] However, he also intimated that these principles are not directly expressed in Australia; instead their content is elaborated in 'provisions of the Act and the corresponding regulations and, subject to the Act and those regulations, the common law'.[216]

3.2.5 Canada: Partial and Overshadowed Grounds of Review for Abuse of Discretion

While Canadian jurisprudence is nowadays characterised by an explicit approach to intensity of review,[217] some general grounds of review were evident during the latter part of the twentieth century in relation to some parts of the supervisory jurisdiction. Prior to the landmark *Baker* decision in 1999, Canadian administrative law adopted a two-track approach to judicial review.[218] Issues of law were governed by what would come to be known as the 'pragmatic and functional framework', where different standards of review were deployed to give effect to the appropriate degree of discretion required in the circumstances (explained in more detail later).[219] This general framework has come to dominate Canadian jurisprudence over the last three decades (albeit subject to some modification) and continues today. However, for a period, a different approach was employed in relation to review of discretion. The exercise of discretion was then governed by a number of specific grounds, deployed under the general ground of abuse of discretion. The specific grounds included matters familiar elsewhere in the Anglo-Commonwealth, such as improper purpose, bad faith, abdication of discretion, and unreasonableness.[220] Indeed, Mullan suggests the restrained attitude mandated by these grounds had

---

[215] *Minister for Immigration and Citizenship* v. *Li* (2013) 297 ALR 225, [14].
[216] *Ibid.*
[217] See Section 4.2.2 and Section 5.2.3.
[218] Geneviève Cartier, 'Keeping a Check on Discretion' in Colleen Flood and Lorne Sossin (eds.), *Administrative Law in Context* (Emond Montgomery, 2008), 269, 275–82. Cartier notes *Roncarelli* v. *Dupllessis* [1959] SCR 121 is usually treated as the 'opening chapter' of review of discretion in Canada (275).
[219] See Section 4.2.2.
[220] See e.g. *Maple Lodge Farms Ltd* v. *Government of Canada* [1982] 2 SCR 2 and *Shell Canada Products Ltd* v. *Vancouver (City)* [1994] 1 SCR 231. See also P.W. Hogg, 'The Supreme Court of Canada and Administrative Law, 1949–1972' (1973) 11 Osgoode Hall LJ 187; D.P. Jones and A.S. de Villars, *Principles of Administrative Law* (5th edn, Carswell, 2009), 139. Unreasonableness as a ground was, however, 'rarely invoked': Cartier, above n. 218, 280.

its origins in the English common law.[221] However, objection to the always vigilant approach to questions of law meant the Supreme Court of Canada 'never considered seriously' adopting a simplified tripartite statement of grounds seen in England and New Zealand.[222]

The deployment of some grounds of review was founded on the law–discretion dichotomy. The grounds applicable to the exercise of discretion 'sought to preserve the freedom of the decision-makers to decide on substance and to limit judicial intervention to policing the legal limits within which such freedom was exercised'.[223] However, review of legal questions authorised 'intrusive judicial control on the substance' (although this was later moderated by the adoption of a more deferential attitude on such matters).[224] L'Heureux-Dubé J explained that the abuse of discretion grounds reflected two key ideas:[225]

> [D]iscretionary decisions, like all other administrative decisions, must be made within the bounds of the jurisdiction conferred by the statute, but that considerable deference will be given to decision-makers by courts in reviewing the exercise of that discretion and determining the scope of the decision-maker's jurisdiction.

In the late 1990s, however, the Supreme Court collapsed the distinction between law and discretion and folded review for abuse of discretion into the pragmatic and functional framework.[226] In *Baker*, a unified theory and approach was adopted for substantive review of all decisions.[227] L'Heureux-Dubé J said:[228]

> It is, however, inaccurate to speak of a rigid dichotomy of 'discretionary' or 'non-discretionary' decisions. Most administrative decisions involve the exercise of implicit discretion in relation to many aspects of decision making ... In addition, there is no easy distinction to be made between interpretation and the exercise of discretion; interpreting legal rules involves considerable discretion to clarify, fill in legislative gaps, and make choices among various options.

---

[221] David Mullan, 'Deference: Is it Useful Outside Canada?' (2006) AJ 42, 56.

[222] *Ibid.*

[223] Cartier, above n. 218, 280.

[224] *Ibid.*

[225] *Baker* v. *Canada (Minister of Citizenship and Immigration)* [1999] 2 SCR 817, [53].

[226] David Mullan, *Administrative Law* (Irwin Law, 2001), 108.

[227] *Baker*, above n. 225. See also *Dr Q* v. *College of Physicians and Surgeons of British Columbia* [2003] 1 SCR 226, [22], [25] ('nominate grounds, ... while still useful as familiar landmarks, no longer dictate the journey').

[228] *Baker*, above n. 225, [54].

Instead, review of discretion was to be subjected to the same three standards of review applicable to questions of law and interpretation: patent unreasonableness, reasonableness simpliciter, and correctness. This did not, though, signal reduction of the degree of deference to be afforded to such matters:[229]

> Incorporating judicial review of decisions that involve considerable discretion into the pragmatic and functional analysis for errors of law should not be seen as reducing the level of deference given to decisions of a highly discretionary nature.

Canada's deployment of grounds of review was therefore partial and temporary. It applied only to review of the exercise of discretion and was overshadowed by the pragmatic and functional framework that applied to review of issues of law. The grounds of review approach was eventually subsumed into the pragmatic and functional framework, with its prescribed standard of review.[230]

3.2.6   Conclusion

The essence of the grounds of review approach is lucidly captured by Fordham:[231]

> The grounds for judicial review are court-recognised rules of good administration: the judges' way of explaining when a public authority has overstepped the mark and when judicial intervention is warranted. They reflect a careful balance between appropriate vigilance and appropriate restraint.

Their expression of standards form a 'framework' for judicial analysis but also permit 'flexibility of response'.[232] This framework has reigned in English and New Zealand law since it was heralded by Lord Diplock in *CCSU*. This type of framework has not infiltrated Australia and Canada, with a more formalistic method being favoured by the former and a more openly circumstantial approach being favoured by the latter.

3.3   Conceptual Underpinnings

The grounds of review schema is treated by many scholars as the current orthodoxy and their scholarship is implicitly predicated on its continuing

---

[229] *Ibid.*, [56].
[230] David Mullan, 'Unresolved Issues on Standard of Review' (2013) 42 AQ 1, 42.
[231] Fordham, 'Grounds', above n. 31, 199.
[232] *Ibid.*, 199.

operation. That is, categorical solutions to questions about the nature and shape of judicial review are presented, typically through the invention or redefinition of different grounds of review (witness the debate about the adoption of the proportionality ground). Craig and Taggart are two scholars with a general commitment to doctrinal grounds of review, framed in a general but evolutionary fashion. Both exhibit support for a role for proportionality as a new ground of review, albeit with differing ambits. Hickman also expresses some support for the categorical method seen in the grounds of review schema. His discussion of the maintenance of a number of discrete 'standards of legality', as he describes them, is discussed in this section.[233] He also strays into contextual review, as he promotes a model of non-doctrinal deference in human rights adjudication, and his contribution on this point is addressed later.[234]

A striking feature of this group of scholars is their commitment to the common law school on the question of judicial review's conceptual underpinnings. Although convergence of the schools makes the distinction a little clouded, Craig, Taggart and Hickman all embrace the power of the courts to fashion (and re-fashion) the principles of judicial review – and their scholarship is designed to tap into that evolutionary character as they promote new and modified grounds of review. And this endeavour is not hindered by the need to link these developments back to a legislative source, indication or hint; the independent values of the common law dominate. That said, they also acknowledge the ultimate trump that the legislature retains even under the common law theory (a position contested by a number of scholars supporting contextual review).[235]

There are some caveats to note in the discussion in this section, due to a reasonable degree of potential overlap at the margins in these scholarly accounts. First, some scholars propose – explicitly or implicitly – a mixture of categorical grounds of review and explicit modulation of intensity. Others propose variable intensity in some areas or in relation to some grounds. A judgement has been made about where they best fit for analytical purposes, based on whether greater or lesser emphasis is placed on indirect categorical grounds or explicit modulation of intensity. For example, Craig promotes a general ground of proportionality, which he acknowledges would have a degree of flexibility to modulate the depth of intensity in order to take account of differing contexts.

---

[233] See Section 3.3.
[234] See Section 5.3.3.
[235] See Section 5.3.

However, first-and-foremost, Craig's vision of judicial review is built on various grounds of review and explicit variability is secondary – hence his discussion in this section. Secondly, I treat those scholars, such as Taggart, promoting a bifurcated vision of judicial review – with different principles and methodologies as between traditional judicial review and human rights adjudication – as also falling within this camp (where they have addressed both).[236] Bifurcation is based on a categorical distinction: in other words, different ground(s) or methodologies of review apply in different classes. While the methodology usually proposed for human rights adjudication – proportionality – is often treated as being flexible in nature, the entry point for the methodology is a ground of review of circumscribed, not general, application. Finally, I acknowledge that some scholars I have addressed under scope of review also seem supportive of the grounds of review schema. Again, as mentioned earlier, any distinction between scope of review and grounds of review tends to be a fine one due to common reliance on doctrinal categorisation; I generally treat the conservatism versus generosity distinction when applying the categories as a stronger ingredient for the purposes of this taxonomy.

3.3.1   Paul Craig: Generalised but Conceptually Precise Categorical Grounds

Craig is one of the most vocal champions of the common law theory, arguing that the courts should be properly understood to be applying substantive values – distilled independently – when fashioning the principles of judicial review. These common law values translate into categorical grounds of review, although Craig's vision for these grounds is generalised, nuanced, and (to the furthest extent possible) faithful to the grounds' underlying conceptual basis.

First, Craig's account of judicial review is grounded in the common law. Judicial review is 'a creation of the common law' and the principles that shape it represent the controls which the courts believe are 'normatively

---

[236] Scholars only advocating explicit and variable deference in relation to proportionality in human rights adjudication are dealt with under variable intensity of review; see Section 4.3. I assume (but cannot be sure) that they are content for the categorical methodologies of traditional judicial review to continue to apply in cases where human rights are not implicated. The mixture of methodologies means they could be addressed in multiple places; however, since their explicit discussion is confined to a naked form of deference in human rights adjudication, I address them under the variable intensity schema.

justified on the grounds of justice and the rule of law'.[237] He is a vocal opponent of the ultra vires or legislative intent theory of judicial review.[238] It is, he says, 'indeterminate, unrealistic, beset by internal tensions, and unable to explain the application of public law principles to those bodies which did not derive their power from statute'.[239] Craig says there is not 'a single doctrinal rule in over four hundred years of judicial review that owes its origin to the existence of the assumed general legislative intent'.[240]

Craig's common law approach is anchored in a judicial assessment of the conceptions of justice or rule of law. It is this, he says, that frames the principles of judicial review and on what the legitimacy of judicial intervention hinges:[241]

> The reality is that the legitimacy of the principles of judicial review at any point in time can only be determined by argument as to whether the conception of justice/rule of law being applied by the courts is warranted in normative terms.

He goes on to say:[242]

> The common law model is not based solely on the proposition that the courts have developed the general heads of review. It is premised on the assumption that the more detailed principles within the heads of review have most commonly been developed by the courts from the rule of law, justice and the like, while accepting also that Parliament can and has made contribution to these principles.

Accordingly, Craig aligns himself with the Dworkinian interpretivist camp.[243] That is, as he explains it, 'propositions of law are true if, subject to questions of fit, they follow from the principles of justice, fairness, and procedural due process that provide the best constructive interpretation of the community's legal practice'.[244]

While grounded in the common law model, Craig accepts that the legislature retains the authority to trump the common law. Although the courts

---

[237] P.P. Craig, 'Fundamental Principles of Administrative Law' in David Feldman (ed.), *English Public Law* (Oxford University Press, 2009), [13.16]. See also Paul Craig, 'Public Law, Political Theory and Legal Theory' [2000] PL 211, 235 and *UK, EU and Global Administrative Law* (Cambridge University Press, 2015), 22–3 and 125–53.

[238] Craig, 'Political Theory', above n. 237, 231.

[239] Craig, 'Fundamental Principles', above n. 237, [13.16].

[240] P.P. Craig, 'The Nature of Reasonableness Review' (2013) 66 CLP 131, 160.

[241] P.P. Craig, 'The Common Law, Shared Power and Judicial Review' (2004) 24 OJLS 237, 244.

[242] *Ibid.*, 245.

[243] P.P. Craig, 'Theory, "Pure Theory" and Values in Public Law' (2005) PL 440, 440.

[244] *Ibid.*, 440.

are the 'creative "drivers" of the legal norms' in judicial review, this does not mean that the courts ignore legislative will when fashioning them.[245] Craig explains that where legislature has manifested a 'specific intent' as to the grounds of review, the courts ought to respect and apply this, just as the courts do in other common law domains where the legislature speaks specifically.[246] The common law model is therefore based, he says, on 'shared power' and does not represent a strong challenge to sovereignty.[247] He argues:[248]

> The fact that Parliament might enact an unequivocal provision that runs counter to pre-existing judicial doctrine concerning the intensity of review, or the consequences of invalidity in a particular area, might simply reflect legitimate disagreement as to what the rule of law requires, not some 'crude' triumph of sovereignty over judicial principle.

Craig explains the basis of limits of judicial intervention in the context of the review of discretion. The principle that the courts should not substitute their view about how a discretion should be exercised for that of the primary decisions is informed by 'basic conceptions of political theory and the allocation of governmental functions'; in other words, doing so would undermine the principle that political and social choices are for the legislature or its delegate, and substitution would amount to a reallocation of power from the legislature and administration to the courts.[249] However, on the other hand, he records that there is also recognition of the fact that administrative discretion should not be uncontrolled. This leads to 'the desire to fashion a criterion that will allow judicial control, without thereby leading to the substitution of judgement or too great an intrusion on the merits'.[250]

Secondly, Craig's scholarship is generally predicated on the existence of doctrinal grounds of review, expressed in their modern, systematised fashion. For example, he is renowned for his promotion of proportionality as a ground of review;[251] similarly, he presents legitimate expectation as a separate and free-standing ground of review.[252] Craig is not, however,

---

[245] Craig, 'Shared Power', above n. 241, 241.
[246] *Ibid.*, 238.
[247] *Ibid.*, 253.
[248] *Ibid.*, 254.
[249] Craig, *Administrative Law*, above n. 43, [21-002].
[250] *Ibid.*, [21-003].
[251] See generally *ibid.*, ch. 21; Craig, 'Rationality', above n. 120; 'Reasonableness', above n. 240; *UK, EU and Global Administrative Law*, above n. 237, 256–60.
[252] Craig, *Administrative Law*, ch. 22; Craig, 'Rationality', above n. 120, 271.

sanguine about variable intensity. He recognises the role that variable intensity plays within a doctrinal schema; in his account, it operates as a gloss or modifier on particular grounds of review. For example, his argument in favour of proportionality acknowledges that the ground of review operates with different intensities of review in different contexts.[253] While he acknowledges the influence of the modulation of the intensity of review, it does not feature directly in the doctrinal schema on which his scholarship is predicated. That continues to be grounded in a series of grounds of review – or categories where judicial intervention is justified.[254] Indeed, in his recent Hamlyn lectures, he briefly addressed the debates about deference and argued that it 'must be located within the standard fabric of judicial review' and 'is not and cannot be a free-standing concept in its own right'.[255] He argues they are not 'tests for reviews', although they may inform and influence the application of other tests for review.[256] Craig's preference for working within generalised categorical grounds of review remains, although he does admit some subsidiary role for modulation of intensity *within* some grounds.

Thus, Craig is content for judicial review and the circumstances of judicial intervention to depend on categories and distinctions, and resists claims that this is unduly formalistic.[257] Boundaries and question-marks about categorisation are, he says, inherent in such an approach. However, he argues, this does not make the methodology or the existence of categories formalistic:[258]

> We use categories and distinctions within the entire body of law, both public and private. It is inherent in the deployment of such categories or distinctions that there will be boundaries, and question marks as to whether a particular case should fall within the relevant category. That does not render the existence of the categories formalistic.

But, as noted before, categorical methodology is necessarily attentive to form and it is difficult for Craig to escape such characterisation. His better

---

[253] See e.g. Craig, 'Rationality', above n. 120, 268.

[254] Note, however, his observation that the earlier, historical development of judicial review was 'inextricably bound up with the development of remedies as opposed to the creation of heads of review': P.P. Craig, 'Administrative Law in the Anglo-American Tradition' in B. Guy Peters and Jon Pierre (eds.), *Handbook of Public Administration* (Sage, 2003), 269, 269.

[255] Craig, *UK, EU and Global Administrative Law*, above n. 237, 245.

[256] *Ibid.*

[257] Craig, 'Shared Power', above n. 241, 252.

[258] *Ibid.* See also P.P. Craig, 'Constitutional Foundations, the Rule of Law and Supremacy' (2003) PL 92, 105.

defence is that his vision of the categorical methodology is not abstract, the categories are generally faithful to their conceptual underpinnings, and the system is alert to, and seeks to resolve, dissonance between the conceptual and doctrinal.[259] In order to avoid denunciation as formalistic, Craig actively works to expose instances of lack of alignment. For example, he recently dissects the nature of reasonableness review.[260] Not content with the mantra that suggests that the assessment of weight and balance has no place in reasonableness review, Craig demonstrates compellingly that the judicial assessment of weight and balance are, in fact, an essential aspect of reasonableness review. Reasonableness review is inescapably tied to the review of relevancy and purpose; 'reasonableness review entails', he says, 'a judicial decision as to whether the weight and balance ascribed by the primary decision-maker to consideration that have been or can be deemed relevant was reasonable'.[261] A good illustration for his desire to expose any conceptual–doctrinal dissonance.

Finally, Craig's commitment to a grounds methodology sees him rebuff criticisms from those who favour non-doctrinal, fully contextual approaches to substantive review. In particular he does not accept Allan's claim that the grounds of review are 'empty vessels' which only assume any meaning when applied in a particular context.[262] Craig says the grounds of review are effectively representative of more detailed principles of review and '[t]hese more detailed principles ... then frame the way in which judicial decisions are made in a particular context'.[263] The fact that the applicable statutory matrix may form a part of the particular context is not a concession to the legislative intent theory. Nor does the fact that the detailed principles may counsel different treatment because of the context mean the grounds themselves lack independent normative force.

In summary, Craig is emblematic of the common law school, committed to the judicial expression (and active re-expression) of the basis for judicial intervention in terms of grounds of review; a task which, for him, channels common law values and morality, while not being ignorant of the statutory setting.

---

[259] Craig, 'Shared Power', above n. 241, 252 (the endeavour to align the conceptual and doctrinal categories is 'the standard fare of academic analysis').

[260] Craig, 'Reasonableness', above n. 240.

[261] *Ibid.*, 166.

[262] Craig, 'Shared Power', above n. 241, 244, responding to T.R.S. Allan, 'The Constitutional Foundations of Judicial Review' (2002) 61 CLJ 87.

[263] Craig, 'Shared Power', above n. 241, 247.

3.3.2   Michael Taggart: (Grudgingly Bifurcated) Suite of Common Law Grounds

Taggart appeared ambivalent towards the debate about the constitutional foundations of judicial review and generally sought to resist philosophical categorisation.[264] However, his work hinted most strongly at the common law model. As a traditional common lawyer,[265] he was also in his element working within a grounds of review schema. While alert to the variable methodologies driven from the human rights domain, he was worried about their effect on traditional administrative law methodology and eventually conceded that each should be compartmentalised.

First, as mentioned, Taggart was not drawn to debate the conceptual underpinnings of judicial review. His early work on theories of invalidity (published before the ultra vires debate took off) skirted around the issue. On the one hand, he described ultra vires as, up to then, operating as the 'organizing principle' in Anglo-Australian administrative law; on the other hand, he noted in a footnote at that time that it was 'challenged by the "error of law" standard'.[266] In his only short piece directly addressing the debate, written for the seminal symposium on the issue, he described it as a 'distraction'.[267] He doubted there was much difference between each side of the debate, especially in practical terms. However, he recognised the significance of a judicially elaborated rule of law – 'a coat of many colours ... contain[ing] many principles, ideas, values, and conventions'.[268] At the same time, he saw that the rule of law 'envelopes and subsumes' the ultra vires doctrine; that is, ultra vires represents the 'rule of law, not men' strand of the rule of law.[269] The invocation of intent of Parliament, while an artificial fig-leaf, added some democratic pedigree to judicial intervention and dodged criticism about judicial overreach. But he seemed content to leave unresolved this tension between the rule of law and democracy; the rights-revolution, internationalisation and privatisation were more pressing. While personally coy about

---

[264] Taggart, 'Proportionality', above n. 105, 425.

[265] See generally Dyzenhaus, Hunt and Huscroft (eds.), *A Simple Common Lawyer*, above n. 123.

[266] Michael Taggart, 'Rival Theories of Invalidity in Administrative Law' in Taggart, above n. 151, 94.

[267] Michael Taggart, 'Ultra Vires as a Distraction' in Christopher Forsyth (ed.), *Judicial Review and the Constitution* (Hart Publishing, 2000), 427.

[268] *Ibid.*

[269] *Ibid.*

which school he subscribed to and the merits of each, his scholarship had a distinctly common law flavour.[270]

Secondly, in terms of the role of deference within the administrative law schema, Taggart argued deference was an essential feature of administrative law, but accepted that it manifest itself in different ways. Indeed, he noted that, until recently, the doctrine of deference had little or no formal recognition in Anglo-Australasian systems – even though 'if you look at what judges did, as well as at what they said they were doing, there was a good deal of deference'.[271] He saw this as a product of contextualism: '[I]n judicial review contextualism and deference mean much the same thing. You really cannot have one without the other'.[272]

Fuelled by a desire for transparency, predictability and a culture of justification, Taggart argued that, if a deference-device was adopted, it was incumbent on judges to articulate and explicitly weigh up relevant deference factors in the particular context of the case.[273] Taggart was very sceptical about abandoning efforts to articulate these principles in doctrinal form. For example, he described Allan's non-doctrinal approach as 'utterly implausible, to say nothing of undesirable'.[274] He regarded it as mandating the courts as 'independent scrutineer[s]' and imposing correctness review across the board.[275]

But Taggart was also reluctant to abandon the traditional common law framework in favour of deploying a grand schema of deference. He saw the expression of deference more as the incremental development of common law principles:[276]

> It is impossible to articulate a clear set of rules in relation to deference. All attempts degenerate into lists of factors, with contestable weights ... [A]ll factorial tests are ultimately indeterminate, because the result is not determined necessarily by a majority of factors pointing one way. Some factors in some circumstances count for more in the balancing. There are no rules, and sometimes precious little guidance or certainty.

---

[270] His focus was often on the judicial supplementation of the statutory scheme and development of principles governing non-traditional public decision-making without any direct statutory mandate. For various accounts of his work, see Dyzenhaus, Hunt and Huscroft, above n. 123.

[271] Taggart, 'Proportionality', above n. 105, 454.

[272] *Ibid.*, 450.

[273] *Ibid.*, 460.

[274] *Ibid.*, 456.

[275] *Ibid.*

[276] *Ibid.*, 458.

This preference for traditional methodologies ultimately led to Taggart conceding to the bifurcation of judicial review – consistent with his commitment to a refined categorical approach. For many years Taggart promoted a unified vision of administrative law and judicial review, along with an openness to variable and flexible notions of deference.[277] But, in his last article on the subject, he argued different approaches to review should be adopted in relation to 'human rights' and 'public wrongs'.[278] In relation to human rights (whether under enumerated bills of rights or common law situations where rights are engaged), he suggested proportionality be adopted as the principal methodology; but while proportionality should operate as a single unitary standard of review, proportionality and deference are necessarily interwoven such that a sliding scale of review operates. On the other hand, in relation to public wrongs (where the question is about public bodies acting illegally or ultra vires, absent any direct issue of human rights), he argued in favour of *Wednesbury* unreasonableness operating as the sole ground of review for abuse of discretion. In particular, he suggested variegated forms of unreasonableness became redundant because variegation was only justified where human rights were engaged; while variegation of unreasonableness was not necessary, he continued to acknowledge a role for (absolute) non-justiciability.

The dividing line he promoted lay between 'human rights' and 'public wrongs', with the human rights side including both cases in which human rights instruments are directly applied and those common law cases where human rights issues arise collaterally. He argued proportionality and deference should apply to the human rights domain, but that the side of public wrongs be governed by the traditional conception of *Wednesbury* unreasonableness, shorn of its intensive iterations.[279] The effect of this book would be to impose a categorical distinction through the centre of the system of judicial review. Variable intensity in its explicit form would

---

[277] See e.g. Michael Taggart, 'Reinventing Administrative Law' in Nicholas Bamforth and Peter Leyland (eds.), *Public Law in a Multi-Layered Constitution* (Hart Publishing, 2003), 311, 334 fn. 144; 'The Tub of Public Law' in David Dyzenhaus (ed.), *The Unity of Public Law* (Hart Publishing, 2004), 455, 466.

[278] Taggart, 'Proportionality', above n. 105.

[279] *Ibid.*, 477. For similar approach, see Jeff King, 'Proportionality' (2010) NZ Law Rev 327, 259. King recently advocated the partial deployment of proportionality, as a sometimes alternative to *Wednesbury* unreasonableness and its high threshold. He bases his 'halfway house' solution on the premise that proportionality generally involves more searching judicial scrutiny. King has also advocated the development of doctrinal principles of deference: see Section 4.3.

be banished from the domain of public wrongs, but would be at the forefront of judicial methodology in the domain of human rights. In the end,
the categorical methodology of traditional administrative law would prevail in most of its traditional domain.

Taggart's common law orientation, combined with his continuing preference for the categorical, means he can be described, using King's label,
as a 'restrictive institutionalist'.[280] Institutionalists are concerned with the
relative competence of the courts to adjudicate; restrictive institutionalists, while rejecting abstract formalism, prefer the retention of some categorical distinctions to take account of judicial competence: 'The net social
consequences of employing bright-line rules (even if occasionally arbitrary) may be superior to allowing multi-factoral judicial weighing to take
place on a case-by-case basis.'[281] Taggart's concession to bifurcate judicial
review and to deploy *Wednesbury* unreasonableness and proportionality
in clearly demarcated domains is particularly illustrative.

3.3.3   Tom Hickman (I): Evolving but
Discrete Standards of Legality

Hickman's approach to the variation of intensity of review is twofold and
does not fall neatly into the different schemata. First, he makes a case
for continuing a categorical approach, where grounds of review supply
the general framework for judicial review and influence the intensity of
review indirectly; to this extent, he exhibits some support for the grounds
of review schema. Secondly, within a doctrinal schema, he promotes the
notion of deference in non-doctrinal form, where factors suggestive of
restraint are taken into account merely as a function of weight in adjudication (this is explained below, under the rubric of contextual review).[282]

In the context of the doctrinal debate about whether proportionality ought to be adopted as a general ground of review (which he rejects),
Hickman shows a continuing commitment to categorical grounds of
review and is dismissive of flexible doctrines which modulate the intensity of review explicitly.[283] His position here is influenced by the distinction he draws between standards of legality and standards of review.[284]

---

[280]   Jeff A. King, 'Institutional Approaches to Judicial Restraint' (2008) 28 OJLS 409, 430.
[281]   *Ibid.*, 431.
[282]   See Section 5.3.3.
[283]   Tom Hickman, 'Problems for Proportionality' (2010) NZ Law Rev 303.
[284]   Hickman, *Public Law*, above n. 66, 99. See text to nn. 319 and 325.

For analytical but not normative purposes, Hickman draws a distinction between rules or principles directed at the administration that must be complied with, over and above the express terms of the statute, on the one hand, and requirements directed at the court about how they review compliance with those rules and principles, on the other. He prefers a focus on the former rather than the latter, which approximates more the grounds of review schema.

In particular, he is sceptical about attempts to fashion monolithic 'flexible meta-principle[s] of substantive review'.[285] Variability should operate not in terms of the depth of judicial scrutiny but in terms of standards of legality (viz. limits on power) that must be adhered to in different circumstances: bad faith, reasonableness, proportionality, strict necessity, or absolute prohibitions. According to Hickman, the identification of the applicable standard should take categorical form, based on the particular context.[286] That is, he rejects – for reasons of legal certainty, legitimacy, and transparency – the notion of sliding scales (whether standards of legality or review).[287] Generalised standards or grounds, where the intensity is manipulable on a case-by-case basis, operate as undesirably as 'opportunities for unstructured judicial discretion'.[288] For example, Hickman is critical of Craig's notion of variable intensity formulations of proportionality. This effectively makes proportionality 'an empty vessel', he argues, allowing the courts to 'simply decide whether in the particular context the merits of one side "press harder" than those on the other'.[289] Hickman's objections here are somewhat overstated though. In particular, he concedes that, even with a focus on categorical standards of legality, the burden of justification that must be met by the administration under each of the standards varies.[290] Although cast in terms of differing norms, variation to the burden that must be met implicitly affects the intrusiveness of the judicial supervision. His concerns about the variable nature of the review process and judicial discretion is equally applicable to his preferred categorical approach for standards of legality as it is to a variable approach for standards of review.

---

[285] Hickman, 'Proportionality', above n. 283, 312.
[286] *Ibid.*, 326.
[287] *Ibid.*, 316.
[288] *Ibid.*, 318.
[289] *Ibid.*
[290] See, for example, his discussion of how the modulation of intensity would differ under irrationality review and strict necessity review: *ibid.*, 316.

Much of Hickman's scholarship focused on the Human Rights Act and the manner in which it, he argues, has transformed public law.[291] His focus on human rights adjudication means his discussion of the legitimacy of judicial review is restricted to legitimacy in the context of protection of human rights norms under statutory bills of rights. He does not directly engage in the ultra vires debate, absent the rights paradigm. However, Hickman comes from a position consistent with the common law school (though he observes the language of ultra vires still remains prevalent amongst the judiciary).[292] He characterises judicial review as an independently created bulwark against government misuse of power:[293]

> Administrative law itself – its existence, its ambit and its doctrines – is a judicial creation which has been forged by creative lawyers and judges in order to provide an effective remedy for government error and unfairness ... [P]ublic law belongs to the judge in a way that private law does not: public law is in its very essence an assertion of judicial independence as a check on government.

His theoretical orientation therefore demonstrates sympathy for the common law theory of judicial review.

Hickman, however, subscribes to a collaborative model of judicial adjudication – what he calls 'a dialogical fertile middle ground'.[294] He rejects the notion of formal legality or pure legal formalism, which limits the courts' role to enforcing the text and intentions of the legislature.[295] He also distances himself from theories of substantive legality, which characterise rights as higher law to be protected by the courts as fundamentals.[296] A supporter of dialogical models founded on interaction between the judges and legislature, he favours a strong form of dialogue. He characterises dialogical theories as enabling the courts to 'propose arguments of principle to other branches' in relation to rights violations and associated issues of balance.[297] However, he argues against weak forms of dialogue which seek to limit the courts' role in proposing arguments on a provisional basis and rely on acceptance or rejection by other branches. His strong dialogical approach extends the courts role beyond mere principle proposing and mandates judicial resolution of these matters (but acknowledges that the

---

[291] Hickman, *Public Law*, above n. 66.
[292] *Ibid.*, 202.
[293] Hickman, 'Proportionality', above n. 283, 303.
[294] Hickman, *Public Law*, above n. 66, 97.
[295] *Ibid.*
[296] Compare Allan's position: see Section 5.3.1.
[297] Hickman, *Public Law*, above n. 66, 69.

line between when this is permissible and when it is not is 'impossible to draw'):[298]

> It is the courts' function to determine questions of principle, but the various branches of the state do not merely counteract protectively but they also interact productively, such as when the courts recognise a degree of latitude for the political branches to make decisions that interfere with protected rights or where they avoid purporting to determine questions of principles and allow matters to remain within the realm of politics.

Hickman aligns himself with the 'liberal legalist' school or close variants.[299] Drawing from Partington, Hickman appreciates 'the desirability and need for the exercise of public power', rejects the idea that 'public law should be seen exclusively in terms of control of such power', and acknowledges a dual role for political and legal accountability (with a bias towards legal accountability due to the perceived inadequacy of political control).[300] Hickman highlights the commitment of liberal legalists to the separation of powers: 'Parliament establishes general rules of executive governance that are interpreted and applied by the courts [and] only by ... dividing the political and the legal ... can liberty effectively be protected.'[301] However, he argues that the responsibilities of the different branches overlap and governance is ultimately a 'joint project';[302] he images notions of give-and-take, collaboration and respect. Hickman goes on to endorse the metaphor of dialogue as representing this collaborative endeavour: 'it ... reflect[s] the idea that the legal constitution can supplement rather than supplant politics.'[303]

Ultimately, though, Hickman is reluctant to endorse any particular moral theory as providing the lodestar for the judiciary when participating in this collaborative enterprise. Law's 'bluntness' means the normative perspectives are numerous, ambiguous and overlap: '[L]aw reflects points of moral consensus and leaves plenty of room for the courts to adapt their moral intuition in future cases, without needing to accept any single moral theory.'[304]

---

[298] *Ibid.*, 97.
[299] Tom R. Hickman, 'In Defence of the Legal Constitution' (2005) 55 UTLJ 981.
[300] *Ibid.*, 987, citing Martin Partington, 'The Reform of Public Law in Britain' in Patrick McAuslan and John F. McEldowney (eds.), *Law, Legitimacy and the Constitution* (Sweet & Maxwell, 1985), 191, 193.
[301] Hickman, 'Legal Constitution', above n. 299, 1004.
[302] *Ibid.*, 1020.
[303] *Ibid.*
[304] *Ibid.*, 1022.

3.3.4   *Conclusion*

The grounds of review approach presents a more flexible and generous model of judicial review than its scope of review sibling. Those scholars commending this approach value its simplified, yet principled, character, along with its aversion to technocratic and conservative common law method. Greater emphasis is placed on the judicial crafting of grounds, based on substantive values, and less weight is placed on linkages with the legislature. While the legislature retains its trumping power, common law judicial authority and developments need not be sourced back to the legislature in order to obtain their legitimacy. Judicial intervention obtains its legitimacy independently and internally.

But the methodology favoured still retains a categorical focus. The grounds of review, with their different and implicit depths of scrutiny, construct a role for the judiciary based on an abstract blueprint. While less limited and more nuanced than the role presented by a scope of review schema, it still has a formalistic character (despite Craig's protests) in that it is based on pre-established categories of intervention and obviates the need for a normative justification to be articulated. Legitimacy is assumed, based on a pre-existing model of the state and law. Here, the scholars manifest slightly different visions of how those allocations ought to be drawn. Taggart tends to favour greater administrative autonomy and generally draws a more deferential schema, underscored by a strong separation of powers sentiment. In contrast, Craig tends to emphasise the judicial role in enforcing the rule of law and promotes a schema of grounds which is more interventionist.

The key point here, and the commonality between these scholars, is a belief that the supervisory jurisdiction can, and should, be doctrinally structured on a pre-emptive basis. The depth of scrutiny and supporting normative arguments are capable of being expressed in an 'off-the-shelf' manner through the proxy of enumerated grounds of review. Line-drawing and categorisation then becomes the workaday method of the judiciary, not normative argumentation.

3.4   Normative Assessment

When assessed against Fuller's principles of efficacy, a grounds of review approach has considerable virtue. The expression of grounds in simplified and generalised form provides rule-structure, clarity, stability and guidance. But the approach also aims to openly acknowledge aspects of the judicial discretion involved, particularly in relation to evolution within the system. The indirect way in which the depth of scrutiny is settled means, however, some judicial judgements are not transparent, thus predictions about the extent of vigilance or restraint are difficult to make. Otherwise, the framework provides good guidance for judges and administrators, and is applied with a reasonable degree of fidelity.

Generality

The grounds of review schema – like its other categorical sibling, scope of review – is based in a regime of rules. The difference between the two lies in the abstractness or specificity of those rules. A grounds of review approach favours a few generalised triggers for judicial intervention over a myriad of specific rules.

In their most basic and practical sense, grounds of review are the bases on which administrative action can be ruled unlawful in judicial review.[305] In other words, as Fordham explains them, a ground represents 'the "flaw" which justifies the Court's interference'.[306] Lord Phillips, in one of the few judicial definitions, characterised the threefold set of grounds as a 'received checklist of justiciable errors'.[307] The definition of grounds of review as the flaw or error justifying judicial intervention is consistent with their common expression in negative terms, as was the case with Lord Diplock's formulation. Thus, the grounds meet Fuller's expectation of generality in the articulation of rules.

When expressed in their positive form, though, grounds represent the principles or norms that regulate administrative decision-making. The inverse of grounds of review may be characterised as 'principles of good administration' (Galligan), 'norms of good public decision-making' (Cane) or 'standards of legality' (Hickman).[308] Nothing particularly hangs on their negative or positive form, at least as the grounds are presently conceived. The failure to comply with a principle of good administration is treated as enabling the courts to intervene by way of judicial review (although, normatively, this need not be so).

---

[305] Peter Cane, *Administrative Law* (4th edn, Oxford University Press, 2004), 131.

[306] *Judicial Review Handbook*, above n. 35, [45.4]. Fordham also describes them as 'a list of recognised "public law wrongs"': Fordham, 'Grounds', above n. 31, 186.

[307] *R (Q) v. Secretary of State for the Home Department* [2004] QB 36, [112] (joint judgment, with Clarke and Sedley LJJ).

[308] D.J. Galligan, 'Judicial Review and the Textbook Writers' (1982) 2 OJLS 257, 261; Cane, *Administrative Law*, above n. 305, 131; Hickman, *Public Law*, above n. 66, 99. See also Fordham, 'Grounds', above n. 31, 199 ('court-recognised rules of good administration').

In terms of the mediation of the balance between vigilance and restraint, each of the tripartite grounds of illegality, procedural impropriety and irrationality presents a fixed, but implicit, depth of scrutiny. In general terms, illegality and procedural impropriety enable correctness review, while irrationality poses a deferential standard. The classes of flaws brought together under each ground share a similar depth of scrutiny. The applicable depth of scrutiny is dependent on the characterisation of the impugned norm; in other words, which ground of review is relied on. Hence, the descriptor of (categorical or doctrinal) grounds of review.[309] As with the scope of review model, classification is still the central judicial function that dictates the depth of review.[310]

The traditional tripartite grounds continue, in many respects, to reflect the hallmarks of the 'classic model' of judicial review.[311] While Lord Diplock's seminal speech in *CCSU* is heralded as significant in the systemisation of judicial review doctrines, the extent of change should not be overstated. As Harlow and Rawlings observe, 'Lord Diplock's three principles still conform largely to the classical grounds as they had evolved over the centuries'.[312] Formal distinctions still dominate, although there is less emphasis on 'rigid legal categories'.[313] The difference lies in Lord Diplock's attempts at developing generalised organisational principles from the doctrinal morass that existed previously.

The doctrinal shape of the grounds of review is more general than seen under the scope of review approach. Each may be divided into various different and more particular sub-principles. For example, illegality may be treated as capturing doctrines addressing matters such as error of law, improper purpose, relevancy, fettering of discretion and so forth. In this respect, the grounds have an aggregating function. This dimension was picked up by Lord Irvine in *Boddington* when he commended the way in which the tripartite grounds 'compendiously grouped' the various types

---

[309] Taggart 'Proportionality', above n. 105, 481 ('doctrinal' grounds); Antony Lester and Jeffrey Jowell, 'Beyond *Wednesbury*' (1988) PL 365, 369 ('categories of review').

[310] Taggart, 'Administrative Law', above n. 47, 82.

[311] Carol Harlow, 'A Special Relationship?' in Ian Loveland (ed.), *A Special Relationship?* (Clarendon, 1995), 79, 83; adopted by Taggart, 'Reinventing', above n. 277, 312. More recently, Rawlings brands this the ('determinedly dull') 'drainpipe model': Rawlings, above n. 85, 98. See ch. 2 above.

[312] Harlow and Rawlings, above n. 9, 107.

[313] D.G.T. Williams, 'Justiciability and the Control of Discretionary Power' in Taggart, above n. 151, 107. See also Fordham, 'Grounds', above n. 31, 195 ('[b]right line distinctions between different functional types' replaced with 'a spectrum of different shades').

of challenges that could be mounted.[314] Others have also emphasised the nature of the grounds as categories of more specific doctrines.[315] Allan goes even further and asks rhetorically whether the grounds of review are anything more than 'labels [that] announce the *conclusions* of legal analysis'?[316] Consistent with his preference for individualised judicial judgement over the application of general doctrine, he says pejoratively that 'the settled grounds of review are really only conclusionary labels for judgments made on the facts of each case – judgments invoking controversial moral and political values'.[317] The conclusionary potential of the grounds echo, to some extent, the indirect and rhetorical style seen under the scope of review method.

The final point about the nature of the doctrinal rules is the question of their intended audience.[318] As noted earlier, the grounds of review have been articulated and applied as if they express public law norms and bases of judicial intervention simultaneously. In other words, these concepts are intertwined and conflated as a single (or series) of grounds of review. As Hickman notes, though, it may be helpful to distinguish between the two different functions of these public law principles, even though the different functions have 'not been clearly distinguished, or even explicitly addressed, in the case law'.[319] Hickman amplifies this distinction when he adopts the language of 'standards of legality' and 'standards of review' for analytical purposes. He explains the terminology in this way. Standards of legality are the rules or principles that are principally directed at the administration; that is, those standards to be satisfied over-and-above the condition expressed in the empowering instrument. In contrast, standards of review speak to the courts, not the administration, expressing how the courts determine whether standards of legality are breached. Thus, in relation to the illegality ground of review, for example, the standard of legality represents the conditions set by the empowering statute.[320] The corresponding

---

[314] *Boddington*, above n. 29, 152.

[315] Allan, 'Foundations', above n. 262, 100 ('open-ended categories') and *Guinness*, above n. 131, 160 (Lord Donaldson) ('currently accepted categorisations').

[316] Allan, 'Foundations', above n. 262, 100.

[317] *Ibid.*, 109. He goes on to argue that then 'the much-celebrated development of our sophisticated administrative law would seem, after all, largely chimerical'.

[318] See further discussion of the hortatory role (text to n. 355).

[319] Hickman, *Public Law*, above n. 66, 101.

[320] This example is borrowed from Hickman, where he only mentioned legislative conditions and not implied common law principles. However, in principle, the analysis holds for implied common law conditions under the guise of illegality.

standard of review imposed by the court in assessing compliance is correctness. 'The question of whether the conditions of the statute had been fulfilled [is] a matter for the courts', Hickman says – in contrast to interfering only if the administration's 'understanding of the statutory requirements was unreasonable'.[321] So, too, with procedural impropriety: the common law principle of natural justice operates as a standard of legality, while a correctness standard of review is adopted when assessing compliance.

Irrationality review is more complicated. Hickman describes *Wednesbury* unreasonableness as (principally) a standard of review. For Hickman, Lord Greene's statement that the courts can quash decisions that are 'so unreasonable that no reasonable authority could ever have come to it' describes 'how the courts should exercise their supervisory jurisdiction over the administration', not 'a substantive principle to which government decisions must conform'.[322] There is some force in Hickman's analysis that *Wednesbury* speaks mainly of a standard of review through the injunction to the courts to exercise restraint. However, a standard of review only makes sense if it is related to a standard of legality, that is, a norm which the administration is charged with satisfying. While at times Hickman's claim is that the tradition in English public law is to not impose substantive standards of legality, he tentatively concedes in a footnote that Lord Greene's test may also implicitly recognise a standard of legality:[323]

> Counsel for the plaintiff had submitted that there was a duty on the authority to act reasonably and that the court should interfere where it considered that a decision was unreasonable. Lord Greene MR accepted that the 'discretion must be exercised reasonably' – a standard of legality – but went on to reject the submission that the court could interfere simply because this standard had not been met. He explained that, given the matter was assigned to the local authority and was within its 'knowledge and expertise', the courts would only intervene if the decision was unsupportable or the unreasonableness 'overwhelming'.

On this analysis, therefore, the standards of legality and review are both reasonableness.[324] This is consistent with the positive formulations of

---

[321] Hickman, *Public Law*, above n. 66, 102 and fn.10. The natural contradistinction to the application of correctness to legal questions is Canada (see Section 4.2.2).

[322] *Ibid.*, 102. Hickman explains the distinction through *Wednesbury* but it is equally applicable to irrationality as described in *CCSU*.

[323] Hickman, *Public Law*, above n. 66, 103 fn. 103.

[324] This analysis may therefore help explain the tautological nature of Lord Greene's statement, a point which is often used to condemn the *Wednesbury* test: Lester and Jowell, above n. 309; *International Traders' Ferry*, above n. 101, 452.

grounds of review and principles of good administration which proclaim an obligation on the administration to act reasonably. For present purposes, it is sufficient to acknowledge that under the grounds of review schema, on an explicit level, the common law does not draw such a distinction and, on an implicit level, standards of review and legality are fused within the grounds of review themselves.

Hickman's distinction between standards of legality and standards of review is only employed for descriptive purposes. He expressly disavows any attempt to fashion the distinction in normative terms.[325] However, my argument is that schemata that explicitly recognise the distinction may be valuable for the purposes of organising judicial review doctrines and determining the circumstances of judicial intervention.

Even though the grounds of review purport to present prescribed and fixed depths of scrutiny, the grounds of review enable significant *variability* in judicial supervision. Judicial discretion is recognised in places in the schema but this is generally subordinate to the guidance provided by the rule-structure. That is, the generalised doctrinal structure of tripartite grounds is the centre-piece of the schema; judicial discretion infiltrates, latently, the classification process where the grounds overlap and operate, patently, in cases where the grounds emerge and evolve. Like the scope of review schema, the embrace of rules promotes *generality*, although the role of judicial discretion places a gloss on this virtue.

First, there is a degree of blurring between the distinctions framing the traditional grounds, explicitly acknowledged by the schema's concession to overlap. In such cases, this enables the depth of scrutiny to be modulated or manipulated, as explained in the doctrinal study. Taylor emphasises the normative dimension to this task in the following metaphor:[326]

> An observer can walk around the outside at such a distance as to be able to see the whole of the building visible from each angle as the observer walks around it. As the observer walks, the building changes its appearance. From some particular views it will look more pleasing and understandable to the observer's eye and brain. The particularly pleasing and understandable views will become more and then less apparent as the observer walks. The art of choosing grounds of review is to identify the grounds that are the most pleasing and understandable on the facts and focus on them. Other grounds which are less pleasing and understandable but still somewhat pleasing or understandable can be added since these may well be the ones the judge finds most pleasing, but adding these grounds can be distracting.

---

[325] Hickman, *Public Law*, above n. 66, 100.
[326] Taylor, above n. 154, [11.06].

Secondly, we have seen other grounds evolve, along with continuing pressure for others to evolve or be reformulated (albeit they are at different stages of genesis). This enlarges the available suite of grounds, bringing more diversity to the supervisory task. The particular incentive to do so is to access a depth of scrutiny that is more intensive than the default deferential review under the irrationality ground. Once again, questions of classification arise. Access to the recognised emergent grounds is generally conditional: in order to rely on the ground, certain categorical preconditions must first be met. Assessment of whether those preconditions exist, provides a degree of judicial discretion and judgement about whether they are satisfied.

Thirdly, in some respects, the departure from established standards of review found in the traditional grounds has seen the adoption of more open-textured and flexible touchstones for intervention, such as abuse of power, fair balance and so forth. In doing so, the reviewing task is imbued with more discretionary judgement, implicitly enabling greater diversity in depth of scrutiny.[327]

For the purposes of assessing the generality of the regime, the significant aspect is that the variability and judicial discretion are both latent and patent. The primary judicial task continues to be categorisation, identifying the appropriate ground of review for the circumstances of the particular case. In this part of the judicial reasoning process, the determination of the depth of scrutiny is indirect and the judicial discretion is latent – although there is some recognition of overlap necessitating judicial judgement and choice. In contrast, the evolutionary and circumscribing aspects of the grounds of review schema more openly disclose a degree of variability and judicial discretion.

Thus, the generality of the schema is relatively mixed, but is more favourable than seen in relation to scope of review. The method is grounded in rules. Judicial discretion is apparent and potent. There is some effort to give judicial discretion explicit doctrinal foundation, but aspects still remain latent.

Public Accessibility and Transparency

The generalised and systemised framework of grounds promotes accessibility and transparency. However, some aspects of the schema still disguise the factors determining the mediation of vigilance and restraint.

---

[327]   See discussion of contextual review (Section 5.2).

The high point for accessibility and transparency is the set of generalised grounds of review. They provide a clear framework guiding the judicial task, supporting the virtues of accessibility and transparency. However, the indirect manner by which the depth of scrutiny is set – by categorisation – means this schema still relies on classification as a proxy for the conceptual factors dictating the appropriate depth of review and takes away from this degree of openness. Judicial justification is generally framed in the language or form on which the grounds are cast, not the underlying conceptual drivers of vigilance and restraint.

The evolutionary aspects of the schema present a mixed degree of transparency. The ability to depart from the traditional and default grounds does not guarantee transparency about the conceptual basis for drawing the balance between vigilance and restraint differently. When judges engage recognised alternative grounds such as substantive legitimate expectations or proportionality, the focus tends to be the doctrinal preconditions which regulate the availability of these other grounds. For example, in the case of establishing a substantive legitimate expectation, it must first be established that an assurance was given in the nature of a promise (that is, triggering the prospect that the substantive expectation based on it may be protected); in the case of proportionality, enumerated rights must be implicated or the circumstances must involve the application of punitive sanctions. Thus, like the classification process, the motives for engaging the non-traditional grounds of review are not always apparent and the schema is not fully transparent; judges need only conclude that those preconditions are established.

The fact the schema sets out a traditional and default framework perhaps creates, at least passively, an expectation of reason and justification when departing from the default position. Certainly, when emerging grounds are forged, judges usually provide extensive and developed reasons justifying the new basis for intervention.[328] There is, though, no guarantee of the provision, nature or extent of the reasoning supporting evolutionary developments. For example, sometimes judges prefer to engage in more subtle doctrinal evolution to avoid taking dramatic steps or highlighting

---

[328] See e.g. the Court of Appeal's judgment in *Coughlan*, above n. 82, where it recognised substantive legitimate expectations in some cases. The judgment is notable for the length and breadth of the conceptual justification for the new ground of review. This type of conceptual reasoning can be compared with the more technical style of reasoning associated with the incremental development of doctrine in 'bottom-up' frameworks such as seen in Australia.

the new developments. Fordham identifies two main techniques whereby the evolution takes place incrementally through two phases: 'temporary masking' (an established principle is stretched to address a new problem but subsequently reinterpreted as a new principle) and 'temporary divergence' (a new principle is developed on a narrow basis and the existing orthodoxy is subsequently overruled in favour of the new principle).[329]

That said, it can be argued that the tripartite grounds also have an explanatory function. The labels – whether conclusory or not – are instrumental in explicating judicial intervention in the circumstances. As Fordham says, the grounds of review are 'the judges' way of explaining when a public authority has overstepped the mark and when judicial intervention is warranted'.[330] In this sense, the grounds operate as a rhetorical device, marking out in shorthand the basis for intervention. As judicial creations,[331] the grounds represent an attempt to express in a generalised way appropriate balances between judicial vigilance and restraint.[332] The grounds therefore have a *legitimising function*.[333] The traditional grounds of judicial review represent, according to received wisdom, balances drawn between vigilance and restraint that are legitimate; emergent grounds must surmount the legitimacy threshold before they are accepted as legitimate alternative expressions of judicial oversight.

To illustrate, the underlying distinctions that infuse the grounds of review can be charted along two axes.[334] First, a strong distinction between

---

[329] Fordham, *Judicial Review Handbook*, above n. 35, [33.3]. The introduction of legitimate expectation through *R (Unilever plc)* v. *Commissioners of Inland Revenue* [1996] STC 681 and then *Coughlan*, above n. 82, is cited as one example of temporary masking. The development of injunctions against the Crown in *Factortame (No 2)* and *M* v. *Home Office* [1994] 1 AC 377 is identified as an instance of temporary divergence.

[330] Fordham, 'Grounds', above n. 31, 199.

[331] Allan, 'Foundations', above n. 262, 97 (regardless of whether one subscribes to the ultra vires or common law school).

[332] Fordham, 'Grounds', above n. 31, 199.

[333] On the centrality of legitimacy to the judicial task of shaping and applying judicial review doctrine, see Thomas Poole, 'Legitimacy, Rights, and Judicial Review' (2005) 25 OJLS 697, particularly 718–22; 'Questioning Common Law Constitutionalism' (2005) 25 LS 142. Poole argues legitimacy is a 'credible rationale' for the exercise of judicial review power ('Legitimacy', 719). Although Craig disagrees with Poole's analysis of legitimacy questions in relation to review of cases involving rights, he still acknowledges the importance of legitimacy; however, he suggests it cannot be disentangled from values: Craig, *Administrative Law*, above n. 43, [1-029]; P.P. Craig, 'Political Constitutionalism and Judicial Review' in Christopher Forsyth and others (eds.), *Effective Judicial Review* (Oxford University Press, 2010), 41–2.

[334] Fordham, 'Grounds', above n. 31, 188–93. See also Fordham, *Judicial Review Handbook*, above n. 35, [45.1].

substance and process is evident. Procedural impropriety is separated from illegality and irrationality because it addresses how the decision is made, not the decision itself. Procedural impropriety, in Fordham's words, 'fits ... with the notion of a truly supervisory jurisdiction' – or, in the present language, 'is legitimate' – because it does not interfere with the substance or merits of the decision.[335] This distinction can be seen in the oft-cited – but nowadays questionable – mantra from *Evans*:[336]

> Judicial review is concerned, not with the decision, but with the decision-making process. Unless that restriction on the power of the court is observed, the court will ... under the guise of preventing the abuse of power, be itself guilty of usurping power.

Similarly, while irrationality addresses the substance of a decision, its inherently deferential threshold means judicial oversight is unlikely to dig into the substance of the decision. Both grounds have 'a built-in merits-avoidance mechanism', as Fordham puts it: 'procedural fairness because it is by nature only procedural, irrationality because its formulation is designed to acknowledge a margin of appreciation.'[337] Secondly, Fordham identifies a dichotomy between 'hard-edged' and 'soft' questions.[338] For those questions which, at least ostensibly, admit only a single and therefore 'correct' answer, it is treated as legitimate for the courts to substitute their view for that of the administration. In the English tradition, questions of law have been treated in this way and the resolution of questions of law remain the sole preserve of the courts.[339] Hence, the strictness of the illegality ground of review. In contrast, matters such as fact, judgement or discretion are treated as soft questions – matters on which it is illegitimate for the courts to intervene when exercising their supervisory review function. Questions of law and the strictness of the illegality ground can be contrasted to soft questions and the deferential *Wednesbury* review under the irrationality ground.

Each ground of review therefore has a central role in addressing questions of legitimacy of the judicial supervision, particularly its interventional legitimacy. Highlighting the trichotomy between review of fact,

---

[335] Fordham, 'Grounds', above n. 31, 188.
[336] *Chief Constable of the North Wales Police* v. *Evans* [1982] 1 WLR 1155, 1165.
[337] Fordham, 'Grounds', above n. 31, 189.
[338] The language of 'hard-edged' was coined, as Fordham notes, in *South Yorkshire Transport Ltd*, above n. 59, 32.
[339] See e.g. *Re Racal Communications Ltd* [1981] AC 374; *Bulk Gas Users Group Ltd* v. *Attorney-General* [1983] NZLR 129. Compare Canada, where deference may apply (Section 4.2.2).

law, and discretion, Taggart says 'the different standards of review in each category [of grounds] reflect functional, institutional, and pragmatic considerations, as well as legitimacy concerns'.[340] Thus, the grounds do, to some limited extent, have a role in rationalising and explicating the basis for intervention. But the explanation is encrypted in a label and therefore lacks transparency.

Prospectivity

This schema, like the others, is generally prospective. There are aspects of the judicial adjudication where there is some retrospective effect, such as when judicial discretion in the classification task affects outcomes or when the evolution of emerging grounds acquires some purchase in particular cases. However, when viewed relative to the other schema, the retrospective effect is not significant. In particular, the evolutionary aspects of the regime are generally not dramatic; emergent grounds are few and their development tends to be foreshadowed before they are actually realised as accepted grounds of review. Adjudicative discretion may generate some retrospective effect but the schema seeks to minimise the latent judicial role by mandating aspects of it and making it transparent.

Clarity

The generalisation and systematisation of the grounds of review aid clarity, avoiding the quagmire of rules that has plagued the scope of review schema. The schema, on its face, aims to present a simple set of principles guiding the circumstances of intervention. It still seeks to promote consistency and predictability, which the criterion of generality seeks to produce. Although not rigidly constructed, the generalised and simplified grounds are designed to be at the forefront of the judicial task and to anchor the questions about whether or not to intervene. The adoption of doctrinal grounds, in lieu of conceptual reasoning, favours clarity over transparency; the conceptual basis for intervention is merely gestured to, in the form of labels which implicitly summarise the legitimacy of intervention in particular circumstances.

Clarity is not universal, however.[341] The admission of overlap, the fact the grounds aggregate a series of more specific sub-grounds, and the role of emergent grounds mean the schema has greater complexity than seen

---

[340] Taggart, 'Administrative Law', above n. 47, 82.
[341] See e.g. Jowell and Lester's criticism of the unreasonableness ground's lack of clarity: Lester and Jowell, above n. 309.

at first blush and greater potential for inconsistency when examined more closely. Moreover, it leaves a distinct role for judicial discretion; however, in contrast to scope of review, this discretion is more apparent on the face of the schema. While there is some departure from the rule-regime ideal of simplicity, clarity and generality, the schema goes some way to exposing the normative judgements involved.

Stability

The schema presents a reasonable degree of stability. For example, the tripartite grounds have endured since their original articulation in the early 1980s. As explained above, the regime provides for some evolution of the grounds. So far, the extent to which emergent grounds have been recognised is modest and limited. Other possible grounds remain inchoate, but are discussed because judicial review jurisprudence has sufficient flexibility to enable them to be explored and promoted in individual cases. The evolution of grounds tends to be measured and generational, rather than frequent and immediate. This means the evolutionary potential does not seriously compromise stability. However, relying on the inherent flexibility of common law review, this longer term evolutionary aspect may allow judges latitude and discretion to seek to deploy novel grounds with increased depths of scrutiny in occasional cases, notwithstanding a ground not yet receiving widespread endorsement. Regardless of whether the novel ground is embraced or disapproved in later cases, in the immediate instance judges may rely on the evolutionary potential to justify its deployment. Again, though, such a practice is not widespread and does not significantly undermine the stability of the schema in the way contemplated by Fuller's virtues.

Non-contradiction and Coherence

The rationale for the systematisation of doctrines into generalised grounds of review was schematic coherence. As explained above, Lord Diplock, in particular, was instrumental in the systemisation project; he proudly proclaimed the systemisation of administration law as the 'the greatest achievement' of the English courts in his judicial lifetime.[342] Lord Donaldson echoed the impact of the tripartite grounds, noting that they were formulated 'in an attempt to rid the courts of shackles bred of the technicalities surrounding the old prerogative writs'.[343] The purpose of

---

[342] *National Federation of Self Employed*, above n. 22, 641.
[343] *Guinness*, above n. 131, 160 (Lord Donaldson).

the systemisation was to move judicial review doctrine beyond its doctrinal morass and to ensure a simple, unified, and coherent framework was adopted. As seen in the explanation of the nature of the rules above, the grounds of review approach is relatively successful in presenting a coherent structure. Moreover, the schematic coherence of the grounds of review approach is illustrated, in part, by the employment of the grounds by textbook writers. The systemised grounds allow the 'orderly exposition' of the bases of intervention.[344] Indeed, an analogy is frequently found between the grounds and the chapter headings of textbooks.[345] As Taylor explains, the grounds provide an analytical structure which is useful for instructive purposes; the groupings – or, again, 'chapters' – avoid the 'unwieldy' exposition of the bases of judicial intervention.[346] Thus, grounds of review performs well under this criterion.

Non-impossibility and Practicality

The simplified, systemised nature of the generalised grounds also ensures litigation is reasonably practical. The litigation process is supported by the operation of the established tripartite grounds, in most cases. These operate as useful guides for the purpose of framing and arguing cases, although non-traditional grounds present some challenges in the litigation process.

The tripartite grounds usefully frame argument in administrative law courts. 'The grounds of review are the arguments which a lawyer can put forward as to why a court should hold a public authority's decision to be unlawful.'[347] The way the grounds of review provide structure in litigation, assisting submissions or judgments to 'focus on the factual features of the decision or action said to be reviewable' has been acknowledged.[348] This is recognised by the rules of civil procedure: claimants are required to identify the grounds on which a judicial review claim is made.[349] The readily understood depth of scrutiny associated with the grounds flows into the evidential corpus required. Like scope of review, review for legality, procedural

---

[344] See *Boddington*, above n. 29, 152.

[345] Le Sueur, Herberg and English, above n. 40, 226; *Brind*, above n. 4, 722; de Smith (5th edn), 294.

[346] Taylor, above n. 154, [11.02].

[347] Le Sueur, Herberg and English, above n. 40, 226.

[348] Taylor, above n. 154, [11.02].

[349] The Civil Procedure Rules Part 54 Practice Direction, cl. 5.6(1) requires claimants to provide 'a detailed statement of the claimant's grounds for bringing the claim for judicial review'. The Judicial Review Procedure Act 2016 (NZ), s. 14(2)(g)(ii) may require an applicant to specify 'the grounds for relief'.

fairness and unreasonableness does not necessitate vast amounts of evidence or cross-examination.[350] The symmetry between the standards of legality and standards of review – that is, their inverse relationship – assists in the deliberation process. Generally, the process of reasoning is simple and uncluttered. Judges' attention is directed to the circumstances of the particular case, and need not engage in lengthy self-reflection about their own methodology or the applicable standards of review.

The simplicity and straightforward nature of litigation is tested because these emergent grounds may unleash different methodologies and different degrees of scrutiny. More vigilant grounds, like proportionality or legitimate expectation, require greater attention to the justification advanced by the administration and greater examination of the reasoning and supporting evidential basis. The classic model of judicial review – expedited and tightly focused in practical terms – does not fit this more vigilant approach. Meeting the evidential demands of greater scrutiny costs time and preparation.

As an example, the *Lab Tests* litigation in New Zealand shows the growth of the court record and the enlargement of time associated with arguments of increased vigilance.[351] The incumbent tenderer for diagnostic testing reviewed a decision of a district health board to award the contract to another provider. Amongst other things, it argued that the Court ought to adopt a 'broad-based probity in public decision-making approach' to reviewing the decision (an approach that was adopted at first instance but overturned on appeal). As a result, the judicial review hearing took ten days to hear at first instance, and a further seven on appeal. The evidential corpus was large (68 affidavits and nearly 12,000 pages of documents) and written submissions lengthy (over 700 pages).[352] Concern was expressed about the unorthodox length of the hearing, prompted especially by the more intensive standard of review and associated factual complexity. For example, Arnold J conceded the appeal court's judgment was 'a lengthy judgment, much longer than is desirable' but pointed to the need to 'examine the evidence in some detail', in the light of the plaintiff's claim for a supervisory approach which mandated 'almost indeterminate scope for intervention by the courts'; his view was that the 'factual and

---

[350] David Abrahams, 'Conflicts of Evidence in Judicial Review Proceedings' [1999] JR 221; Harlow and Rawlings, above n. 9, 704.

[351] *Lab Tests*, above n. 169. See also *Powerco*, above n. 159.

[352] *R (Rossminster) v. Inland Revenue Commissioners* [1980] AC 952; *Geary v. Psychologists Board* (2009) 19 PRNZ 415.

other subtleties' were 'too great to be dealt with in what is supposed to be "a relatively simple, untechnical and prompt procedure".[353] This can be compared to the experience and expectation of litigation under a classic model, where proceedings would often be heard in a day or so.[354]

The procedural style of litigation associated with increased scrutiny is markedly different and more involved; we can describe it as the 'plenary' style of procedure, in contrast to the more modest 'constrained' style of procedure. The existence of two procedural styles raises the question of how the courts can accommodate each within the ordinary framework of review. In other words, practically, how can the courts modulate the quality of procedure in cases in which that is required? On the one hand, it is not desirable or feasible for the plenary style of procedure to be employed in every case. The costs associated with this would be significant. And presenting a full evidential corpus for intensive review in cases where traditional review only applies risks encouraging judges to engage in more vigilant review, without any normative basis. On the other hand, it may be difficult to anticipate those cases where increased scrutiny is justified; nor is it easy to demarcate evidence between low-intensity and high-intensity grounds, or to separate factually dependent grounds from abstract grounds. This compromises predictability and therefore the lessens the clarity of the schema.

That said, the conditional or partial nature of emergent grounds does ameliorate this to some extent. None of the emergent grounds is universal; as mentioned above, preconditions must be first satisfied before they can be reached and they have, to date, been relatively confined in operation. Thus, the courts must first be persuaded that the emergent ground is applicable in the circumstances of the particular case before the high-intensity procedural review is deployed. This limits, to some degree, the need for, and reliance on, high-intensity procedural review. However, these decisions are often not made at or before the substantive hearing of the case, diluting this gate-keeper function. It is possible that more sophisticated and robust examination of the claimed grounds of review at the preliminary permissions stage (where this is available) could improve this gate-keeping function and ensure the evidential corpus is commensurate with the realistically arguable grounds of review. However, there may be some

---

[353] *Lab Tests*, above n. 169, 344, referring to *Minister of Energy* v. *Petrocorp Exploration Ltd* [1989] 1 NZLR 348.

[354] See further Harlow and Rawlings, above n. 9, 703–10 for the impact of the expansion of judicial review on the fact base of proceedings.

reluctance to make judgements like this based on the sparse evidence available at preliminary hearings.

Congruence and Candour

The grounds of review schema performs relatively well in term of congruence and candour, balancing a need for consistency with flexibility – and generally encouraging congruence and candour on the part of judges. However, the ability to manipulate some of the key classifications takes away from congruence and candour. As explained earlier, doctrinal classification can obfuscate the unstated normative reasons for the classification.

Hortatory Versatility

Finally, the grounds of review schema is well-suited as a hortatory framework. The hortatory function is exemplified by the production of the various bureaucratic manuals, such as the *Judge Over Your Shoulder* guides produced in England and New Zealand, based on the simplified and systemised grounds of review.[355] The aim is to seek to improve awareness of the principles of good administration and promote compliance. The grounds of review are often cast in inverse terms to represent what have been described as principles of good administration or standards of legality.[356] They represent norms which ministers, public bodies and officials must comply with when exercising discretion. In other words, the corollary of grounds of review enabling intervention on the basis of illegality, irrationality and procedural impropriety (as per Lord Diplock) is an obligation on the part of decision-makers to act legally, rationally and with procedural propriety. This helps explain the usefulness of the ground for bureaucrats and their prominence in administrative guidance.

It is commonly observed that the number of administrative decisions which are subject to external review, particularly judicial review, is minuscule compared to the vast number of decisions actually made by the administration.[357] Thus, the hortatory role is important because it has the potential to reach parts of the administration that are not frequently exposed to external review and supervision. Moreover, these principles

---

[355] Treasury Solicitor, *The Judge Over Your Shoulder* (4th edn, 2006); Crown Law Office, *A Judge Over Your Shoulder* (2005). See Harlow and Rawlings, above n. 9, 734; Dawn Oliver 'Judge Over Your Shoulder – Mark II' [1994] PL 514; de Smith (7th edn), 31.

[356] See text to n. 308. For examples of formalised accounts of these principles, see United Kingdom Ombudsman, *Principles of Good Administration* (2007) and European Union, *Code of Good Administrative Behaviour* (2012).

[357] Cane, *Administrative Law*, above n. 305, 26.

of good administration may be utilised by other public functionaries which have a grievance-remedying role, such as ombudsmen, auditors or administrative tribunals. Again, the simple expression of three bases of intervention supports this function.

The increasing complexity of the circumstances of judicial intervention, however, means a simple inversion of the grounds of intervention to articulate principles of good administration is no longer adequate. The growth in emergent grounds, with different depth of scrutiny review in different circumstances, creates tension between the statement of grounds in terms of standards of legality and standards of review. Take, for instance, the legitimate expectation ground. In some circumstances, defeating a legitimate expectation in a way that creates resultant unfairness or an abuse of power justifies judicial intervention. As a standard of review, the intensity may be approximated to simple unreasonableness (or, as some argue, proportionality), if the circumstances justify; if not, the default *Wednesbury* unreasonableness standard applies.[358] But how does this translate into a general standard of legality? The contingent and contextual nature of the ground inversion of the standard or ground does not readily translate into a general standard or norm that decision-makers should comply with. Instead, further reflection is required to elaborate a norm. Here, it is one of consistency or legal certainty (either acting consistently with promulgated policies or established practices on the one hand, or not reneging on promises or other assurances on the other) – this is the gist that runs through legitimate expectation. Thus there are some limits to the hortatory role of the grounds, particularly when the emergent grounds are engaged.

3.5   Conclusion

The framework of grounds of review provides a few generalised grounds to guide, indirectly, the determination of the depth of scrutiny. Born out of Lord Diplock's expression of three grounds, the tripartite formulation provides the structure for the later editions of de Smith's textbook and continues to be orthodox in England and New Zealand. Some of the potential for the addition of more grounds has been realised and further potential remains.

The articulation of standards, drawn from the common law without being dressed up in the cloak of vires or legislative intent, means the

---

[358] See text to n. 86 above.

approach satisfies those from the common law school. However, those scholars supporting the approach prefer the expression of values be given some structure, crystallised in the form of key markers of judicial depth of review.

The normative value of this approach comes from its attempts to simplify and systematise the basis of intervention, without pretending the generalisations are perfect or rigid. Thus, more abstract rules encourage coherence, congruence and practicality, without significantly diminishing generality. Elements of residual judicial discretion – sometimes unexposed – leave a gloss on the rule-based virtue of the schema, particularly its transparency, clarity and stability.

Overall, the delivery of administrative justice through grounds expressed with a degree of abstraction provides an honest and workable framework. A balance is drawn between providing lights to assist those affected through the supervisory process and judicial flexibility in order to respond to the circumstances of particular cases. The schemata's continuing currency – in England and New Zealand especially – therefore comes as no surprise.

4

Intensity of Review

4.1 Introduction

Intensity of review brings questions of the depth of scrutiny into the foreground. The hallmark of this style of review is the explicit calibration of the depth of review as a preliminary step in the supervisory process. The language and style of intensity of review is increasingly evident through the fifth, sixth and seventh editions of de Smith's textbook although it has not yet eclipsed the organisational framework provided by grounds of review.

This approach takes schematic form and also exists as a method within a particular doctrine. Its schematic form is seen most vividly in Canada's framework of explicit standards of review (most prominently before its recent rationalisation); under this framework the depth of review was calibrated explicitly based on forms of reasonableness and correctness review. Elsewhere in English and New Zealand judicial review, the methodology is evident in particular grounds or doctrines for substantive review. Notions of 'hard look', variegated forms of unreasonableness and structured forms of deference all exhibit the transparent mediation of the balance between vigilance and restraint, based on various constitutional, institutional and functional factors. While not yet assuming full schematic form in England and New Zealand, it is increasingly engaged on matters of substantive review and has the potential to provide a competing framework to other schemata such as grounds of review.

Intensity of review draws support from both sides of the conceptual underpinnings debate about judicial review. Some from the ultra vires school acknowledge the categorical distinctions of formalism are unable to cope with the complexity of judicial review. For them, more conceptual reasoning is supported, but only when circumscribed by doctrine to ensure judicial values do not overtake legislative intent. This approach also finds favour amongst some from the common law school. While acknowledging the role judges have in articulating administrative law norms and the circumstances of judicial intervention, they are also acutely aware of judicial limitations. Although the judicial judgement unavoidably takes centre-stage in the complex domain of administrative law, so too should the limitations of the judicial function – in this case, realised in doctrinal form.

Intensity of review scores highly on a number of the principles of efficacy. Transparency, coherence and candour are aided by the centrality of conceptual reasoning to the determination of depth of review. A rule-structure is present – and hence generality is honoured – but the focus is on rules about *how* the depth of review is to be determined. This brings a more open-textured judicial methodology, making it more difficult to predict substantive outcomes. Although the approach tries to ameliorate this, the lack of certainty diminishes the prospectivity, clarity and practicality of the schema.

4.2   Doctrinal Manifestation

I begin by tracing the language of intensity of review in de Smith's textbook; absent from the first four editions, it becomes increasingly prominent thereafter. I then turn to the way the approach has provided the schematic form for Canadian administrative law for many years, before drawing out its role in relation to substantive review in England and New Zealand.

4.2.1   De Smith Derivation

The concept and language of 'intensity of review' makes a brief cameo appearance in the fifth edition, but gains a much stronger foothold in the sixth and seventh editions. The authors increasingly resort to the language of intensity of review for analytical purposes and embrace the notion that the depth of review modulates in different situations; but that the discussion of intensity of review still occurs within a general schema or framework of grounds of review.

In the fifth edition, a number of paragraphs are dedicated to a discussion of intensity of review in the context of the unreasonableness ground of review.[1] The concept is also alluded to in the discussion of justiciability and proportionality.[2] In its formative appearance, its genesis is often attributed to the 'margin of appreciation' concept employed in European

[1] De Smith (5th edn), 586–592.
[2] *Ibid.*, 314 and 598–600 respectively.

Community law and European Convention jurisprudence; the phraseology of intensity and margin/latitude are often used interchangeably.[3]

Not nearly as developed as in the editions that followed, the commentary highlighted two circumstances – at different extremes – illustrative
of the idea that the subject-matter of the decision under review may
influence the threshold of intervention. Managerial and policy decisions
involving calculations of social and economic preference were said to be
an area where the intensity of review would be low.[4] Two cases involving challenges to ministerial control of local authority expenditure were
cited in support of this form of light-handed review: *Nottinghamshire* and
Hammersmith.[5] In both cases, the high degree of policy content supported
this very deferential approach, along with the parliamentary ratification of
the ministerial action.[6] In contrast, Woolf and Jowell said the courts would
'look significantly harder' at cases involving infringements of human or
fundamental rights.[7] The seeds of the principle of legality are hinted at.
Based on the *Leech* case,[8] it is suggested (baldly) the courts will infer that,
in the absence of clear authorisation, statutory powers were not intended
to infringe fundamental rights.[9] A lower threshold of unreasonableness is
also alluded to. Relying on *Brind*, it was suggested that where legislation
unambiguously confers a discretionary power to interfere with a fundamental right, '[r]eview is stricter'; rather than reasonableness analogous to
perversity or absurdity being deployed, a simpler expression of reasonableness is adopted.[10] Further, in one short, passing sentence, the possibility
of 'most anxious scrutiny' is also referred to; cases later assuming greater
significance, *Bugdaycay* and *Smith*, are dotted in a supporting footnote.[11]

---

[3] *Ibid.*, e.g., 552, 605, 606.
[4] *Ibid.*, 586–7.
[5] *Nottinghamshire City Council* v. *Secretary of State for the Environment* [1986] AC 240, 247
     and *R (Hammersmith and Fulham London Borough Council)* v. *Secretary of State for the
     Environment* [1991] 1 AC 521, 597. See Section 4.2.3.
[6] The significance of a decision having a democratic mandate was expanded later in the com-
     mentary: de Smith, 590 (relevant to the assessment of reasonableness, but should not be
     taken as conclusive proof, referring to *Bromley London Borough Council* v. *Greater London
     Council* [1983] AC 768; *Secretary of State for Education and Science* v. *Tameside Metropolitan
     Borough Council* [1977] AC 1014; *Nottinghamshire*, above n. 5; *Hammersmith*, above n. 5).
[7] De Smith (5th edn), 588–90.
[8] *R (Leech)* v. *Secretary of State for the Home Department* [1994] QB 198.
[9] De Smith (5th edn), 589.
[10] *Ibid.*
[11] *Ibid.*, 589 and fn. 26. See Section 4.2.3.

Finally, the variability of the standard of unreasonableness and intensity of review is most squarely identified in the context of statutory unreasonableness.[12] Pointing to a number of cases where the approach to review a decision where the statute itself insisted the decision be reasonable, Woolf and Jowell conclude that depth of review adopted was diverse: 'The term "unreasonable", in its *Wednesbury* or any other sense, is no magic formula; everything must depend upon the context.'[13]

In the sixth and seventh editions, 'intensity of review' is given significant prominence and subjected to extensive analysis. Again afforded its own subsection in the rebranded section on substantive review and justification, the direct treatment of intensity of review grows to eight pages, along with a further half-dozen pages of comparative comment.[14] As well as the extent of direct coverage increasing, the commentary itself highlights the centrality of intensity of review in substantive review. The terminology is also dotted throughout the commentary elsewhere.[15]

In their introductory passage, the authors acknowledge and explain their avoidance of the style previously attributed to this ground: 'unreasonableness' and 'irrationality'.[16] The imprecision of these terms, tautological nature of unreasonableness, and the overlap with the emerging concept of proportionality are promoted as the reason for adopting the broader and more generic title of 'substantive review and justification'.[17] Pitched as engaging the substance of the decision and the sufficiency of its justification, the authors admit the importance of intensity of review – or rather, as they describe it, 'the appropriate measure of deference, respect, restraint, latitude or discretionary area of judgement (to use some of the terms variously employed)'.[18]

In their subsequent, extended commentary (under the heading 'Intensity of Review'), they develop further the role of latitude and uniformity in judicial review.[19] The authors endorse the principle of

---

[12] De Smith (5th edn), 592.

[13] *Ibid.*, 593.

[14] De Smith (6th edn), 591–8; (7th edn), 635–42.

[15] De Smith (6th edn), 630–3; (7th edn), 685–9, notably referring to 'deference' and a 'sliding scale of review', along with *R (Begbie)* v. *Secretary of State for Education and Employment* [2000] 1 WLR 1115, above ch. 3 n. 91 (proposing a proportionality assessment).

[16] De Smith (6th edn), 543; (7th edn), 585.

[17] De Smith (6th edn), 543–4; (7th edn), 585–7.

[18] De Smith (6th edn), 544 and fn. 14; (7th edn), 587 and fn. 14. The footnote to this passage equates the various terms to 'intensity of review'.

[19] Two questions are posed: 'To what extent should the courts allow a degree of latitude or leeway to the decision-maker? And to what extent should it be uniform?': de Smith

contextualism expressed by Lord Steyn in *Daly* and admit that the 'willingness' of the courts to invalidate a decision on substantive grounds will depend on a number of factors such as respective institutional competence and practical considerations.[20]

Significantly, intensity is depicted in terms of a complete schema. A number of different formulations of variable intensity were identified, from 'full intensity review' on the one hand, to non-justiciable decisions on the other:[21]

Full Intensity Review	Structured Proportionality Review	Variable Intensity Unreasonableness Review Depending on the nature of the subject-matter ⟵——————————————⟶			Non-justiciable
Court decides 'correctness' and whether power abused	Intensity of review may vary according to the context Burden of justification on public authority	**Anxious scrutiny unreasonableness review** Burden on public authority	**Standard** *Wednesbury* **unreasonableness review** Burden on claimant	**'Light touch'** **unreasonableness review** Burden on claimant	But adequacy of justification still required

Full intensity, or correctness, review is described as arising in three main fields: (a) decisions made where no evidence exists to support it or an established fact is ignored; (b) decisions which offend the principle of consistency; and (c) some (but not all) decisions which undermine legitimate expectations.[22] The authors recount that the language of 'abuse of power' is often employed in these cases, rather than the language of unreasonableness or proportionality.

In between the two poles of full intensity review and non-justiciability, a number of different manifestations of variable depth of scrutiny are plotted. 'Variable intensity unreasonableness review' is described as allowing the 'broadest spectrum of intensity'; the authors explain that some

---

(6th edn), 591. While there is reference to uniformity, the commentary which follows makes it clear variability is embraced.

[20] De Smith (6th edn), 591; (7th edn), 635.

[21] De Smith (6th edn), 592; (7th edn), 636.

[22] De Smith (6th edn), 592; (7th edn), 636. See discussion of abuse of power: Section 5.2.4.

cases require the courts to allow the administration 'a degree of latitude' or, in other words, 'a sliding scale of review'.[23] The authors identify the default position – 'at the time of writing' – is still the *Wednesbury* formulation of unreasonableness.[24] They suggest there has been a subtle reformulation, a softening of the extremity of *Wednesbury*'s language to a simpler test of whether the decision falls 'within the "range of reasonable responses"'.[25] Lord Cooke's promotion of a simpler formulation of the test (and his contempt for *Wednesbury* unreasonableness) is identified as being influential and a number of cases adopting this simplified approach are also recounted.[26]

On each side of *Wednesbury* unreasonableness, two further classes of case are described. The first is characterised as a form of 'heightened scrutiny unreasonableness review', available where a decision interferes with a 'fundamental right or important interest'.[27] The deployment of 'anxious scrutiny' in *Bugdaycay* and the insistence of more extensive justification in cases involving human rights in *Smith* (both more prominent in this edition) are instanced, along with *Brind* and *Saville* where similar remarks are made.[28] A further class of cases, described as 'light-touch review', is identified within the rubric of variable intensity of review.[29] '[C]onsiderable latitude' – and, importantly, more deference than found in the default *Wednesbury* test – may be afforded to some administrative decisions.[30] This class of case is equated with the triggering language of 'outrageous' employed in *CCSU* and 'arbitrary' in *Pro-Life Alliance*.[31] Oddly, the *Nottinghamshire* and *Hammersmith* cases referred to in earlier editions are not cited in this context; rather, they appear in an earlier more generic discussion on the constitutional context of substantive review.[32]

---

[23] De Smith (6th edn), 594; (7th edn), 638.

[24] De Smith (6th edn), 554 and 596; (7th edn), 596 and 640.

[25] De Smith (6th edn), 554; (7th edn), 596.

[26] De Smith (6th edn), 554 and fn. 72; (7th edn), 596 and fn.73; citing, notably, *Ala* v. *Secretary of State for the Home Department* [2003] All ER (D) 283; *Huang* v. *Secretary of State for the Home Office* [2007] 2 AC 167.

[27] De Smith (6th edn), 594; (7th edn), 638.

[28] De Smith (6th edn), 595; (7th edn), 639; *R (Bugdaycay)* v. *Secretary of State for the Home Department* [1987] AC 514, 531; *R (Smith)* v. *Ministry of Defence* [1996] QB 517; *R (Brind)* v. *Secretary of State for the Home Department* [1991] 1 AC 696; *R (A)* v. *Lord Saville of Newdigate* [2000] 1 WLR 1855.

[29] De Smith (6th edn), 596; (7th edn), 640.

[30] De Smith (6th edn), 596; (7th edn), 640.

[31] De Smith (6th edn), 596; (7th edn), 640.

[32] De Smith (6th edn), 546; (7th edn), 589.

The treatment of light-touch review is relatively modest and quickly shades into a discussion of the principle of non-justiciability, which is identified earlier as the high-water mark in terms of judicial restraint.[33] While it is said that 'no power – whether statutory or under the prerogative – is any longer inherently unreviewable', it is accepted that there are certain decisions which the courts 'cannot or should not easily engage'.[34] Two situations are identified: the first where the courts are 'constitutionally disabled from entering on review' and the second where the courts lack ... 'relative institutional capacity to enter into a review of a decision'.[35] A need for judicial caution is expressed on constitutional grounds in relation to policy matters requiring the weighing of social, economic and political preferences. Similarly, decisions on which the courts are ill-equipped to review are identified as being 'not amenable to the judicial process' (adopting the words of Lord Diplock in CCSU), based on institutional limitations.[36] The evaluation of matters of preference, matters on which the courts lack (relative) expertise, and matters which are polycentric are expressed as decisions which 'are not ideally justiciable'.[37] Ultimately, the authors do not profess 'any carefully calibrated theory' about the circumstances in which the courts should recognise their constitutional and institutional limitations by adopting very deferential forms of review.[38] But their animus towards non-justiciability as an absolute concept is obvious.[39]

One form of proportionality, namely 'structured proportionality review', is also presented on the schema of variable intensity, between full intensity review and variable intensity of review.[40] The identification of variable intensity in the context of proportionality fits with other analysis in the text of the nature of proportionality review. Different roles are discussed: (a) the implicit potential role for proportionality at common law; (b) its established role for assessing whether limitations on rights are justified under the Human Rights Act 1998; and (c) its role in relation to directly effective

---

[33] De Smith (6th edn), 597; (7th edn), 641.
[34] De Smith (6th edn), 15, 597; (7th edn), 641
[35] De Smith (6th edn), 597; (7th edn), 641.
[36] De Smith (6th edn), 18, 597; (7th edn), 19, 641.
[37] De Smith (6th edn), 18; (7th edn), 19.
[38] De Smith (6th edn), 549; (7th edn), 592.
[39] At a number of points, the authors argue the courts should be slow to relinquish their supervisory role, even in situations when faced with constitutional and institutional limitations: see e.g. de Smith (6th edn), 17, 548–50 and 597; (7th edn), 21, 591–3 and 641.
[40] De Smith (6th edn), 592; (7th edn), 636.

European Community law.[41] The latter two roles are explained as instances where structured proportionality applies. This form of review is characterised, on the one hand, as 'more searching' because of the closer attention to justification for the decision than found in reasonableness review.[42] On the other hand, the authors acknowledge that proportionality does not displace the role for deference: 'Varying levels of intensity of review will be appropriate in different categories of case'.[43] Two instances of a more deferential approach are presented: decisions involving complex economic assessment under European Community law cases;[44] and Convention right cases involving social policy or questions of resource allocation.[45]

An alternative formulation, proportionality as a test of 'fair balance', is also discussed but, oddly, it is not specifically identified on the authors' variable intensity schema. This formulation is described as mandating judicial intervention when disproportionate weight it placed on a consideration or a decision amounts to a disproportionate interference with a person's rights or interests.[46] It requires the defect to be manifest and requires a claimant to establish a basis for intervention. This style of (dis)proportionality is described as an 'implicit explanation' for judicial intervention under the unreasonableness ground.[47] Its implicit relationship with unreasonableness perhaps explains its omission from the variable intensity schema; in any event, it lines up as a further instance of variability within proportionality, even if not explicitly presented as such by the authors.

4.2.2   Canada: Standards of Review

Explicit calibration of intensity of review has been commonplace in Canada for many decades.[48] Since 1979, Canadian courts have

---

[41] De Smith (6th edn), 584; (7th edn), 627.

[42] De Smith (6th edn), 593; (7th edn), 636; citing, notably, *Tweed* v. *Parades Commission for Northern Ireland* [2007] 1 AC 650.

[43] De Smith (6th edn), 592–3; (7th edn), 635–6.

[44] De Smith (6th edn), 593; (7th edn), 636; citing, notably, *R (Astonquest)* v. *Ministry of Agriculture, Fisheries and Food* [2000] Eu LR 371.

[45] De Smith (6th edn), 594; (7th edn), 636; citing, notably, *R (Alconbury Developments Ltd)* v. *Secretary of State for the Environment, Transport and the Regions* [2003] 2 AC 295 and *Begbie*, above n. 15.

[46] De Smith (6th edn), 585; (7th edn), 629.

[47] De Smith (6th edn), 585; (7th edn), 629; citing, notably, *R (Hook)* v. *Barnsley Metropolitan Borough Council* [1976] 1 WLR 1052; *R (Uchendu)* v. *Highbury Corner Justices* (1994) 158 JP 409.

[48] For extended background to the development of the framework, see D.P. Jones and A.S. de Villars, *Principles of Administrative Law* (5th edn, Carswell, 2009), 489–522;

adopted a framework of variable standards of review, identifying the appropriate depth of review as a preliminary step in the supervisory process. As originally developed, it applied only to review for error of law; in the late 1990s, it was also extended to review of the exercise of discretion.[49] Notably, unlike other Anglo-Commonwealth jurisdictions, this means that deference also applies explicitly to questions of law – that is, resolving matters of interpretation is not regarded as being the sole constitutional preserve of the courts.

Initially, in *Canadian Union of Public Employees Local 963* v. *New Brunswick Liquor Corporation*, the Supreme Court identified two discrete standards of review – 'correctness' and 'patent unreasonableness' – mimicking the depth of review applied in England and New Zealand under the grounds of review schema.[50] In the late 1990s, the space between these two discrete standards was filled by an intermediate standard of review: 'reasonableness *simpliciter*'.[51] Again, this more vigilant form of reasonableness echoed the more intensive forms seen in England and New Zealand, setting a test for intervention 'more deferential than correctness but less

---

Audrey Macklin, 'Standard of Review' in C.M. Flood and L. Sossin (eds.), *Administrative Law in Context* (Edmond Montgomery, 2008), 197; David Mullan, 'Deference: Is it Useful Outside Canada?' (2006) AJ 42, 48–50; Michael Taggart, 'Outside Canadian Administrative Law' (1996) 46 UTLJ 649; Paul Daly, *A Theory of Deference in Administrative Law* (Cambridge University Press, 2012), 15–16. See also recent moves within this framework towards more contextual forms of unreasonableness: Section 5.2.3.

[49] Procedural fairness is addressed separately: that is, a correctness standard always applies, although the assessment of the content of the obligation sometimes mimics the assessment of deference for substantive review: *Nicholson* v. *Haldimand-Norfolk Regional Police Commissioners* [1979] 1 SCR 311; *Canada (Citizenship and Immigration)* v. *Khosa* [2009] 1 SCR 339; *Mission Institution* v. *Khela* [2014] 1 SCR 502; Grant Huscroft, 'The Duty of Fairness' in Flood and Sossin, above n. 48, 115, 135. For recent moves, where Charter rights are engaged, to subject some (individualised) administrative decision-making to reasonableness review rather than the traditional proportionality test, see *Doré* v. *Barreau du Québec* [2012] 1 SCR 395.

[50] [1979] 2 SCR 227. Matters which were 'preliminary and collateral' on which the decision-maker's jurisdiction depended were reviewed according to the correctness standard. In contrast, other matters within the decision-maker's jurisdiction, on which the legislature intended the decision-maker's decision should be final, were assessed according to a patent unreasonableness standard.

[51] *Canada (Director of Investigation & Research)* v. *Southam Inc* [1997] 1 SCR 748 and *Pushpanathan* v. *Canada (Minister of Employment & Immigration)* [1998] 1 SCR 982. The Supreme Court had earlier toyed with the concept of a 'spectrum of standards of review' in *Pezim* v. *British Columbia (Superintendent of Brokers)* [1994] 2 SCR 557, although in that case, as Jones and de Villars note, 'the Supreme Court actually only referred to two possible standards of review – correctness and patent unreasonableness (which it selected)': Jones and de Villars, above n. 48, 490 fn. 5. See also Macklin, above n. 48, 210.

deferential than "not patently unreasonable".[52] With the addition of this intermediate standard, the Supreme Court, as Jones and de Villars describe it, 'effectively trad[ed] a toggle switch for a dimmer switch'.[53] The Supreme Court encouraged a 'functional and pragmatic' approach to the settling of the appropriate standard, based on four key factors: (a) the presence or absence of a privative clause; (b) the comparative expertise of the decision-maker and court; (c) the purpose of the Act and provision in issue; and (d) the nature of the problem, namely whether it was one of law, fact, or mixed law and fact. As explained above, the Supreme Court in *Baker* also brought review for abuse of discretion (previously reviewable on a number of largely deferential grounds of review) within this framework.[54]

This basic framework endured for over a decade, until the Supreme Court in *Dunsmuir* v. *New Brunswick* collapsed the distinction between patent unreasonableness and reasonableness *simpliciter*.[55] Following a major review of the jurisprudence on standards of review, the Supreme Court ruled the two standards of review should be: (a) correctness review; and (b) a 'single form of "reasonableness" review'.[56] In other words the different forms of unreasonableness were replaced with a unified, but context-specific, reasonableness standard.[57] The Supreme Court indicated that this more generalised form of unreasonableness would be simpler and enable review in cases where justice required it.[58] Notably, the majority rejected any suggestion of reverting to the pre-*Southam* 'all-or-nothing' days prior to the creation of the intermediate reasonableness *simpliciter* category.[59] The new unified standard of unreasonableness is broader and would continue to capture the depth of review previously undertaken in the names of patent unreasonableness and reasonableness *simpliciter*.

The Supreme Court in *Dunsmuir* retained a factorial approach to the determination of the appropriate standard (under the new regime, either correctness or unreasonableness), but with some modification. The factors

---

[52] *Southam Inc*, above n. 51, [54].
[53] Jones and de Villars, above n. 48, 490.
[54] *Baker* v. *Canada (Minister of Citizenship and Immigration)* [1999] 2 SCR 817, [55]. See Section 3.2.5 above.
[55] [2008] 1 SCR 190. See generally David Mullan, '*Dunsmuir* v. *New Brunswick*' (2008) 21 Can J Admin L & Prac 117; Laverne Jacobs, 'Developments in Administrative Law' (2008) 43 SCLR (2d) 1; along with the Supreme Court's account in *Dunsmuir* ([34]–[42]).
[56] *Dunsmuir*, above n. 55, [45].
[57] *Ibid.*, [34], [134] and [167].
[58] *Ibid.*, [43].
[59] *Ibid.*, [44].

were reiterated, with only subtle rewording.[60] Notably, the Court said an 'exhaustive review' of the factors to determine the applicable standard was not required in every case.[61] If existing jurisprudence 'already determined in a satisfactory manner the degree of deference to be accorded with regard to a particular category of question', this standard is to be applied;[62] only if this 'proves unfruitful', is it necessary to analyse the mandated contextual factors to ascertain the applicable standard of review.[63] A number of questions were marked out as 'generally' requiring correctness review:[64] constitutional issues;[65] general and important questions of law outside the primary decision-maker's area of expertise; 'true' questions of jurisdiction;[66] and competing authority between specialised tribunals. In contrast, questions of fact, discretion or policy, a specialist tribunal's interpretation of their home statute, and cases involving privative clauses will 'usually' signal a reasonableness standard.[67] While employing the

---

[60] *Ibid.*, [64]. Alice Woolley, 'The Metaphysical Court' (2008) 21 CJALP 259, 263–4.

[61] *Dunsmuir*, above n. 55, [57].

[62] *Ibid.*, [62].

[63] *Ibid.* For subsequent discussion of the scope of the presumptive categories, see e.g. *Smith v. Alliance Pipeline* [2011] 1 SCR 160; *Canada (Canadian Human Rights Commission) v. Canada (Attorney-General)* [2011] 3 SCR 471; *Nor-Man Regional Health Authority Inc v. Manitoba Association of Health Care Professionals* [2011] 3 SCR 616; *Doré v. Barreau du Québec* [2012] 1 SCR 395; *Communications, Energy and Paperworkers Union of Canada, Local 30 v. Irving Pulp & Paper Ltd* [2013] 2 SCR 458; *McLean v. British Columbia (Securities Commission)* [2013] SCC 67; *Agraira v. Canada (Public Safety and Emergency Preparedness)* [2013] SCC 36. See generally Mullan, '*Dunsmuir*', above n. 55; Paul Daly, 'The Unfortunate Triumph of Form Over Substance in Canadian Administrative Law' (2012) 50 Osgoode Hall LJ 317; Andrew Green, 'Can There Be Too Much Context in Administrative Law?' (2014) 47 UBC Law Rev 443; Paul Daly, 'The Scope and Meaning of Reasonableness Review' (2015) 52 Alta Law Rev 799.

[64] *Dunsmuir*, above n. 55, [58]–[61].

[65] The Supreme Court in *Doré*, above n. 63, subsequently ruled that the Charter analysis undertaken by administrative decision-makers should be subjected to reasonableness, not correctness, review; cf. *Multani c. Commission scolaire Maguerite-Bourgeoys* [2006] 1 SCR 256. See Lewans, 'Administrative Law, Judicial Deference, and the *Charter*' [2014] 23 Constitutional Forum 19; Macklin, 'Charter Right or Charter-Lite? Administrative Discretion and the Charter' (2014) 67 SCLR (2d) 561 and Geiringer, 'Process and Outcome in Judicial Review of Public Authority Compatibility with Human Rights' in Hanna Wilberg and Mark Elliott, *The Scope and Intensity of Substantive Review* (Hart Publishing, 2015), 349.

[66] The reference to jurisdiction was intended to be read narrowly and robustly, capturing the 'the narrow sense of whether or not the tribunal had the authority to make the inquiry' – not the meaning that had 'plagued' jurisprudence for years ([59]). See Mullan, 'Unresolved Issues on the Standard of Review' (2013) 42 AQ 1 and Thomas Lipton, 'Justifying True Questions of Jurisdiction' (2015) 46 Ottawa Law Rev 275.

[67] *Dunsmuir*, above n. 55, [51]–[54].

language of categories, these presumptions do not repudiate the commitment to an intensity-centred approach. First, they represent situations where the factorial 'analysis required is already deemed to have been performed and need not be repeated'.[68] Secondly, the presumptions can be seen, as Mullan explains, as the application of precedent in circumstances when one or two factors are treated as being determinative.[69] Thirdly, they are generally indicative and rebuttable; that is, they are qualified by words like 'generally' and 'usually'.[70] Finally, they apply in tandem with a factorial test, in the first stage of the supervisory process, where the courts are required to explicitly consider the intensity of review that should be applied.[71] Thus, so-called 'categorisation' in this context operates differently than, say, under the scope of review schema.

The present Canadian approach, in summary, straddles the intensity of review and contextual review models. On the one hand, in the first instance, the intensity of review – either correctness or reasonableness – is settled explicitly; calibration is based on a set of factors and related presumptive categories. The tradition of bringing issues of deference to the fore and addressing them on a preliminary basis continues. On the other hand, if the unreasonableness standard is adopted, a second and further iteration is required. Unreasonableness is context-dependent, such that the depth applied in particular cases turns on the circumstances. This emphasis on contextual reasonableness review bears a stronger allegiance to the unstructured and circumstantial review seen elsewhere in English and New Zealand law, and is discussed in more detail below.[72]

4.2.3   England: Heightened Scrutiny, Light-touch Unreasonableness and Doctrinal Deference

English law's experience with intensity of review, cast in its most explicit form, is most vivid in three particular areas. The first two instances involve variations to the reasonableness principle where the intensity differs from the traditional *Wednesbury* standard. First, a form of heightened scrutiny under which decisions are scrutinised more deeply has been deployed,

---

[68] *Ibid.*, [57].

[69] Mullan, *'Dunsmuir'*, above n. 55.

[70] See e.g. *McLean* v. *British Columbia (Securities Commission)* [2013] 3 SCR 895.

[71] See Green, above n. 63 (only 'partial move to categories'); Diana Ginn, 'New Words for Old Problems' (2010) 37 AQ 317 ('halfway house'). Compare Paul Daly, 'Form Over Substance', above n. 63.

[72] See Section 5.2.3.

under rubrics such as anxious scrutiny, hard look and heightened scrutiny. Secondly, light-touch review has also been relied on, presenting an even more deferential standard than *Wednesbury*. Thirdly, the depth of review in human rights adjudication is often acknowledged to be dependent on context and the proportionality calculus is frequently teamed with the notion of deference to reflect this. There have been some efforts to structure this process by giving the principle of deference doctrinal form (although the non-doctrinal expression of deference is presently preferred).[73]

Heightened scrutiny

The common law's attempts to deviate from the *Wednesbury* form of unreasonableness have been well documented.[74] One of the most heralded developments was the effort taken to afford greater protection to human rights than evident in traditional administrative law. In the years before the Human Rights Act 1998 came into force, the courts began to develop more intensive forms of review under the unreasonableness rubric when (so-called[75]) 'fundamental' or 'constitutional' rights were engaged.[76]

This lowering of the threshold of unreasonableness took a number of different guises. The concept of anxious scrutiny was seeded by the House of Lords in *Bugdaycay*.[77] When considering a series of challenges to the refusal of applications for asylum by refugee, Lord Bridge said:[78]

> [T]he court must, I think, be entitled to subject an administrative decision to the more rigorous examination, to ensure that it is in no way flawed, according to the gravity of the issue which the decision determines. The most fundamental of all human rights is the individual's right to life and when an administrative decision under challenge is said to be one which may put the applicant's life at risk, the basis of the decision must surely call for the most anxious scrutiny.

---

[73] See below.

[74] See e.g. Tom Hickman, *Public Law after the Human Rights Act* (Hart Publishing, 2010); Andrew le Sueur, 'The Rise and Ruin of Unreasonableness?' [2005] JR 32; Paul Craig, 'Judicial Review and Anxious Scrutiny' [2015] PL 60.

[75] For discussion of the contested nature of the adjective, see ch. 3, n. 66.

[76] Hickman, *Public Law*, above n. 74, 18 and 105; David Dyzenhaus, Murray Hunt and Michael Taggart, 'The Principle of Legality in Administrative Law' (2001) 1 OUCLJ 5, 19; Michael Taggart, 'Proportionality, Deference, *Wednesbury*' [2008] NZ Law Rev 424, 433–5; P.P. Craig, 'Substantive Legitimate Expectations in Community and Domestic Law' (1996) 55 CLJ 289, 292; Michael Fordham, 'Surveying the Grounds' in Peter Leyland and Terry Woods (eds.), *Administrative Law Facing the Future* (Oxford University Press, 1997), 184, 197.

[77] *Bugdaycay*, above n. 28, 531.

[78] *Ibid.*, 531. See also Lord Templeman's remarks (537). These sentiments were subsequently echoed by Lord Ackner in *Brind*, above n. 28, 757.

The flexibility of the unreasonableness principle, along with the need for the administration to provide greater justification in cases where human rights are affected, was also acknowledged in *Smith*, where service men and women sought to overturn a policy preventing gays and lesbians from serving in the military:[79]

> This Court may not interfere with the exercise of an administrative discretion on substantive grounds save where it is satisfied that decision is unreasonable in the sense of being beyond the range of responses open to a reasonable decision maker. But in judging whether the decision maker has exceeded this margin of appreciation, the human rights context is important. The more substantial the interference with human rights the more the Court will require by way of justification before it is satisfied that the decision was reasonable ...

The Court accepted that the fact that the policy concerned 'innate qualities of a very personal kind' and had a 'profound effect on their careers and prospects' weighed in favour of greater scrutiny of the basis for the policy.[80] However, while this factor supported the need for increased scrutiny, it was not decisive; the judges did not engage in the probing analysis contemplated by that approach and dismissed the challenge. Other factors noted by the Court pointed towards a more deferential approach (such as significant policy content, limited judicial expertise on the issue, and legislature progressing reform of policy).[81] One reading is that the countervailing values of both vigilance and restraint cancelled each other out.[82] Regardless, the principle in *Smith* continues be relied on to support intense scrutiny of the substance of the decision.

This principle was built on and later characterised as a 'sliding-scale of review'.[83] For example, in *Mahmood*, Laws LJ commended the language of a continuum:[84]

> [A] fundamental right ... is engaged in the case ... There is ... what may be called a sliding scale of review; the graver the impact of the decision in

---

[79] *Smith*, above n. 28, 554 (adopting the submissions of Pannick QC, counsel for the service men and women). For subsequent endorsement, see e.g. *Lord Saville*, above n. 28, 1872.

[80] *Smith*, above n. 28, 554.

[81] *Ibid.*, 556.

[82] Aileen Kavanagh, *Constitutional Review under the UK Human Rights Act* (Cambridge University Press, 2009), 250; le Sueur, 'Unreasonableness?', above n. 74, 39 and 42; Jeffrey Jowell, 'Beyond the Rule of Law' [2000] PL 671, 682 (the Court 'paid lip service to heightened scrutiny').

[83] *Begbie*, above n. 15, 1130; *R (Mahmood)* v. *Secretary of State for the Home Department* [2001] 1 WLR 840, 849; *R (Asif Javed)* v. *Secretary of State for the Home Department* [2002] QB 129, [49]; *Sheffield City Council* v. *Smart* [2002] EWCA Civ 4, [42].

[84] *Mahmood*, above n. 83, [16] and [19].

question upon the individual affected by it, the more substantial the justification that will be required. It is in the nature of the human condition that cases where, objectively, the individual is most gravely affected will be those where what we have come to call his fundamental rights are or are said to be put in jeopardy.

Again, while the circumstances suggested increased intensity of review (impact on the applicant's family life), even this deeper scrutiny did not lead to the vitiation of the decision (deportation of an illegal entrant).

Since the Human Rights Act 1998 came into force, reliance on this approach diminished.[85] The more direct protection and intensive review under the Human Rights Act was seen as being more powerful than its common law equivalent.[86] However, somewhat out of the blue, the Supreme Court in *Kennedy* v. *Charity Commission* returned to, and explicitly embraced, the variable form of unreasonableness and more intensive scrutiny.[87] In relation to the review, on substantive grounds, of the Charity Commission's refusal to allow a journalist access to information about a particular charity, Lord Mance recorded that the 'common law no longer insists on the uniform application of the rigid test of irrationality once thought applicable under the so-called *Wednesbury* principle'.[88] A more contextual approach is required, he said, notably endorsing remarks from Lord Carnwath in an earlier case where he spoke of the determination of a particular 'intensity of review'.[89] The constitutional context in the case, particularly the principles of accountability and transparency raised, justified the Court 'plac[ing] itself so far as possible in the same position as

---

[85] See e.g. *R (Gibson)* v. *Crown Court at Winchester* [2004] 1 WLR 1623; *R (Razgar)* v. *Secretary of State for the Home Department* [2004] 2 AC 368; *R (da Silva)* v. *Director of Public Prosecutions* [2006] All ER (D) 215; *R (OM)* v. *Secretary of State for Home Department* [2012] EWHC 3395. For non-human rights cases, see e.g. *IBA Healthcare Ltd* v. *Office of Fair Trading* [2004] ICR 1364; *R (Bradley)* v. *Work and Pensions Secretary* [2009] QB 114, [71]–[72]; *R (Equitable Members Action Group)* v. *H.M. Treasury* [2009] NLJR 1514, [66] (review of decisions to reject recommendations of Ombudsman).

[86] Mark Elliott, *Beatson, Matthews and Elliott's Administrative Law* (4th edn, Oxford University Press, 2011), 249 and 252; le Sueur, 'Unreasonableness?', above n. 74, [9]–[17].

[87] [2014] 2 WLR 808.

[88] *Ibid.*, [51] (Lord Mance; Lord Neuberger, Lord Clarke, Lord Sumption agreeing); see also [133] (Lord Toulson).

[89] *Ibid.*, [53], referring to *IBA Healthcare Ltd* v. *Office of Fair Trading* [2004] ICR 1364, [90]–[92]. On this point, Lord Carnwath himself stood by his then comments but noted that 'the jurisdictional basis for the more flexible approach, and its practical consequences in different legal and factual contexts, remain uncertain and open to debate' ([246]). Lord Mance also raised, but did not decide, whether proportionality (overlaid with varying intensity) may provide useful structure for the analysis ([54]).

the Charity Commission' when reviewing the request for information.[90] In other words, the Court applies a style of correctness review – but one in which the Court may still give 'weight' to the Commission's original evaluation.[91] This acknowledgement of variable intensity in the unreasonableness ground was also echoed, soon after, in *Pham* v. *Secretary of State for the Home Department*.[92]

Light-touch review

The second instance of the test for unreasonableness being treated as a sliding-scale of review is in the class of cases described as 'light-touch review'.[93] Sometimes described as 'super-*Wednesbury*',[94] the courts have occasionally applied an even more deferential test for unreasonableness than found in *Wednesbury*. The judicial focus is more on any flagrant impropriety on the part of the decision-maker, rather than any defects in the decision itself.[95] As noted earlier, it is possible to treat this as amounting to a variegation of unreasonableness or circumscription of the grounds of review; I prefer the former because the development of this method has generally been undertaken in the name of irrationality or unreasonableness.[96]

In *Nottinghamshire*, presented with a challenge to the funding formula for local authorities ultimately approved by the House of Commons, Lord Scarman said the decision was 'not open to challenge on the grounds of irrationality short of the extremes of bad faith, improper motive, or

---

[90] *Kennedy*, above n. 87, [56].

[91] *Ibid.*, [56], [132]. This approach picks up the role of the weight principle in contextual review (see Section 5.2.4) but it is unclear whether the Supreme Court intended this to be a style of review of general application or merely a feature of the more intensive depth of scrutiny.

[92] [2015] 1 WLR 1591, [60], [94] and [109], citing *Kennedy*, above n. 87.

[93] De Smith (6th edn), 596.

[94] Elliott, *Administrative Law*, above n. 86, 248. However, confusingly, the term is also used by a few commentators to describe more intensive forms of unreasonableness: le Sueur, 'Unreasonableness?', above n. 74, 39; T.R. Hickman 'The Reasonableness Principle' (2004) 63 CLJ 166, 186.

[95] De Smith, oddly, appears to equate the language of 'outrageous' employed in *CCSU* v. *Minister of Civil Service* [1985] AC 374 and 'arbitrary' in *R (Pro-Life Alliance)* v. *British Broadcasting Corporation* [2004] 1 AC 185. While these cases undoubtedly pose a high threshold, unlike *Nottinghamshire*, above n. 5, and *Hammersmith*, above n. 5, they are not markedly different from *Wednesbury*. Indeed, there is no suggestion in his speech in *CCSU* that Lord Diplock intended that he was contemplating a threshold that differs from the *Wednesbury* approach from before.

[96] See Section 3.2.2 above.

manifest absurdity".[97] Similarly, in *Hammersmith*, in the context of the capping of local authority charges by a minister ultimately approved by the House of Commons, Lord Bridge spoke of intervention only when the decision-maker 'acted in bad faith, or for an improper motive, or [the actions were] so absurd that he must have taken leave of his senses".[98] In both cases, the high degree of policy and involvement of the elective body were critical factors supporting this very deferential approach.

Doctrinal deference

Since the adoption of the Human Rights Act, English courts have grappled with different devices to operate in conjunction with proportionality in order to recognise and reflect concerns about the legitimacy of judicial adjudication on human rights questions.[99] Some manifestations of deference in this context emulate the intensity of review method (others, which are more unstructured, are discussed later in relation to contextual review).

Once the Human Rights Act became operative, the courts spoke of the need for some form of deference or respect towards the balance drawn by the administration on rights-matters.[100] Early cases tended to express the concept in terms of a 'discretionary area of judgement'.[101] However, this zonal or categorical approach fell out of favour. Instead, in the *Belmarsh Prison* case, Lord Bingham said questions of deference were better seen in terms of a continuum:[102]

> The more purely political (in a broad or narrow sense) a question is, the more appropriate it will be for political resolution and the less likely it is to be an appropriate matter for judicial decision. The smaller, therefore, will

[97] *Nottinghamshire*, above n. 5, 247. See recently, perhaps, *R (Rotherham Borough Council)* v. *Secretary of State for Business, Innovation and Skills* [2014] WLR(D) 338.

[98] *Hammersmith*, above n. 5, 597.

[99] Kavanagh, *Constitutional Review*, above n. 82, 240; Conor Gearty, *Principles of Human Rights Adjudication* (Oxford University Press, 2005), 141 (unusually preferring the terms 'judicial restraint' or 'institutional competence' in relation to whether protected rights have been infringed; but 'judicial deference' in relation to the remedial choice under ss. 3 and 4).

[100] See P.P. Craig, 'The Courts, the Human Rights Act and Judicial Review' (2001) 117 LQR 589, 589–95. Notably, the courts eschewed the European Convention concept of 'margin of appreciation' developed by the Strasbourg court to reflect the structural subsidiarity underlying the European system. See *R (Kebeline)* v. *Director of Public Prosecutions* [2000] 2 AC 326 and *Brown* v. *Stott* [2003] 1 AC 681, rejecting the language from *Handyside* v. *United Kingdom* (1976) 1 EHRR 737 and *Sunday Times* v. *United Kingdom* (1979) 2 EHRR 245.

[101] *Kebeline*, above n. 100, 380. See e.g. *R* v. *Lambert* [2002] QB 1112, [16]; *Brown* v. *Stott*, above n. 100; and *R (Pretty)* v. *Department of Public Prosecutions* [2002] 1 AC 800, [2].

[102] *A* v. *Secretary of State for the Home Department* [2005] 2 AC 68, [29].

be the potential role of the court ... Conversely, the greater the legal content
of any issue, the greater the potential role of the court ...

This characterisation bears a strong analogy with the sliding-scale form
of unreasonableness. An explicit role is marked out for the determination
of the depth of review, the degree of which modulates along a continuum.
This style of approach has been described by commentators as *doctrinal
deference*.[103] Laws LJ's dissenting judgment in *International Transport* is
also often cited in support of a doctrinal role for deference.[104] He argued
there 'is a sufficient citation of authority from which to draw together the
principles now being developed by the courts for the ascertainment of the
degree of deference which the judges will pay, or the scope of the discretionary area of judgment which they will cede, to the democratic powers
of government'.[105] In the particular case, the existence of several factors
weighing in favour of deference persuaded Laws LJ to reject a challenge
under the Human Rights Act to a regime which penalised lorry drivers,
on a reverse onus basis, for carrying clandestine illegal entrants into the
country.[106]

   While the courts continue to afford deference to judgements made
by the administration in some circumstances, manifesting that restraint
in doctrinal form has since fallen out of favour. The current preference,
expressed by the House of Lords in *Huang*, is for questions of deference,
restraint or respect to be treated merely as matters of weight, without
being given any particular form of doctrinal scaffolding.[107] The nature and
form of judicial deference or restraint continues, however, to be vigorously

---

[103] Hickman, *Public Law*, above n. 74, 172; Jeff A. King, 'Institutional Approaches to
     Judicial Restraint' (2008) 28 OJLS 409, 411. See also Richard Gordon, 'Two Dogmas of
     Proportionality' [2011] JR 18 and Alan D.P. Brady, *Proportionality and Deference under the
     UK Human Rights Act* (Cambridge University Press, 2012), 24.
[104] *International Transport Roth GmbH* v. *Secretary of State for the Home Department [2003]*
     QB 728. The principles articulated by Laws LJ were later endorsed by other Court of Appeal
     judges: see e.g. *Shala* v. *Secretary of State for the Home Department* [2003] INLR 349, [12]
     (Keene LJ) and *A* v. *Secretary of State for the Home Department* [2004] QB 335, [40] and
     [81] (Lord Woolf CJ and Brooke LJ).
[105] *International Transport*, above n. 104, [81]. Laws LJ identified four key factors relevant
     to the assessment of the amount of deference to be applied: in general terms, democratic
     genesis; balancing or qualified questions; constitutional responsibility for subject-matter;
     and relative expertise.
[106] *Ibid.*, [209]. Simon Brown and Parker LJJ both ruled, however, that Convention rights
     were breached by the regime.
[107] *Huang*, above n. 26. See also *R (Animal Defenders International)* v. *Secretary of State for
     Culture, Media and Sport* [2008] 1 AC 1312, [33] (restraint as 'weight'). See generally
     Section 5.2.4.

debated amongst the academy and bar, suggesting that the last word may not yet have been spoken on deference in this context.[108]

4.2.4   New Zealand: Variegated Unreasonableness

New Zealand courts have also promoted and deployed a number of different formulations of the reasonableness ground.[109] Resorting to increased intensity of review based on a sliding scale or reliance on the intermediate category of unreasonableness is now commonplace in the High Court and, to a lesser extent, the Court of Appeal. Justice Wild's endorsement of the concept of the sliding-scale of unreasonableness in *Wolf* v. *Minister of Immigration* has assumed particular currency, despite the remarks at High Court level not yet receiving direct endorsement at higher levels.[110] After canvassing domestic and overseas authority, he said 'the time has come to state – or really to clarify' that the tests for unreasonableness expressed in *CCSU* and its local equivalent, *Woolworths*, 'are not, or should no longer be, the invariable or universal tests of "unreasonableness" applied in New Zealand public law'.[111] Instead, Wild J commended an intermediate standard of simple unreasonableness, with the selection of the appropriate form depending on context.[112] Other courts have also referred to or applied similar increased intensity of review under the reasonableness ground, adopting a variety of labels: 'hard look' or 'anxious scrutiny', 'sliding scale', or Wild J's intermediate standard of reasonableness.[113]

---

[108] Notable members of the doctrinal camp include Jeffrey Jowell, Murray Hunt, Aileen Kavanagh, Alison Young and Paul Daly (see Section 4.3). Those advocating non-doctrinal deference include Tom Hickman, T.R.S. Allan and Richard Gordon (see Section 5.3). See also King, 'Restraint', above n. 103.

[109] See generally Dean R. Knight, 'A Murky Methodology' (2008) 6 NZJPIL 117; 'Mapping the Rainbow of Review' (2010) NZ Law Rev 393; Taggart, 'Proportionality', above n. 76.

[110] [2004] NZAR 414. See also Baragwanath J's articulation of multi-layered expressions of unreasonableness and substantive review: *Ports of Auckland Ltd* v. *Auckland City Council* [1999] 1 NZLR 601; *Tupou* v. *Removal Review Authority* [2001] NZAR 696; *Progressive Enterprises* v. *North Shore City Council* [2006] NZRMA 72; *Mihos* v. *Attorney-General* [2008] NZAR 177.

[111] *Wolf*, above n. 110, [47]; referring to *CCSU*, above n. 95, and *Wellington City Council* v. *Woolworths New Zealand Ltd (No 2)* [1996] 2 NZLR 537.

[112] *Wolf*, above n. 110), [47]. Wild J expressly pointed to the following aspects of the decision: '[U]pon who made it; by what process; what the decision involves (that is, its subject matter and the level of policy content in it) and the importance of the decision to those affected by it, in terms of its potential impact upon, or consequences for, them.'

[113] See e.g. *Pharmaceutical Management Agency Ltd* v. *Roussel Uclaf Australia Pty Ltd* [1998] NZAR 58 ('hard look'); *Pring* v. *Wanganui District Council* [1999] NZRMA 519;

Appellate courts have so far been more coy about variegated unreasonableness. The Court of Appeal has occasionally remarked that unreasonableness must be treated as a contextual concept, something that inevitably varies in the circumstances.[114] The Supreme Court has not directly addressed common law unreasonableness; the indications are that, on the one hand, the Court will readily accept that unreasonableness is contextual but, on the other hand, will be sceptical about attempts to structure that contextualism under rubrics like anxious scrutiny or sliding scales of intensity.[115]

4.2.5   Conclusion

Intensity of review brings the mediation of the balance between restraint and vigilance into the foreground of the supervisory jurisdiction. Huscroft, speaking of the Canadian framework, distils the approach down to an explicit style of reasoning:[116] 'It is simply a means of structuring the discourse on deference.' Openness in the reasoning and calibration process is prioritised, with conceptual considerations brought to the fore.

In Canada the determination of the appropriate degree of judicial restraint (for many years, expressed in terms of forms of reasonableness and correctness, and based on a set of enumerated 'pragmatic and functional factors') is the first step in the supervisory process. This variegation of unreasonableness, and potential that the depth of review may be explicitly modulated to take into account the circumstances, has also found its way into aspects of English and New Zealand law – particularly where human rights are engaged.

4.3   Conceptual Underpinnings

The intensity of review schema captures those scholars who argue for an even more flexible and transparent approach to supervisory review. While

---

B v. *Commissioner of Inland Revenue* [2004] 2 NZLR 86; *Huang* v. *Minister of Immigration* [2007] NZAR 163; *Wright* v. *Attorney-General* [2006] NZAR 66; *S* v. *Chief Executive of the Department of Labour* [2006] NZAR 234; *Dunne* v. *CanWest TVWorks Ltd* [2005] NZAR 577.

[114] See e.g. *Waitakere City Council* v. *Lovelock* [1997] 2 NZLR 385; *Pharmaceutical*, above n. 113; *Pring*, above n. 113; *Discount Brands Ltd* v. *Northcote Mainstreet Inc* [2004] 3 NZLR 619 (CA); *Conley* v. *Hamilton City Council* [2008] 1 NZLR 789.

[115] Knight, 'Mapping the Rainbow of Review', above n. 109.

[116] Grant Huscroft, 'Judicial Review from *CUPE* to *CUPE*' in Grant Huscroft and Michael Taggart (eds.), *Inside and Outside Canadian Administrative Law* (University of Toronto Press, 2006), 296, 297.

still favouring a doctrinal approach, scholars such as Daly, Elliott, King and Hunt contend that the inherently variable nature of judicial review ought to be manifest. The modulation of review ought to be embraced, either through explicit standards of review, continuums of intensity or explicit principles of deference/restraint. In doing so, a more complicated and normative judicial role is envisaged. Questions of legitimacy cannot be solved on a priori basis and must be confronted in individual cases; however, this must not lead to unfettered judicial discretion and the assessment of intensity of review must be structured, through doctrinal principles, in order that it reflects the limitations of the judicial role.

4.3.1   Paul Daly: Tripartite Standards Informed by Legislative Intent

Daly argues for the crystallisation of principles of restraint into doctrinal form, in the form of schema of three standards of review (like the former Canadian position). Notably, he rejects unstructured or non-doctrinal forms of deference (what he describes as epistemic deference). But legislative intent looms large in Daly's normative framework. Selection of the appropriate standard, he argues, should be exclusively determined according to the legislative language and sources. Although he seeks to avoid such categorisation, his doctrinal framework is born of the ultra vires school.

First, Daly only makes a brief explicit foray into the ultra vires debate, self-styling himself as 'chart[ing] a middle course between two extremes'.[117] For him, the common law school is too ready to ignore statutory provisions in the pursuance of principles of good administration based independently on the rule of law. On the other hand, he characterises the approach of the ultra vires school as being artificial in its treatment of legislative intent:[118]

> [I]f the ultra vires principle can be relied upon to justify any decision reached by a reviewing court, the judicial obligation to give effect to legislative intent may be dissolved into an elixir of judicial creativity.

His approach, he contends, takes legislative intent more seriously, while still recognising that the responsibility for fashioning the principles of good administration falls on the courts. But his embrace of legislative

---

[117] Paul Daly, *A Theory of Deference in Administrative Law* (Cambridge University Press, 2012), 290.
[118] *Ibid.*

intent, the centrality of delegation theory, and the general tenor of his scholarship suggest a stronger alignment with the ultra vires school. The key ingredient in the determinant of the applicable judicial approach is the statutory text; to that extent, he echoes the analysis of modified ultra vires proponents like Forsyth and Elliott. '[C]ourts must give effect to legislative intent.'[119] Not only is legislative intent the guiding principle for Daly, his conception of legislative intent is cast narrowly, based on the text: '[legislative intent] is the "formal specification of the act" ... not to the literal intentions of legislators'; in other words, '[w]hat is relevant is the language of the statute'.[120]

Part of this might be explainable by the fact he approaches the principles of good administration, in some respects, with a partial lens. He locates his analysis in judicial restraint and deference, and assumes the courts have some role in reviewing the substance of administrative decisions.[121] He excludes questions of procedural fairness on the basis that, according to him, the current orthodoxy provides that these are matters properly within the province of the judiciary on which the courts have the 'final say'. The principles of good administration are negative in character, circumscribing the mandate of the courts to review. He does not address the positive dimension, namely, from where the courts acquire their mandate to review generally. This is consistent with the orientation of North American jurisprudence, on which he relies heavily, where judicial restraint is the starting point. This contrasts with Anglo-Australasian jurisprudence where scrutiny and intervention, expressed in generalised grounds of review, dominate.[122]

Secondly, Daly's preferred schematic model is based on the adoption of a doctrinal form of deference.[123] He argues that existing judicial review doctrine which requires the application of a variable standard of review (namely, jurisdictional questions, interpretations of law, exercises of discretion, and political questions) should be reformed to reflect the three standards of curial deference.[124] The model (or 'ideal-type'[125]) he promotes for adoption in Canada, England and the United States manifests three

---

[119]　*Ibid.*, 38.

[120]　*Ibid.*, 43.

[121]　*Ibid.*, 3.

[122]　For Daly's own contrast between grounds and standards of review, see *ibid.*, 258–62.

[123]　*Ibid.*, ch. 4.

[124]　Like Canadian courts, Daly treats procedural fairness as sitting outside any deference regime.

[125]　*Ibid.*, 288.

variable standards of review: correctness, unreasonableness and manifest unreasonableness.

The legislative intent principle operates as the lodestar for his justification of deference and his development of a general schema. Variable intensity of review – which he supports – is justified (only) by legislative intent. In rare cases, where the legislature has directed a variable standard of review, the courts ought to apply this; similarly, in the absence of an express direction, 'a variable standard of review may nonetheless be required, based on a proper consideration of the relevant statutory provisions'.[126] He elaborates:[127]

> The process of interpretation of a statute may indicate that the legislature intended to delegate power for particular reasons; because the extent of the delegation of power and at least some of the reason for the delegation of power will be ascertainable from the statute, reviewing courts should take them into account in developing the general principles of judicial review.

Daly dismisses the separation of powers as providing an alternative justifying principle (drawing particularly on scholarship addressing deference in the United States).[128] For him, (judicial) deference is the corollary of (legislative) delegation. It is the nature and extent of the legislative delegation of power to the administration which counsels in favour of judicial restraint:[129]

> First, because of the existence of a delegation of power to a delegated decision-maker, courts should adopt a secondary, reviewing stance relative to the delegated decision-maker. Secondly, because of the existence of variable delegations of power, courts should follow an approach which is capable of varying from case to case ... If powers of varying extent have been delegated to delegated decision-makers, courts should develop and follow a variable approach in general to judicial review.

Thirdly, Daly argues a doctrinal form of deference is to be preferred and, specifically, to be preferred over what he describes as 'epistemic' or unstructured deference.[130] He suggests it has the potential to 'induce a greater degree of rigour on the part of reviewing courts' and that doctrinal analysis is 'a valuable means of giving guidance to judges as to how to fulfil

---

[126] Daly, above n. 117, 37.
[127] *Ibid.*, 37.
[128] *Ibid.*, 44.
[129] *Ibid.*, 60.
[130] In general terms, epistemic deference describes judicial restraint given effect to through the application, on an unstructured basis, of weight and judgement by judges. See the discussion of contextual review in ch. 5.

the substantive values underlying their legal system'.[131] Daly is also quick to reject grounds of review as a possible means to give effect to deference, even though he admits that 'they can perhaps be described as constituting an example of doctrinal deference in their own right'.[132] His main objections are that grounds are ad hoc, are too interventionist, and bear little relationship to legislative intent.[133] Daly also summarily rejects deference deployed by reasoning directly from constitutional principle (in other words, instinctive or non-doctrinal deference, or what he labels 'epistemic' deference). For him, deference without doctrine is 'troubling' and 'carries with it the possibility of inconsistency and uncertainty'.[134]

Finally, the selection of the appropriate standard of review should, Daly says, principally be informed by the extent of the legislative delegation. Legislatures delegate variable extents of power to public bodies and officials, which he says 'counsels not only judicial restraint, but variable amounts of judicial restraint'.[135] The corollary of this variable grant of authority is that, he argues, reviewing courts must adopt a variable or nuanced standard of review. The courts must respect the legislature's choice to delegate authority to the administration and not to the courts.[136] 'A delegation of power to a delegated decision-maker', he says, 'functions as a directive to courts to follow a restrained approach.'[137] However, if no delegation of power has been made, then no deference is required.[138] And the plethora of types of administrative decisions, differing processes for making such decisions and various accountability mechanisms translates into 'variable degrees of power'.[139] Daly argues this variability mandates variable standards of review; otherwise, 'the decision to delegate varying degrees of power would be undermined'.[140] Ultimately, then, a conservative version of the separation of powers underscores his position.

---

[131] Daly, above n. 117, 34, 137.
[132] *Ibid.*, fn. 187 and 258–62. The 'grounds' he describes are numerous, beyond the tripartite formulation (259–60). He also goes on to accept that grounds might still be useful as indicia of unreasonableness (262).
[133] *Ibid.*, 261.
[134] *Ibid.*, 34.
[135] *Ibid.*, 5.
[136] Daly argues delegation to the courts may happen in one of two ways: *directly* (vesting the decision in them) or indirectly (providing for a de novo right of appeal) (*ibid.*, 54).
[137] *Ibid.*, 55.
[138] *Ibid.*, 54.
[139] *Ibid.*, 55.
[140] *Ibid.*

He adds that 'practical justifications', as evidenced in the statutory scheme, may also justify judicial restraint.[141] Practical considerations related to the judicial function – such as expertise, complexity, democratic and procedural legitimacy – are often deployed to support a more circumspect judicial role.[142] But Daly contends these matters should only influence the extent of curial deference if 'it can plausibly be inferred that the practical justifications influenced the decision to delegate power'.[143] Daly's singular focus on legislative intent means he concedes the practical considerations relevant to curial deference are restricted to those that 'can only be ascertained by means of a proper consideration of the relevant statutory provisions'.[144] In other words, not only must a reviewing court assess the extent of the power delegated, it must also assess the reasons for the delegation.[145]

Daly therefore presents an unusual mix: a commitment to an old-fashioned model of legislative intent based in a formalistic allocation of functions, but overlaid on top of modern framework for judicial adjudication.

4.3.2   Mark Elliott: Calibration of Intrinsic and Adjudicative Deference

A long-standing and passionate defender of the ultra vires theory, Elliott too favours a doctrinal approach to deference. His normative framework for giving effect to deference in doctrinal form is relatively formative and undeveloped, though he draws an interesting distinction between the types of deference which may arise in the supervisory process and a possible need for different treatment (starting point deference versus adjudicative deference).

First, Elliott, together with Forsyth,[146] has been instrumental in making a case for ultra vires being the foundation of judicial review. Legislative

---

[141] *Ibid.*, 5.

[142] *Ibid.*, ch. 3, esp. 72–134.

[143] *Ibid.*, 72.

[144] *Ibid.*

[145] *Ibid.*, 70. The expertise and democratic legitimacy of the delegated decision-maker, along with complexity of the problem and procedural legitimacy, are to be taken into account, but in terms of what was 'contemplated by the legislature'. He accepts that not every aspect will be evident in the statutory provisions, so 'reliance on some background understandings will be necessary'.

[146] Christopher Forsyth and Mark Elliott, 'The Legitimacy of Judicial Review' [2003] PL 286. However, Elliott's scholarship nowadays tends to be more progressive and is less committed to the formalist endeavour than Forsyth.

intent, they say, continues to be the foundation stone. It applies indirectly, though, through a presumption of compliance with the rule of law:[147]

> [W]hen Parliament enacts legislation which (typically) confers wide discretionary power and which makes no explicit reference to the controls which should regulate the exercise of the power, the courts are constitutionally entitled – and constitutionally right – to assume that it was Parliament's intention to legislate in conformity with the rule of law principle. This means that Parliament is properly to be regarded as having conferred upon that decision-maker only such power as is consistent with that principle.

However, the implementation of the legislature's general intention – 'transforming ... into detailed, legally enforceable rules of fairness and rationality' – is for the courts 'through the incremental methodology of the forensic process'.[148] This presumption is deployed by Elliott to distance himself from traditional ultra vires or direct legislative intent theory, particularly 'the implausible assumption that Parliament directly intends the myriad principles of judicial review'.[149] However, Elliott is forced to acknowledge there remains an artificiality about this presumption.[150]

The corollary of the ultra vires theory promoted by Elliott, even when modified from its stricter origins, is the centrality of a jurisdictional analysis: '[A]ll of judicial review is about jurisdiction: is the action under scrutiny within or outside the power of the decision-maker?'[151] If within those limits, then the courts should not interfere; if outside, the courts should. The limits identified here by Elliott are not restricted to express legislative terms though; they also include general principles developed by the courts in accordance with the powerful, but artificial, legislative presumption. This requires Elliott to acknowledge that the expression of the constitutional principles which govern judicial intervention have inherent and intrinsic normative value independent of legislative intention. However, his attempt to draw some connection between those values and the legislature is aimed at presenting some form of harmonious constitutional order:[152]

---

[147] Mark Elliott, *The Constitutional Foundations of Judicial Review* (Hart Publishing, 2000), 109.

[148] *Ibid.*

[149] Mark Elliott, *Beatson, Matthews and Elliott's Administrative Law* (4th edn, Oxford University Press, 2011), 22.

[150] Elliott, *Foundations*, above n. 147, 24.

[151] Elliott, *Administrative Law*, above n. 149, 33.

[152] Elliott, *Foundations*, above n. 147, 113.

> [S]uch an approach recognises the pervasiveness of the values on which
> the constitution is founded, such that judicial vindication of the rule of
> law through judicial review is seen to fulfil, rather than conflict with, the
> endeavours of the legislature.

In other words, legislative intent operates, in his vision, as a legitimising
device to promote collaboration rather than combat between the branches
of government.

Elliott's scholarship has traditionally assumed the currency of a categorical framework based on grounds of review. However, his more recent
work on the role of deference suggests a move away from existing legal
division in favour of an explicitly variable approach, where the calibration
of intensity of review takes centre-stage.

The existing grounds of review and traditional dichotomies have fea-
tured prominently in Elliott's scholarship and he has engaged in debates
which assume the continuance of that style of reasoning.[153] His ultra vires
orientation often means the analysis also manifests a concern for the
maintenance of the jurisdictional demarcation.[154] Within that framework,
Elliott has always been prepared to recognise the role that variability and
deference plays in judicial review.[155]

His more recent work takes an interesting turn though, away from the
categorical towards the explicitly variable. On the question of variability or deference in relation to substantive review, he argues in favour of
independent and explicit recognition of deference.[156] He encourages us to
'move beyond a doctrinal focus which results (depending on one's preferences) either in a bifurcated approach or one wedded to a specific doctrine
(such as proportionality)'; instead he calls on us to concentrate 'on calibrating substantive review by reference to the normative and institutional
and constitutional considerations which ought properly shape it'.[157]

Elliott's solution distinguishes between two different types of deference:
(a) intrinsic deference; and (b) adjudicative deference. *Intrinsic deference* is

---

[153] See e.g. Mark Elliott, 'Unlawful Representations, Legitimate Expectations and Estoppel in
Public Law' [2003] JR 71; 'Legitimate Expectation, Consistency and Abuse of Power [2005]
JR 281; '*Wednesbury* and Proportionality' [2002] JR 97; 'Proportionality and Deference' in
Christopher Forsyth and others (eds.), *Effective Judicial Review* (Oxford University Press,
2010), 264.

[154] See e.g. Elliott, *Administrative Law*, above n. 149, ch. 2.

[155] See e.g. Elliott, 'Proportionality and Deference', above n. 153; 'Judicial Review's Scope,
Foundations and Purposes' [2012] NZ Law Rev 75.

[156] Mark Elliott, 'From Bifurcation to Calibration' in Hanna Wilberg and Mark Elliott, *The
Scope and Intensity of Substantive Review* (Hart Publishing, 2015), 61.

[157] *Ibid.*, 71.

explained as the judicial assessment of the appropriate operative standard of justification. In other words, what is the nature of the burden or benchmark that must be met by the decision-maker in any particular case? Elliott argues that 'the operative burden of justification ought to be informed by the normative significance of the value impacted by the impugned decision'.[158] The general principle, he says, is 'the more important the norm threatened by a decision, the greater should be the onus on the decision-maker to justify it' – echoing Lord Bridge's remarks in *Bugdaycay*.[159] Such burden-setting and intrinsic deference, Elliott argues, 'are merely two sides of one coin'.[160] Elliott contrasts intrinsic deference arising from burden-setting with *adjudicative deference*, which he suggests arises later when the court is assessing whether or not that burden has been discharged.[161] Adjudicative deference focuses on the institutional and constitutional relationship between the court and the primary decision-maker; that is, whether the decision-maker's view should be respected or given particular weight because the decision-maker is in a better position than the court to assess whether the burden has been sufficiently discharged. Thus, adjudicative deference captures concerns about relative expertise, institutional competence and democratic legitimacy. While having some sympathy with the idea of epistemic deference, where the views of others are given respect in the course of the deliberation process,[162] Elliott seems to contemplate that such deference will assume a more tangible role in the reasoning process.

Elliott's main goal in this contribution is to animate these different types of deference, although he acknowledges 'the two types of deference exist not as entirely separate concepts, but as distinct-yet-related aspects of a single concept'.[163] There may be some interaction or elision between the two. For example, if a heavy burden is set, issues of institutional competence when assessing whether the burden has been discharged may become more acute and may necessitate doses of adjudicative deference; in contrast, if a low justification-burden is set, questions of relative expertise and competence may not arise.[164] But Elliott strongly argues that the

---

[158] *Ibid.*, 76.
[159] *Ibid.* Notably, Elliott makes a plea for greater granularisation than a simple rights and non-rights dichotomy seen in the bifurcation debate though, arguing that the 'normative pull' of some rights will be stronger than others, as will be true in non-rights cases too.
[160] *Ibid.*, 80.
[161] *Ibid.*
[162] See ch. 5.
[163] *Ibid.*, 87.
[164] *Ibid.*, 83.

relatively abstract burden-setting task should not to be conflated with the fact-laden burden-discharge assessment:[165]

> Separating out intrinsic and adjudicative deference is helpful because it acknowledges the distinction between, on the one hand, the level of review that is normatively justified and, on the other, the level of review that can appropriately be supplied given the particularities of the individual case.

Elliott's analysis assumes that modulation of the depth of scrutiny infiltrates the curial task. Indeed, he seeks to dissect the process of modulation into discrete concepts. He leaves the question of how that modulation should be expressed unanswered but his preference for a doctrinal solution is obvious. On the one hand, he acknowledges existing doctrinal grounds of review implicitly seek to do much of the intrinsic deference, pointing especially to the understanding that the justification-burden is heavier in cases where proportionality applies rather than unreasonableness.[166] But he suggests this distinction is too crude because it 'merely clothes a deeper level of complexity evidenced by significant differences *within* those categories' and the associated labels 'obscure more than they illuminate'.[167] On the other hand, he rejects 'an adoctrinal approach' based in unstructured contextualism – expressly disapproving of the simplicity school's embrace of the 'contextualist impulse'.[168] Instead, he sees his two forms of deference as 'doctrinal constructs' providing a degree of 'structural rigour', although ultimately 'subsidiary to, and reflective of, the deeper considerations – normative, institutional and constitutional that are necessarily in play'.[169] Although only expressed in broad-brush terms, he thus favours a method of modulation that is explicit, doctrinal and brings conceptual considerations into the foreground. Deference should, Elliott argues, occupy 'centre stage, as a tool that helps give concrete meaning to the core concept of justification, and doctrinal shape to the performance of a necessarily contextual judicial task'.[170]

   In general terms, Elliott's work is interesting because it seeks to marry the legislative intent theory with modern notions of deference, in a similar fashion to Daly. Elliott acknowledges the need to move away from existing doctrinal mechanisms controlling and defining the respective allocation

---

[165] *Ibid.*, 84.
[166] *Ibid.*, 73.
[167] *Ibid.*, 74.
[168] *Ibid.*, 88. He names Lord Cooke, Elias CJ and Lord Carnsworth as key proponents of this approach. See the discussion of contextual review (ch. 5).
[169] *Ibid.*, 89.
[170] *Ibid.*, 89.

of authority. More pliant and nuanced – albeit still doctrinal – methodologies are needed to ensure the normative, institutional and constitutional considerations are adequately engaged with when assessing whether a particular decision is sufficiently justified.

4.3.3   Murray Hunt: Due Deference
Elaborated Across-the-Board

Hunt has spoken in favour of the adoption of a doctrine of due deference, not just in human rights adjudication, but also more generally throughout public law.[171] He resists attempts to bifurcate judicial review into rights and non-rights categories and argues that a developed form of due deference is capable of bridging the two territories.[172] Otherwise, he is coy on the ultra vires debate, preferring a collaborative approach to the legislative–judicial relationship which seeks to avoid the source of power question.

First, as noted, Hunt has no enthusiasm for the debate about the source of constitutional authority for judicial review. This, he says, buys into the 'alluring idea of "sovereignty" as a foundational concept' and 'a conceptualisation of public law in terms of competing supremacies'.[173] He labels the competing schools of thought, in relation to the debate as it relates to human rights, as 'democratic positivism' and 'liberal constitutionalism', with their claims for sovereignty of Parliament and the courts respectively. To the contrary, he argues, public power is dispersed and shared amongst a role of constitutional actors and questions of supremacy are inapt. Instead he promotes a collaborative enterprise:[174]

> [A]n alternative approach [is to] not seek to delineate respective zones of competence, or to decide who has the power to define those boundaries, but which begin from the premise that in today's conditions both the courts and the political branches share a commitment *both* to representative democracy and to certain rights, freedoms and basic values.

He argues that it is more productive to abandon the language of sovereignty in favour of the language of justification. Public law discourse should 'reconceive our conceptions of law and legality away from

---

[171] Murray Hunt, 'Sovereignty's Blight' in Nicholas Bamforth and Peter Leyland (eds.), *Public Law in a Multi-Layered Constitution* (Hart Publishing, 2003), 337; 'Against Bifurcation' in David Dyzenhaus, Murray Hunt and Grant Huscroft (eds.), *A Simple Common Lawyer* (Hart Publishing, 2009), 99. For his earlier work on the role of human rights in administrative law, see Murray Hunt, *Using Human Rights in English Courts* (Hart Publishing, 1997).
[172] Hunt, 'Sovereignty's Blight', above n. 171.
[173] *Ibid.*, 339.
[174] *Ibid.*, 340.

formalistic concepts such as the historic will of Parliament, the separation of power and ultra vires towards more substantive concepts of value and reason.[175] Deference then becomes, he contends, the 'crucial mediating concept', where a primary decision-maker earns judicial respect or restraint through the force of their reasoning and justification.[176]

Hunt, accordingly, implicitly rejects an account of judicial review grounded in ultra vires or legislative intent, but his account of the judicial role is also qualified. The judicial supervisory role is self-limited by the concept of justification, grounded in democratic considerations.[177]

Secondly, Hunt has been a long-standing advocate – especially in relation to human rights adjudication – for the adoption of an explicit and doctrinal notion of deference.[178] When deference-talk became fashionable, he attempted to chart a middle ground, between the early 'no-go zone' or non-justiciability type approaches on the one hand, and the strong objections to any role for deference on the other. He argues for a nuanced approach to deference, where restraint is settled on a case-by-case basis through reference to various factors. Notably, Hunt's vision also dictates that particular prominence be given to the assessment of deference in judicial adjudication:[179]

> This will require the explicit articulation of a number of matters which at present are too often buried beneath inappropriate doctrinal tools: the sorts of factors that might warrant a degree of deference from a judicial decision-maker; the specific factors which are in play in a particular case; why the court considers that they require a degree of deference to a particular decision, or an aspect of it; and just how much deference the court considers to be due in the circumstances.

This contemplates the principles being expressed transparently in doctrinal form.

Thirdly, in relation to the factors which influence the variation of intensity or application of deference, Hunt casts the net widely, identifying factors such as relative expertise, the degree of democratic accountability of the decision-maker and the existence of other accountability mechanisms for any judgement made.[180] Particular emphasis is put on the quality of justificatory reasons and the corresponding deference that may arise.[181]

---

[175] *Ibid.*
[176] *Ibid.*
[177] *Ibid.*
[178] Hunt, 'Sovereignty's Blight', above n. 171.
[179] *Ibid.*, 370.
[180] *Ibid.*, 353–4. See also Hunt, 'Bifurcation', above n. 171.
[181] Hunt, 'Sovereignty's Blight', above n. 171; 'Bifurcation', above n. 171, 114. On this point, Hunt echoes Dyzenhaus; see discussion at Section 5.3.4.

Finally, Hunt rejects a bifurcated public law as well. As one of Taggart's former collaborators in the unity project,[182] he laments Taggart's concession to bifurcation. He argues that the unification of public law and reconciliation of methodologies within judicial review should not be abandoned.[183] Again, he sees the solution in reason-giving, justification and due deference:[184]

> [T]o avoid bifurcation we must seek to enshrine a constitutional require-
> ment to give reasons, to understand proportionality as a flexible methodol-
> ogy for ascertaining whether adequate justification for interference with
> fundamental values has been made out, and to redouble our efforts both
> to explain why public law needs a concept of due deference and to provide
> an account of it capable of constraining judges without collapsing into a
> non-justiciability doctrine.

Hunt, therefore, is notable for promoting a vision of due deference, across-the-board, crystallised into doctrinal form. This approach is con-sistent with a number of other human rights scholars who have advocated a doctrinal form of deference in the human rights adjudication,[185] along with the position of some other public law scholars.[186]

---

[182] See e.g. Dyzenhaus, Hunt and Taggart, above n. 76, 19.

[183] Hunt, 'Bifurcation', above n. 171.

[184] *Ibid.*, 120.

[185] Kavanagh, for example, observes that the proportionality enquiry and deference are nec-essarily intertwined. While the sequential structuring of proportionality provides the method for supervisory review, deference provides the intensity by which that method is applied. In other words, she contends proportionality is necessarily a variable standard 'because it can be applied more or less deferentially' and the intensity of application 'will vary according to the multiplicity of factors which obtain in the context of an individual case'. In her work, she then attempts to articulate the various grounds for judicial defer-ence and contexts in which deference is most pronounced. See Kavanagh, *Constitutional Review*, above n. 82, 237; 'Deference or Defiance?' in Grant Huscroft (ed.), *Expounding the Constitution: Essays in Constitutional Theory* (Cambridge University Press, 2008), 184; 'Judicial Restraint in the Pursuit of Justice' (2010) UTLJ 23; 'Defending Deference in Public Law and Constitutional Theory' (2010) 126 LQR 222. Similarly, Young also promotes a doctrinal model where deference is framed in terms of respect and where appropriate weight is given to the opinions of the legislature or executive 'when dealing with contest-able rights-issues'. She argues that whether or not weight should be given depends on an assessment of institutional factors, such as the administration have greater knowledge or expertise or where their decision-making process has greater legitimacy. Young doubts the ability of a non-doctrinal approach to deference to provide necessary coherence, arguing the doctrinal form 'aims to make the judicial process more transparent, thus promoting a culture of justification in both judicial and administrative decision-making.' See Alison L. Young, 'In Defence of Due Deference' (2009) 74 MLR 554; 'Deference, Dialogue and the Search for Legitimacy' (2010) 30 OJLS 815; 'Will You, Won't You, Will You Join in the Deference Dance' (2014) 34 OJLS 375.

[186] See e.g. King, 'Restraint', above n. 103, and Jeffrey Jowell, 'Judicial Deference' [2003] PL 592; 'Judicial Deference and Human Rights' in Paul Craig and Richard Rawlings (eds.),

4.3.4   David Mullan: Effective
and Practical Deference

Mullan's scholarship on deference is generally internally focused: that is, his contribution assumes the existence of a doctrine of deference (as has long been the case in Canada where his writing is generally grounded) and his analysis concentrates on operational aspects of the doctrine. He is generally supportive of the regime centred around deference, where the calibration of intensity is settled explicitly, although he is conscious of efforts to convert this into a fully contextual evaluation.

First, Mullan has not directly entered the ultra vires versus common law debate which has occupied other jurisdictions. However, his leanings towards the common law school can be partly gleaned from his analysis of the constitutional pedigree of deference in Canada (although he observes that these constitutional considerations have not preoccupied the development of a deference framework).[187] Mullan detects a possible tension between the principle of deference and the constitutional mandate of the courts in the Canadian constitution, suggestive perhaps of a judicial duty to assess *all* questions of law according to a correctness standard.[188] However, he concludes that the prevailing view is that correctness review is not actually constitutionalised, at least for intra-jurisdictional questions, and endorses the Supreme Court decision which implies such a conclusion.[189]

Law and Administration in Europe (Oxford University Press, 2003), 67. King supports an 'institutional' approach to deference lying between a formalist model (lacking nuance and constructed on abstract categories based on unrealistic distinctions) and non-doctrinal models (too reliant on judicial discretion, too unpredictable, and too open to accusations of arbitrariness). Accordingly, to King, institutionalists 'focus on the comparative merits and drawbacks of the judicial process as an institutional mechanism for solving problems' and argues the answer lies in recognising these limitations through the adoption of deference (or, as he prefers to call it, restraint) in doctrinal form and the development of principles to structure its application. Jowell, while advocating the development of additional (constitutionally informed) grounds of review, he also recognises a need for an explicit and structured notion of deference, endorsing for example the factors outlined by Laws LJ in *International Transport.*

[187] David Mullan, 'Deference: Is it Useful Outside Canada?' (2006) AJ 42, 47. He says: 'In reality, the constitutional dimensions of the issue had little to do with the emergence ... and prevalence of deference'. See generally David Dyzenhaus, 'David Mullan's Theory of the Rule of (Common) Law' in Grant Huscroft and Michael Taggart, above n. 116.

[188] Mullan, 'Deference', above n. 187, 45.

[189] *Ibid.*, endorsing *Crevier* v. *Attorney-General (Québec)* [1981] 2 SCR 220.

As a supporter of deference, Mullan is content for the courts to develop these principles independently, subject to the power of the legislature to provide otherwise:[190]

> [S]eemingly ... both the legislatures and the courts [are] free to develop common law principles as to the scope of judicial review ... Included within this authority is the development of principles of deference without attracting constitutional attention.

His analysis is therefore consistent with the common law school.[191] Indeed, he acknowledges the role that the rule of law occupies in Canadian administrative law jurisprudence and the potential for it to support different conceptions of the judicial role, either vigilant or deferential. He also notes that it is possible that a case for deference could be mounted on the basis of either parliamentary sovereignty (giving effect to 'the legislature's intention regarding the appropriate relationship between the statutory authority and reviewing court') or the separation of powers (whereby deference could be justified by reference to 'Canada's constitutional tradition of a strong executive with broad prerogatives over policy-making').[192] In the end, Mullan leaves the constitutional arguments unresolved and assumes that some form of deference is constitutionally defensible.

Secondly, in terms of a preferred schema, Mullan stands as a qualified supporter of the deference-centred framework which exists in Canada. 'Operating at its best, the Canadian standard of review analysis ... does provide a ... sophisticated, constitutionally coherent regime of judicial review of administrative action'.[193] In other words, he embraces the explicit modulation of depth of scrutiny that is synonymous with the variable intensity schema. Mullan justifies the deference regime on the grounds of institutional pluralism and administrative practicality. He argues 'an increasingly diversified and pluralistic legal world' means the courts cannot claim a monopoly on legal interpretation and application, especially relative to statutory authorities.[194] Similarly, administrative regimes increasingly include error-correction and abuse-detection mechanisms,

---

[190] Mullan, 'Deference', above n. 187, 46.
[191] Although the convergence of the schools means the passage could be read either way, elsewhere Mullan has proclaimed his allegiance (without detailed explanation) to the common law school: David Mullan, 'The Canadian Charter of Rights and Freedoms' in Linda Pearson, Carol Harlow and Michael Taggart (eds.), *Administrative Law in a Changing State* (Hart Publishing, 2008), 123, 126.
[192] Mullan, 'Deference', above n. 187, 47.
[193] *Ibid.*, 61.
[194] *Ibid.*, 57.

diminishing the need for a judicial supervisory role. Finally, mandating full-scale, resource-intensive judicial supervision may not be the most efficient or effective means to achieve administrative justice.

Thirdly, on the issue of the factors which ought to be influential, Mullan recounts the standard factors influential in the Canadian framework: legislative choice (that is 'the right or entitlement [of the legislature] to put certain issues beyond the ken of the regular courts', manifest in the purpose of legislation, privative clauses or conferral of broad and unstructured discretion), comparative institutional competence and practical advantage.[195] Mullan worries, though, that the Canadian system of calibration is too focused on legislative choice and expertise and too divorced from circumstances of the particular context in issue;[196] his concern was partly ameliorated by some rebalancing of the factors to determine the standard of review and the adoption of a broad-church reasonableness standard of review in *Dunsmuir*.[197] While Mullan employs Allan in support of his claim that closer attention ought to be paid to the individual interests impugned by the decision in the particular context, one does not detect a strong desire to repudiate some sort of two-stage calibration process (whether in the selection of a standard of review or the determination of how deferential (or not) the application of the reasonable standard should be).[198] Finally, Mullan commends Dyzenhaus' framing of deference as respect and the need for close attention to the justification advanced by the administration.[199] But, unlike Dyzenhaus, Mullan discloses a preference for doctrine. He seems eager for a blueprint to be provided to the judiciary to guide the process of determining the degree of deference and to ensure the application of reasonableness is faithful to the justificatory aims.

Mullan is committed to the deference-project and the explicit calibration of intensity of review. He brings with this a penchant for doctrinal

---

[195] David Mullan, 'Deference from *Baker* to *Suresh* and Beyond' in David Dyzenhaus (ed.), *The Unity of Public Law* (Hart Publishing, 2004), 21, 52.

[196] Mullan, 'Deference', above n. 187, 59.

[197] Mullan, '*Dunsmuir*', above n. 55, and 'Unresolved Issues', above n. 66.

[198] On the former, see Mullan, 'Deference', above n. 187, 60 (support for a framework which commences with 'the identification in the abstract of what standard of review should apply', with a 'situational specific enquiry' looking at the statutory basis of the decision and nature of the interests at stake). On the latter, see Mullan, 'Unresolved Issues', above n. 66, 76 and 81 (support for 'intensity of reasonableness review depending on context', but a plea for 'greater clarity' about the practical application of this contextual reasonableness standard).

[199] Mullan, 'Deference', 60 and Section 5.3.4.

structure, conscious of the demands of contextualism, but worries, too, about the dangers of too much judicial discretion and uncertainty.

4.3.5   Conclusion

Support for an intensity of review schema is drawn from quite different theoretical domains. The transparent calibration of intensity of review, through doctrinal devices, finds favour from both sides of the ultra vires debate.

On the one hand, there are those who continue to argue linkage back to the legislature is essential to the democratic legitimisation of judicial review. Here Daly and Elliott acknowledge the general trajectory away from the categorical towards more direct and circumstantial means of settling the depth of review, but are reluctant to repudiate the model of government that underpins the ultra vires. Instead, the judicial role is warned away from areas which they regard as unsuitable for judicial super-vision – but through the consideration of essentially institutional factors which counsel different degrees of deference. Daly translates this into three differing standards of review, with selection based on an assessment of the legislative text. Elliott supports the project to construct operational principles to guide the process of calibration and, presumably, to maintain the linkages to legislative intent. However, he has yet to crystallise this into a normative schema, save for suggesting the task may be complicated by the fact that deference arises at two points in the supervisory process; in other words, the schema may need to differentiate between what he labels starting point deference and adjudicative deference.

On the other hand, those with some sympathy for a common law position are also drawn to the explicit calibration of intensity under this schema. For example, Mullan continues to support a schema whereby the depth of review is modulated in individual cases, but by reference to a suite of doctrinal factors. Others who seek to avoid the ultra vires debate in favour of a collaborative legislative–judicial endeavour, like Hunt, also sign onto a schema with elaborated factors for settling the depth of review in individual cases.

The factors that influence the calibration exercise are relatively common to all: factors which speak to the legislative allocation of power, complexity, relative expertise and practical disadvantage. That is a mixture of con-siderations reflecting legislative supremacy and curial limitations. Those from the ultra vires school would emphasise the extent of discretion dele-gated to the administrative actor, while also considering issues of expertise and practicality evident in the legislative text. Those from the common law school would echo this set of considerations, but not find it necessary to ground the assessment in the terms of the statute. Hunt would also build in considerations which look to other means of accountability and the quality of the justification advanced by the administration. Importantly, this schema seeks to align the conceptual and the doctrinal. Rather than working through indirect categories and ritualistic mantra, the constitutional relationship between primary decision-maker and supervisory court is front-and-centre. The factors provide tools for the courts to assess the appropriate equilibrium in individual cases and provide a language for them to elaborate their reasoning.

The intensity of review schemata manifests a strong alertness to the limitations of the judicial oversight, along with a belief that these limitations are best addressed on a dynamic basis within the supervisory jurisdiction through the structuring of judicial discretion. As King observes, institutionalists 'focus on the comparative merits and drawbacks of the judicial process as an institutional mechanism for solving problems'.[200] And, here, King's label of 'contextual institutionalists' is apt;[201] those scholars commending this intensity of review approach seek to develop tools – pliant doctrine directives – which allow the limitations of the judicial oversight process to be recognised and reflected in the supervision process, without delimiting territorial exclusion zones.

4.4 Normative Assessment

Intensity of review moves away from an indirect and categorical approach to the explicit calibration of the depth of scrutiny and brings variability into the foreground. '[F]ormalist methodology of bright lines and either/or propositions [give] way to a balancing of multiple factors and a spectrum of possibilities.'[202] Rules about *how* the courts ought to deliberate on the depth of scrutiny are favoured over rules which indirectly dictate particular depths of scrutiny.

A degree of generality is still evident; as well as providing rules to guide the calibration process, the schema acknowledges, but seeks to structure, the judicial judgement. The focus on transparent deliberation about the depth of scrutiny means the schema brings transparency, coherence and

---

[200] King, 'Restraint', above n. 103, 410.
[201] *Ibid.*
[202] Macklin, above n. 48, 224, speaking of the Canadian experience in particular.

candour. Moving the focus away from outcomes to method hinders pro-spectivity, clarity, stability and practicality. These virtues all depend on a degree of predictability, which cannot be guaranteed; the approach puts its faith in open reasoning to provide the necessary cues and desirable con-sistency, which has had mixed results.

Generality

The schema is doctrinal, in that its operation is governed by rules. However, the rules dictate the consideration of certain factors, rather than outcomes, and therefore rely on significant judicial discretion in the assessment of weight and influence when determining the appropriate depth of review. In some respects, therefore, the schema disappoints in terms of *generality*. However, the schema seeks to ameliorate inconsistency and lack of pre-dictability (circumstances which the principle of generality seeks to avoid).

There are three key aspects to the rule structure of this schema.[203] First, there is the identification of the factors which should be taken into account. Secondly, there is the weight to be given to those factors in the overall mix. Finally, there is the translation of those weighted factors into a particular depth of scrutiny. Doctrine governs some, but not all, parts of that process; judicial judgement occupies an important role.

On the first part of the process, there is a growing accord about the types of factors which should shape the balance drawn between restraint and vigilance.[204] Factors such as relative expertise and institutional compe-tence are generally regarded as being appropriate drivers of the depth of review. The magnitude of the effect of the decision, particularly whether it engages questions of human rights, is implicitly treated as an impor-tant consideration (although some argue for a more nuanced account). Others emphasise more formal characteristics such as recognition of the legislative allocation of power and the nature of the particular impugned decision. Others are attentive to the availability of other accountability avenues. Finally, some argue that the cogency of the justification advanced by the administration ought to be taken into account. While there is an emerging set of considerations, it is important to note that there is, and will continue to be, debate about the factors which ought to be influential.

---

[203] This is not the only possible means to calibrate intensity but it is the dominant means evident in the jurisprudence. Compare the move to recognise presumptive categories in *Dunsmuir*, text to n. 55 above.

[204] See Section 4.3 above; see also the generalised expression of factors in *International Transport*, above n. 104.

Or how they should be expressed, given they overlap and sometimes draw out similar considerations. This may impact on the stability of the schema, which is discussed below.

The Canadian approach has been to attempt to synthesize and generalise the factors that inform the appropriate degree of deference.[205] Two of the key factors relied on during the high-point of the pragmatic and functional era squarely placed issues of legitimacy on the agenda, namely, comparative expertise and the nature of the problem; the other two factors – privative clauses and the purpose of the provision – are nods back to legislative intent. For present purposes, the important point is that the factors which inform the judicial calibration of intensity are more directly connected to the conceptual basis for review. In other words, the factors are denotative, not reliant on proxies for their instrumentality.

In England and New Zealand, the factors which drive the modulation have not been systemised and remain ad hoc. However, more vigilant supervision is usually supported by reference to the impact of the decision on an individual, particularly in terms of fundamental or human rights, or the engagement of some other higher-order norm. Those factors which condition restraint are generally centred on questions of judicial competence, in a relative sense, to adjudicate on the matter before them. Such factors include high policy content, a decision of a polycentric nature, particular administrative expertise on the issue, and so forth. Weight is also given to the nature of the judicial forum and administrative processes, particularly where the development of a policy or position is more legitimate if the product of a democratic process, or where other non-judicial processes provide adequate checks-and-balances against abuse.

For present purposes, it is sufficient to acknowledge that at least some or most of these factors ought to inform the calibration exercise. The focus of this book is principally on the *method* and *form* of the calibration exercise, not the resolution of conceptual questions about *which* factors ought to inform that process of calibration. First, the latter question is a vast one beyond the scope of this project which requires consideration in its own right. Secondly, it is a question on which there is already a growing body of literature and analysis. Thirdly, because of the focus on the definition of these factors in this literature, there is a lack of attention to schematic aspects of modulation of intensity; hence, the focus of this book. The operation of a variable intensity schema does not, in general terms, differ

---

[205] This applies both pre- and post-*Dunsmuir*; see Section 4.2.2 above and Section 5.2.3.

based on the factors which feed into the schema. It is therefore possible to assume the existence of a suite of factors to test the operation of that schema, without definitively settling on the content of that suite of factors. Finally, the suite of factors have a traditional common law character, which means they are capable of definition and re-definition over time.

The second aspect of the process is the question of the weight to be attributed to each factor when mediating the balance between vigilance and restraint. Like the traditional relevancy principle, the factors are treated like mandatory relevant considerations, that is, as matters which should be taken into account. It follows though that questions of weight and balance between the factors are matters for the decision-maker (here, the supervisory judge). Unlike the formalistic approaches under scope and, to a lesser degree, the grounds of review schemata, this schema does not attempt to construct strict rules or typologies. Other than marshalling the factors that must be taken into account, factorial tests generally do not specify the weight to be afforded to each factor.[206]

Realised in its purest form, this schema recognises that weight, balance and counter-balance are contextual and the operational framework can do no more than ensure that judges turn their mind to these factors and reason through their influence. Some are critical of this approach. For example, Taggart worried about the absence of rules and lack of guidance and certainty.[207] This is caused, he argued, by the fact that factorial tests are comprised of 'lists of factors with contestable weights'.[208] In other words, 'the result is not determined necessarily by a majority of factors pointing one way' and '[s]ome factors in some circumstances count for more in the balancing'.[209] Similarly, others have argued that factorial tests are overly complicated.[210] The pre-*Dunsmuir* practice was sharply criticised for becoming 'unduly burdened with law office metaphysics'.[211]

This part of the schema departs from the ideal of general rules and instead utilises discretion; to this extent, it compromises *generality*. However, this is a deliberate compromise. Trying to develop rigid and

---

[206] Jacques de Ville, 'The Rule of Law and Judicial Review' [2006] AJ 62, 63.

[207] Taggart, 'Proportionality', above n. 76, 460. See also Philip A. Joseph, 'Exploratory Questions in Administrative Law ' (2012) 25 NZULR 75, 82.

[208] Taggart, 'Proportionality', above n. 76, 458, citing de Ville, above n. 206, 63.

[209] Taggart, 'Proportionality', above n. 76, 458. See also Hickman, *Public Law*, above n. 74, 137.

[210] Sian Elias, 'Righting Administrative Law' in Dyzenhaus, Hunt, Huscroft, above n. 171, 68, 72.

[211] *Dunsmuir*, above n. 55, [122]. See also Lorne Sossin and Colleen Flood, 'The Contextual Turn' (2007) 57 UTLJ 581.

universal rules simply revives the problems of categories that plagued the scope and grounds of review schema. The reliance on a model of relevant considerations, teamed with an obligation to explicitly justify their influence, acknowledges contextualism but also seeks to ameliorate loss of consistency, predictability and clarity associated with increased judicial discretion. The method is one drawn from established judicial review principle. The courts themselves have assumed that relevant considerations and reason-giving go some way to encouraging consistency and predictability.[212]

Secondly, once these factors are brought into the foreground and their application in particular cases is justified and reasoned, jurisprudence about their influence will develop and mature over time, enabling more consistent application. Taggart argued in favour of this style of mapping project: 'We must get beyond simply talking about context and actually contextualize in a way that can generate generalizable conclusions'.[213] He worried that otherwise 'the law will continue to be rather chaotic, unprincipled, and result-orientated'.[214] Adoption as a general schema would therefore allow the common law to develop more precision as it evolves, thereby supporting a more disciplined approach. Appellate review will also be able to monitor the role the factors play. In principle, a balance is drawn, where the influence of factors assumes a degree of predictability, without foreclosing on difference balances being struck in particular (especially unusual) cases.

The final part of the process turns to the practical translation of the balance between vigilance and restraint into a particular depth of review. This part of the process raises a particular issue about how precisely, as a matter of doctrine, a particular depth of review should be calibrated. There are two key ways the depth of review can be expressed: as a continuum of limitless possibilities, or as a number of pre-defined standards of review. We can describe them as 'finite' and 'infinite' scales respectively. An infinite scale allows the intensity of review to float or slide between two extremes, but without defining specific calibrations along the way. This is the essence of doctrinal developments which promoted, in general terms, more intensive ('anxious') scrutiny or a 'sliding-scale' of review,[215] as well as the formative concepts of deference under the Human Rights

---

[212] P.P. Craig, *Administrative Law* (6th edn, Sweet & Maxwell, 2008), [19-015].
[213] Taggart, 'Proportionality', above n. 76, 454.
[214] *Ibid.*, 453.
[215] See text to n. 83.

Act.[216] It is also the style of modulation evident in the second stage of the standards of review analysis in Canada, if reasonableness is adopted in the particular case.[217] The lack of structure or precision in the calibration process also means there is little light between it and the contextual review schema which operates absent doctrine. In contrast, a finite scale seeks to define or label specific depths of review. This approach seeks to generalise the different intensity of review into different methodologies or judicial touchstones. It is evident in the pre-*Dunsmuir* regime in Canada, where a distinction was drawn between the patent unreasonableness and reasonableness simpliciter standards of review. It is also consistent with some of the efforts to variegate the unreasonableness ground into separately identified grounds or standards of review, such as super-*Wednesbury* review,[218] or simple unreasonableness.[219]

The different forms of calibration have different virtues. An infinite scale maximises adaptability and flexibility, but comes at the expense of generality (and clarity). A discrete scale emphasises the reverse. In my view, a finite scale is more efficacious and has stronger virtue.[220] First, the schema needs to recognise the practical reality of the supervision task. Modulation is not an exact or precise science. Setting calibrations too finely may mean the distinctions become meaningless. Allowing the depth of review to be settled anywhere on an indeterminate continuum risks collapsing the calibration of intensity into mere judicial judgement, as seen in contextual review. When generalised into discrete standards, different methodologies become apparent. For example, the simple unreasonableness approach is understood to open up the scrutiny of the balance drawn by the decision-maker, in contradistinction to the traditional approach under the *Wednesbury* test.[221] Likewise, super-*Wednesbury* focuses on the motivations or propriety of the decision-maker ('bad faith, corruption and fraud').[222] Secondly, calibration by reference to generalised depths of

---

[216] See text to n. 108.
[217] See text to n. 48.
[218] See text to n. 94.
[219] See text to n. 110.
[220] Compare Sossin and Flood, above n. 211, who favour a 'flexible spectrum of review' over 'fixed categories' but with a stronger emphasis on particularised judicial explanation of why intervention is justified (that is, 'balancing the discretion accorded to the minister with the consequences of error').
[221] P.P. Craig, 'The Nature of Reasonableness Review' (2013) 66 CLP 131; Daly, above n. 117, 166–81.
[222] Knight, 'Murky Methodology', above n. 109.

review is more likely to exact control of the judicial discretion and ensure operational coherence. The existence of a few but distinct points on a continuum tends to structure the judicial discretion by restricting the number of choices available. In doing so, it downplays the instinct of individual judges and encourages consistency across the supervisory jurisdiction. The hope is that this, in turn, helps make the determination of the depth of scrutiny more predictable. As Le Sueur said of variegated forms of unreasonableness, this makes 'it easier for there to be a principled and more certain approach to the court's role' and avoids 'slithering around in grey areas'.[223] Thirdly, generalised calibrations are more faithful to the principle of generality and do not unduly undermine flexibility. A move from a grounds of review approach to an explicit intensity of review approach unlocks the judicial lens and, in principle, allows context to determine a balance between vigilance and restraint, not formalistic categories. On a meta-level, panoptic flexibility is ensured; on a micro level, any loss of flexibility associated with limited precision is marginal.

Once the depth of review is settled an evaluative judgement is also settled, as the facts of the particular cases are assessed in the light of the standard of review. That is, rather than a structured method of analysis being imposed (such as with a proportionality calculus), the judicial method continues to be an 'overall evaluation'.[224] A judgement in the round is made, coloured in this model by a notional depth of scrutiny. As Fordham and de la Mare rightly acknowledge: 'It is inescapable that the very fact of a substantive unreasonableness doctrine, *wherever* the threshold is to be found, will involve the Court in a degree of value-judgment.'[225] Significantly, the 'formal veneer' of *Wednesbury* is retained – perhaps, some argue, in order to bolster the legitimacy of more intrusive review.[226] Some have argued the judicial method of more intense reasonableness review

---

[223] Le Sueur, 'Unreasonableness?', above n. 74, [30]. Similarly, in relation to the pre-*Dunsmuir* framework, Bryden says the difference between the standards of review 'offers a distinction in kind rather than merely one of degree': Philip Bryden, 'Understanding the Standard of Review in Administrative Law' (2005) 54 Uni New Brun LJ 75, 93. Compare David Dyzenhaus, 'Dignity in Administrative Law' (2012) 17 Rev Const Stud 87, 106.

[224] Joseph, 'The Demise of Ultra Vires' [2001] PL 354, 371. See also Elliott, *Administrative Law*, above n. 86, 288 ('generally regarded as more amorphous').

[225] Michael Fordham and Thomas de la Mare, 'Identifying the Principles of Proportionality' in Jeffrey Jowell and Jonathan Cooper (eds.), *Understanding Human Rights Principles* (Hart Publishing, 2001), 32, [14].

[226] Paul Craig, 'Unreasonableness and Proportionality in UK Law' in Evelyn Ellis (ed.), *The Principle of Proportionality in the Laws of Europe* (Hart Publishing, 1999), 85, 95; Taggart, 'Proportionality', above n. 76, 433; Hickman, *Public Law*, above n. 74, 200.

mimics the essence of proportionality review because it involves a candid assessment of the balance struck or relative weight applied.[227] While there is a degree of truth to the analogy, the courts have been reluctant to equate anxious scrutiny or simple unreasonableness with the structured form of proportionality.[228]

So while the regime involves a mix of process-style rules and judicial discretion, the method does not surrender to judicial whim. Structure and discipline are still imposed in the judicial method. While factorial tests are not determinate mathematical formulae, the obligation to have regard to certain factors represses some judicial discretion. Calibration must be reasoned and reasoned explicitly.[229] A culture of justification is imposed on judicial discretion. This mimics the same culture of justification that has been heralded as instrumental in checking and controlling administrative discretion.[230] Similarly, while the assessment of the circumstances of the individual case are assessed in the round, the calibration of depth of review moderates any instinct on the part of judges to merely apply their own view. Of course, it can be argued this is an abstract and weak control because even different depths of review may not calibrate universally and it may be difficult to assess when an articulated depth of review is not in fact applied in practice. These are fair criticisms. However, the model goes some way to address these concerns.

Finally, the rule-regime is agnostic to the depth of review; it does not dictate particular outcomes. A curious feature of the current manifestation of this style of regime is that it has developed with different emphases in different parts of the Anglo-Commonwealth. In England and New Zealand, it generally supports more vigilant review; in Canada, it is treated as counselling more deferential review. Much of this is attributable to the locus of its principal development. In England and New Zealand, variegation

---

[227] Craig, 'Unreasonableness and Proportionality', above n. 226, 97. See also Knight, 'Murky Methodology', above n. 109, 210.

[228] In England, see *R (Daly)* v. *Secretary of State for the Home Office* [2001] 2 AC 532, [27] (Lord Steyn) and [32] (Lord Cooke). Both relied on this same conclusion being reached by the European Court of Human Rights in *Smith and Grady* v. *United Kingdom* (1999) 29 EHRR 493, in the European Convention sequel to *R (Smith)* v. *Ministry of Defence* [1996] QB 517. However, this conclusion has been criticised for failing to recognise the deferential factors and application in *Smith*: Kavanagh, *Constitutional Review*, above n. 82, 251. In New Zealand, see *Wolf*, above n. 110; compare *Ye* v. *Minister of Immigration* [2010] 1 NZLR 104.

[229] Dyzenhaus, Hunt and Taggart, above n. 76, 27.

[230] David Dyzenhaus, 'Law as Justification' (1998) 14 SAJHR 11; Taggart, 'Proportionality', above n. 76, 461; Dyzenhaus, Hunt and Taggart, above n. 76, 29.

of unreasonableness has generally (but not exclusively) been adopted as a means to circumvent *Wednesbury*'s deferential threshold on substantive review. In contrast, the Canadian developments have promoted restraint on legal or jurisdictional questions (and otherwise reinforced deference in relation to review of discretion).[231] These different backdrops, though, give rise to different lexical character. The execution of this method of review in England and New Zealand is emblazoned with the language of 'scrutiny'. However, in the Canadian context, the language of 'deference' dominates, as it does also in the particular sphere of human rights adjudication in England. In principle, though, the regime does not inherently favour, either way, vigilance and restraint – the open-textured nature of the regime leaves the full range of possibilities open.

Prospectivity

Like the other schema, the intensity of review schema is generally prospective because the regime governing judicial supervision is articulated in advance. However, the degree of judicial discretion in adjudication does create some retrospective effect. Again, this is a feature of all the schemata due to the circumstantial variability involved. The open-textured schema – based on a factorial test and weight – does intensify the effect somewhat, although, as discussed in relation to the principle of generality, the schema does seek to mitigate any lack of clarity and predictability associated with this.

Public Accessibility and Transparency

One of the key virtues of the intensity of review schema is the way it provides transparency in the judicial method. Rather than modulation of intensity operating in the shadows of categorisation or being collapsed into an instinctive reaction, the calibration exercise is brought into the foreground. The openness of the process by which the depth of review is set avoids resort to furtive techniques; judges are empowered to be candid and to grapple explicitly with the factors that influence the depth of review. This has a number of positive consequences. First, it is likely to ensure greater conformity between doctrinal outcomes and conceptual underpinnings. In other words, it improves the quality of decision-making. Secondly, it helps promote trust and confidence in the judicial process and enhances the legitimacy of judicial review. It helps remove a sense that

---

[231] Mullan, 'Deference', above n. 187, 49.

doctrine is being manipulated in order to achieve particular outcomes; while it is probably inevitable that some scepticism will remain, the refrain of candour and intellectual honesty that runs through this schema means it generally performs better than other schema on this point.[232]

This style of review also seeks to clearly delineate first-order and second-order issues in the supervisory task. A distinction is drawn between 'primary issues' such as the propriety of some administrative action or the treatment of a citizen by the state and 'second-order issues' about the legitimacy of the courts to definitively adjudicate on such matters.[233] Speaking to rights-adjudication, Kavanagh adopts slightly different language: the assessment of the merits of the substantive legal issue – namely, whether rights have been violated or not – is described as the 'substantive evaluation', while the assessment of relative institutional competence, expertise and legitimacy is described as the 'institutional evaluation'.[234] The separate distillation of principles informing the degree of deference in Canada was undertaken for 'pragmatic and functional' reasons,[235] but those reasons echo the legitimacy issues driving the two-step method in other jurisdiction. The approach signalled 'attention to context and issues of relative institutional competence'.[236]

While transparency is generally welcomed, it has been questioned whether candour might have some unintended consequences in this context. Endicott, for example, warns that 'if judges did ask the pertinent questions ... judicial review would be a battleground for competing understandings'.[237] There may be a certain degree of truth in this observation. However, we should be cautious about placing too much significance on it for normative purposes. Competing understandings about the nature and purpose of judicial review are rife and cannot be avoided, whether the differences manifest themselves explicitly or not. Transparency and

---

[232] It is arguable that contextual review also shares similar candidness; however, the internal and non-doctrinal nature of the reasoning process means it does provide the same degree of transparency as the intensity of review schema. See chapter 5.

[233] Thomas Poole, 'Legitimacy, Rights, and Judicial Review' (2005) 25 OJLS 697, 709.

[234] Kavanagh, 'Defending Deference', above n. 185, 231.

[235] The label was first deployed by in *UES Local 298* v. *Bibeault* [1988] 2 SCR 1048, [122]. See Mullan, 'Deference', above n. 187, fn. 2.

[236] Dyzenhaus, 'David Mullan's Theory of the Rule of (Common) Law', above n. 187, 458. See also David Mullan, *Administrative Law* (Irwin Law, 2001), 81 (a focus on the 'respective qualifications of court and tribunal concerning the issue in question'); Mary Liston, 'Governments in Miniature' in Flood and Sossin, above n. 48, 105.

[237] Timothy Endicott, *Administrative Law* (Oxford University Press, 2009), 221, endorsed by Jeff King, 'Proportionality' (2010) NZ Law Rev 327, 259.

openness about those understandings are essential if we are to have any hope of working towards a shared understanding and harmonising the differences – or, if agreement cannot be reached, acknowledging the impact of the lack of agreement.

Clarity

The clarity of the intensity of review schema is mixed. One the one hand, the method for mediating vigilance and restraint is clearly and simply articulated. It is to be determined based on the assessment of a number of relatively uncontentious factors. On the other hand, the implementation of that assessment is less clear because it is reliant on the undefined judicial assessment of weight and influence based on the circumstances.

Again, it needs to be acknowledged that the application of the factorial test has been strongly criticised in Canada for its lack of clarity and cumbersome nature.[238] The reasons for the confusion are, perhaps, complex. It has been suggested that the courts failed to deliver on the 'bold' pragmatic and functional philosophy required under this approach and 'slip[ped] into old ways of thinking'[239] and that judges 'have not actually internalized and committed to the principles underlying curial deference'.[240] Or, alternatively, that some of the complexity is simply a natural consequence of the expansion of the framework into domains where the deference enterprise is inevitably complicated.[241] Regardless, this open-textured but structured assessment has been challenging to implement.

Clarity may be compromised further by the calibration of the depth of scrutiny. A finite scale with a few pre-defined degrees of intensity is more likely to present a clear and understandable basis for supervision and review. However, if an infinite continuum is favoured, then this compromises clarity further, as explained in relation to the principle of generality above.

The language is relatively clear too. Expressed as standards of review, not legality, the orientation of the schema is on the judicial method, with variability and the mediation of vigilance and restraint assuming

---

[238] Sossin and Flood, above n. 211; Macklin, above n. 51; Mark D. Walters, 'Jurisdiction, Functionalism, and Constitutionalism in Canadian Administrative Law' in C. Forsyth and others (eds.), *Effective Judicial Review: A Cornerstone of Good Governance* (Oxford University Press, 2010), 300; David J. Mullan, 'Establishing the Standard of Review' (2004) 17 CJALP 59.

[239] Walters, above n. 238, 307.

[240] Macklin, above n. 51, 226.

[241] Mullan, 'Standard of Review', above n. 238.

prominent roles. The language – such as correctness, reasonableness and non-reviewability – is faithful to this task. And it is neither unduly pejorative nor particularly obscure.

Stability

This schema is relatively stable. The holistic nature of the schema means it can accommodate evolution within its framework without repudiating its methodological essence. Evolving conceptions about the role of certain factors and the influence of particular circumstances can be readily addressed in the factorial test, either through the articulation of factors to be considered or the weight they should be accorded. The relatively open-textured nature of the factorial test means significant rule-changes are unlikely.

The judicial discretion in the framework, particularly as to the weight to be afforded to the different factors, does potentially create some potential for contemporary instability; however, as discussed above, the framework seeks to ameliorate this by aiming, through reasoning, to give this a more predictable character.

Non-contradiction and Coherence

A strong feature of the intensity of review schema is its coherence. It presents a monolithic and consistent framework for the supervisory framework. A common methodology is utilised to determine the depth of review and it is flexible enough to accommodate different circumstances and contexts. In other words, it is comprehensive. This contrasts with other doctrinal methods under scope and grounds of review which utilise a range of different (and indirect) techniques to access different intensities of review. Although there is no central or overarching substantive principle evident, unity is achieved through a focus on relativity between the administration, as primary decision-makers, and the courts, as secondary reviewers, and the consequent modulation of intensity of review to reflect that relationship.

Non-impossibility and Practicality

The intensity of review schema is generally practical, but presents a number of challenges. The method of calibration is transparent and therefore allows the evidence and argumentation to be focused on essential questions relating to the depth of intensity to be deployed. The explicit calibration focuses attention of the depth and modulation of review and the

factorial approach provides doctrinal scaffolding to support deliberation on it.

The first challenge lies in ensuring the two-stage approach does not
become overly obsessed by the first stage, to the exclusion of the second
stage. Calibration of intensity is important, but so too is the application
of the appropriate standard to the facts of the case. Over-emphasising the
standard of review carries risks. Judicial review doctrines which mostly
concentrate on judicial methodology, without strongly elaborating norms
for the administration, undermine its effectiveness. Again, the Canadian
experience illustrates this criticism, particularly the consequential costs of
uncertainty. For example, Binnie J in *Dunsmuir* was critical of the energy
devoted to the 'threshold debate' about which reasonableness standard
should apply and argued that the courts should 'get the parties away from
arguing about the tests and back to arguing about the substantive merits
of their case'.[242] He lamented the 'lengthy and arcane discussions' about
standards of review and the amount of 'unproductive "lawyer's talk"'
involved in resolving cases.[243] His concern was expressed in terms of the
financial costs to litigants, but the point resonates more generally in terms
of the workability, predictability and coherence of the schema. Indeed,
part of the criticism was based on the fact that an applicable standard
often is not settled beyond doubt unless and until the Supreme Court rules
definitively. As Binnie J noted, the outcome of cases 'may well *turn* on the
choice of the standard of review', hence there is a significant incentive to
litigate the standard or review whenever possible.[244]

The second challenge is related and arises from the definition of the
evidential corpus and nature of argumentation required for the second
stage of the supervision process. Both of these differ markedly based on
what depth of scrutiny is mandated.[245] Supervision which is focused on
correctness requires great weight of evidential material to resolve it and
the nature of argument is different because matters of secondary review
and deference need not be addressed. In contrast, if a more deferential
approach is adopted, the evidential corpus is more modest and the style

---

[242] *Dunsmuir*, above n. 55, [145]. This attitude is also evident in recent remarks from Lord
Carnwath: 'Perhaps we as judges should cut out the theorising and concentrate on doing
justice in real cases.' ('From Judicial Outrage to Sliding Scales' (ALBA annual lecture,
London, November 2013), 19.)

[243] *Dunsmuir*, above n. 55, [133]. See also Daly, above n. 117, 182.

[244] *Dunsmuir*, above n. 55, [133].

[245] Mark Aronson, 'Process, Quality and Variable Standards' in Dyzenhaus, Hunt and
Huscroft, above n. 171, 28.

of argumentation is more relative and respectful of the secondary nature of review.

The challenges raised essentially relate to the timing and predictability of the calibration exercise. There are some ways to ameliorate these issues. First, we can look to strengthen the predictability of the calibration exercise. One of the steps taken to address this in Canada is to encourage better use of precedent to avoid the need for a full-blown standards of review analysis in each and every case, with some working presumptions also being developed.[246] These start to provide a degree of predictability, without foreclosing on a particularised assessment in tricky cases. In many respects, this builds on the idea of a flexible jurisprudence developing around the influence of the factors.[247] Secondly, as explained above, the crystallisation of a framework that explicitly manifests variable intensity is expected to, over time, allow the jurisprudence to mature and refine itself – with the hope that it therefore becomes more predictable and practical.

Congruence and Candour

This schema encourages congruence in implementation and judicial candour. The absence of firm substantive rules, where the depth of scrutiny is set indirectly through categorical proxies, avoids the need for covert manipulation by judges. Fidelity to the schema is encouraged by the open-textured approach which brings the conceptual factors relevant to the depth of scrutiny to the foreground. The normative nature of the supervisory task is acknowledged and mandated. Variability, based on the circumstances, is encouraged but within a framework which seeks to channel and structure the mediation between restraint and vigilance. The constraints imposed on judges are more procedural than substantive; the primary obligation is to deliberate and justify the calibration by reference to the mandated factors. Thus, while the framework is open-textured and 'malleable',[248] there is little incentive for judges to depart from the framework.

Hortatory Versatility

This schema's primary focus on the intensity or standards of review means it provides only weak hortatory guidance. The framework speaks

---

[246] *Dunsmuir*, above n. 55, [62]; see also Binnie J's suggestion of stronger use of presumptions ([145]).

[247] Taggart, 'Proportionality', above n. 76, 453.

[248] Dyzenhaus, 'Dignity', above n. 223, 106.

to the judiciary and provides little guidance to the administration about the norms which should be respected by the administration. It is essentially a judicial charter. For example, noticeably understated in Canadian administrative law cases is a clear articulation of the norms and expectations applicable to decision-makers. There are few occasions on which the courts have elaborated the expectations on decision-makers in general terms, and these are so rhetorical and ecumenical that they provide little value.[249] Moreover, the concept of grounds of review – from which norms could implicitly be drawn – fell out of favour when the pragmatic and functional framework was extended in *Baker* from questions of law to include discretionary decision-making.[250] The striking feature of Canadian administrative law jurisprudence is that the judicial rhetoric is heavily self-referential, even following the *Dunsmuir* reform.

The intensity of review schema is still capable of sending some messages to the administration, but the missives are more subdued and cryptic. The modulation of review intensity transmits judicial directives about the extent of administrative autonomy. As Halliday explains, a deferential judicial approach tells a public agency that it is empowered to 'follow its instincts and preferences, and to have confidence in the finality of its judgements'.[251] This, he argues, changes the nature of agency deliberations, obviating the need to look externally to the courts for guidance and allowing them to 'be more introspective, develop their expertise and enjoy the broad scope of their own discretion'.[252] In other words, law evaporates in favour of bureaucratic instinct. In contrast, when more interventionist review is deployed, public agencies are forced to 'discover the courts' preferences on pertinent issues and to take the lead from them'.[253] Law's influence survives, even when the judges are not present, as administrators seek to emulate their methodology and analysis. Thus, messaging which is predominantly framed in terms of modulation of judicial intensity resonates in terms of bureaucratic discretion: autonomy or hyponymy. But this messaging lacks the sophistication and precision needed in modern administrative law.

---

[249] See e.g. *Baker* v. *Canada (Minister of Citizenship and Immigration)* [1999] 2 SCR 817, [56].
[250] See Section 3.2.5 above.
[251] Simon Halliday, *Judicial Review and Compliance with Administrative Law* (Hart Publishing, 2004), 131.
[252] *Ibid.*, 131.
[253] *Ibid.*, 158.

The framework will still have some collateral value for other public functionaries, such as tribunals and Ombudsmen, charged with the external review of administrative decisions. However, institutional differences – the nature of the reviewing body and its relationship with the administration – mean the approach will need to be tailored to those circumstances. In a general sense, therefore, the schema and the broad principles running through the calibration of intensity will be of some value for those reviewing bodies too.

4.5 Conclusion

Intensity of review openly embraces the determination of the depth of scrutiny. Direct consideration of the factors influencing the balance between vigilance and restraint is favoured over attention to categories and form. The importance of context is acknowledged, but so too is doctrinal structure and reasoning. Rules still seek to guide, not through dictating outcomes, but through requiring transparent consideration and deliberation. This aims to strike a balance between adaptability of the judicial task and the limitations of the courts' secondary role.

Scholars supporting intensity of review acknowledge that the demands of context cannot be met by strict doctrinal categories, but they remain unwilling to allow the supervisory task to dissolve into judicial judgement alone. Hence, a case is made for doctrinal scaffolding to focus the judicial assessment and to encourage reasoned elaboration. A culture of justification for judges too.

The approach performs relatively well against the principles of efficacy. Its strength lies in its embrace of the conceptual factors governing the depth of review and the central role they assume. This encourages transparency, coherence and candour. Doubts about the predictability of outcomes – given the prominence of judicial judgement within the rule-framework – means it scores less well in terms of prospectivity, clarity, stability and practicality.

This schema, on the whole, provides a workable alternative to the grounds of review approach, with a different flavour. It provides a reasoning process that foregrounds constitutional and practical considerations about the nature of the relationship between the primary decision-maker and supervisory court. Thus, it has strong conceptual credentials, albeit the judicial method tends to be self-referential. As a supervisory framework, it is relatively nimble, yet it resists the collapse of judicial method into an overall unstructured evaluation.

5

Contextual Review

5.1 Introduction

Contextual review resists categorical approaches to judicial supervision. The strong refrain about context and its importance signals an emergent trend towards this open-textured and discretionary style of judicial supervision. This form of unstructured contextualism, where the judges assess the circumstances in the round without any doctrinal scaffolding to control the depth of scrutiny, finds some favour in some parts of English, New Zealand and Canadian administrative law. In its strong form, it suggests judicial instinct and discretionary judgement is, and should be, the essential litmus test for judicial intervention. In its weaker form, it captures doctrinal frameworks which are so open-textured that their essential feature is an overall evaluative judgement on the part of the judiciary. While not prominently featuring in de Smith's textbook, this methodology has been promoted in the academic literature and there are a few comments in de Smith's text that recognise its existence.

The powerful judicial role in this schema means it draws its support from some scholars from the common law school or those recognising or supporting a stronger judicial role. Doctrine is seen as unsuitable for the supervisory task; normative reasoning is required and should be mandated. The rejection of rules means, however, it performs poorly against Fuller's principles of efficacy. On a superficial level, it scores well in terms of clarity, coherence and candour because the basis for intervention is plainly framed in terms of judicial judgement; but when that judgement is exposed and picked apart, even these virtues disintegrate. Judicial discretion prevails, without any guarantee of the underlying normative reasoning becoming apparent.

5.2   Doctrinal Manifestation

This approach has limited purchase, both in de Smith's textbook and generally. I identify some seeds in de Smith, before providing some instances from New Zealand, Canada and England where the style of reasoning – a broad unstructured judicial judgement – is evident. This style operates, most obviously, within existing doctrinal constraints although it has the potential to be realised more broadly as a general lodestar for intervention as well.

5.2.1   De Smith Derivation

This style of review is, unsurprisingly, not prominently referenced in de Smith's text. However, its character is recognisable from a few passages in the later editions.

First, in the discussion of the constitutional context of judicial review, the authors discuss the balance stuck between certainty and flexibility. Reference is made to how many of the standards applied in judicial review are necessarily 'open-textured'.[1] The content of the values may not, the authors say, be defined with precision and 'will always need to be accompanied by a recognition of the particular circumstances of a special case'.[2] The circumstances which colour these standards are listed as 'the breadth of the power conferred upon the decision-maker; the conditions of its exercise; the availability of alternative procedural protections, and the fairness to the parties involved (and to others affected by the decision)'.[3]

Secondly, in the context of irrationality and substantive review, the authors seed the idea that the courts may engage in full intensity correctness review under the rubric of 'abuse of power'.[4] The concept is not developed in detail other than giving a handful of instances of when it may arise.[5] They explain the absence of constitutional or institutional reasons for the application of any deference may mean the courts are 'in as good a position as the primary decision-maker', allowing them to 'assess the relevant factors'.[6] In some respects, the resort to the abstract label 'abuse of

---

[1] De Smith (6th edn), 14; (7th edn), 17.
[2] De Smith (6th edn), 14; (7th edn), 17.
[3] De Smith (6th edn), 14; (7th edn), 17.
[4] De Smith (6th edn), 546, 592; (7th edn), 589, 636.
[5] Cases where no evidence for a decision exists, decisions offending against consistency, and some instances of disappointing legitimate expectations are cited: de Smith (6th edn), 592; (7th edn), 636.
[6] De Smith (6th edn), 592; (7th edn), 641.

power' and injunction to the courts to review the decision in the round captures the notion of contextual review of the kind discussed below.

Thirdly, in a number of passages there is recognition of the role of deference, especially in its unstructured formulation, in relation to human rights adjudication.[7] The *Huang* case, where the House of Lords endorse this approach to deference, is discussed on a number of occasions.[8] Aspects of the discussion relate to the basis for such deference, but in a couple of places the unstructured and non-doctrinal nature of this style of deference is acknowledged.[9] For example, under the heading of 'culture of justification' and citing *Huang*, the authors say:[10]

> Even where the courts recognise their lack of capacity or expertise to make the primary decision, they should nevertheless not easily relinquish their secondary function of probing the quality of the reasoning and ensuring that assertions are properly justified.

They suggest that, when an equilibrium is to be drawn between competing interests, the proper approach is for the courts to show 'respect' to the balance struck by a 'person or institution with special expertise in that area'.[11]

5.2.2 New Zealand: Cookeian Simplicity and Instinctive Review

Within New Zealand's legal system, one finds a strong undercurrent of support for broadly framed and unconstrained supervisory review. This is undoubtedly attributable to the significance of Lord Cooke and his simplicity project.[12] The preference for simplicity over complexity, substance over form, and discretion over structure continues to have a degree of currency today.

Over many decades Lord Cooke promoted a model of judicial review that was shorn of formalism and technicalities. Instead he encouraged

---

[7] De Smith (6th edn), 587; (7th edn), 636.

[8] De Smith (6th edn), 547, 549, 555, 597; (7th edn), 590, 592, 598, 641.

[9] De Smith (6th edn), 549–50, 555, 597; (7th edn), 589–90; 598, 641.

[10] De Smith (6th edn), 592; (7th edn), 641.

[11] De Smith (6th edn), 597; (7th edn), 641; repeating a passage from *Bato Star Fishing Ltd* v. *Chief Director of Marine Coastal Management* (2004) 4 SA 490.

[12] Dean R. Knight, 'Simple, Fair, Discretionary Administrative Law' (2008) 39 VUWLR 99; Michael Taggart, 'The Contribution of Lord Cooke to Scope of Review Doctrine in Administrative Law' in Paul Rishworth (ed.), *The Struggle for Simplicity in the Law* (Butterworths, 1997), 189; Janet McLean, 'Constitutional and Administrative Law' in Rishworth (ed.), *Struggle for Simplicity*, 221; Philip A. Joseph, 'The Contribution of the Court of Appeal to Commonwealth Administrative Law' in Rick Bigwood, *The Permanent New Zealand Court of Appeal* (Hart Publishing, 2009), 41.

the notion that judges ought to retain the broad power to intervene to address injustice wherever it was seen. Lord Cooke's simplified statement of the tripartite grounds has already been highlighted.[13] His other targets were many: the language of jurisdiction and jurisdictional error (a 'rather elusive thing'),[14] formalist natural justice ('fairness' to be preferred),[15] narrow defined standing (echoing Lord Diplock's condemnation of 'outdated technical rules of locus standi'),[16] and *Wednesbury* unreasonableness (a 'tautologous formula' and an 'unfortunately retrogressive decision'),[17] to highlight just a few. Emblematic of his style, of course, was his strong advocacy in support of 'substantive fairness', as a legitimate ground of judicial review, 'shading into but not identical with unreasonableness'.[18] Substantive fairness allowed judges, he said, to consider 'the adequacy of the administrative consideration given to a matter and of the administrative reasoning' and enabled 'a measure of flexibility enabling redress for misuses of administrative authority which might otherwise go unchecked'.[19] Consistent with this theme, he also signalled his support for Lord Donaldson's analogous 'innominate' ground of review.[20]

Others have since continued his campaign in favour of broad and unconstrained supervisory review. A few examples demonstrate his legacy endures. First, open-textured and discretion-laden judicial review doctrines continue to marshal strong support. Lord Cooke's substantive fairness has already been mentioned; although the drive for a ground of that name has since diminished, the campaign has shifted to other doctrines.[21]

---

[13] See ch. 3, text to n. 151.

[14] *Bulk Gas Users Group Ltd* v. *Attorney-General* [1983] NZLR 129, 136.

[15] *Daganayasi* v. *Minister of Immigration* [1980] 2 NZLR 130.

[16] *Environmental Defence Society Inc* v. *South Pacific Aluminium Ltd (No 3)* [1981] 1 NZLR 216.

[17] *R (International Traders' Ferry Ltd)* v. *Chief Constable of Sussex* [1999] 2 AC 418, 452; *R (Daly)* v. *Secretary of State for the Home Department* [2001] 2 AC 532, 549.

[18] *Thames Valley Electric Power Board* v. *NZFP Pulp & Paper Ltd* [1994] 2 NZLR 641, 653. See also *Northern Roller Milling Co Ltd* v. *Commerce Commission* [1994] 2 NZLR 747. Despite Lord Cooke's efforts in the late 1980s and early 1990s, it failed to gain any real traction as a ground in itself: see Joseph, 'Commonwealth Administrative Law', above n. 12, 65.

[19] *Thames Valley*, ibid.

[20] Robin Cooke, 'Fairness' (1989) 19 VUWLR 421, 426; 'The Discretionary Heart of Administrative Law' in Christopher Forsyth and Ivan Hare (eds.), *The Golden Metwand and the Crooked Cord* (Claredon, 1998), 203, 212; 'Foreword' in G.D.S. Taylor *Judicial Review* (Butterworths, 1991), iv; 'Foreword' in Philip A. Joseph, *Constitutional and Administrative Law in New Zealand* (2nd edn, Brookers, 2001), vi; 'The Road Ahead for the Common Law' (2004) 53 ICLQ 273, 284.

[21] Dean R. Knight, 'Mapping the Rainbow of Review' (2010) NZ Law Rev 393.

Others have echoed his support for a simplified and unified form of unreasonableness: Thomas J's plea in *Waitakere City Council* v. *Lovelock*, for a simpler expression, being a notable instance.[22] Similarly, the innominate ground from *Guinness* has been deployed, with the Court of Appeal recommending its 'more flexible approach' when reviewing quasi-public decisions of unincorporated bodies.[23] This innominate ground therefore seems to have acquired greater currency in New Zealand than in England where it was first deployed.[24]

Secondly, amongst the senior judiciary, there is little appetite for structured formulations of deference, either in substantive review at common law or in human rights adjudication under the New Zealand Bill of Rights Act 1990. Much of the opposition is headed by the present Chief Justice, Dame Sian Elias, who has been a vocal critic of doctrinal forms of deference and variable intensity. She described deference as 'dreadful'[25] and said spectrums of unreasonableness were 'a New Zealand perversion of recent years'.[26] She has also rejected attempts to articulate structured forms of curial deference, both in judicial review cases,[27] and in statutory appeals.[28] Like Lord Cooke, she prefers simple and discretionary standards for intervention. '[T]here is no need for any amplification of reasonableness or fairness', she said, as 'both [take] their shape from context'.[29] These

---

[22] [1997] 2 NZLR 385, 403 ('whether a reasonable authority acting with fidelity to its empowering statute could have arrived at the decision it did in the circumstances of that case').

[23] *Electoral Commission* v. *Cameron* [1997] 2 NZLR 421. See also its recognition in *Health Authority Trust* v. *Director of Health and Disability Consumer Advocacy* [2008] NZCA 67; *Wilkins* v. *Auckland District Court* (1997) 10 PRNZ 395; *Issac* v. *Minister of Consumer Affairs* [1990] 2 NZLR 606; *Taiaroa* v. *Minister of Justice* (CP 99/94, High Court, 4.10.1994); *Shaw* v. *Attorney-General (No 2)* [2003] NZAR 216; *Te Runanga o Ngai Tahu* v. *Attorney-General* (CIV-2003-404-1113, 6.11.2003).

[24] See text to n. 53.

[25] *Ye* v. *Minister of Immigration* (NZSC, transcript, 21-23 April 2009, SC53/2008), 179 (Elias CJ), quoted in Knight, 'Rainbow of Review', above n. 21, 400.

[26] *Astrazeneca Ltd* v. *Commerce Commission* (NZSC, transcript, 8 July 2009, SC 91/2008), 52.

[27] *Discount Brands Ltd* v. *Westfield (New Zealand) Ltd* [2005] 2 NZLR 597, [5] (questions not 'helpfully advanced by consideration of the scope and intensity').

[28] *Austin, Nichols & Co Inc* v. *Stichting Lodestar* [2008] 2 NZLR 141 and *McGrath* v. *Accident Compensation Corporation* [2011] 3 NZLR 733. See Andrew Beck, 'Farewell to the Forum Otiosum?' [2011] NZLJ 269 and Edward Willis, 'Judicial Review and Deference' [2011] NZLJ 283.

[29] Sian Elias, 'Administrative Law for Living People' (2009) 68 CLJ 47, 48. See also Sian Elias, 'Righting Administrative Law' in David Dyzenhaus, Murray Hunt and Grant Huscroft (eds.), *A Simple Common Lawyer* (Hart Publishing, 2009), 55. See also Sian Elias, 'The Unity of Public Law?' (Public Law conference, September 2016, Cambridge), 1 (characterising

sentiments have been echoed by other members of the Supreme Court.[30] One particularly notable example is the rhetorical remark of Tipping J (in the course of oral argument), asking whether, as a judge, 'in the end, you interfere if you think you should.'[31] Again, this reflects the instinctive test for intervention expressed in the innominate ground. In addition, the concept of deference in human rights adjudication is relatively fledgling. In the leading decision on assessment of justified limitations under the NZ Bill of Rights Act, judges only made passing reference to any influence deference should have;[32] when mentioned, it was characterised as a general form of latitude, which may vary in the circumstances.[33]

Finally, leading members of the academy and bar continue to crusade strongly in favour of simple and discretionary approaches to judicial supervision. For example, Professor Joseph speaks strongly against the 'terminological congestion' and 'pedagogical confusion' in judicial review.[34] Part of his solution is exposing the 'instinctive impulse' as the chemistry of the judicial task (an approach discussed further below).[35] Leading silk Francis Cooke applauds Joseph's rationalisation,[36] as well as speaking – in a similar vein to his judge father – about the importance of simplicity: 'Notions of intensity simply obscure the real task, which is to ensure the law is being followed.'[37] The small nature of the legal community mean such views are particularly influential.

5.2.3   Canada: Broad Church Unreasonableness

Canada's long-standing commitment to explicit standards of review has already been examined.[38] The doctrinal prominence given to the calibration of intensity or deference means the regime is catalogued under the intensity of review model, with other approaches which seek to manifest intensity in a preliminary and structured fashion. However, one aspect of Canada's

---

New Zealand as taking 'the simple path of optimistic contextualism' and asking rhetorically whether 'the search for better doctrine is ultimately doomed').

[30] Knight, 'Rainbow of Review', above n. 21, 402. Further, the judgments in *Austin* and *McGrath* were judgments for the whole court.

[31] *Ye* (transcript), above n. 25.

[32] *Hansen* v. *R* [2007] 3 NZLR 1.

[33] See e.g. *ibid.*, [111] (Tipping J) and [268] (Anderson J).

[34] Philip A. Joseph, 'Exploratory Questions in Administrative Law' (2012) 25 NZULR 75, 81.

[35] *Ibid.*, 74 and 101.

[36] Francis Cooke, 'The Future of Public Law in New Zealand' in *Administrative Law* (New Zealand Law Society, 2011), 75 (proclaiming Joseph 'New Zealand's own Voltaire').

[37] Francis Cooke, 'A Personal Word' (2008) 39 VUWLR 15, 19.

[38] See Section 3.2.5 and Section 4.2.2.

post-*Dunsmuir* regime perhaps has greater affinity with the contextual review model. In particular, following the collapse of the different forms of unreasonableness, the new broad church formulation of unreasonableness presents a more discretionary and open-textured approach.[39] Therefore, apart from cases where the correctness of review is appropriate, the determination of the depth of review takes an implicit and floating character. Bastarache and LeBel JJ framed reasonableness review in classic terms:[40]

> Reasonableness is a deferential standard animated by the principle that ... certain questions that come before administrative tribunals do not lend themselves to one specific, particular result. Instead, they may give rise to a number of possible, reasonable conclusions. Tribunals have a margin of appreciation within the range of acceptable and rational solutions.

They went on to say that a reviewing court needs to be attentive to the quality of reasons and the diversity of outcomes:[41]

> [R]easonableness is concerned mostly with the existence of justification, transparency and intelligibility within the decision-making process. But it is also concerned with whether the decision falls within a range of possible, acceptable outcomes which are defensible in respect of the facts and law.

The new category of unreasonableness does not, though, mandate more intensive review than previous.[42] Deference is still a crucial ingredient to the supervisory task: 'Deference is both an attitude of the court and a requirement of the law of judicial review.'[43] Once again, the Dyzenhaus characterisation of 'deference as respect' was endorsed;[44] the concept of

---

[39] *Dunsmuir* v. *New Brunswick* [2008] 1 SCR 190. See generally Paul Daly, '*Dunsmuir's* Flaws Exposed' (2012) 58 McGill LJ 1; Mullan, '*Dunsmuir*', below n. 48; 'Unresolved Issues', below n. 48; Gerald P. Heckman, 'Substantive Review in Appellate Courts Since *Dunsmuir*' (2009) 47 Osgoode Hall LJ 751; Andrew Green, 'Can There Be Too Much Context in Administrative Law?' (2014) 47 UBC Law Rev 443; Paul Daly, 'The Scope and Meaning of Reasonableness Review' (2015) 52 Alta Law Rev 799; David Stratas, 'The Canadian Law of Judicial Review' (2016) Queen's LR 27. See Section 4.2.2.

[40] *Dunsmuir*, above n. 39, [47].

[41] *Ibid.*

[42] *Ibid.*, [48]. See, however, Robert Danay, 'Quantifying *Dunsmuir*: An Empirical Analysis of the Supreme Court of Canada's Jurisprudence on Standard of Review' (2016) 66 UTLJ 55, where it is suggested that the Supreme Court may be more deferential following *Dunsmuir*, albeit acknowledging that such a trend may not necessarily be inherent in the *Dunsmuir* framework itself.

[43] *Dunsmuir*, above n. 39.

[44] David Dyzenhaus, 'The Politics of Deference' in Michael Taggart (ed.), *The Province of Administrative Law* (Hart Publishing, 1997), 279, 286; referred to in *Dunsmuir*, above n. 39, [48] and previously endorsed in *Baker* v. *Canada (Minister of Citizenship and Immigration)* [1999] 2 SCR 817, [65]; *Law Society of New Brunswick* v. *Ryan* [2003] 1 SCR 247, [49].

deference, 'imports *respect* for the decision-making process of adjudicative bodies with regard to both the facts and the law'.[45] In other words, issues of deference are resolved through the application of weight: 'Deference in the context of the reasonableness standard therefore implies that courts will give due consideration to the determinations of decision makers.'[46] This approach, Bastarache and Le Bel JJ said, provided sufficient on-the-ground guidance, while still allowing review where justice required it.[47]

It is fair to say, though, that the *Dunsmuir* approach modifies the location of the deference analysis. As Binnie J said in his separate reasons in *Dunsmuir*:[48]

> 'Contextualizing' a single standard of review will shift the debate (slightly) from choosing *between* two standards of reasonableness that each represent a different level of deference to a debate *within* a single standard of reasonableness to determine the appropriate level of deference.

Binnie J continued to highlight the amount of discretion the singular formulation of reasonableness provides. '"Reasonableness" is a deceptively simple omnibus term', he said in *Alberta Teachers' Association*, 'which gives reviewing judges a broad discretion to choose from a variety of levels of scrutiny from the relatively intense to the not so intense.'[49]

Indeed, since *Dunsmuir*, the breadth of the reasonableness standard has become readily apparent; in successor cases in the Supreme Court, the effective depth of scrutiny has varied from something close to correctness, to ordinary reasonableness, to manifest (*Wednesbury*-style) unreasonableness.[50] But rather than taking explicitly doctrinal form as in the pre-*Dunsmuir* days, the calibration of depth of review remains inchoate and at large. Reasonableness, in its post-*Dunsmuir* form now 'floats' along an infinite spectrum of deference – a judicial method once condemned in the

---

[45] *Dunsmuir*, above n. 39, [48] (emphasis added).

[46] *Ibid.*, [49].

[47] *Ibid.*, [43].

[48] *Ibid.*, [139]. See also David Mullan, '*Dunsmuir* v. *New Brunswick*' (2008) 21 CJALP 117, 134 ('reasonableness is a standard that admits of varying levels on intensity of review depending on the context'); 'Unresolved Issues on the Standard of Review' (2013) 42 AQ 1.

[49] *Alberta (Information and Privacy Commissioner)* v. *Alberta Teachers' Association* [2011] 3 SCR 654, [87]. See also *Canada (Attorney-General)* v. *Canadian Human Rights Commission* [2013] FCA 75, [12].

[50] *Canada (Canadian Human Rights Commission)* v. *Canada (Attorney-General)* [2011] 3 SCR 471; *Alberta Teachers'*, above n. 49; *Catalyst Paper Corp* v. *North Cowichan (District)* [2012] 1 SCR 5, discussed by Daly, '*Dunsmuir's* Flaws', above n. 39.

prologue to *Dunsmuir*.[51] As the Court put it in *Catalyst Paper*, reasonableness 'is an essentially contextual inquiry'.[52]

5.2.4   England: Review in the Round and Non-doctrinal Deference

The emblematic case for the strong form of contextual review is *R (Guinness plc)* v. *Panel on Take-overs and Mergers*, although its subsequent application is rare.[53] Lord Donaldson spoke of the courts stepping in when 'something had gone wrong of a nature and degree which required the intervention of the court'.[54] The body subject to review – a private, unincorporated, self-regulatory body – was described as unique and *sui generis*. The absence of a legislative template on which to base review meant the Court of Appeal was driven to generate a more generalised basis for supervising the Panel's activities (in the particular case, the refusal to adjourn a hearing about a potential breach of the Panel's code on take-overs and mergers). This justified review, Lord Donaldson said, 'more in the round than might otherwise be the case and, whilst basing its decision on familiar concepts, should eschew any formal categorisation'.[55]

Recently, a member of the Supreme Court expressly commended the instinctive approach in extra-judicial remarks.[56] Lord Carnwath dismissed the notion of sliding scales of intensity and *Wednesbury*'s traditional deferential approach; instead he confessed that while on the bench his approach was much closer to the 'characteristically pragmatic approach' set out in *Guinness*.[57]

---

[51] *Ryan*, above n. 44, [20] and [44]. After *Dunsmuir*, the majority in *Canada (Citizenship and Immigration)* v. *Khosa* [2009] 1 SCR 339 was anxious, though, to avoid the language of a spectrum ([108]): 'these are single standards, not moving points along a spectrum'; compare Binnie J: reasonableness is 'a single standard that takes its colour from the context' ([59]).

[52] *Catalyst Paper*, above n. 50, [18]. See also *Khosa*, above n. 51, [59].

[53] [1990] 1 QB 146. See also *R (Camelot Group plc)* v. *National Lottery Commission* [2001] EMLR 3. For cases in which it was acknowledged but not made out, see e.g. *R (Niazi)* v. *Secretary of State for the Home Department* [2007] EWHC 1495; *R (A)* v. *Lord Saville of Newdigate* [2000] 1 WLR 1855. See discussion the 'innominate ground' (ch. 3 n. 131) above.

[54] *Guinness*, above n. 53, 160. I have distinguished the *Guinness* approach from variegated forms of unreasonableness because the *Guinness* approach has a broader ambit and more general character, unlike the forms of unreasonableness which try to express particularised degrees of scrutiny. See Section 4.2.3 above.

[55] *Ibid.*, 159.

[56] Lord Carnwath, 'From Judicial Outrage to Sliding Scales' (ALBA Annual Lecture, November 2013), 19.

[57] *Ibid.*

In its weaker form, unstructured contextualism is also represented in England by the current approach to deference in human rights adjudication under the Human Rights Act. The genesis of different approaches to judicial restraint applied in the assessment of whether limitations on rights are justified was discussed earlier.[58] In particular, doctrinal formulations which initially attracted some favour and continue to be supported by many scholars were identified. The present judicial approach to deference, however, has a non-doctrinal character.

The ground was laid in *Daly*, with Lord Steyn's now famous concluding remark about the nature of the proportionality test: 'In law context is everything'.[59] This signalled the move towards a free-floating principle of contextualism that was ultimately to colour the preference for a non-doctrinal form of deference through the weight principle. The leading authority on this point is Lord Bingham's speech in *Huang*, with which all other members of the appellate committee in that case joined.[60] The House was called on to determine the proper approach to be applied when appellate immigration authorities assessed whether the ministerial refusal of leave to remain breached the applicants' right to family life under the Human Rights Act.[61] In essence, the House of Lords ruled that any questions of deference should simply be determined on a case-by-case basis in the ordinary way by applying 'weight' to the views of the administration. Lord Bingham was critical of attempts to structure these considerations by reference to various devices: 'due deference', 'discretionary areas of judgment', 'margin of appreciation', 'democratic accountability', 'relative institutional competence', and so forth.[62] He said doing so had the tendency to 'complicate and mystify what is not, in principle, a hard task to define, however difficult the task is, in practice, to perform'.[63] Instead, a non-doctrinal approach was preferred:[64]

> The giving of weight to factors ... is the performance of the ordinary judicial task of weighing up the competing considerations on each side and according appropriate weight to the judgment of a person with responsibility for a given subject matter and access to special sources of knowledge and advice. That is how any rational judicial decision-maker is likely to proceed.

58 See Section 4.2.3 above.
59 *Daly*, above n. 17, [28].
60 *Huang* v. *Secretary of State for the Home Department* [2007] 2 AC 167.
61 Lord Bingham treated the question as the same for all authorities: the adjudicator, Immigration Appeal Tribunal, and Court of Appeal.
62 *Huang*, above n. 60, [14].
63 *Ibid.*
64 *Ibid.*, [16].

The language and label of deference was expressly disavowed: this weighing process 'is not, in our opinion, aptly described as deference'.[65] The preference for non-doctrinal deference and weight has been reinforced subsequently by the House of Lords and Supreme Court in a number of cases.[66]

5.2.5   Conclusion

Under contextual review, normative reasoning is preferred over doctrinal reasoning. Joseph characterises the method in the following way:[67]

> The forensic exercise is 'inherently discretionary' and cannot be reduced to formulaic rules for producing predictable and mechanical outcomes ... 'Has something gone wrong?' is the litmus test for determining which cases are deserving of the court's intervention, and cases which are not.

In its strong form, a singular basis for intervention is posed, based on judicial judgement and instinct. In its weaker form, it recognises that context may require the courts to respect and give weight to the views of others, but avoids giving this restraint or deference any doctrinal form. This style of approach, while not widespread, appears in parts of Canadian, English and New Zealand jurisprudence.

5.3   Conceptual Underpinnings

The contextual review schema, generally based on unstructured judgement on the part of judges, comes through in the scholarship of Allan, Joseph, Hickman and Dyzenhaus. All four are eager to eschew doctrinal frameworks to vary the supervisory lens; instead, they see matters of deference or restraint as forming part of the ordinary course of judging in the

---

[65] *Ibid.*

[66] See e.g. *R (SB)* v. *Governors of Denbigh High School* [2007] 1 AC 100; *Belfast City Council* v. *Miss Behavin' Ltd* [2007] 1 WLR 1420; *Animal Defenders, R (Animal Defenders International)* v. *Secretary of State for Culture, Media and Sport* [2008] 1 AC 1312, [33] (and, in that context, 'great weight'); *R (Quila)* v. *Secretary of State for the Home Department* [2012] 1 AC 621; *R (Nicklinson)* v. *Ministry of Justice* [2014] 3 WLR 200 [166]–[171], [348]; *R (Lord Carlile)* v. *Secretary of State for the Home Department* [2014] UKSC 60. See also *Kennedy* v. *Charity Commission* [2014] 2 WLR 808 (correctness review, along with an emphasis on 'weight', in the context of common law unreasonableness review) and *Pham* v. *Secretary of State for the Home Department* [2015] 1 WLR 1591 (especially the emphasis on 'context' determining intensity and weight to the primary decision-maker's view); ch. 4 text to n. 87 above.

[67] Joseph, 'Exploratory Questions', above n. 34, 75, 79.

particular context. However, the models they propose for judicial deliberation have different aspects and emphases.

Allan argues it is the constitutional duty of the courts to assess the propriety of the administrative decisions in the circumstances of the individual case, based on rule of law principles. Joseph constructs supervisory review around the notion of a judicial instinct – an entirely unstructured approach to the assessment of the circumstances. Hickman argues in favour of the employment of non-doctrinal deference, in the form of a basic assessment of the weight to be given to the views of others, in human rights adjudication.[68] Dyzenhaus also favours a non-doctrinal appraisal of a decision in context, but believes the focus ought to be the reasonableness (not correctness) of the relationship between the decision and its justification.

5.3.1 Trevor Allan: Unstructured and Normative Contextualism

One of the strongest advocates for unstructured contextualism – and against giving principles of deference or restraint doctrinal form – is Allan. The model of government and judicial methodology he promotes is based on a thick and judicially enforced version of the rule of law with a qualified approach to legislative supremacy. His condemnation of absolute legislative supremacy takes him outside the usual terrain of the ultra vires debate.

First, Allan is reluctant to be drawn into either of the main schools of thought,[69] although he admits the constitutional foundation of judicial review is a question of great significance.[70] For him, 'the match has been fixed'; the tacit agreement that ultimately parliamentary sovereignty trumps, he says, 'threatens the coherence of the debate' and leads to practically no difference between the two main schools.[71] Allan argues that limits and conditions of legislative supremacy must also be debated and absolute sovereignty ought to be rejected. He would shuffle these questions into his contextual treatment in the supervisory process.

---

[68] Compare his position more generally; see Section 3.3.3.

[69] T.R.S. Allan, *The Sovereignty of Law* (Oxford University Press, 2013), 229. Allan says a 'misguided focus on competing *sources* of administrative law, characteristic of legal positivism, has deflected attention away from subtle practicalities of legal interpretation in particular circumstances'.

[70] *Ibid.*, 211.

[71] *Ibid.*, 209.

Allan's objection to the ultra vires theory, as well as its embrace of parliamentary supremacy, is the artificiality of legislative intent, although he accepts that statutory context can (and should) play a role in the supervisory jurisdiction. The ultra vires theory is to attempt to – in Allan's view, problematically – reconcile legislative supremacy and the rule of law.[72] The central presumption that Parliament intends the rule of law to be observed means any breach of the rule of law is treated as a breach of the limits of the power delegated to the decision-maker. The 'standards of legality' (grounds of review) cannot be engaged without the decision-maker losing their jurisdiction because the standards are treated as inherent limits on the power conferred; framed in terms of policing the boundaries of power, the ultra vires theory therefore presents no threat to parliamentary supremacy. But, Allan argues, this formal rationalisation provides inadequate substantive guidance or legitimacy because 'the ultra vires doctrine is consistent with whatever limits on administrative discretion the court decides that the rule of law requires'.[73] In other words, the strong presumptive role of the rule of law effectively means Parliament's authority, while absolute in theory, is practically constrained. The courts will, Allan argues, not acknowledge attempts by Parliament to confer unreasonable, unfair or unfettered powers.[74] Further, Allan laments the pretence of the jurisdictional reasoning based on ultra vires and the grounds of review method; for him, this method is ultimately dependent on context and is inevitably manipulable:[75]

> The doctrinal heads and categories of public law are quintessentially markers for the role of constitutional principle in the appraisal of executive action. They indicate the nature of the argument necessary, in each case, to show that such action satisfies the demands of legality; and they obtain their concrete content from application to the circumstances of a specific complaint of illegality.

Allan suggests that, if legislative supremacy is put to one side, the ultra vires theory is capable of being recast in narrower and more plausible terms – merely emphasising the link between judicial review and statutory interpretation.[76] In other words, he is content for some emphasis to be placed on 'the specific statutory context in which the general grounds of

---

[72] *Ibid.*, 213.
[73] *Ibid.*, 214.
[74] *Ibid.*, referring to the circumvention of privative clauses as a prime example.
[75] *Ibid.*, 237.
[76] *Ibid.*, 215.

review must be applied'.[77] This is consistent, he argues, with his overarching conception of contextualism: 'judgements of fairness or reasonableness or proper purposes are necessarily attuned to all the circumstances'.[78]
And the latter necessarily includes judicial consideration of the statutory
background ('the enacted provisions and the policies and purposes that
best appear to animate them').[79]

The powerful authority of the courts under Allan's preferred model of
contextualism is suggestive of the common law school. However, Allan
takes issue with the impotence of the model and the common law label
that comes with it. Allan observes that the grounds of review – 'articulated
and developed by the judges' – are part of the common law and 'exemplify
the common law's commitment to constitutionalism'– a clear nod to the
common law school.[80] At the same time, he dismisses the notion, generally
accepted in the common law school, that these common law expressions
of legality are subservient to the decree of the legislature. Drawing on Sir
John Laws,[81] Allan characterises the grounds of review as 'constitutional
fundamentals ... impervious to any purported legislative abrogation'.[82] As
Parliament 'invokes the idea of law', when it makes law 'it cannot logically
repudiate the basic principle of legality';[83] any conception of legislative
intent must therefore, he says, operate consistently with the principle of
legality and the rule of law. Hence, he argues, the common law and the
ultra vires theories converge. Allan is also critical of the emphasis that the
common law theory places on 'free-stranding criterion of administrative legality, independent of context'.[84] Its proponents 'underestimate the
pliability of the grounds of review, which in many cases serve mainly to
summarize a finding of illegality closely dependent on all the circumstances'.[85] Moreover, the common law approach is also a 'threat to democracy'
because there is '[t]oo much emphasis in the independent operation of the
common law, separately from statute'.[86]

---

[77] Ibid.
[78] Ibid.
[79] Ibid.
[80] Ibid., 221.
[81] John Laws, 'Illegality' in Michael Supperstone and James Goudie (eds.), Judicial Review
(2nd edn, Butterworths, 1997), 51.
[82] Allan, Sovereignty, above n. 69, 216 and 217.
[83] Ibid., 217.
[84] Ibid., 224.
[85] Ibid., 224.
[86] Ibid., 235.

Despite the logic of his argument, Allan argues that his theory does not amount to common law prevailing over statute or vice versa; they are not external fetters on the grant of power.[87] Rather, he frames the principles of administrative legality or other constitutional norms as 'essential presuppositions'; in his language, they are 'internal to the correct construction of the legislative powers conferred'.[88] Seeking to avoid the language of supremacy, he instead seeks to present an integrated approach. 'Parliament and courts cooperate to preserve the integrity of liberal democracy'.[89] He argues the *Cart* case (where the courts adopted a nuanced and residual review approach in the light of an alternative adjudicative structure, protected by a privative clause) demonstrated 'the court permit[ting] a statutory tribunal to exercise the authority (including interpretative authority) appropriate to the constitutional function conferred by Parliament in ... its legitimate democratic role'.[90] In other words, although not in words Allan would use, a more deferential standard of review allowed the relative authority of the tribunal to be squared with the constitutional role of the court in relation to standards of legality.

Allan's solution to the legitimacy question lies in contextualism: '[P]rinciples of legality must be sensitive to context'.[91] The legitimacy of judicial review turns on its 'manner of exercise' as much as its underlying principles.[92] Moreover, he characterises the dynamic and case-by-case 'integration of legislative aim and structure, on the one hand, and the constraints of legality, on the other' as the *raison d'être* of public law adjudication.[93] In other words, the principles and their application must 'tread a delicate line between unwarranted interference with a public agency's functions ... and failure to protect the victim of an abuse of power'.[94] However, ostensibly inconsistent with this position, Allan maintains that the courts are still obliged to intervene if they conclude there has been an abuse of power, because, in his eyes, failing to do so would involve the courts 'giving up on law' and would amount to abdication of responsibility.[95]

---

[87] *Ibid.*, 229.
[88] *Ibid.*
[89] *Ibid.*, 223.
[90] *Ibid.*, referring to *R (Cart)* v. *Upper Tribunal* [2012] 1 AC 663.
[91] Allan, *Sovereignty*, above n. 69, 226.
[92] *Ibid.*, 234.
[93] *Ibid.*, 234.
[94] *Ibid.*, 226.
[95] *Ibid.*

One of Allan's central themes is hostility to judicial deference or restraint. He concedes, though, that while the common law grounds of review are fundamentally important, there may be a limited role for democratically grounded restraint in some cases. In reality, this vanishes quickly. Allan suggests there may be instances when the courts may might need to exercise restraint or deference for reasons of constitutional legitimacy or institutional expertise; however, he strongly resists that any consequent restraint be given independent doctrinal form.[96] His claim is that these matters are, if one accepts his internal and contextual approach, already factored into the supervisory process. That is, an independent and external doctrine of deference is redundant. But the concession to contextual deference is hollow and is ultimately overshadowed by an injunction that the courts must step in to address abuse.

Allan's vision for judicial review, as developed above, is contextualism, rather than any specific schema or organising principles. Context is the essential mediating device; in Allan's eyes, the contextual sensitivity of judicial review 'dissolves' any antagonism between the rule of law and parliamentary supremacy.[97] Doctrine – whether in the form of grounds, categories or other structuring methodologies – is frowned upon; however, the concept of grounds of review is not entirely obliterated and continues to serve a modest, subordinate role:[98]

> From an appropriately internal, interpretative stance, many of the distinctions and categories invented for purpose of analytical exposition lose their force – or at least serve only as very rough guides to the making of an evaluative legal judgement, dependent on all the circumstances.

The essential commitment is to a judgement-based approach. While contextual review is seen by Allan as legitimate as acceptable methodology, he also acknowledges that it may benefit from having some explicit analytical reasoning added.[99] To this extent, his model of judicial adjudication is not as instinctive as Joseph's.

---

[96] *Ibid.*, 241.

[97] *Ibid.*, 228.

[98] *Ibid.*, 249. The contextual adaptability of the principles of legality/grounds of review is a key part of Allan's logic that the common law principles are omnipotent and need not be seen as being suspended or curtailed by the legislature. Indeed, he rejects the characterisation of his approach in terms of a principle of legality. For him, constitutional rights or fundamental norms are not capable of abrogation; they are 'an implicit condition of the validity of both administrative action and parliamentary enactment' (243).

[99] *Ibid.*, 242.

A particular consequence of the instinctive approach is, for example, that Allan shows little interest in the debates between unreasonableness and proportionality, seeing little difference between the two.[100] These grounds only operate as 'convenient labels for a form of review that must press as far, in each case, as is necessary to satisfy the court ... that the action in question is truly justified'.[101]

Allan rebels against efforts to give judicial deference any tangible and independent role, as noted earlier.[102] First, he argues a separate doctrine is unnecessary in light of the contextual methodology he promotes:[103]

> The appropriate degree of deference is dictated, in each case, by analysis of the substantive legal issues arising. If properly conducted, the analysis will indicate the correct division of responsibilities between court and agency, making all due allowance for the exercise of administrative discretion and recourse to specialist expertise. That division of responsibilities is itself the outcome of legal analysis attuned to the specific questions of legality arising; it cannot determine these questions, a priori, on the basis of general features of the separation of powers divorced from the specific constitutional context.

Secondly, he rejects the suggestion that the courts ought to weigh up the various factors relevant to deference in order to calibrate the intensity of review, even if done on a case-by-case basis.[104] Allan's claim is that constructing deference in this way amounts to the abdication of the judicial function to determine the legality of the action. He would avoid the language of deference altogether (a court 'does not "defer" to Parliament or Government in any ordinary sense of that term'); 'deference' for him merely marks the situation where an administrative decision is accepted by the courts as 'fall[ing] within the proper scope of the relevant powers'.[105] True deference only arises where there is a range of outcomes that all meet

---

[100] *Ibid.*, 244, suggesting there is no difference between the two: 'a public authority that imposes a disproportionate burden on the relevant individual interests has necessarily acted unreasonably, overlooking (or disregarding) the special status of those interests.' Notably, Allan expressly parts company with Lord Steyn in *Daly* on this point.

[101] Allan, *Sovereignty*, above n. 69, 245.

[102] *Ibid.* See also Allan, 'Human Rights and Judicial Review' (2006) 65 CLJ 671, 675; 'Deference, Defiance, and Doctrine' (2010) 60 UTLJ 41. Young argues Allan's position is mistakenly based on deference amounting to submission, rather than respect: Alison Young, 'In Deference of Due Deference' (2009) 72 MLR 554.

[103] Allan, *Sovereignty*, above n. 69, 268.

[104] *Ibid.*, 269.

[105] *Ibid.*, 269, 246.

the test of justification; only in those circumstances is it legitimate, he says, for a court to defer on constitutional or expertise grounds.[106]

Thirdly, he objects to the development of standards of review or independent calibration of the supervisory lens. They are, in his view, cut from the same cloth and undermine the particularised contextual judgement he believes judges must deploy. He rejects Hickman's distinction between standards of legality and standards of review: 'the former ought to be a direct reflection of the latter'.[107] He also criticises the notion that grounds such as unreasonableness and proportionality can be calibrated by reference to independent intensity of review.[108] 'It supposes that the court must determine the appropriate form of review, within the available spectrum, on criteria quite separate from the substantive issue of *justification*, which inevitably depends on all the circumstances.'[109]

Allan's essential complaint appears to be that crystallising deference involves double-counting; the constitutional and expertise factors relevant to intensity of review are, in his view, already properly engaged in the particular question of whether the action is justified. That is not to say, though, that relative expertise might not limit the scope of a court's enquiry or the constitutional values engaged are irrelevant. It is merely that these considerations do not need separate expression from the contextual evaluation of justification. Deference moves from a doctrinal or methodological consideration to an evidential and evaluative burden: 'Judicial deference must be based on evidence and argument, in support of the decision or measure under review, that the complainant has not been able effectively to undermine.'[110] Put another way, deference is explained as the '*hesitat[ion] to condemn* as unlawful' (especially when, 'examined in the light of relevant expert knowledge, applied to the facts by an appropriately crafted procedure', the course of action may be demonstrated to be shown to be necessary and justified).[111] In this form, the judicial circumspection is seen as a function of due process, which Allan argues is the quid pro quo for any

---

[106] *Ibid.*, 246. Allan is anxious to avoid equating this to the principle of non-justiciability, which would violate his vision of the judicial imperative to adjudicate (274).

[107] *Ibid.*, 241. The distinction, 'while useful perhaps for limited purposes of exposition, is potentially misleading' (250).

[108] *Ibid.*, 246.

[109] *Ibid.*

[110] *Ibid.*, 249.

[111] *Ibid.*, 276 (emphasis added). Compare with Elliott's 'adjudicative deference' (ch. 4, text to n. 161).

judicial deference.[112] That is, a public authority must deliberate on balance in the particular circumstance (not necessarily in a quasi-judicial way); if it fails to do so, then any subsequent claim that its decision was justified is less likely to satisfy the burden of persuasion for the courts. On this account, substance and process are necessarily intertwined.

Behind the deference-sceptic analysis, Allan's analysis discloses a number of factors which may weigh in favour of judicial restraint (albeit he would object to their abstract and separate identification and would admit them only as part-and-parcel of the individualised assessment of legality he proposes).[113] For example, special deference to Parliament merely because it has elected status is improper, but sometimes Parliament's ability to address questions of public opinion or confidence may put it at a relative advantage to the courts. The nature of the question may influence, though not merely because a question is complex or polycentric; only the existence of numerous lawful courses of action, following proper legal analysis, counsels restraint (and then only because the existence of 'no uniquely right answer' means a challenge based on legality is misconceived).[114] Considerations of democratic accountability – including the availability of other avenues to address the issue – are seen as improper and, again, as the abdication of the judicial obligation to adjudicate and uphold the rule of law.[115] As mentioned, he is dismissive of attempts to articulate those factors in advance of the individualised analysis:[116]

> The extent to which considerations of expertise and competence should constrain or circumscribe judicial deliberation, however, must depend on all the circumstances; and the proper limits of judicial inquiry cannot be determined as an independent matter, divorced from those circumstances.

Despite this, he observes that the differences between his non-doctrinal account and other doctrinal versions might not be as great as first appears.[117] For example, he suggests that King's institutional model of doctrinal deference does not differ much from his own non-doctrinal version

---

[112] Allan, *Sovereignty*, above n. 69, 262.
[113] *Ibid.*, 272. See also Allan, 'Deference, Defiance, and Doctrine', above n. 102, 51; 'Human Rights', above n. 102, 688.
[114] Allan, *Sovereignty*, above n. 69, 271.
[115] The constitutional duty of the courts, he says, 'is to decide each case, after hearing evidence and argument, in accordance with the reasons it finds persuasive': Allan, 'Human Rights', above n. 102, 683.
[116] Allan, *Sovereignty*, above n. 69, 275.
[117] Compare a similar observation from the opposite perspective from Taggart: 'Proportionality', above n. 76, 456.

(he singles out King's model, but his comments are equally applicable to Hunt's).[118] He says King's approach offers 'a largely external, analytic description of an adjudicative process that, from an internal, interpretative viewpoint, is substantially "non-doctrinal"'.[119] Although deference is given an explicit role, Allan argues that this approach means the calibration of intensity is not divorced from the particular context, thereby more resembling the non-doctrinal contextual models.

While Hickman and Allan share a preference for a fact-sensitive and non-doctrinal approach to deference, Allan objects to Hickman's suggestion that the factors relevant to deference influence the judicial interpretation.[120] '[S]uch factors operate legitimately only in determining whether the right is infringed *in all the circumstances*; they should not operate independently, as second-order considerations that specify a distinct judicial approach or standard of review'.[121]

So, in essence, Allan's position on deference and the factors which may underscore judicial restraint is that these matters are 'wholly internal to the ordinary legal question' and fall to be determined 'based on established tests of legality'; in other words, 'there is no separate conceptual space for any doctrine of deference to occupy'.[122]

5.3.2   Philip Joseph: Common Law-Inspired Instinctive Judgement

Joseph is one of the most vocal proponents of the contextual approach in its strong form. He crusades against formalism and rejects attempts to justify judicial intervention under legislative intent. His support of the common law and a judicially enforced rule of law translates into a desire to free the judicial supervisory eye from any constraint; embraced, instead, is the ultimate non-doctrinal solution in the form of the instinctive impulse.

First, Joseph is a die-hard common law theorist and argues vehemently against the ultra vires theory of judicial review. It is, he says, repeating Craig's well-known objections, ahistorical, fictional and contrived.[123]

---

[118]   Allan, *Sovereignty*, above n. 69, 280.

[119]   *Ibid.*

[120]   Compare Tom Hickman, *Public Law after the Human Rights Act* (Hart Publishing, 2010).

[121]   Allan, *Sovereignty*, above n. 69, 276 fn. 124.

[122]   *Ibid.*, 278.

[123]   Philip A. Joseph, 'The Demise of Ultra Vires' [2001] PL 354, 354, 376. See also Philip A. Joseph, 'The Demise of Ultra Vires – A Reply' (2002) 8 Canta LR 463. For Craig's critique, see Section 3.3.1.

Instead, drawing on Allan, he promotes the rule of law as the legitimising and organising principle of judicial review: '[J]udicial review is founded on normative considerations of justice and the rule of law', he says, mandating the courts 'to check organised public power and to vouchsafe vital freedoms that promote individual human worth'.[124]

For him, the rule of law is 'a metaphor for principles of liberty and social justice and the "correct" organisation of the state (representative democracy and a system of independent courts)'.[125] While aspirational and contested,[126] the rule of law eclipses positivist legal method and releases a form of normative argumentation:[127]

> The rule of law represents the default 'setting' for guiding the judicial intuition where no applicable principle of law is directly in point. Constitutional norms remain partially indeterminate and obscured until actual situations of injustice arise. Such situations materialise fundamental principles in tangible form and give concrete definition to the rule of law.

Notably, Joseph invests his faith in the judiciary and is not troubled by the definitional tasks being left to the judiciary. The 'forensic mind-wrestle' – the framing and testing of competing propositions – is an adequate legal method to solve the contestability and indeterminacy of the rule of law.[128]

Secondly, in the administrative law context, Joseph's emphasis on the rule of law and 'normative argumentation' translates into what he characterises the 'instinctive impulse'.[129] The forensic exercise is 'inherently discretionary' and '[n]o amount of rule formalism can relieve the courts of their instinctual task in judicial review', he argues.[130] The limits of judicial intervention are ultimately a function of trust – we are asked to trust the cautiousness of the judiciary and their innate concern not to overstep the mark.[131]

Although a strong advocate for the recognition of the instinctive impulse at the 'nub' of judicial review, Joseph is unable to unhook his normative vision from the comfort of the grounds of review schema. Even

---

[124] Joseph, 'Ultra Vires', above n. 123, 376.
[125] Philip A. Joseph, 'The Rule of Law' in Richard Ekins (ed.), *Modern Challenges to the Rule of Law* (LexisNexis, 2011), 47, 58.
[126] *Ibid.*, 58, drawing particularly from Ronald Dworkin, *Justice in Robes* (Belknap, 2008).
[127] Joseph, 'Rule of Law', above n. 125, 60.
[128] *Ibid.*, 61.
[129] Joseph, 'Exploratory Questions', above n. 34, 74.
[130] *Ibid.*, 75 and 80. See also Joseph, 'Commonwealth Administrative Law', above n. 12, 67 ('discretionary and subjective judgment').
[131] Joseph, 'Exploratory Questions', above n. 34, 81.

though the judicial instinct dominates, judges need to 'fit applications for judicial review within an established ground of review'.[132] The decision to intervene must be cloaked into the doctrinal schema to provide it with a degree of legitimacy – the charade of legal reasoning is preserved (despite Joseph's condemnation of formalism and doctrinal method). This retention of some form of grounds of review schema by Joseph sits uncomfortably with his condemnation of doctrinal developments. Judicial review, particularly substantive review, has, he says, become a 'pedagogical morass'.[133] In the pursuit of 'simplicity', he argues that *Wednesbury* unreasonableness could simply be abandoned. He targets particularly the 'terminological congestion' associated with variegation of unreasonableness.[134] For him, many of the standards express the same notion of more intensive review and 'clutter the administrative law curriculum but offer no guidance for bench or bar'.[135] Joseph toys with two possible approaches to rationalisation – Taggart's bifurcation and Craig's proportionality – but in the end concludes unreasonableness should be dispensed with altogether in favour of his instinctive method. His complaint about the retention of *Wednesbury* unreasonableness is that, in its traditional low-intensity formulation, it never provides an independent basis for intervention. This, he argues, makes it superfluous ('forensically parasitic');[136] he is only interested in the doctrine's role in mandating intervention, not its role in tempering restraint. Proportionality holds more appeal to him, because of its structure, precision and sophistication. But he argues it, too, is redundant. Illegality and procedural impropriety (implicitly cast very broadly) cover the field.

Ultimately, Joseph contends unstructured contextualism and the judicial judgement provide the answer, without any doctrinal glosses like deference delimiting the constitutional and institutional competence of the courts. 'The courts respect the ambit of administrative discretion and limits of the adjudicative role', he says, 'without imposing yet more distracting doctrine'.[137]

---

[132] *Ibid.*, 74, 80.
[133] *Ibid.*, 81.
[134] *Ibid.*, 82. Joseph lists 11 different standards, including proportionality, although his list is deliberately exaggerated.
[135] *Ibid.*
[136] *Ibid.*, 85.
[137] *Ibid.*, 87.

5.3.3   Tom Hickman (II): Non-doctrinal Deference in Human Rights Adjudication

Hickman curiously adopts a divergent approach on the intensity of review, as explained earlier.[138] On the one hand, Hickman expresses a preference for categorical approaches to the determination of the applicable standard of legality (rejecting flexible forms of unreasonableness or proportionality). On the other hand, he goes on to argue in favour of non-doctrinal forms of deference, particularly in the context of human rights adjudication. Hickman's position on the former has already been explained; here we turn to his argument in favour of non-doctrinal deference and its parallels with contextual review.

Hickman's non-doctrinal approach to deference arises in his discussion of the narrower question of substantive review in human rights adjudication: that is, 'how the standards of legality fall to be applied by the courts', in the context of 'applying Convention rights and constitutional common law rights'.[139] Here, he resists efforts to give the principles underlying judicial restraint or deference any further doctrinal foundation.[140] Instead, he argues it is up to the courts to exhibit deference to the views of primary decision-makers on a case-by-case basis:[141]

> [T]he courts [should] take account of the various considerations that require [them] to give weight to the views of another person on a case-by-case basis, without needing to go through a process of categorisation and without needing to apply prescriptive principles to structure whether and how much weight to afford to them ... [W]e can call this a non-doctrinal approach, since the task of the courts is not regulated by any doctrine, but is simply part of the ordinary business of judging.

Doctrinal deference, he argues, 'would at best unnecessarily complicate human rights litigation, and at worst would undermine human rights protection'.[142] He advances a number of reasons why a non-doctrinal approach is to be preferred. He argues that the application of weight is a familiar curial technique.[143] 'When [judges] recognise their lack of knowledge or competence relative to another person, they understandably give

---

[138] See Section 3.3.3 above.
[139] Hickman, *Public Law*, above n. 120, 128.
[140] *Ibid.*, 130 fnn. 4–6, expressly rejecting the argument that deference should be crystallised.
[141] *Ibid.*, 128. His normative approach echoes the House of Lords' approach in *Huang*, above n. 60, and Hickman expressly endorses it (130).
[142] Hickman, *Public Law*, above n. 120, 172.
[143] *Ibid.*, 137.

weight to their views.'[144] But Hickman argues it is inappropriate to label this as 'deference', particularly because those judging have 'the responsibility of making up their own mind and [are] not relinquishing that responsibility, in substance if not in form, by accepting the opinion of another after deciding that that person is in a better position to judge'.[145] The terminology of weight is more faithful, he argues, to the curial technique. However, in making this observation, Hickman overstates the linguistic infidelity of deference, especially in light of the generally accepted framing of deference as respect, not submission. He is also critical of the apparent bluntness of deference (or that its language is suggestive of bluntness): it 'fails to capture the way that the amount of significance afforded to the views of others will vary'.[146] Again, this claim is based on a false construct; (doctrinal) deference need not be binary in nature and is capable of being applied in a nuanced fashion.

Hickman's rejection of doctrinal deference and embrace of weight is underscored by three key reasons, all based on the 'pervasive and inherently fact-sensitive nature' of deference in the adjudicative process.[147] First, he argues that the principles underlying deference can only be articulated as a high level of abstraction; they become, he argues, only 'examples of where on the particular facts and in particular circumstances and given the particular procedures, such superiority has been found to exist in a relevant respect, given the particular legal issue to be determined by the court'.[148] In other words, reasoning from generalisations is unsafe. Secondly, doctrinal deference would, he repeats, be insufficiently nuanced to capture degrees of weight or deference arising from particular facts and issues; and, if it could, it would be unduly complicated. Thirdly, the relative institutional capacity of the courts may vary within a case or across of range of cases, and again he argues that a doctrine of deference will lack sophistication to take account of this. For example, he observes that the procedures for determining an issue may vary (say, as a result of cross-examination or expert evidence), or the constitution of courts and supervisory tribunals may vary (say, through expertise-mandated appointments) and suggests a more responsive version of deference is required.

---

[144] *Ibid.* Compare with Elliott's 'adjudicative deference': ch. 4, text to n. 161.
[145] Hickman, *Public Law*, above n. 120, 137.
[146] *Ibid.*
[147] *Ibid.*
[148] *Ibid.*, 138.

While sharing Allan's critique of doctrinal approaches to deference, Hickman parts company from Allan on how deference factors ought to be reflected in a non-doctrinal approach. In particular, Hickman disagrees with Allan's parsing of deference factors in terms of external and internal and thus impermissible and permissible. Hickman argues that the distinction is 'untenable' and 'unreal'.[149] Hickman conveniently catalogues the permissible and impermissible 'reasons' for affording weight (that is, deference factors – although his non-doctrinal orientation means he avoids such language).[150] The reasons advanced by him are relatively orthodox and generally accord with those who have advocated a doctrinal form of deference in human rights adjudication.[151]

The key factors he identifies are practical reasons supporting the application of weight. First, he argues relative expertise and experience is a permissible reason, but only if it is 'relevant and superior in relation to a particular aspect of the decision' – it cannot simply be assumed by dint of the office.[152] Secondly, the rigour of the process by which the decision is made similarly may be a reason for deference, in that it may have enabled a decision-maker to assume particular expertise on a particular issue. Thirdly, the strength of the reasons given, Hickman argues, should not be a basis for affording weight; this would lead to circularity because the task of the courts is ultimately to determine whether or not those reasons ought to be accepted or rejected.[153] The nature and comprehensiveness of reasons may only serve as evidence of superior knowledge and expertise on the issues – but the latter should not be assumed from the former alone. Fourthly, the inaptness of the supervisory process to address the issues in question is a permissible reason for weight, on the basis that it affects the relative expertise of the court to adjudicate.

Notably Hickman is cautious about 'constitutional' reasons for affording weight.[154] He argues that it should not be assumed that weight is afforded merely because the decision has been made by a democratic or representative body. That is, he rejects the automatic application of weight merely based on respecting the 'allocation of functions'. However, he accepts that the particular nature of the primary decision-maker – its electoral

---

[149] *Ibid.*, 142.
[150] *Ibid.*, 145–67.
[151] See Section 4.3 above.
[152] Hickman, *Public Law*, above n. 120, 146.
[153] Compare the emphasis placed on the strength of justification by Hunt, text to n. 181, and Dyzenhaus, text to 183.
[154] Hickman, *Public Law*, above n. 120, 166.

or democratic character – may mean the courts should afford their determination some weight on the basis that it may have led to some superior
expertise on the particular issue. The basis for this should, though, be
'unpicked' – deference should not be based merely on the 'shorthand' of
democratic credentials and should be interrogated closely.[155]

Hickman is also doubtful that the importance of the impugned right –
'the fact that an administrative decision has a particularly severe impact
on an individual' – is a direct reason against affording weight or deference to the primary decision-makers.[156] As he sees it as the duty of the
courts to adjudicate and this factor does not speak to relative expertise,
Hickman deems it irrelevant. However, he concedes it may still have indirect influence. If a decision has grave impact, it may be 'legitimate and
appropriate ... for individuals on whose shoulders the decision falls to be
made to make additional efforts to acquaint themselves with the relevant
facts'.[157] This may affect the relative expertise balance as the secondary
decision-maker acquired 'enhanced decision-making capacities'.[158] So,
while the impact of the decision on an individual may not be a direct reason for deference per se, it may cause the courts to 'modify their scrutiny
and adapt their procedures' thereby ameliorating any lack of expertise.[159]

Hickman's approach to human rights adjudication (in contrast to his
approach in relation to traditional judicial review) is based on a non-
doctrinal formulation of deference: expressed in its most basic form, it is
the ordinary application of varying weight being afforded to the views of
others.

5.3.4   David Dyzenhaus: Respectful, Deferential and Non-doctrinal Appraisal

Dyzenhaus is renowned for his account of 'deference as respect'.[160] His
characterisation of deference in this way has been influential in the
Canadian development of the deference-based framework.[161] Like other

---

[155] *Ibid.*
[156] *Ibid.*, 167.
[157] *Ibid.*
[158] *Ibid.*
[159] *Ibid.* Hickman reluctantly acknowledges, though, that there are differing ways the court can give effect to factors other than through his weight principle, including through the notion of enhanced scrutiny (168).
[160] Dyzenhaus, 'Deference', above n. 44, 286.
[161] See e.g. Canadian judicial endorsements at n. 44 above.

contextualists, he favours non-doctrinal approaches to deference. However, he nominates a more reserved role for the judiciary and would charge the courts with reviewing administrative decisions according to a lens of unreasonableness, rather than correctness.

Dyzenhaus is dismissive of the ultra vires/legislative intent versus common law debate.[162] He argues the debate – and both sides of the debate[163] – unduly founders in formalism, with little substantive difference between the two schools of thought. He characterises it as a debate about 'an issue that makes no difference', which cannot therefore be resolved.[164] He explains:[165]

> All that the two camps divide on is whether [common law] values are themselves the legitimating basis for review or whether legislative intent is what legitimates judicial reliance on those values.

Both sides, he says, ultimately agree on the formal nature of the rule of law engaged in judicial review; namely, the conception of the rule of law 'sketches very distinct roles' for the different legal institutions, 'does not build in any moral values into its structure' and 'maintains the integrity of the separation of powers, formally understood'.[166] The debate therefore cannot, he laments, escape 'Dicey's "clammy spectre"'.[167]

Dyzenhaus joins the common law school in their critique of the legislative intent school, on the usual grounds. He also rejects a 'plain fact' conception of the rule of law – that is, judges are supposed to 'faithfully reflect the content of what the legislature in fact decided' – in favour of a

---

[162] David Dyzenhaus, 'Formalism's Hollow Victory' [2002] NZ Law Rev 525. For his contribution to the seminal symposium on this issue, see David Dyzenhaus, 'Form and Substance in the Rule of Law' in Christopher Forsyth (ed.), *Judicial Review and the Constitution* (Hart Publishing, 2000), 141.

[163] Dyzenhaus labels the ultra vires/legislative intent and common law schools as 'democratic positivists' and 'liberal anti-positivists' respectively: Dyzenhaus, 'Deference', above n. 44, 280. Democratic positivists seek to uphold the primacy of legislative will: law enacted by Parliament obtains its legitimacy from the accountability of Parliament to the people. Anti-positivists, in contrast, emphasise the common law and its values: these values, typically liberal values, have legitimacy because they reflect the moral values of the people and form a background against which legislation is to be interpreted.

[164] Dyzenhaus, 'Hollow Victory', above n. 162, 550. See also Dyzenhaus, 'Deference', above n. 44, 285.

[165] Dyzenhaus, 'Hollow Victory', above n. 162, 528.

[166] *Ibid.*, 527. He complains the theory of the rule of law is 'on the one hand substantive – a theory of judicial review built on the values of the common law – and on the other hand purely formal – a theory about Parliament's authority to do anything it pleases', with both camps conceding the formal component has the 'upper hand' (539).

[167] *Ibid.*, 528, drawing on Stephen Sedley, 'Foreword' in Michael Taggart, *The Province of Judicial Review* (Hart Publishing, 1997), vii, viii.

value-based conception of the rule of law committed to individual dignity (the former connoting the legislative intent school and the latter the common law school).[168] But he goes on to say that the common law argument ultimately collapses into an ultra vires argument because it recognises Parliament's legislative supremacy, something he says the common law school has provided no answer to:[169]

> [A]ny recognition that Parliament can formally exclude the operation of the common law is tantamount to a recognition that ultra vires remains the justification for judicial review. Since Parliament can assert itself over the judges, judicial review depends upon, and is therefore legitimated by, Parliament's silence.

Like Allan, Dyzenhaus is anxious that the debate about the constitutional underpinnings of judicial review be conducted without the shadow of legislative supremacy being cast over it.[170] He posits that, drawing on Pocock's language, 'consubstantiality' might be a better way to conceive of the relative authority of the legislative and judiciary; in other words, 'both Parliament and the judiciary are engaged in the same task of using reason to give expression to a common order of fundamental values'.[171] Dyzenhaus is therefore drawn to the notion of an 'internal morality' of law, compliance with which is essential for law-making authority.[172]

Moreover, Dyzenhaus argues formalism – and legitimacy accounts based on separation of powers – cannot describe the complex reality of administrative law.[173] In particular, he takes issue with the formalism, and the artificial process–substance dichotomy, which underlies the tripartite grounds of review, as generalised and systematised by Lord Diplock.[174] In the context of illegality, Dyzenhaus is particularly concerned about formalism's claims of a judicial monopoly on legal interpretation and a legislative monopoly on law-making – both of which are problematic for him because they fail to recognise the administrative state as having a legitimate role within the legal order.[175] He also condemns *Wednesbury*

---

[168] David Dyzenhaus, 'Dignity in Administrative Law' (2012) 17 Rev Const Stud 87, 104.

[169] Dyzenhaus, 'Hollow Victory', above n. 162, 538.

[170] *Ibid.*, 555.

[171] *Ibid.*, 555, citing J.G.A. Pocock, *The Ancient Constitution and the Feudal Law* (2nd edn, Cambridge University Press, 1987), 271.

[172] Dyzenhaus, 'Hollow Victory', above n. 162, 556, drawing on Lon L. Fuller, *The Morality of Law* (Yale University Press, 1964), ch. 3.

[173] Dyzenhaus, 'Hollow Victory', above n. 162, 528.

[174] *Ibid.*, 543–9.

[175] This is influenced by the Canadian context where the idea of a judicial monopoly on resolving questions of law has long since evaporated; see ch. 4 text to n. 48.

unreasonableness as a 'toothless box-ticking exercise', driven by what he describes as the 'rationality paradox'.[176] While the courts have asserted the independent power to review decision for rationality – inescapably moving them into the substantive domain – they cannot avoid the fact that their sense of rationality is modelled on 'the way in which judges think decisions should be made'; hesitant about then stepping into the shoes of the administration on matters of substance ('impos[ing] judicial standards of rationality'), the courts have de-powered the standard for intervention (that is, they have 'creat[ed] a non-legal test for illegality').[177]

Dyzenhaus' template for administrative law is based on a single standard of review: reasonableness.[178] The courts should, he says, interrogate the reasons for the decision and relationship with the conclusion reached.[179] But, unlike Allan, his proposed trigger for judicial intervention has a deferential flavour:[180]

> The court should therefore intervene only if it is prepared to discharge the onus of showing, not that it would have reached another decision, but that the decision reached is not reasonably supportable.

While the supervisory lens is calibrated according to reasonableness, Dyzenhaus still acknowledges that this will, in effect, enable variable intensity across a wide range of modulation, that is, 'more or less intense scrutiny of the reasons, depending on the nature of the interest at stake'.[181]

He is critical about the continuing ubiquity of a 'mantra-like' taboo against 'reweighing' or 'review on the merits'.[182] This prohibition, he argues, is impossible to observe, is founded on the misapprehension of a plain fact model of legislative intent, and is inconsistent with the reason-giving duty that lies at the heart of the culture of justification. The courts 'must ask whether the official's reasons do justify the conclusion – and that cannot be done ... without considering whether the official gave appropriate weight to important factors'.[183] He is therefore in agreement with scholars

---

[176] Dyzenhaus, 'Hollow Victory', above n. 162, 548.

[177] *Ibid.*, 549.

[178] Dyzenhaus, 'Dignity', above n. 168, 109.

[179] *Ibid.*

[180] Dyzenhaus, 'Deference', above n. 44, 304. He says the courts should not apply a correctness standard, 'a question that would permit them to first work out the answer and then check to see whether the official's answer coincided without any need to inspect the reasons offered by the official': Dyzenhaus, 'Dignity', above n. 168, 113.

[181] Dyzenhaus, 'Dignity', above n. 168, 113.

[182] *Ibid.*, 110.

[183] *Ibid.*, 113.

like Craig who proclaim that substantive review necessarily involves an assessment of weight.[184]

Responding to concerns about undue judicial activism and discretion, Dyzenhaus relies on an abstract ideal to temper the judicial judgement. Initially, Dyzenhaus posited the value of equality as the supervisory lodestar;[185] however, he subsequently modified this to dignity (with equality remaining as an indirect value).[186] The substantive focus on dignity – while abstract – sits awkwardly with the lens of reasonableness though. The substantive overlay risks encouraging correctness review where fidelity with the dignity objective is assessed – thereby undercutting the focus on the reasonableness of the justification proffered. If a dignity touchstone is intended to be instrumental in ameliorating judicial discretion then it must have substantive influence (over-and-above merely providing a conceptual basis for the focus on the justification); it is left unexplained how the multiple mandates can be harmonised in practice.

The adoption of the reasonableness standard, Dyzenhaus says, necessarily reflects and subsumes reasons for deference (expressly referring to the allocation of the task to a tribunal not a court, a tribunal's proximity to the dispute, and its expertise).[187] He argues the requirement of reason-giving and justification makes his approach inherently democratic;[188] the essence of citizenship is 'the democratic right [of those governed] to require an accounting for acts of public power' and the ability of the governors to 'offer adequate reasons' is central to the justification of public power.[189] Put another way, the rule of law 'depends, in the first instance, on the ability of the legal order to bring the excesses of politics to the surface and to force those who wish to violate fundamental democratic values to be explicit about it'.[190]

So, ultimately, Dyzenhaus echoes other contextualists to the extent he strips the supervisory task of detailed doctrinal constraints in favour of universal judicial judgement, assessed in the particular circumstances. However, he differs from them to the extent that the universal standard or instinct is more deferential: namely, reasonableness par excellence.

---

[184] See ch. 3 text to n. 261 above.
[185] Dyzenhaus, 'Deference', above n. 44, 305.
[186] Dyzenhaus, 'Dignity', above n. 168, 104.
[187] Dyzenhaus, 'Deference', above n. 44, 304.
[188] Ibid., 305.
[189] Ibid., 307.
[190] David Dyzenhaus and Evan Fox-Decent, 'Rethinking the Process/Substance Distinction' (2001) 51 UTLJ 193, 241.

5.3.5   Conclusion

Contextual review translates into non-doctrinal approaches to judging.[191] Judges are mandated to make their own assessment in the circumstances. Absent doctrinal directives or guidelines, the appraisal is undoubtedly normative. Judges are called on to deploy visions of administrative justice by reference only to constitutional principles such as the rule of law. And the diverse conceptions of the rule of law and administrative law lead to different versions of this appraisal.

The most prominent non-doctrinal proponent, Allan, emphasises a rule of law which is sensitive to context. A sceptic of legislative supremacy and consequential critic of a loaded ultra vires debate, he argues it is the duty of the courts – acting under law – to address any abuses of administrative power they perceive. Deference for him only operates residually, where law runs out, in relation to a range of options all of which pass scrutiny under the rule of law; only then may the courts defer to the administration's choices. In other words, correctness review. Joseph similarly promotes, again by reference to the rule of law, a model of judicial review where the courts make a judgement about whether to intervene based on the circumstances as a whole. Here, correctness review takes the form of an instinctive judgement. Hickman is also eager to strip the judicial supervisory lens of constraint, at least in relation to human rights adjudication. Instinct is cloaked in a traditional adjudicative language, though. Any deference is manifest in the form of the affording of weight to the views of others; while Hickman identifies a number of reasons why courts should be deferential (generally based on relative expertise), the process of doing so is left to the implicit weighting process. Finally, Dyzenhaus also seeks to strip the supervisory process of detailed doctrinal constraint. But he favours a more deferential enquiry: rather than a correctness assessment, Dyzenhaus argues for the relationship between a decision and its justification to be subjected to an assessment based on its reasonableness (informed by the abstract notion of human dignity).

Contextual review presents a constitutional vision of judicial review, animated by higher-order – albeit perhaps nebulous – principles. Doctrine is rejected as the primary judicial tool in the supervisory jurisdiction; instead

---

[191] King recognises a non-doctrinal version of restraint, as a counterpoint to the formalist and institutionalist approaches: Jeff A. King, 'Institutional Approaches to Judicial Restraint' (2008) 28 OJLS 409, 411. While not a supporter of the non-doctrinal approach, King suggests that this approach is neither wild nor unorthodox and perhaps captures how many courts operate.

the embedded wisdom of judges guides the pursuit of administrative justice in individual cases. Contextual review is not unconcerned with the appropriate relationship between primary decision-maker and reviewing court; however, views on this question are manifest in a generalised background philosophy about the nature of judicial adjudication and need not be specifically articulated or canvassed in individual cases.

5.4   Normative Assessment

Contextual review captures, as mentioned earlier, two types of method. First, it manifests itself in a strong form, where the terms of intervention are cast in the broadest terms so as to capture the instinctive impulse of judges. Secondly, it has a weaker form, where the emphasis is on context rather than doctrinal reasoning; the decision about whether to intervene is framed in terms of deliberation about the nature of weight and respect that ought to be afforded to the views of the primary decision-maker. Measured against Fuller's virtues it performs poorly – unsurprisingly, because its eschews rule-structure.

Generality

This method is highly sceptical about rules seeking to guide the judiciary's supervisory eye. Both forms of contextual review avoid doctrine, but there are subtle differences in the way the (extra-legal) judicial task is conducted.

In its strong form, this form of judicial supervision can be equated with, as Joseph labels it, an 'instinctual impulse'.[192] Shorn of any constraints or limiting parameters, the task of the supervising judge is to assess, in the round, whether there is any basis for judicial intervention. Joseph argues it is this inarticulate premise – not principles or doctrines or curriculum – that lies at the heart of the judicial role.[193] Characterising it in its baldest form, the method can be described (whether colloquially or pejoratively) as a 'sniff test':[194]

> An impugned decision may invite a demonstrable reaction; a decision, viewed in the round, may be 'whiffy'. Seasoned litigators apply the 'sniff test' where the decision-making goes palpably awry.

---

[192] Joseph, 'Questions', above n. 34, 74. See also Joseph C. Hutcheson, 'The Judgment Intuitive' (1929) 14 Cornell LR 274 ('judicial hunch').
[193] Joseph, 'Questions', above n. 34, 74.
[194] *Ibid.*, 77.

The method can also be cloaked in more law-like terms, such as 'over-all evaluation',[195] the innominate ground,[196] and 'abuse of power'.[197] But the essence is the same. Everything is up for grabs, in the light of context and circumstances: judicial review reduces to 'what the whole shebang is'.[198] The forensic exercise is 'inherently discretionary', Joseph says: '[n]o amount of rule formalism can relieve the courts of their instinctual task in judicial review'.[199]

Thus, it is based on discretion, rather than rules, and unashamedly so. Seen pejoratively, the schema enables and commends 'palm tree justice';[200] extensive judicial discretion such as this was criticised by Lord Scarman in *Duport Steels Ltd* v. *Sirs*: 'Justice in [developed] societies is not left to the unguided, even if experienced, sage sitting under the spreading oak tree.'[201]

The variability of this method is self-evident. Strong form contextual review is inherently discretionary, with infinite possibilities of depths of review. While unstructured normativism associated with contextual review frees the reviewing eye from formal restraints, it does not explicitly manifest a particular intensity of review. To the extent that curial discretion is not limited by any doctrine, there is a degree to which this form of review promotes more intensive supervision. The judge may decide for themselves whether there is any basis for intervention. However, the method of review may also result in review which is, in substance, still deferential. This will not be dictated or assured by law's immediate structure. Instead, it will turn on the values and vision of the reviewing judge – especially as administrative law lacks a generally mandated purpose and objective. While other methods of review inevitably enable the judicial method to also be influenced by the reviewing judge's values (sometimes covertly), the contextual model tends to amplify those values because its essence is constructed around value-judgements. That said, proponents of this method all seek to colour the value judgement by reference to higher-order principles such as the rule of law (Allan and Joseph) and equality/dignity (Dyzenhaus). The abstract and/or contested nature of

---

[195] *Ibid.*, 79. See also Joseph, 'Ultra Vires', above n. 123, 371.
[196] See text to n. 53 above.
[197] Joseph, 'Questions', above n. 34, 77. See text to n. 4 above.
[198] *Ibid.*, 80.
[199] *Ibid.*, 75, 80.
[200] The palm tree justice metaphor is drawn from Judges 4:5 ('And she dwelt under the palm tree of Deborah between Ramah and Bethel in Mount Ephraim: and the children of Israel came up to her for judgment.')
[201] *Duport Steels Ltd* v. *Sirs* [1980] 1 WLR 142, 168.

these principles may, however, limit their influence relative to individual judicial values.

In its weaker form, contextual review manifests deference in terms of respect and weight. Context and circumstances dominate, but doctrinal structure is eschewed. Unlike its stronger, instinctive sibling, deference takes a deliberative role in the judicial process. That is, the importance of the notion of deference is acknowledged. However, it is not marked out for special treatment. Instead, it is introduced implicitly into the balance, through the familiar practice of attributing weight to the views of others.

This method is described in different ways. In contradistinction to the doctrinal deference camp, it has been described as 'non-doctrinal deference'.[202] Daly adopts the label 'epistemic deference', again in contrast to doctrinal deference.[203] Allan draws a helpful distinction in the nature of the deliberative process: this method adopts a 'single-level integrated analysis', rather than a 'two-level theory of adjudication'.[204] All these descriptors seek to capture the notion that questions form part of the 'ordinary business of judging', where any variation in the depth of review is settled implicitly on a case-by-case basis through existing judicial methods.[205]

Thus, weight and respect are at the centre of this weaker form of contextual review. Epistemic deference means, Daly argues, 'the paying of respect to the decisions of others by means of according weight to those decisions'.[206] The language of 'weight' is perhaps confusing though because, as Hickman explains, weight is also used to described that balancing of countervailing factors. In the context of 'affording weight' to those with greater relative expertise and knowledge, as was the case in *Huang*, the process is more akin to respecting another's views.[207] Indeed, this method appears to

---

[202] Hickman, *Public Law*, above n. 120, 172; King, 'Restraint', above n. 191, 411. See also Richard Gordon, 'Two Dogmas of Proportionality' [2011] JR 18 and Alan D.P. Brady, *Proportionality and Deference under the UK Human Rights Act* (Cambridge University Press, 2012), 26.

[203] Paul Daly, *A Theory of Deference in Administrative Law* (Cambridge University Press, 2012), 7.

[204] T.R.S. Allan, 'Judicial Deference and Judicial Review' (2011) 127 LQR 96, 98 and 108. Compare the two-stage process under intensity of review (chapter 4) and Poole's identification of primary and secondary issues: Thomas Poole, 'Legitimacy, Rights, and Judicial Review' (2005) 25 OJLS 697, 709.

[205] Hickman, *Public Law*, above n. 120; King, 'Restraint', above n. 191, 411. See also Gordon, above n. 202.

[206] Daly, above n. 203, 7. Daly identifies the method as being analogous to the 'Skidmore deference' applied in the United States in some circumstances: see *Skidmore* v. *Swift and Co* 323 US 134 (1944).

[207] Hickman, *Public Law*, above n. 120, 129.

strongly embrace and adopt Dyzenhaus' famous characterisation of 'deference as respect'.[208]

The language differs a little in the Canadian context, even though the method is similar. The Canadian courts start from an environment of deference, rather than scrutiny first and foremost. While respect and weight are still central to the supervisory method, the reasonableness enquiry poses the question of whether the administration has presented sufficient justification to warrant deference. As the majority in *Dunsmuir* said, 'reasonableness is concerned mostly with the existence of justification, transparency and intelligibility within the decision-making process';[209] the courts must pay 'respectful attention to the reasons offered or which could be offered in support of the decision'.[210] This process has been characterised as a 'burden of justification', something that is more or less demanding depending on the circumstances.[211] Equally, though, this exhibits similar characteristics to the affording of weight. The views of the administration are afforded instrumental weight, as and when the courts are satisfied that the administration has advanced sufficient justification in support of them (although the extent of justification required varies in different contexts).

The style of review also enables significant variability in the depth of review. The deployment of deference or variability through the vehicle of weight does not dictate particular depths of review. Anything is possible. There can be more or less scrutiny, depending on the context and circumstances. 'Weight is, by its very nature, variable.'[212]

In both its strong and weak form, contextual review strongly prioritises adaptability and flexibility over consistency and predictability. The banishing of doctrinal structure opens the field to judicial intervention. Under this schema the courts have an imprimatur to intervene as and when they assess it is necessary. But this has a vivid trade-off with consistency and predictability. The triggers for intervention are an individualised judicial assessment about whether the circumstances justify intervention – thresholds which are difficult to predict and prone to inconsistent outcomes based on the preferences of different judges. Proponents of this approach are not troubled by this though. For example, Joseph's embrace of the instinctive

---

[208] Dyzenhaus, 'Deference', above n. 44, 286.

[209] *Dunsmuir*, above n. 40, [47].

[210] *Ibid.*, [48].

[211] Matthew Lewans, 'Deference and Reasonableness since *Dunsmuir*' (2012) 38 Queen's LJ 59, 98.

[212] Hickman, *Public Law*, above n. 120, 137.

impulse is openly dismissive of the value of predictability in the judicial function.[213]

With the absence of doctrinal scaffolding, contextual review must look to other methods to provide guidance and bridle judicial discretion. However, these methods are generally amorphous and weak. Judicial discipline remains the principal controlling mechanism. Joseph, for example, argues that the impulse is tempered by the implicit constraints of the 'judicial mindset':[214] namely, a 'judge's knowledge and experience of the law, the disciplines of the judicial role and the commitment to do practical justice'.[215] He argues that '[d]emocracy imposed limits to the acceptability of judicial review' weigh heavily on judges, meaning matters such as the separation of powers and relative expertise must be factored in. 'The imperative to uphold the rule of law legitimises judicial review but does not condone a judicial usurpation.'[216] Sometimes judges may 'experience the instinctual impulse', Joseph explains, but still may decide not to intervene 'for fear of overstepping the judicial function'.[217] To these implicit constraints, he adds the need to follow the instinctive impulse with the language of law, that is, the expectation that the instinctive impulse will be cloaked in 'familiar administrative law language'.[218] We are encouraged to trust the judiciary's – 'generally ... pragmatically cautious' – judgement.[219]

The difficulty with these constraints is that they are not manifest – we are asked to trust judges to get things right, without any obvious comfort being provided. As is evident in both the doctrinal and theoretical discussion in this book, the concepts of law, justice and the key principles of public law (such as sovereignty, the separation of powers and the rule of law) are contested. Judicial figures are not homogeneous. While these matters may cause judges some pause on an individual basis, their ability to promote consistency and predictability is poor. In days gone by when most judicial applications were heard by a common bench or small pool of judges,[220] consistency and predictability arose from the stable personnel charged with adjudication. But nowadays the number of superior court

---

[213] Joseph, 'Questions', above n. 34, 75, 81.

[214] *Ibid.*, 80.

[215] *Ibid.*, 79.

[216] *Ibid.*, 80.

[217] *Ibid.*

[218] *Ibid.*, 79.

[219] *Ibid.*, 81.

[220] See e.g. Louis Blom-Cooper, 'The New Face of Judicial Review' [1982] PL 250 (Eng); Joseph, 'Commonwealth Administrative Law', above n. 12 (common membership of the New Zealand Court of Appeal for long periods).

judges has expanded and is drawn from judges with increasingly diverse backgrounds and an array of different experiences.[221] Thus, contextual review does little to ameliorate the absence of rules and to promote consistency or predictability.

Public Accessibility and Transparency

Contextual review gives the appearance of judicial candour and honesty, but the mediation of the balance between vigilance and restraint remains latent. The identification and application of the depth of review need not be a feature of judicial reasoning and exposition.

Strong form contextual review, which channels the judicial impulse, does not provide an open and transparent basis for judicial intervention. It is imbedded in the mind of the judge. While the judicial impulse that there is something awry that requires judicial attention is colloquially candid, it does not disclose a legal or intellectual justification for overturning a decision. Law's style and language is eschewed in favour of sensation and human reaction. The result is a trigger which is internal and individual to the judge. While sincere, it is not lucid. Any value of candour is lost because the language of law is shunned and the basis for intervention is not translatable for external observers. Sure, judges may still seek to express the nature of the instinct in their reasons, but the sniff test does not dictate they do so.

Indeed, the judgement about intervention risks being explained *ex post facto*, with the veneer of law-like justifications that did not directly inform the original decision to intervene: in other words, reverse-reasoning. As explained above, Joseph argues in favour of the judicial instinct being subsequently justified through the language of law. While he argues the instinctive impulse provides 'insight into the true nature of judicial review', he later qualifies himself by suggesting judges should still 'fit applications for judicial review within an established ground of review'.[222] This is a confession of support for the principle of reverse-reasoning:[223]

> Has something gone *wrong* that calls for judicial intervention and correction? If the answer is 'yes', the judge must translate the instinctual impulse into 'legal' language that can explain and justify the court's intervention. The judge must identify a recognised ground of review and show how the decision-maker has failed to comply with the law.

---

[221] See e.g. A.W. Bradley and K.D. Ewing, *Constitutional and Administrative Law* (14th edn, Pearson, 2007), 388; Judicial Working Group, *Justice Outside London* (2007), [42]; Richard Clayton, 'New Arrangements for the Administrative Court' [2008] JR 164.

[222] Joseph, 'Questions', above n. 34, 74, 80.

[223] *Ibid.*, 74.

The potential dissonance between instinct and principle is also seen in Laws LJ's unusually candid judgment in *Abdi*.[224] An issue arose about whether the applicants' claim to a legitimate expectation, founded on an administrative policy, that their application for asylum would be determined in the United Kingdom prevented their deportation. The doctrinal test for legitimate expectation – 'abuse of power' – mimics the approach of contextual review.[225] Laws LJ admitted that he was inclined to determine the case 'on the simple ground that the merits of the Secretary of State's case press harder than the appellant's'.[226] However, his Honour described it as 'very unsatisfactory' to conclude on that basis:[227]

> The conclusion is not merely simple, but simplistic. It is little distance from a purely subjective adjudication ... It is superficial because in truth it reveals no principle. Principle is not in my judgment supplied by the call to arms of abuse of power. Abuse of power is a name for any act of a public authority that is not legally justified. It is a useful name, for it catches the moral impetus of the rule of law ... But it goes no distance to tell you, case by case, what is lawful and what is not. I accept, of course, that there is no formula which tells you that; if there were, the law would be nothing but a checklist. Legal principle lies between the overarching rubric of abuse of power and the concrete imperatives of a rule-book.

Laws LJ's candour is to be applauded. But his remarks expose the potentially venal nature of the judging process. As Poole says, it points to a 'decision based upon an assessment of the arguments presented by counsel, and/ or judicial instinct, propped up ex post – almost laughably – on the vague invocation of even vaguer principles'.[228] The deployment of 'principled patina' does not disguise the original instinctive judgement.[229] Thus, where contextual review takes its nakedly instinctive form, we have reason to be sceptical about any reasons which accompany the decision to intervene.

Weak form contextual review, which is built around the weight principle, performs slightly better due to weight typically being a concept expressly deliberated on by judges. Again, the mediation of the balance between vigilance and restraint is largely latent. The variation of intensity

---

[224] Thomas Poole, 'Between the Devil and the Deep Blue Sea' in Linda Pearson, Carol Harlow and Michael Taggart (eds.), *Administrative Law in a Changing State* (Hart Publishing, 2008), 15, 39 and *R (Abdi & Nadarajah)* v. *Secretary of State for the Home Department* [2005] EWCA Civ 1363.

[225] See ch. 3, text to n. 84.

[226] *Abdi*, above n. 224, [67].

[227] *Ibid.*

[228] Poole, 'Deep Blue Sea', above n. 224, 40.

[229] *Ibid.*, 26.

does not necessarily take explicit form. Variation and deference are not showcased under this method. The dominant ingredient is the weight to be afforded, based on the circumstances. However, as the judicial process of weighting has a deliberative dimension, the factors informing the weight afforded will often merit mention in the judicial reasoning process. To this extent, the weak form of unstructured contextualism parts company with its stronger sibling. But here using weight as an anchor has limitations. First, even within existing judicial practice, the application of weight can have a relatively amorphous character, as discussed earlier in relation to the intensity of review schema. Secondly, the schema does not demand transparency; it is merely incidental. Explicit deliberation on the factors influencing weight, and therefore the depth of scrutiny, is not guaranteed.

Moreover, while this form of contextual review is anchored by an existing legal device (weight), it is still strongly informed by judicial discretion and judgement.[230] Notably, Hickman links weight directly back to the judicial instinct: it is 'something that courts do *instinctively* as part of the exercise of judging'.[231] Indeed, Hickman suggests it is something that any rational decision-maker does when presented with a person who has knowledge and expertise that the decision-maker lacks. 'When they recognise their lack of knowledge or competence relative to another person, they understandably give weight to their views.'[232] This connection to judicial instinct suggests a reasonable degree of synergy between the strong and weak forms of this supervisory method. Given this discretion, it is again inevitable that the weight or latitude to be afforded is, at least in part, dependent on the self-perception of the judicial role and corresponding values.

Prospectivity

Like the other schema, no direct issues of retrospective rules apply. However, because this schema performs poorly in terms of generality and clarity (due to the prominence of judicial discretion and lack of predictability), the inevitably retrospective effect of judicial adjudication becomes more acute.

Clarity

The contextual review schema scores relatively poorly in terms of clarity, both in its strong instinctive form and its weaker form as weight and

---

[230]   King, 'Restraint', above n. 191, 411.
[231]   Hickman, *Public Law*, above n. 120, 135 (emphasis added).
[232]   *Ibid.*, 137.

respect. Here, the concern lies in the lack of certainty arising from reliance on value and indeterminate standards or triggers for intervention. The incorporation of general standards was not condemned out of hand by Fuller.[233] 'Common sense standards of judgement' – ordinary language that has meaning outside law – are treated as acceptable means of providing clarity, especially where the nature of the subject-matter is not suitable for more specificity.[234] However, he warned against too readily employing standards, when these standards are capable of conversion into rules with greater clarity – otherwise, the elaboration of meaning is delegated, undesirably, to adjudicative bodies to determine on a case-by-case basis.[235]

Here, where contextual review is equated with generalised standards like abuse of power or unreasonableness (framed in its abstract, meta formulation), their use does not meet the expectations demanded. While the adoption of standards such as these – or the colloquial judicial instinct – mandates a clearly stated judicial trigger for intervention, the case-by-case style that results brings vagueness and indeterminacy to the supervisory task, generating a lack of legal certainty about its operation and its likely outcomes.

Similarly, resort to weight and respect in the weaker form of contextual review also brings a lack of clarity. Notions of weight and respect, while not foreign concepts in themselves, do not promote legal certainty. The influence of other views or the extent of respect to be afforded by the reviewing judges remain a discretionary judgement: both in terms of whether to give weight or respect and, if so, how much. Again, as explained above, predictability is not enhanced by this method.

Stability

This schema does not make explicit provision for evolution or modification of the rules. This is because the framework adopts contextual judicial discretion at its core. Changes to judicial philosophy or the accommodation of novel circumstances present no impediment to this schema – they are readily accommodated internally within the existing judicial methodology, conditioned by instinct or weight and respect. Again, though, the lack of explicit instability does not mean this schema performs well under this criterion; as discussed under other criteria, the prominence of

---

[233] Lon L. Fuller, *The Morality of Law* (Yale University Press, 1964), 64, instancing standards such as 'good faith' and 'due care'.
[234] *Ibid.*
[235] *Ibid.* Here, Fuller highlights the instances the problematic use of the standard of 'fairness' in commercial dealings.

unarticulated judicial discretion means, in effect, those affected have little ability to predict outcomes and are faced with the potentially shifting sands of judicial judgement.

Non-contradiction and Coherence

As is evident, contextual review rejects schematic structure, at least from a doctrinal perspective; there is no attempt to promote coherence through legal devices. Traditional legal techniques which encourage consistency, connectedness and unity of approach and doctrine are absent. To this extent, this schema appears incoherent.

An alternative view, though, is that the singular criterion for interference – albeit cast in terms of instinct or other abstract values – has a certain neatness about it. While the absence of legal doctrine means the singular criterion is not amplified, the existence of a meta-principle governing judicial intervention manifests unity, even if it is drawn in esoteric terms. On the other hand, unity and coherence tend to erode in implementation. As discussed above, the practical application of this standard is prone to much more individual interpretation by judges based on their personal preferences and values. The discretionary nature of judgement risks inconsistency and coherence being collapsed as individual judges apply this standard in different ways. Coherence is difficult to produce, given the lack of law.

Non-impossibility and Practicality

On a simplistic level, contextual review is eminently practical. On its face, simplicity in the supervisory lens is suggestive of simplicity in procedure. Unconstrained by doctrine seeking to circumscribe the judicial eye, procedural restrictions become unnecessary as *de novo* review is encouraged. It follows that the evidential corpus should not be restricted, else something that may trigger the judicial instinct could be lost. Filtering the lines of argument and analysis is left to the judicial gut-instinct: 'Has something gone wrong that calls for judicial intervention and correction?'[236] While simple in form, this entails a plenary style of procedure and evidence, with consequent costs.

On a deeper level, the workability of this schema is undermined by its enigmatic character. The supervisory process is reactive and adversarial, not inquisitorial. For the power of the judicial instinct to be harnessed,

[236] Joseph, 'Questions', above n. 34, 74.

litigants must provide evidence which piques or alleviates the judicial interest, along with argument which explains it. But this is dependent on a reasonable degree of alignment between litigants and the supervisory judges – hence unpredictable 'gut-feelings' dominate.

How then do litigants – private plaintiffs and state actors – shape their case in anticipation? The lack of predictability risks litigants bombarding the courts with the highest order of evidence in every case, and extending the argumentation accordingly. No stone is left unturned. This has significant procedural implications in terms of the cost and length of hearings. A prudent plaintiff will have no choice but to seek to advance each and every argument that might trigger a judge's instinct. Faced with wide-ranging arguments that are difficult to anticipate, a prudent defendant will be forced to similarly mount a wide-ranging defence. This has the potential to ratchet up the evidential corpus required in any particular case.

So too with the style of argument. The standard involved is ultimately abstract – dependent on the intuition and values of individual judges. So much turns on the type of judge allocated to the particular case, a factor which is often not known in advance of the hearing. While realists rightly argue that this is a feature of all adjudication, the schema amplifies this problem because it does not limit or structure the judicial personality. The absence of doctrine means there is no legal scaffolding to limit, anchor or structure the dynamics of argument. The judicial predilections shape the argument in a way which litigants must be prepared to meet.

Moreover, the instinctive approach risks removing the language of law, in which advocates are trained and skilled. If judicial deliberation need not be expressed in or be constrained by law, then so too the argument of advocates.[237]

Congruence and Candour

Like adherence to the other principles of efficacy, contextual review presents the appearance of congruence. However, at a deeper level its operation is more troublesome.

The embrace of the judicial instinct and the resort to the judicial assessment of weight and respect mean incongruence is unlikely to specifically arise. But that is because the 'rules' capture and manifest the judgement made on implementation. Thus, there is unlikely to be any separation

---

[237] For similar arguments about the problems of open-ended moral reasoning and the value of legally directed adjudication in the context of the proportionality test, see Francisco J. Urbina, 'A Critique of Proportionality' (2012) 57 Am J Juris 49.

between the two. Candour is encouraged and, indeed, given a prominent place with the supervisory process – but to the exclusion of declared rules.

To the extent that reasoning and deliberation is recognised within this schema (at best in a limited fashion), it brings with it the risks of reverse-reasoning, as discussed above. If this results, then the reasons risk masking the true basis for intervention, disclosing a lack of judicial candour.

Hortatory Versatility

Contextual review does not manifest clear educative principles which are capable of being deployed elsewhere or performing the hortatory role. Adjudication is value-based and normative; the absence of doctrinal principles means the schema does not readily provide a means to educate or structure bureaucracy in other contexts. The legal methodology is unspecific and internal to the supervisory judge. The method is one grounded in higher-order values, such as the rule of law, rather than operational principles. The heavily contested nature of the rule of law means it does not send clear messages. The emphasis on abstract values over doctrine comes at a cost. As Harlow and Rawlings notes, the hortatory role of judicial review is threatened by the 'imprecise application of ... imprecise principle[s]'.[238] They sympathise with complaints from the administration that some principles of judicial review are too vague, contextual or uncertain, such as is apparent under contextual review: '[T]he "intuitive judgement" of courts can be difficult to fathom, let alone predict!'[239] Similarly, Halliday warns that the impact of judicial review on the administrative attenuates if doctrine fails to send consistent and clear messages, particularly when the doctrine is 'uncertain and contingent on context'.[240]

Here, the judicial methodology is circumstantial and normative. It generates little, if any, operational guidance for the bureaucracy. Its emphasis is on judicial-rightness, deployed in *ex post facto* review in particular cases. While over time, it might be argued, the corpus of cases may manifest trends about when the judicial instinct is engaged, this still may not provide reliable guidance. First, it is reliant on the very thing contextual review objects to – the generalisation of principles over the circumstantial assessment in particular cases. Secondly, contextual assessment cannot

---

[238] Carol Harlow and Richard Rawlings, *Law and Administration* (3rd edn, Cambridge University Press, 2009), 728.

[239] *Ibid.*

[240] Simon Halliday, *Judicial Review and Compliance with Administrative Law* (Hart Publishing, 2004), 143.

guarantee consistent and coherent outcomes, because the judicial instinct is by definition circumstantial. Inconsistent and contradictory outcomes and trends may result.

5.5   Conclusion

Under the contextual review approach, normative reasoning is heralded and doctrinal structure condemned. Based around a broad judicial assessment of whether anything has gone wrong which justifies intervention, unstructured normativism can be seen in a number of aspects of Anglo-Commonwealth jurisprudence: the judicial hunch, the innominate ground, the abuse of power principle, non-doctrinal deference and umbrella forms of unreasonableness. It is supported by some from the common law school and others who champion a potent and explicitly normative role for the courts. Assessed against the principles of efficacy, unsurprisingly, it performs poorly. Its rejection of doctrine in favour of normative judicial judgement or instinct is anathema to Fuller's conception of the rule of law.

At its heart, contextual review has a strong vision of the courts being active and instrumental in addressing administrative justice and ensuring constitutional righteousness. Attempts to shackle that judicial power or to insist on explicit consideration of the limitations of judicial supervision in individual cases are rejected. The expertise and values of judges provide the necessary, albeit inconspicuous, comfort that the courts will appropriately discharge their supervisory functions. Yet this requires large doses of trust – something that sits uncomfortably with the culture of justification which has become a key catch-cry of administrative law in recent decades.

6

Conclusion

6.1 Introduction

At the outset, I introduced the modulation of the depth of scrutiny in judicial review in terms of the mediation of the balance between *vigilance* and *restraint*. On the one hand, the courts are called on to rule on primary issues such as the propriety of administrative action or the treatment of a citizen by the state.[1] This generates a judicial impulse to be vigilant, to ensure the action or treatment is appropriate and justified. On the other hand, the supervisory or review function of the courts raises second-order issues about the legitimacy of the courts to definitively adjudicate on such matters. The judicial process may be ill-suited for the determination of the primary issues raised. For example, the relative knowledge or expertise of the administration may be superior, the judicial processes may not adequately accommodate the breadth of the issues raised, or it may be more legitimate for the propriety of the administrative action to be settled through more democratic processes. This counsels restraint on the part of the reviewing judge. Hence, the courts must mediate this tension between vigilance and restraint.

But, as we have seen, this tension is necessarily dynamic. The vast terrain of administrative law brings before the courts a wide array of different actions, decision-makers and circumstances. The equilibrium drawn between restraint and vigilance is conditioned by, and must accommodate, these differences. It is not possible to generalise in any meaningful way where the equilibrium should be drawn. '[C]ontext is everything', perhaps more so here than in any other area of law.[2]

---

[1] For the difference between 'primary issues' and 'second-order' issues, see Thomas Poole, 'Legitimacy, Rights, and Judicial Review' (2005) 25 OJLS 697, 709. See also Peter Cane, *Administrative Tribunals and Adjudication* (Hart Publishing, 2009), 142 (performance vs supervision).

[2] *R (Daly)* v. *Secretary of State for the Home Department* [2001] 2 AC 532, [28]. For discussion of the rise of contextualism, see Michael Taggart, 'Outside Canadian Administrative Law'

In this book I have focused on different ways the courts can mediate this balance between vigilance and restraint. In particular, I have drawn out four schemata – scope, grounds, intensity and context – which exhibit different methods for modulating the depth of scrutiny. Analysing the schemata across three dimensions – doctrinal, conceptual, normative – my aim has been to assess the different strengths of each approach. I return to these three dimensions and consider the conclusions that I have reached about the different schemata.

6.2   Doctrinal Manifestation

Over the last fifty years and more, the *manner* in which English and other Anglo-Commonwealth courts have mediated the balance between vigilance and restraint has evolved significantly. My study of these jurisdictions over this period – aided by reference to the language and structure of one of the leading judicial review textbooks – has identified four different approaches to the modulation of the depth of review: scope of review, grounds of review, intensity of review, and contextual review.

The *scope* and *grounds* of review schemata are both built around the indirect and categorical modulation of the depth of scrutiny. The classi-fication of a decision or defect into certain categories or bases for review ultimately determines the balance between restraint and vigilance. Scope of review depends on numerous complex distinctions, many of which are difficult to apply with fidelity. Grounds of review simplifies and systema-tises the categories, to present generalised grounds more in the nature of overarching principles of good administration.

The approaches of *intensity* of review and *contextual* review embrace a more direct and circumstantial approach. The context of the case, broadly framed, determines the depth of scrutiny and thus whether judicial inter-vention is justified. This brings the modulation of the balance between vigilance and restraint to the foreground and showcases the extent of judi-cial discretion and variability involved in judicial review. The difference between the two circumstantial approaches lies in the role of doctrine. The intensity of review schema provides scaffolding for the calibration of the depth of review and the deployment of the supervisory lens. While recognising the supervisory jurisdiction, in effect, captures a full range of

---

(1996) 46 UTLJ 649, 653; Michael Taggart, 'Proportionality, Deference, *Wednesbury*' [2008] NZ Law Rev 423, 450; Timothy Endicott, *Administrative Law* (Oxford University Press, 2009), 10.

possibilities between restraint and vigilance, contextual review abandons doctrine in favour of judicial instinct, judgement and the assessment of weight.

A key observation from this study is the fact that variability in the depth of scrutiny is omnipresent. *Modulation of the depth of review is a prominent feature of all Anglo-Commonwealth systems of judicial review.* This is a basic point but one that should not be lost sight of in the often heated debates about techniques of variable intensity. It is the *manner* in which it is expressed which differs across those jurisdictions, not the *fact* that the depth of review is modulated.

Some other patterns can be identified, although the jurisdictional diversity makes it difficult to draw out strong trends over time. First, the doctrinal form that filled the first edition of de Smith's textbook has fallen out of favour, except in Australia. Tightly framed doctrinal categories are no longer regarded as suitable for signalling the circumstances in which the courts are prepared to intervene. Despite their appearance, the key distinctions are too unstable and the multifarious categories too complex. The rule-structure creates a disconnect between expression and application, and masks the extent of judicial discretion involved. Only Australia continues the abstract formalism of old. However, there is perhaps a tacit understanding that this is more about dressing up the reasoning in ritual, the language of jurisdiction and so forth must be employed to express the conclusions to (unstated) more normative reasoning.

Secondly, the extent of the departure from this original method differs depending on the jurisdiction in focus. The moves away from scope of review to grounds of review in England and New Zealand are modest. Some of the character of scope of review remains, especially the emphasis on the indirect and categorical modulation of the depth of scrutiny. Simplification, rationalisation and greater emphasis on general principles (legality and rationality) over rules (jurisdiction and vires) mark out the difference between the definition of the categories.

Canada moved to direct and circumstantial approaches to the calibration of the depth of review, elements of which can also be detected in particular parts of English and New Zealand law. The more open-textured methodologies – more sensitive to the influence of context – provide a greater role for constitutional, institutional, functional and procedural considerations to directly influence the closeness or otherwise of forensic scrutiny.

Thirdly, a pattern – albeit inexact – can be detected in the preferred style of reasoning: from doctrinal, to conceptual, to normative. The scope of review approach embeds an ostensibly formal approach to doctrinal reasoning. The grounds of review approach is framed by categorical doctrine, but is more generalised, more open-textured and leaves some space for conceptual reasoning. Intensity of review brings conceptual reasoning to the foreground, openly encouraging the consideration of constitutional, institutional and functional demands; normativity is unavoidable but needs to be structured. Contextual review whole-heartedly embraces normative reasoning.

Fourthly, these general trends are punctuated by emphasising context and, correspondingly, the dynamic of the judicial method. The growth of the modern administrative state and the proliferation in the way in which public power is exercised have required more nuanced and sophisticated judicial supervision. Witness the greater prominence given to the notion of variable depth of review, the growth in circumstantial approaches to the determination of the depth of review, and refinement of the potential balances between vigilance and restraint. Blunt tools are no longer fit for purpose.

Finally, the linkages between the jurisdictions are stronger than they appear on the face of the doctrine. The diversity of form gives the appearance of difference or disconnected jurisprudence. However, the schemata I have identified allow us to reconcile and connect the different approaches, while still being alert to their difference. For example, Australia is regularly shamed for being out-of-step with Anglo-Commonwealth jurisprudence but I detect greater variability in method and stronger resemblance to its cognate jurisdictions, once the veneer of abstract formalism is pierced and understood. Similarly, the prominence of the language of deference in Canadian law, while off-putting for some, is simply a different means of expressing the conceptual dynamics that underscore the categorical approaches elsewhere.

That is not to claim that the jurisdictions exhibit a unified jurisprudence though. Their relationship is more in the nature of a syndicate bound by a common aim (mediating vigilance and restraint), some unique ideas, and some borrowed practice – creating a loose association of jurisdictions exhibiting some family resemblance. Hence, the usefulness of the de Smith textbook in providing a centre-point of the analysis, anchored in the English experience but recognising the connections and divergence elsewhere in the Anglo-Commonwealth.

In marking these key trends, I am equivocal about the role of human rights in developments in the manner by which depth of review is modulated. Trends associated with judicial restraint and vigilance are traditionally traced by reference to human rights. In particular, increased judicial scrutiny tends to be associated with increased attentiveness to fundamental rights and the growth of a culture of human rights protection. While I do not discount the role of human rights as a catalyst for some developments, I do not align human rights with particular schemata or approaches. In the context of my focus on the *manner* by which the depth of review is modulated, the influence of human rights is less directly correlative. Human rights have brought an extra layer of complexity to the mediation of vigilance and restraint. Greater judicial vigilance, especially on the merits, begins to strain the secondary nature of judicial review and brings an acute focus on the limitations of the judicial role. The need to recognise these limitations – constitutional, institutional and functional – has encouraged some changes to the style of reasoning noted above. Human rights have been but one catalyst of change.

6.3   Conceptual Underpinnings

Doctrinal diversity is matched by conceptual diversity. The different schemata which manifest the modulation in different ways can be justified from a range of conceptual perspectives. I have examined the different ways scholars have sought to legitimise different approaches to variability in judicial review and sought to align those arguments with the different organising schemata. Through the lens of the meta-level debate about the constitutional underpinnings of the system of judicial review as a whole, I have sought to distil the conceptual arguments supporting the different mechanisms which modulate the depth of scrutiny. The original debate on the conceptual underpinnings of the system itself has provided a rich debate from which to address the latter question. Higher-order legitimacy and legitimacy of the aspects of the minutiae are related, although not necessarily directly aligned. But the analysis generates a number of conclusions.

First, the constitutional underpinnings debate generally distributes into three groupings: the original two schools (ultra vires versus common law – both under the shadow of legislative supremacy), along with those who reject the debate's concession to ultimate legislative supremacy.

The ultra vires school is grounded in formalism and, unsurprisingly, its scholars argue in favour of stronger linkages between the judicial methodology and legislative mandate. Judicial discretion is to be minimised. In categorical schemata, this means the ultra vires formalists (Forsyth; Aronson) generally favour the drawing of strict and narrow categories, ultimately labelled and linked back to Parliament through the (purported) legitimising device of ultra vires. In more contextual schema, those from the ultra vires school (Daly; Elliott) take on a more progressive character and are prepared to move away from rigid categories. However, there remains an emphasis on the structuring of judicial discretion in order to downplay the influence of the particular circumstances of the case. This school dislikes the substantive or normative reasoning that a dynamic, case-by-case approach requires. A free-ranging judicial eye upsets the balance of the constitutional order and steps on the toes of a sovereign Parliament. If a line-drawing, categorical approach is no longer sophisticated enough to address the modern demands of the administrative state, then the answer is modest doctrinal evolution. The conceptual basis of the old categories needs to be brought to the foreground, and should be carefully deployed and strictly applied in a way that still respects the division of duties of old. Structured judicial evaluation, teamed with a legislative lodestar, is a concession – a modest one – to administrative law's evolving modernity and contextualism.

In contrast, the common law school exhibits more faith in the judicial role and readily admits the influence of substantive values. In the categorical domain, these scholars (Craig; Taggart) embrace generalised and evolving grounds of review, albeit to differing degrees. Normative argumentation by judges is fine, but generally only in relation to the architecture of judicial review. In other words, judicial review may evolve and redefine itself on a systemic basis. But this does not translate into unfettered judicial authority and judgement. The specific directives of the legislature must still be respected. The institutional morality of the system itself is still better expressed in a carefully designed blueprint for judicial supervision.

In the more contextual domain, some common law scholars (Mullan) favour more individualised treatment, whereby the depth of review is modulated in individual cases, but by reference to a suite of doctrinal factors in a compromise between generalism and the particularism. So, while the calibration of intensity is brought to the foreground, its deployment continued to be controlled, not by the drawing of categories, but through a moderated and transparent reasoning process. Factors, settled on an abstract and systemic basis, must be taken into account, reasoned through, and balanced. The limitations of the supervisory jurisdiction (relative expertise and practical disadvantage) are factors which are readily identified as influential, along with factors which are reflective of institutional arrangements (legislative allocation of power and existence of other means to enable accountability) and the gravity of the effect on the individual concerned.

Others (Joseph; in part Hickman) trust the judicial judgement to get things right: either through instinctive reaction to the circumstances of the case or the ordinary assessment of the weight to be given to the views of others, driven by the rule of law but implicitly respectful of judicial inadequacies and overreach. No need for doctrine to guide or complicate. Contextualism unfettered.

Those who stand outside the standard terms of engagement of the ultra vires debate (Allan; Dyzenhaus) object to the assumption of legislative supremacy. They charge the courts with the general defence of the rule of law, without any formal or particularised doctrinal matrix as guidance. Again, contextualism dominates; an appraisal of all the circumstances is required. But there is some divergence about the intensity of this assessment, between a de novo assessment of consistency with substantive liberal values or a reasonableness assessment of the reasoning and justification informed by the notion of dignity. Hunt's orientation is perhaps a little unusual. He too is anxious not to be drawn into the competing parameters of the ultra vires versus common law debate, but then argues in favour of an elaborated and detailed regime of due deference.

Thus a number of key points of contest can be identified. First, differences are evident as to whether the appropriate depth of scrutiny can be generalised for particular classes of decision or whether an individualised and circumstantial assessment is required. Secondly, if individualised assessment is required, the role of doctrine is disputed: some argue deliberation ought to be guided by doctrine; others suggest it falls for consideration in the round as part of context. Thirdly, and related to the role of doctrine, should the determination of the depth of scrutiny be subject to judicial reasoning and justification, or can it be left to the judgement or instinct of judges? Finally, the appropriate degree of precision is subject to debate. Should the categories defining the depth of scrutiny be cast tightly or more generally? Should the depth of review be expressed as a sliding scale, defined trigger-points or discrete standards? Or should depth be conditioned solely by abstract, overarching values? As we have seen, these questions involve trade-offs between different normative values.

6.4 Normative Assessment

Each of the different schemata has been assessed using Fuller's principles of legality, with a range of results. The employment of Fuller's principles is justified on the basis that the definition of judicial methodology in the supervisory jurisdiction is akin to rule-definition and rule-application.

Thus, one way of assessing the normative value of the different schemata is to measure the schemata against orthodox rule of law expectation about the efficacy of rules. This does not ignore judicial review's role in promoting administrative propriety and delivering administrative justice. The inherent variability of judicial review, across all schemata, leaves the achievement of that goal open. The focus here has been on the *manner* in which that variability is expressed, not its existence.

The criteria – generality, public accessibility and transparency, prospectivity, clarity, stability, non-contradiction and coherence, non-impossibility and practicality, congruence and fidelity, and hortatory versatility – provide a basis for testing the effectiveness and virtue of the different schemata. Performance against Fuller's criteria varies; some schemata perform better than others in some respects but worse in others. As noted at the outset, some trade-offs are inevitable. However, isolating these different aspects allows us to expose these trade-offs and be cognisant of their impact.

In general terms, their performance can be depicted as set out in the table:

	Scope of Review	Grounds of Review	Intensity of Review	Contextual Review
Generality	Mixed: High–Low	High	Medium	Low
Public accessibility and transparency	Mixed: High–Low	Medium	High	Low
Prospectivity	High	High	Medium	Medium
Clarity	Mixed: Medium–Low	Medium	Medium	Mixed: High–Low
Stability	Mixed: High–Low	Medium	Medium	Medium
Non-contradiction and coherence	Low	Medium	High	Mixed: High–Low
Non-impossibility and practicality	Medium	High	Medium	Low
Congruence and candour	Low	Medium	High	Mixed: High–Low
Hortatory versatility	Low	High	Medium	Low

Those schemata built around doctrinal categories perform best (subject to some caveats) in terms of *generality* and *prospectivity*. These schemata condition the supervision task by the promulgation of categories (viz. rules) which dictate the depth of scrutiny in particular cases. However, there remains a danger that the doctrinal rules merely camouflage judicial discretion. This is especially acute with the scope of review schema because the undue complexity and conceptual dissonance provides incentives to escape the formalist categories. The formalised categories therefore risk being conclusory only, as labels attached after the fact in order to justify and legitimise more normative reasoning. The grounds of review schema is less prone to this covert manipulation, but only because its categories are less rigid and value-based variability is sanctioned to some degree. The intensity of review schema also relies on rules, but rules which structure the judicial calibration of the depth of scrutiny, rather than dictate the depth of scrutiny to be applied in particular cases. Contextual review repudiates any need for rules or law. Instead, instinct, judgement and respect regulate judicial decisions about whether to intervene, based implicitly on the mediation of the balance between restraint and vigilance.

Public accessibility and transparency is similarly enhanced by those schemata which favour the expression of rules, namely scope, grounds and intensity of review. However, in some cases, this is undermined by the extent of judicial discretion; unless explicitly reasoned, the judgement compromises the transparency of the schema. The intensity of review schema, while open-textured, urges the reasoned elaboration of the calibration of review and performs well. The grounds of review schema encourages explicit judicial deliberation in some circumstances, but frequently leaves the determination of the depth of review to the opaque classification exercise. The ostensibly formal reasoning of the scope of review schema is tainted by its amenability to subversion by unstated normative influences. Contextual review creates a rule-void and therefore maximises judicial discretion. In its stronger formation as instinct, any transparency is lost, hidden in the hunches of judicial figures; in its weaker form of weight and respect, there remains space for judicial reasoning to be explicit, but there is little schematic guarantee of this.

Clarity, along with *non-contradiction and coherence*, depend on the extent to which the schemata present clear, understandable, predictable and harmonious legal regimes. Scope of review suffers from rule-based complexity, indeterminacy and paradox; this lack of clarity and coherence is further exacerbated when overlaid with possible judicial contrivance. The grounds of review schema was championed in order to present systematised simplicity and therefore clarity and coherence. This is achieved, to a large degree, by the tripartite formulations of the heads of intervention; however, reliance on classification in circumstances of overlap and the role of contingent and emergent grounds complicate this simplicity and add a gloss of uncertainty. Intensity of review identifies a clear and coherent process for determining the depth of review, but its application and outcomes are less certain. Contextual review has a degree of coherence: the naked reliance on judicial instinct or judgement presents, in a formal sense, a singular litmus for judicial intervention, therefore avoiding any contradiction or incoherence. However, the absence of law and prioritisation of judicial discretion makes outcomes uncertain, unpredictable and inevitably inconsistent.

The objective of *stability* does not raise significant issues because each schema is assessed in isolation, assuming its prevalence as an organisational schema. However, in a marginal sense, those schemata incorporating large doses of judicial discretion – intensity of review and contextual review, and, latently, scope of review – manifest a degree of instability. Further, the explicit recognition of evolution of grounds under the grounds of review schema provides some instability; however, evolution tends to be generational and the degree of changeability is not undue.

In the context of self-developed judicial methodologies, *non-impossibility and practicality* focuses mainly on the workability of the different schemata in the litigation and adjudication process. The two-track nature of scope of review means the ostensible practicality of the formalised rule-system, based on defined categories of intervention, is undermined by the amorphous role of judicial discretion. While the schema appears to be based on formal distinctions, resolvable without resort to much evidence, the reality is that litigants must also confront the possible impact of more normative and value-laden argumentation. The grounds of review schema is heralded for its forensic simplicity, at least when argumentation takes place on the territory of the traditional grounds of review. The practicality is tested a little, though, when argumentation roams into the realm of emergent grounds, where greater depth of scrutiny – and thus greater evidence – characterises the adjudicative task. The more circumstantial schemata (intensity of review and contextual review) provide less advanced substantive guidance about the appropriate depth of scrutiny, making it more difficult to predict the nature of the evidence, forensic analysis and argument. Contextual review presents little, if anything, to ameliorate the open-textured nature of the supervisory task. The intensity of review schema seeks to off-set the open-textured evaluation by providing some doctrinal scaffolding to guide its operation. At its strongest, a set of mandated considerations inform the calibration exercise and the depth of review is calibrated by reference to a finite continuum of possibilities, presenting clear reference points and distinct supervisory tasks. While not eradicating procedural uncertainty, this goes some way to making the nature and shape of the supervisory task more predictable. Other formulations of intensity of review, such as with an infinite continuum of depths of review, suffer from the same impracticality concerns as contextual review.

The *congruence and candour* of the schemata – the extent to which the legal regime and its rules are honoured in application – varies. Scope of review performs poorly, with its complexity and conceptual dissonance, encouraging latent manipulation of the critical distinctions which determine the depth of review. The grounds of review schema performs better. Its simplified framework, open tolerance of variability and potential for normative evolution provides less incentive for incongruence, although the classification task in relation to overlapping grounds may still camouflage judicial discretion. The intensity of review schema brings the underlying conceptual drivers of the vigilance–restraint dynamic to the foreground and leaves their weight and influence to the supervisory judge. In doing so, congruence and candour on the part of judges is strongly promoted, with the courts ultimately empowered to make a normative assessment in the light of those factors. Contextual review is more enigmatic. On the one hand, the regime embraces the judicial instinct and judgement, avoiding any incongruence; on the other hand, the absence of rules means any congruence is artificial. Moreover, if reasons for intervention are given, the prioritisation of the judicial hunch encourages reverse-reasoning – distracting from congruence and candour.

Finally, *hortatory versatility* examines the suitability of the norms generated on judicial review as guidance in other administrative law domains. Those schemata generating complex and confusing sets of rules (scope of review) or generating no rules at all (contextual review) perform poorly against this criterion. Intensity of review fails to generate specific norms or values that are readily applicable elsewhere; however, it does give some – albeit perhaps cryptic – indication about administrative autonomy (both the circumstances where it arises and the factors informing it). The best performing schema is grounds of review. It has an established practice of articulating administrative norms for domains beyond judicial review; the emergent grounds are less lucid and slightly counteract the hortatory guidance though. But generally the norms articulated under the grounds of review schema have a strong and helpful reach beyond the supervisory jurisdiction.

Based on the foregoing analysis, it becomes apparent that the grounds of review and intensity of review schemata are generally the strongest performing schemata. As I noted at the outset, however, it is not my intention to commend one of the schemata based merely on the greater compliance with the most factors. First, the characteristics tend to overlap and are not necessarily equivalent or additive. Secondly, trade-offs inevitably arise and do not get captured in a mere numerical count. Thirdly, the schemata are drawn from existing jurisprudence, described in the terms by which they are generally applied; the normative task is not so constrained and can readily accommodate some amalgamation of some features of each schema. The analysis is important, though, as it exposes the strengths and weaknesses of the different approaches and allows us to better understand the compromises each method involves. For example, a marked difference is evident in structuring the circumstantial assessment of the depth of review through doctrine. Under the intensity of review framework, transparency, coherence and congruence are enhanced by the way the judgement about depth is framed by rules; these virtues are lost if the judgement dissolves into the judicial hunch or the inconspicuous application of respect and weight. The normative dimension employed here is also useful for analysing aspects internal to each schema. For example, the intensity of review schema has considerable value but the clarity and predictability is compromised if an infinite scale of review is adopted, rather than a few discrete and recognisable calibrations.

The analysis also provokes some jurisdiction-specific observations, albeit the meta-level approach means I am cautious about making strong normative claims about possible pathways for each jurisdiction; such claims require deeper investigation within each jurisdiction in the light of their particular historical context and current settings. Subject to those caveats, though, a number of general comments can be made.

Australia's strong embrace of abstract formalism has been well documented – a tradition worn almost as a badge of honour. My normative analysis suggests it performs poorly when judged in rule-of-law terms, although it still enables (largely latent) variability in the depth of scrutiny. The analysis suggests some evolutionary pathways to alternative frameworks though – such as grounds of review or intensity of review. These approaches, on the one hand, still involve judges reasoning through doctrine but, on the other hand, more fully embrace a nuanced approach. Such evolution is less dramatic than the Australian 'exceptionalism' brand suggests; while the style of reasoning differs, my analysis suggests there is more communality or variability than others tend to admit. Thus, the natural pathway might be towards a grounds of review approach – still based in categorical reasoning. Such a transition, like England and New Zealand before, retains the indirect approach to calibration of depth of scrutiny. Importantly, it need not, in and of itself, necessitate any philosophical change to the judicial willingness to intervene or not. The institutional context and settings which generate an Australian tendency towards restraint are still readily accommodated with the top-down grounds of review schema (and other schemata).

England's experience has spanned the different schemata. Grounds of review remains the prominent method in common law judicial review, although large doses of intensity of review and contextual review are also evident, especially in the last decade or so; this is consistent with the overall trajectory towards more manifestly circumstantial methodologies. But this pluralism means the overall meta-structure is in a somewhat unsettled state. The analysis provides some additional fodder for normative debates about which method should prevail, along with a means to recognise commonality and difference. Rule of law values suggest that continuing to work through grounds of review (whether expanded or not) or explicitly reflecting on the intensity of review as a preliminary question are both feasible alternatives for embracing variability. Certainty, the allure of contextual review ought to be resisted, whether as a general basis for common law intervention or as a deference gloss in human rights adjudication. But it is difficult to predict where England's tradition might turn next. Indeed, it may be that the jurisdiction is suited to more blended schemata, as discussed below, where features of grounds of review are explicitly employed in combination with intensity of review calibration. The long experience of working through an expanded suite of grounds, along with judicial appetite for engaging with issues of deference, mean a richer framework might be a more suitable fit.

New Zealand's style has evolved past its old English parent: from the scope to grounds of review, at least as a starting point. Pressure for circumstantial and context-sensitive supervision has seen New Zealand adopt some more open-textured doctrine – along with pressure to reject doctrine altogether. The analysis here warns of the dangers of abandoning doctrine as a means to increase variability. Indeed, experience shows that New Zealand is quite proficient at the modulation of depth of scrutiny through doctrinal tools. Whether that ought to be through indirect means (grounds of review) or directly (intensity of review) is perhaps less important given the strengths of both. The key mission might be more one of recognition – recognition that schemata based in doctrine still provide rich frameworks to deliver administrative justice which are sensitive to the facts and relationships of any particular case. Contextual review has currency, in part, because of a belief that it is the most nimble judicial method. However, the analysis here suggests, first, contextual review does not have a monopoly on variability, and, secondly, such an approach falls short in a number of other ways.

Canada's supervisory experience in recent decades has been very circumstantial. And very self-referential – almost obsessively preoccupied with judicial method and deference, often overshadowing the circumstances of the particular case and the primary issues which arise. My analysis effectively questions the *Dunsmuir* move from intensity of review (in the form of the pragmatic and functional framework with different standards, including different standards of reasonableness) to contextual review (in the form of a unified approach where a broad-church form of reasonableness does much of the heaving lifting). The relative virtues of each schema in rule of law terms suggests contextual review has significant drawbacks.

As mentioned, the analysis also allows us to explore other combinations and possibilities. For example, one possible approach is to seek to amalgamate the methods found in the grounds and intensity of review schemata. That is, a generalised statement of grounds could be incorporated into the supervisory task *in combination with* the explicit determination of intensity. The grounds of review would then provide a presumptive framework, with corresponding depths of scrutiny; however, when the context demands otherwise, a more generalised assessment of the depth of scrutiny is enabled. Thus, the grounds of review provide default analytical anchors, but the open-textured virtue of intensity of review is retained. This increased predictability and guidance greatly improves clarity and practicality. Giving the judicial discretion a more secondary and residual role in atypical cases also marginally improves generality, prospectivity and stability. The retention of generalised principles of good administration also improve the hortatory versatility of the schema. This doctrinal solution emulates the distinction Hickman draws between standards of legality and standards of review (albeit Hickman intended this to be only descriptive, not deployed in normative frameworks). The key distinction is that the former identify norms which administrators ought to respect, while the latter address the method by which the courts review compliance. Incorporating both standards of legality and review allows for the development of presumptions in order to ameliorate uncertainty. On the one hand, presumptions provide a degree of predictability which make the forensic process more predictable. On the other hand, some presumptions (as opposed to rules or rigid categories) retain judicial discretion and explicitly allow the particular circumstances to be given effect to if that is necessary. Overall configuration requires further reflection but this is one example of how the analysis here can be usefully deployed.

6.5 Conclusion

The mediation of the balance between vigilance and restraint is a fundamental feature of judicial review of administrative action in the Anglo-Commonwealth. Modulation of the depth of scrutiny is ubiquitous in the system of judicial review, but takes different shapes and forms. These different shapes and forms risk obscuring the variability of the judicial lens in the supervisory jurisdiction. The isolation of the key schemata for mediating the balance between vigilance and restraint allows us to confront the question of how we – judges, lawyers, litigants, bureaucrats and scholars – might best have conversations about the appropriate depth of review in particular cases. The normative question about *depth* of review should not be clouded by disagreement about the basis for *calibrating* the depth of review.

In this book I have identified the key schemata in Anglo-Commonwealth judicial review over the last fifty years (and beyond) that have been used to modulate the depth of scrutiny. I have identified their conceptual foundations and exposed their commonality and differences. I have then judged the schemata against rule of law-based criteria in order to assess their efficacy. In my study, the grounds of review and intensity of review schemata display the greatest efficacy, albeit with emphasis on different virtues.

The main value of this analysis, however, lies in isolating the strengths and weaknesses of the different approaches and identifying the various compromises they involve. The hope is that this analysis helps illuminate questions about the *manner* by which the depth of review is modulated in judicial review and allows our conversations to return, more fruitfully, to normative questions about the appropriate depth of review in particular cases.

BIBLIOGRAPHY

Abrahams, D., 'Conflicts of Evidence in Judicial Review Proceedings' [1999] JR 221

Ahmed, F. and A. Perry, 'Expertise, Deference, and Giving Reasons' [2012] PL 221

Airo-Farulla, G., 'Rationality and Judicial Review of Administrative Action' (2000) 24 MULR 543

Alder, J., *Constitutional and Administrative Law* (6th edn, Palgrave Macmillan, 2007)

Allan, T.R.S., 'Fairness, Equality, Rationality: Constitutional Theory and Judicial Review' in C. Forsyth and I. Hare (eds.), *The Golden Metwand and the Crooked Cord: Essays in Honour of Sir William Wade QC* (Oxford University Press, 1998), 15

 Constitutional Justice: A Liberal Theory of the Rule of Law (Oxford University Press, 2001)

 'The Constitutional Foundations of Judicial Review: Conceptual Conundrum or Interpretative Inquiry?' (2002) 61 CLJ 87

 'Constitutional Dialogue and the Justification of Judicial Review' (2003) 23 OJLS 563

 Constitutional Justice: A Liberal Theory of the Rule of Law (Oxford University Press, 2003)

 'Legislative Supremacy and Legislative Intent: A Reply to Professor Craig' (2004) 24 OJLS 563

 'Human Rights and Judicial Review: A Critique of Due Deference' (2006) 65 CLJ 671

 'Deference, Defiance and Doctrine: Defining the Limits of Judicial Review' (2010) 60 UTLJ 41

 'Judicial Deference and Judicial Review: Legal Doctrine and Legal Theory' (2011) 127 LQR 96

 The Sovereignty of Law: Freedom, Constitution and Common Law (Oxford University Press, 2013)

Allars, M., 'On Deference to Tribunals, With Deference to Dworkin' (1994) 20 Queen's LJ 163

 '*Chevron* in Australia, A Duplicitous Rejection?' (2002) 54 Ad L Rev 569

Allison, J., 'Transplantation and Cross Fertilisation in European Public Law' in J. Beatson and T. Tridimas (eds.), *New Directions in European Public Law* (Hart Publishing, 1998)

The English Historical Constitution: Continuity, Change and European Effects (Cambridge University Press, 2007)

Anderson, S., 'Judicial Review' [2010] NZLJ 373 (book review)

Anonymous, 'Professor SA de Smith' (1974) 33 CLJ 177

Anthony, G., *Judicial Review in Northern Ireland* (2nd edn, Hart Publishing, 2008)

Arancibia, J., *Judicial Review of Commercial Regulation* (Oxford University Press, 2011)

Aronson, M., 'The Resurgence of Jurisdictional Facts' (2001) 12 PLR 17

'Is the ADJR Act Hampering the Development of Australian Administrative Law?' (2005) 15 PLR 202

'Jurisdictional Error without the Tears' in M. Groves and H. Lee (eds.), *Australian Administrative Law* (Cambridge University Press, 2007), 330

'Process, Quality and Variable Standards: Responding to an Agent Provocateur' in D. Dyzenhaus, M. Hunt and G. Huscroft (eds.), *A Simple Common Lawyer: Essays in Honour of Michael Taggart* (Hart Publishing, 2009), 5

Aronson, M. and M. Groves, *Judicial Review of Administrative Action* (5th edn, Thomson Reuters, 2013)

Arthurs, H., 'Jonah and the Whale: The Appearance, Disappearance and Reappearance of Administrative Law' (1980) 30 UTLJ 225

Austin, R., 'Administrative Law's Reaction to the Changing Concepts of Public Service' in P. Leyland and T. Woods (eds.), *Administrative Law Facing the Future* (Blackstone, 1997), 30

Bamforth, N. and P. Leyland (eds.), *Accountability in the Contemporary Constitution* (Oxford University Press, 2013)

Basten, J., 'The Supervisory Jurisdiction of the Supreme Court' (2011) 85 ALJ 273

'Jurisdictional Error After *Kirk*: Has it a Future?' (2012) 23 PLR 94

Beatson, J., 'The Scope of Judicial Review for Error of Law' (1984) 4 OJLS 22

'The Discretionary Nature of Public Law Remedies' (1991) *NZ Recent Law* 81

Beck, A., 'Farewell to the Forum Otiosum?' [2011] NZLJ 269

Beloff, M.J., 'The Concept of "Deference in Public Law"' [2006] JR 213

Bennett, M., 'Hart and Raz on the Non-Instrumental Moral Value of Law: A Reconsideration' (2011) 30 Law & Phil 603

Bingham, T., *The Business of Judging: Selected Essays and Speeches* (Oxford University Press, 2000)

'The Human Rights Act' [2010] EHRLR 568

The Rule of Law (Penguin, 2011)

Birkinshaw, P., 'De Smith's Judicial Review' (2009) 15 EPL 279 (book review)

Blake, N., 'Importing Proportionality: Clarification or Confusion' [2002] EHRLR 19

Boughley, J., 'Administrative Law: The Next Frontier for Comparative Law' (2013) 62 ICLQ 55

'The Reasonableness of Proportionality in the Australian Administrative Law Context' (2015) 43 Fed L Rev 59

Bradley, A. and K. Ewing, *Constitutional and Administrative Law* (14th edn, Pearson Longman, 2007)

Brady, A.D., *Proportionality and Deference under the UK Human Rights Act: An Institutionally Sensitive Approach* (Cambridge University Press, 2012)

Burnton, S., 'Proportionality' [2011] JR 179

Cameron, B., 'Legal Change over Fifty Years' (1987) 3 Canta LR 199

Cane, P., 'Merits Review and Judicial Review – The AAT as Trojan Horse' (2000) 28 Fed L Rev 213

'The Making of Australian Administrative Law' (2003) 23 Aust Bar Rev 114

Administrative Law (4th edn, Oxford University Press, 2004)

'Understanding Judicial Review and its Impact' in M. Hertogh and S. Halliday (eds.), *Judicial Review and Bureaucratic Impact* (Cambridge University Press, 2004), 15

Administrative Tribunals and Adjudication (Hart Publishing, 2009)

Cane, P. and L. McDonald, *Principles of Administrative Law* (Oxford University Press, 2008)

Carnwath, R., 'Tribunal Justice – A New Start' [2009] PL 48

'From Judicial Outrage to Sliding Scales' (ALBA Annual Lecture, November, 2013)

Cartier, G., 'Keeping a Check on Discretion' in C. Flood and L. Sossin (eds.), *Administrative Law in Context* (Emond Montgomery, 2008), 269

Chan, C., 'Deference and the Separation of Powers: An Assessment of the Court's Constitutional and Institutional Competences' (2011) 41 HKLJ 7

Clayton, R., 'Legitimate Expectations, Policy, and the Principle of Consistency' (2003) 62 CLJ 93

'Judicial Deference and Democratic Dialogue: The Legitimacy of Judicial Intervention under the Human Rights Act 1998' [2004] PL 33

'Principles for Judicial Deference' [2006] JR 109

'New Arrangements for the Administrative Court' [2008] JR 164

Clyde, L. and D. Edwards, *Judicial Review* (W. Green, 2000)

Cochrane, T., 'A General Public Law Duty to Provide Reasons: Why New Zealand Should Follow the Irish Supreme Court' (2013) 11 NZJPIL 517

Cohen, F.S., 'Transcendental Nonsense and the Functional Approach' (1935) 35 Colum L Rev 809

Cohen-Eliya, M. and I. Porat, 'American Balancing and German Proportionality: The Historical Origins' (2010) 8 ICON 263

Cooke, F., 'A Personal Word' (2008) 39 VUWLR 15

'The Future of Public Law in New Zealand' in *Administrative Law* (NZ Law Society, 2011), 75

Cooke, R., 'The Struggle for Simplicity in Administrative Law' in M. Taggart (ed.), *Judicial Review of Administrative Action in the 1980s* (Oxford University Press, 1986)

'Fairness' (1989) 19 NZULR 421

Turning Points of the Common Law (Sweet & Maxwell, 1997)

'The Discretionary Heart of Administrative Law' in I. Hare and C. Forsyth (eds.), *The Golden Metwand and the Crooked Cord: Essays on Public Law in Honour of Sir William Wade QC* (Clarendon, 1998), 203

'Foreword' in P.A. Joseph (ed.), *Constitutional and Administrative Law in New Zealand* (2nd edn, Brookers, 2001)

'The Road Ahead for the Common Law' (2004) 53 ICLQ 273

Corder, H., 'Administrative Justice Across the Commonwealth: A First Scan' [2006] AJ 1

Craig, P.P., 'The Common Law, Reasons and Administrative Justice' [1994] CLJ 282

'Substantive Legitimate Expectations in Community and Domestic Law' (1996) 55 CLJ 289

'Unreasonableness and Proportionality in UK Law' in E. Ellis (ed.), *The Principle of Proportionality in the Laws of Europe* (Hart Publishing, 1999), 85

'Public Law, Political Theory and Legal Theory' [2000] PL 211

'The Courts, the Human Rights Act and Judicial Review' (2001) 117 LQR 589

'Constitutional Foundations, the Rule of Law and Supremacy' (2003) PL 92

'Administrative Law in the Anglo-American Tradition' in B.G. Peters and J. Pierre (eds.), *Handbook of Public Administration* (Sage, 2003), 269

'Judicial Review, Appeal and Factual Error' [2004] PL 788

'The Common Law, Shared Power and Judicial Review' (2004) 24 OJLS 237

'Legislative Intent and Legislative Supremacy: A Reply to Professor Allan' (2004) 24 OJLS 585

'Theory, "Pure Theory" and Values in Public Law' (2005) PL 440

'Administrative Law' in B. Dickson and G. Drewry (eds.), *The Judicial House of Lords 1876–2009* (Oxford University Press, 2009), 524

'Fundamental Principles of Administrative Law' in D. Feldman (ed.), *English Public Law* (Oxford University Press, 2009)

'Judicial Review and Questions of Law: A Comparative Perspective' in S. Rose-Ackerman and P. Lindseth (eds.), *Comparative Administrative Law* (Edward Elgar, 2010)

'Proportionality, Rationality and Review' [2010] NZ Law Rev 265

'The Nature of Reasonableness Review' (2013) 66 CLP 131

UK, EU and Global Administrative Law (Cambridge University Press, 2015)

'Judicial Review and Anxious Scrutiny' [2015] PL 60

Administrative Law (8th edn, Sweet & Maxwell, 2016)

Craig, P.P. and R. Rawlings (eds.), *Law and Administration in Europe: Essays in Honour of Carol Harlow* (Oxford University Press, 2003)

Crown Law Office, *A Judge Over Your Shoulder: A Guide to Judicial Review of Administrative Decisions* (Crown Law Office (NZ), 2005)

Daley, J., 'Defining Judicial Restraint' in T. Campbell and J. Goldsworthy (eds.), *Judicial Power, Democracy and Legal Positivism* (Ashgate, 2000), 279

Daly, P., 'Deference on Questions of Law' (2011) 74 MLR 649

'Wednesbury's Reasoning and Structure' [2011] PL 238

A Theory of Deference in Administrative Law (Cambridge University Press, 2012)

'*Dunsmuir's* Flaws Exposed' (2012) 58 McGill LJ 1

'The Unfortunate Triumph of Form over Substance in Canadian Administrative Law' (2012) 50 Osgoode Hall LJ 317

'The Scope and Meaning of Reasonableness Review' (2015) 52 Alta Law Rev 799

Davis, D.M., 'To Defer and then When? Administrative Law and Constitutional Democracy' [2006] AJ 23

De Smith, S., '*Judicial Review of Administrative Action: A Study in Case Law*' (London School of Economics and Political Science, 1959)

Judicial Review of Administrative Action (Stevens & Sons, 1959)

Judicial Review of Administrative Action (2nd edn, Stevens & Sons, 1968)

Judicial Review of Administrative Action (3rd edn, Stevens & Sons, 1973)

De Smith, S. and Evans, H.M., *Judicial Review of Administrative Action* (4th edn, Stevens & Sons, 1980)

De Ville, J., 'The Rule of Law and Judicial Review' [2006] AJ 62

Diplock, K., 'Administrative Law' (1974) 33 CLJ 233

Dodek, A.M. and D.A. Wright, 'The McLachlin Court's First Decade – A Dynamic Time for Public Law' in A.M. Dodek and D.A. Wright (eds.), *Public Law at the McLachlin Court* (Irwin Law, 2011), 1

Douglas, R. and M. Jones, *Douglas and Jones' Administrative Law* (6th edn, Federation Press, 2009)

Dworkin, R., *Taking Rights Seriously* (Harvard University Press, 1978)

Law's Empire (Harper Collins, 1998)

Dyzenhaus, D., 'The Politics of Deference: Judicial Review and Democracy' in M. Taggart (ed.), *The Province of Administrative Law* (Hart Publishing, 1997), 279

'Law as Justification: Etienne Mureinik's Conception of Legal Culture' (1998) 14 SAJHR 11

'Form and Substance in the Rule of Law' in C. Forsyth (ed.), *Judicial Review and the Constitution* (Hart Publishing, 2000)

'Constituting the Rule of Law: Fundamental Values of Administrative Law' (2002) 27 Queens LJ 445

'Formalism's Hollow Victory' [2002] NZ Law Rev 525

'*Baker*: Unity of Public Law' in D. Dyzenhaus (ed.), *The Unity of Public Law* (Hart Publishing, 2004)

'The Genealogy of Legal Positivism' (2004) 24 OJLS 39

(ed.), *The Unity of Public Law* (Hart Publishing, 2004)

'David Mullan's Theory of the Rule of (Common) Law' in G. Huscroft and M. Taggart (eds.), *Inside and Outside Canadian Administrative Law: Essays in Honour of David Mullan* (Toronto University Press, 2006), 448

'The Legitimacy of the Rule of Law' in D. Dyzenhaus, H. Murray and G. Huscroft (eds.), *A Simple Common Lawyer: Essays in Honour of Michael Taggart* (Hart Publishing, 2009), 33

'The Very Idea of a Judge' (2010) 60 UTLJ 61

'Dignity in Administrative Law: Judicial Deference in a Culture of Justification' (2012) 17 Rev Const Stud 87

'Proportionality and Defence in a Culture of Justification' in G. Huscroft, B.W. Miller and G. Webber (eds.), *Proportionality and the Rule of Law* (Cambridge University Press, 2014), 234

'Process and Substance as Aspects of the Public Law Form' (2015) 74 Camb LJ 284

Dyzenhaus, D. and E. Fox-Decent, 'Rethinking the Process/Substance Distinction' (2001) 51 UTLJ 193

Dyzenhaus, D., M. Hunt and G. Huscroft (eds.), *A Simple Common Lawyer: Essays in Honour of Michael Taggart* (Hart Publishing, 2009)

Dyzenhaus, D., M. Hunt and M. Taggart, 'The Principle of Legality in Administrative Law: Internationalisation as Constitutionalisation' (2001) 1 OUCLJ 5

Dyzenhaus, D. and M. Taggart, 'Judicial Review, Jurisprudence and the Wizard of Oz' (1990) 1 PLR 21

Edwards, R.A., 'Judicial Deference under the Human Rights Act' (2002) 65 MLR 859

Elias, S., 'Administrative Law for Living People' (2009) 68 CLJ 47

'Righting Administrative Law' in D. Dyzenhaus, M. Hunt and G. Huscroft (eds.), *A Simple Common Lawyer: Essays in Honour of Michael Taggart* (Hart Publishing, 2009), 55

'National Lecture on Administrative Law' (Australian Institute of Administrative Law Conference, Canberra, 2013)

'The Unity of Public Law?' (Public Law conference, September 2016, Cambridge)

Elliott, M., 'The Human Rights Act 1998 and the Standard of Substantive Review' (2001) 60 CLJ 301

'*Wednesbury* and Proportionality: Complementary Principles of Substantive Review' [2002] JR 97

'Unlawful Representations, Legitimate Expectations and Estoppel in Public Law' [2003] JR 71

'Legitimate Expectation, Consistency and Abuse of Power' [2005] JR 71

'Legitimate Expectations and the Search for Principle: Reflections on *Abdi & Nadarajah*' [2009] JR 281

'Proportionality and Deference: The Importance of a Structured Approach' in C. Forsyth and others (eds.), *Effective Judicial Review: A Cornerstone of Good Governance* (Oxford University Press, 2010), 264

Beatson, Matthews and Elliott's Administrative Law (4th edn, Oxford University Press, 2011)

'Has the Common Law Duty to Give Reasons Come of Age Yet?' [2011] PL 56

'Judicial Review's Scope, Foundations and Purposes' [2012] NZ Law Rev 75

'Justification, Calibration and Substantive Judicial Review' (working paper, September 2013)

'Proportionality and Deference' (working paper, September 2013)

'From Bifurcation to Calibration' in H. Wilberg and M. Elliott, *The Scope and Intensity of Substantive Review* (Hart Publishing, 2015), 61

Elster, J., 'Deliberation and Constitution Making' in J. Elster (ed.), *Deliberative Democracy* (Cambridge University Press, 2001)

Endicott, T.A., 'Questions of Law' (1998) 114 LQR 292

'The Impossibility of the Rule of Law' (1999) 19 OJLS 1

'Are There Any Rules?' (2001) 5 Legal Ethics 199

Vagueness in Law (Oxford University Press, 2001)

Administrative Law (Oxford University Press, 2009)

Feldman, D., 'Judicial Review: A Way of Controlling Government?' (1998) 66 Pub Admin 21

Fenwick, H., G. Phillipson and R. Masterman (eds.), *Judicial Reasoning Under the UK Human Rights Act* (Cambridge University Press, 2011)

Flood, C. and L. Sossin (eds.), *Administrative Law in Context* (Emond Montgomery, 2008)

Administrative Law in Context (2nd edn, Emond Montgomery, 2012)

Foley, B., 'Diceyan Ghosts – Deference, Rights, Policy and Spatial Distinctions' (2006) 28 DULJ 77

Deference and the Presumption of Constitutionality (Institute of Public Administration, Dublin, 2008)

Fordham, M., 'Surveying the Grounds' in P. Leyland and T. Woods (eds.), *Administrative Law Facing the Future* (Blackstone, 1997)

'Common Law Proportionality' [2002] JR 110

'Common Law Rights' [2011] JR 14

Judicial Review Handbook (6th edn, Hart Publishing, 2012)

Fordham, M. and T. de la Mare, 'Anxious Scrutiny, the Principle of Legality and the Human Rights Act' [2001] JR 40

'Identifying the Principles of Proportionality' in J. Jowell and J. Cooper (eds.), *Understanding Human Rights Principles* (Hart Publishing, 2001), 32

Forsyth, C., 'Of Fig Leaves and Fairy Tales: The Ultra Vires Doctrine, the Sovereignty of Parliament and Judicial Review' (1996) 55 CLJ 122; also published in C. Forsyth (ed.), *Judicial Review and the Constitution* (Hart Publishing, 2000), 29

'The Metaphysics of Nullity' in C. Forsyth and I. Hare (eds.), *The Golden Metwand and the Crooked Cord* (Oxford University Press, 1998), 141

'Showing the Fly the Way Out of the Flybottle: The Value of Formalism and Conceptual Reasoning in Administrative Law' (2007) 66 CLJ 325

'Legitimate Expectations Revisited' (2011) 16 JR 429

Forsyth, C. and M. Elliott, 'The Legitimacy of Judicial Review' [2003] PL 286

Forsyth, C. and I. Hare (eds.), *The Golden Metwand and the Crooked Cord: Essays in Honour of Sir William Wade QC* (Oxford University Press, 1998)

Forsyth, C. and L. Whittle, 'Judicial Creativity and Judicial Legitimacy in Administrative Law' (2002) 8 Canta L Rev 453

Forsyth, C. and others (eds.), *Effective Judicial Review: A Cornerstone of Good Governance* (Oxford University Press, 2010)

Franklin, C.N.K., 'The Burgeoning Principle of Consistency in EU Law' (2011) 30 YEL 42

Freckleton, A., 'The Concept of Deference in Judicial Review of Administrative Decisions in Australia – Part 1' (2013) 73 AIAL Forum 52

'The Concept of Deference in Judicial Review of Administrative Decisions in Australia – Part 2' (2013) 73 AIAL Forum 48

French, R., 'Administrative Law in Australia: Themes and Values Revisited' in M. Groves (ed.), *Modern Administrative Law in Australia: Concepts and Context* (Cambridge University Press, 2014), 24

Fuller, L.L., *The Morality of Law* (Yale University Press, 1964)

The Anatomy of Law (Greenwood Press, 1976)

Gageler, S., 'The Underpinnings of Judicial Review of Administrative Action: Common Law or Constitution?' (2000) 28 Fed L Rev 303

'Impact of Migration Law on the Development of Australian Administrative Law' (2010) 17 AJ Admin L 92

Galligan, D., 'Judicial Review and the Textbook Writers' (1982) 2 OJLS 257

Discretionary Powers: A Legal Study of Official Discretion (Oxford University Press, 1990)

Gardbaum, S., *The New Commonwealth Model of Constitutionalism* (Cambridge University Press, 2013)

Gearty, C., *Principles of Human Rights Adjudication* (Oxford University Press, 2005)

Geiringer, C., '*Tavita* and All That' (2004) 21 NZULR 66

'International Law Through the Lens of *Zaoui*: Where is New Zealand At?' (2006) 17 PLR 300

'The Principle of Legality and the Bill of Rights Act: A Critical Examination of *R v. Hansen*' in C. Geiringer and D. Knight (eds.), *Seeing the World Whole: Essays in Honour of Sir Kenneth Keith* (Victoria University Press, 2008), 69

'Sources of Resistance to Proportionality Review of Administrative Power Under the New Zealand Bill of Rights Act' (2013) 11 NZJPIL 123

Gleeson, M., 'Judicial Legitimacy' (2000) 20 Aust Bar Rev 4

Gordon, R., 'Two Dogmas of Proportionality' [2011] JR 18

Graham, C., 'Judicial Review of Administrative Action' (1997) 3 EPL 149 (book review)

Green, A.J., 'Can There Be Too Much Context in Administrative Law? Setting the Standard of Review in Canadian Administrative Law' (2014) 47 UBC Law Rev 443

Griffith, J., 'Judicial Review of Administrative Action' (1960) 18 CLJ 228 (book review)

Grimm, D., 'Proportionality in Canadian and German Constitutional Jurisprudence' (2007) 57 UTLJ 393

Groves, M., 'Treaties and Legitimate Expectations – The Rise and Fall of Teoh in Australia' [2010] JR 323

  'Should We Follow the Gospel of the ADJR Act?' (2010) 34 MULR 736

  (ed.), *Modern Administrative Law in Australia: Concepts and Context* (Cambridge University Press, 2014)

Groves, M. and H.P. Lee (eds.), *Australian Administrative Law: Fundamentals, Principles and Doctrines* (Cambridge University Press, 2007)

Habermas, J., *Between Facts and Norms* (MIT Press, 1996)

Halliday, S., *Judicial Review and Compliance with Administrative Law* (Hart Publishing, 2004)

Hare, I., 'The Separation of Powers and Judicial Review for Error of Law' in C. Forsyth and I. Hare (eds.), *The Golden Metwand and the Crooked Cord* (Oxford University Press, 2008), 113

Harlow, C., 'Politics and Principles: Some Rival Theories of Administrative Law' (1981) 44 MLR 114 (book review)

  'Changing the Mindset: The Place of Theory in English Administrative Law' (1994) 14 OJLS 419

  'A Special Relationship? American Influences on Judicial Review in England' in I. Loveland (ed.), *A Special Relationship? American Influences on Public Law in the UK* (Oxford University Press, 1995), 79

  'Export, Import: The Ebb and Flow of English Public Law' [2000] PL 240

Harlow, C. and R. Rawlings, *Law and Administration* (3rd edn, Cambridge University Press, 2009)

Harris, B., 'Judicial Review, Justiciability and the Prerogative of Mercy' (2003) 62 CLJ 631

Hartogh, M. and S. Halliday, *Judicial Review and Bureaucratic Impact* (Cambridge University Press, 2004)

Hayne, K., 'Deference: An Australian Perspective' [2011] PL 75

Heckman, G., 'Substantive Review in Appellate Courts Since *Dunsmuir*' (2009) 47 Osgoode Hall LJ 751

Hertogh, M. and S. Halliday (eds.), *Judicial Review and Bureaucratic Impact* (Cambridge University Press, 2004)

Hickman, T., 'The Reasonableness Principle' (2004) 63 CLJ 166

  'The Reasonableness Principle: Reassessing its Place in the Public Sphere' (2004) 63 CLJ 166

'In Defence of the Legal Constitution' (2005) 55 UTLJ 981

'Problems for Proportionality' (2010) NZ Law Rev 303

Public Law after the Human Rights Act (Hart Publishing, 2010)

Hogg, P.W., 'The Supreme Court of Canada and Administrative Law, 1949–1971' (1973) 11 Osgoode Hall LJ 187

Hood, Phillips O., 'Book Review: Judicial Review of Administrative Action' (1960) 23 MLR 458 (book review)

Hunt, M., *Using Human Rights in English Courts* (Hart Publishing, 1997)

'Sovereignty's Blight: Why Contemporary Public Law Needs a Concept of Due Deference' in N. Bamforth and P. Leyland (eds.), *Public Law in a Multi-Layered Constitution* (Hart Publishing, 2003), 337

'Against Bifurcation' in D. Dyzenhaus, M. Hunt and G. Huscroft (eds.), *A Simple Common Lawyer: Essays in Honour of Michael Taggart* (Hart Publishing, 2009), 99

Huscroft, G., 'The Duty of Fairness' in C. Flood and L. Sossin (eds.), *Administrative Law in Context* (Emond Montgomery, 2008), 115

'Judicial Review from *CUPE* to *CUPE*' in G. Huscroft and M. Taggart (eds.), *Inside and Outside Canadian Administrative Law* (University of Toronto Press, 2009), 296

Huscroft, G. and M. Taggart (eds.), *Inside and Outside Canadian Administrative Law: Essays in Honour of David Mullan* (Toronto UP, 2006)

Hutcheson, J.C., 'The Judgment Intuitive: The Function of the Hunch in Judicial Decision' (1929) 14 Cornell L Rev 274

Illingworth, G., 'Fundamental Rights and the Margin of Appreciation' [2010] NZLJ 424

Jaffe, L.T., 'Book Review: Judicial Review of Administrative Action' (1961) 74 Harv Law Rev 636 (book review)

Jones, D. and A. de Villars, *Principles of Administrative Law* (5th edn, Carswell, 2009)

Jones, T.H., 'Judicial Review and Codification' (2006) 20 LS 517

Jones, T.H. and J.M. Williams, 'Wales as a Jurisdiction' [2004] PL 78

Joseph, P.A., 'The Demise of Ultra Vires: Judicial Review in the New Zealand Courts' [2001] PL 354

'The Demise of Ultra Vires – A Reply to Christopher Forsyth and Linda Whittle' (2002) 8 Canta LR 463

'The Contributions of the Court of Appeal to Commonwealth Administrative Law' in R. Bigwood (ed.), *The Permanent New Zealand Court of Appeal: Essays on the First 50 Years* (Hart Publishing, 2009), 41

'The Rule of Law' in R. Ekins (ed.), *Modern Challenges to the Rule of Law* (LexisNexis, 2011), 47

'Exploratory Questions in Administrative Law' (2012) 25 NZULR 75

Constitutional and Administrative Law (4th edn, Brookers, 2014)

'False Dichotomies in Administrative Law' [2016] NZ Law Rev 127

Jowell, J., 'Proportionality' in J. Jowell and D. Oliver (eds.), *New Directions in Judicial Review* (Steven & Sons, 1988), 51

'Is Equality a Constitutional Principle' (1994) 7 CLP 1

'Of Vires and Vacuums: The Constitutional Context of Judicial Review' [1999] PL 448

'Beyond the Rule of Law: Towards Constitutional Judicial Review' [2000] PL 671

'Judicial Deference: Servility, Civility or Institutional Capacity?' [2003] PL 592

'Judicial Deference and Human Rights' in P. Craig and R. Rawlings (eds.), *Law and Administration in Europe* (Oxford University Press, 2003), 67.

'Administrative Law' in V. Bogdanor (ed.), *The British Constitution in the Twentieth Century* (Oxford University Press, 2003), 373

'The Democratic Necessity of Administrative Justice' [2006] AJ 13

'The Rule of Law and its Underlying Values' in J. Jowell and D. Oliver (eds.), *The Changing Constitution* (6th edn, Oxford University Press, 2007), 5

Jowell, J. and A. Lester, 'Beyond *Wednesbury*: Substantive Principles of Administrative Law' [1988] PL 368

'Proportionality: Neither Novel nor Dangerous' in J. Jowell and D. Oliver (eds.), *New Directions in Judicial Review* (Steven & Sons, 1988), 51

Kaplow, L., 'Rules Versus Standards: An Economic Analysis' (1992) 42 Duke LJ 557

Kavanagh, A., 'The Elusive Divide Between Interpretation and Legislation Under the Human Rights Act 1998' (2004) 24 OJLS 259

'Deference or Defiance? The Limits of the Judicial Role in Constitutional Adjudication' in G. Huscroft (ed.), *Expounding the Constitution: Essays in Constitutional Theory* (Cambridge University Press, 2008), 184

Constitutional Review under the UK Human Rights Act (Cambridge University Press, 2009)

'Defending Deference in Public Law and Constitutional Theory' (2010) 126 LQR 222

'Judicial Restraint in the Pursuit of Justice' (2010) UTLJ 23

Keene, D., 'Principles of Deference Under the Human Rights Act' in H. Fenwick, G. Phillipson and R. Masterman (eds.), *Judicial Reasoning Under the UK Human Rights Act* (Cambridge University Press, 2007), 206

Kenall, D., 'De-Regulating the Regulatory Compact: The Legacy of *Dunsmuir* and the "Jurisdictional" Question Doctrine' (2011) 24 CJALP 115

King, J.A., 'The Justiciability of Resource Allocation' (2007) 70 MLR 197

'Institutional Approaches to Judicial Restraint' (2008) 28 OJLS 409

'Proportionality: A Halfway House' (2010) NZ Law Rev 327

'The Instrumental Value of Legal Accountability' in N. Bamforth and P. Leyland (eds.), *Accountability in the Contemporary Constitution* (Oxford University Press, 2013), 124

Kirk, J., 'The Concept of Jurisdictional Error' in N. Williams (ed.), *Key Issues in Judicial Review* (Federation Press, 2014), 11

Klinck, J.A., 'Reasonableness Review: Conceptualizing a Single Contextual Standard from Divergent Approaches in *Dunsmuir* and *Khosa*' (2011) 24 CJALP 41

Knight, D.R., 'A Murky Methodology: Standards of Review in Administrative Law' (2008) 6 NZJPIL 117

'Simple, Fair, Discretionary Administrative Law' (2008) 39 VUWLR 99

'Mapping the Rainbow of Review' [2010] NZ Law Rev 393

Kress, K., 'Coherence and Formalism' (1993) 16 Harv J L & Pub Pol'y 639

Kumm, M., 'The Idea of Socratic Contestation and the Right to Justification' (2010) 4 *Law and Ethics of Human Rights* 147

Laws, J., 'De Smith, Woolf and Jowell' (1996) 1996 JR 49 (book review)

'Illegality' in M. Supperstone and J. Goudie (eds.), *Judicial Review* (2nd edn, Butterworths, 1997), 51

'*Wednesbury*' in C. Forsyth and I. Hare (eds.), *The Golden Metwand and the Crooked Cord* (Oxford University Press, 1998), 141

Lawson, G. and S. Kam, 'Making Law Out of Nothing at All' (2013) 65 Admin LR 1

Le Sueur, A., 'The Judicial Review Debate: From Partnership to Friction' (1996) 31 *Government and Opposition* 8

'Legal Duties to Give Reasons' (1999) 52 CLP 150

'The Rise and Ruin of Unreasonableness?' [2005] JR 32

Le Sueur, A., J. Herberg and R. English, *Principles of Public Law* (Cavendish, 1999)

Leigh, I., 'Taking Rights Proportionately' (2002) 47 PL 265

'The Standard of Judicial Review after the Human Rights Act' in H. Fenwick, G. Phillipson and R. Masterman (eds.), *Judicial Reasoning Under the UK Human Rights Act* (Cambridge University Press, 2007), 174

Lewans, M., 'Deference and Reasonableness since *Dunsmuir*' (2012) 38 Queen's LJ 59

Lewis, C., *Judicial Remedies in Public Law* (5th edn, Sweet & Maxwell, 2014)

Leyland, P. and T. Woods (eds.), *Administrative Law Facing the Future* (Blackstone, 1997)

Textbook on Administrative Law (4th edn, Oxford University Press, 2003)

Lipton, T., 'Justifying True Questions of Jurisdiction' (2015) 46 Ottawa Law Rev 275

Liston, M., 'Governments in Miniature' in Flood, C. and L. Sossin (eds.), *Administrative Law in Context* (Emond Montgomery, 2008), 105

Loughlin, M., 'A Study of the Crisis in Administrative Law Theory' (1978) 28 UTLJ 215

'The Pathways of Public Law Scholarship' in G.P. Wilson (ed.), *Frontiers of Legal Scholarship* (Wiley, 1995), 163

The Idea of Public Law (Oxford University Press, 2004)

Foundations of Public Law (Oxford University Press, 2010)

Loveland, I., *Constitutional Law, Administrative Law and Human Rights* (5th edn, Oxford University Press, 2009)

MacCormick, N., *Rhetoric and The Rule of Law: A Theory of Legal Reasoning* (Oxford University Press, 2005)

Macklin, A., 'Standard of Review: Back to the Future?' in C. Flood and L. Sossin (eds.), *Administrative Law in Context* (2nd edn, Emond Montgomery, 2012), 279

Mason, A., 'Mike Taggart and Australian Exceptionalism' in D. Dyzenhaus, M. Hunt and G. Huscroft (eds.), *A Simple Common Lawyer: Essays in Honour of Michael Taggart* (Bloomsbury, 2009), 179

Mason, K., 'What is Wrong with Top-Down Legal Reasoning?' (2004) 78 ALJ 574

McCrudden, E., 'Equality and Non-Discrimination' in D. Feldman (ed.), *English Public Law* (2nd edn, Oxford University Press, 2009), 499

McDonald, L., 'Rethinking Unreasonableness Review' (2014) 25 PLR 117

McGarry, J., 'Effecting Legal Certainty under the Human Rights Act' [2011] JR 66

McMillan, J., 'Judicial Restraint and Activism in Administrative Law' (2002) 30 Fed L Rev 335

Meazell, E., 'Deference and Dialogue in Administrative Law' (2011) 111 Colum L Rev 1722

Mullan, D.J., 'Judicial Review of Administrative Action' [1975] NZLJ 154
  Administrative Law (Irwin Law, 2001)
  'Establishing the Standard of Review: the Struggle for Complexity?' (2004) 17 CJALP 59
  'Deference from *Baker* to *Suresh* and Beyond' in D. Dyzenhaus (ed.), *The Unity of Public Law* (Hart Publishing, 2004), 21
  'Deference: Is it Useful Outside Canada?' (2006) AJ 42
  'The Canadian Charter of Rights and Freedoms: A Direct Driver of Judicial Review of Administrative Action in Canada?' in L. Pearson, C. Harlow and M. Taggart (eds.), *Administrative Law in a Changing State: Essays in Honour of Mark Aronson* (Hart Publishing, 2008), 123
  '*Dunsmuir v. New Brunswick,* Standard of Review and Procedural Fairness for Public Servants: Let's Try Again!' (2008) 21 CJALP 117
  'Judicial Review of the Executive: Principled Exasperation' (2010) 8 NZJPIL 1
  'Proportionality – A Proportionate Response to an Emerging Crisis in Canadian Judicial Review Law?' [2010] NZ Law Rev 233
  'Unresolved Issues on the Standard of Review in Canadian Judicial Review of Administrative Action – the Top Fifteen!' (2013) 42 AQ 1

Mullan, D.J., M. Taggart and G. Huscroft, *Inside and Outside Canadian Administrative Law: Essays in Honour of David Mullan* (University of Toronto Press, 2006)

Mureinik, E., 'A Bridge to Where?' (1994) 10 SAJHR 31

Murphy, C., 'Lon Fuller and the Moral Value of the Rule of Law' (2005) 24 Law & Phil 239

Murray, P., 'Process, Substance and the History of Error of Law Review' in J. Bell and others, *Public Law Adjudication in Common Law Systems* (Bloomsbury, 2016), 87

Neill, P., 'The Duty to Give Reasons' in C. Forsyth and I. Hare (eds.), *The Golden Metwand and the Crooked Cord* (Oxford University Press, 1998)

Neuberger, L., P.K. Thompson and L. Di Mambro, *Civil Court Practice 2009 (The Green Book)* (LexisNexis, 2009)

Oliver, D., 'Is the Ultra Vires Rule the Basis of Judicial Review?' [1987] PL 543

'The Judge Over Your Shoulder' (1989) 42 Parliamentary Affairs 302

'Judge Over Your Shoulder – Mark II' [1994] PL 514

Orsi, S.D., 'Legitimate Expectations: An Overview' [2010] JR 388

Pearson, L., C. Harlow and M. Taggart (eds.), *Administrative Law in a Changing State: Essays in Honour of Mark Aronson* (Hart Publishing, 2008)

Phillipson, G., 'Deference, Discretion and Democracy in the Human Rights Act Era' (2007) 60 CLP 40

Picinali, F., 'Two Meanings of "Reasonableness": Dispelling the "Floating" Reasonable Doubt' (2013) 76 MLR 845

Pocock, J., *The Ancient Constitution and the Feudal Law* (2nd edn, Cambridge University Press, 1987)

Poole, T., 'Justice, Rights and Judicial Humility: *ex p Simms*' [2000] JR 106

'Back to the Future? Unearthing the Theory of Common Law Constitutionalism' (2003) 23 OJLS 454

'Legitimacy, Rights and Judicial Review' (2005) 25 OJLS 697

'Tilting at Windmills? Truth and Illusion in "The Political Constitution"' (2007) 70 MLR 250

'Between the Devil and the Deep Blue Sea: Administrative Law in an Age of Rights' in L. Pearson, C. Harlow and M. Taggart (eds.), *Administrative Law in a Changing State: Essays in Honour of Mark Aronson* (Hart Publishing, 2008), 15

'The Reformation of English Administrative Law' (2009) 68 CLJ 142

'Judicial Review at the Margins' (2010) 60 UTLJ 81

'Proportionality in Perspective' [2010] NZ Law Rev 369

Posner, E.A., 'Standards, Rules, and Social Norms' (1997) 211 Harvard Journal of Law & Public Policy 101

Posner, R.A., 'Legal Reasoning From the Top Down and From the Bottom Up' [1992] U Chicago LR 433

'The Rise and Fall of Judicial Self-Restraint' (2012) 100 CLR 519

Rawlings, R., 'Modelling Judicial Review' (2008) 61 CLP 95

Rawls, J., *The Law of Peoples* (Harvard UP, 2001)

Raz, J., 'The Rule of Law and its Virtue' (1977) 93 LQR 195

The Authority of Law (Clarendon, 1979)

Rishworth, P. (ed.), *The Struggle for Simplicity in the Law: Essays for Lord Cooke of Thorndon* (Butterworths, 1997)

Rivers, J., 'Proportionality and Variable Intensity of Review' (2006) 65 CLJ 174

Robson, W.A., 'Administrative Law in England, 1919–1948' in G. Campion (ed.), *British Government Since 1918* (Allan and Unwin, 1950), 85

'Administrative Law' in M. Ginsberg (ed.), *Law and Opinion in England in the 20th Century* (University of California Press, 1959), 193

Rodriguez Ferrere, M., 'The Unnecessary Confusion in New Zealand's Appellate Jurisdictions' (2012) 12 OLR 829

Rose-Ackerman, S. and P.L. Lindseth, 'Comparative Administrative Law: Outlining a Field of Study' (2010) 28 Windsor YB Access Just 435

(eds.), *Comparative Administrative Law* (Edward Elgar, 2010)

Sales, P., 'A Comparison of the Principle of Legality and Section 3 of the Human Rights Act 1998' (2009) 125 LQR 598

Sales, P. and J. Clement, 'International Law in Domestic Courts' [2008] LQR 388

Samuel, G., 'Can the Common Law be Mapped?' (2005) 55 UTLJ 271

Saunders, C., 'Apples, Oranges and Comparative Administrative Law' [2006] AJ 423

'Constitution, Codes and Administrative Law' in C. Forsyth and others (eds.), *Effective Judicial Review* (Oxford University Press, 2010)

'Constitution as Catalyst: Different Paths within Australasian Administrative Law' (2012) 10 NZJPIL 143

Schlag, P.J., 'Rules and Standards' (1985) 33 UCLA L Rev 379

Schønberg, S., *Legitimate Expectations in Administrative Law* (Oxford University Press, 2000)

Sedley, S.S., 'The Sound of Silence' in V. Bogdanor (ed.), *The British Constitution in the Twentieth Century* (Oxford University Press, 2003), 373

Smith, M., 'Embracing Proportionality Review' [2011] NZLJ 224

The New Zealand Judicial Review Handbook (2nd edn., Thomson Reuters, 2016)

Soper, P., *The Ethics of Deference: Learning from Law's Morals* (Cambridge University Press, 2002)

Sossin, L. and C. Flood, 'The Contextual Turn' (2007) 57 UTLJ 581

Spiegelman, J., 'The Centrality of Jurisdictional Error' (2010) 21 PLR 77

Stern, K., 'Substantive Fairness in UK and Australian Law' (2007) 29 Aust Bar Rev 266

Steyn, J., 'Deference: A Tangled Story' [2005] PL 346

Stratas, D., 'The Canadian Law of Judicial Review' (2016) Queen's LR 27

Sumption, J., 'Judicial and Political Decision-making: The Uncertain Boundary' [2011] JR 301

Sunkin, M. and G. Richardson, 'Judicial Review: Questions of Impact' (1996) PL 79

Taggart, M., 'Rival Theories of Invalidity in Administrative Law' in M. Taggart (ed.), *Judicial Review of Administrative Action in the 1980s* (Oxford University Press, 1986), 93

(ed.), *Judicial Review of Administrative Action in the 1980s* (Oxford University Press, 1986)

'Outside Canadian Administrative Law' (1996) 46 UTLJ 649

'Introduction to JR in New Zealand' [1997] JR 236

'The Contribution of Lord Cooke to Scope of Review Doctrine in Administrative Law: A Comparative Common Law Perspective' in P. Rishworth (ed.),

The Struggle for Simplicity in the Law: Essays for Lord Cooke of Thorndon (Butterworths, 1997), 189

The Province of Administrative Law (Hart Publishing, 1997)

'Reinvented Government, Traffic Lights and the Convergence of Public and Private Law' [1999] PL 124

'Ultra Vires as a Distraction' in C. Forsyth (ed.), *Judicial Review and the Constitution* (Hart Publishing, 2000), 427

'Reinventing Administrative Law' in N. Bamforth and P. Leyland (eds.), *Public Law in a Multi-Layered Constitution* (Hart Publishing, 2003), 311

'The New Zealandness of New Zealand Public Law' (2004) 15 PLR 81

'The Tub of Public Law' in D. Dyzenhaus (ed.), *The Unity of Public Law* (Hart Publishing, 2004)

'Prolegomenon to an Intellectual History of Administrative Law in the Twentieth Century: the Case of John Willis and Canadian Administrative Law' (2005) 43 Osgoode Hall LJ 224

'Administrative Law' [2006] NZ Law Rev 75

'"Australian Exceptionalism" in Judicial Review' (2008) 36 Fed LR 1

'Proportionality, Deference, Wednesbury' [2008] NZ Law Rev 424

Taylor, G.D.S., 'May Judicial Review Become a Backwater?' in M. Taggart (ed.), *Judicial Review of Administrative Action in the 1980s* (Oxford University Press, 1986), 153

Taylor, G.D.S. *Judicial Review: A New Zealand Perspective* (3rd edn, LexisNexis, 2014)

Thomas, R., *Legitimate Expectations and Proportionality in Administrative Law* (Hart Publishing, 2000)

Thwaites, R. and D.R. Knight, 'Review and Appeal of Regulatory Decisions' in S. Frankel (ed.), *Learning from the Past, Adapting for the Future* (LexisNexis, 2011)

Treasury Solicitor, *The Judge Over Your Shoulder* (4th edn, Government Legal Service, 2006)

Urbina, F.J., 'A Critique of Proportionality' (2012) 57 Am J Juris 49

Varuhas, J.N., 'Keeping Things in Proportion: The Judiciary, Executive Action and Human Rights' (2006) 22 NZULR 300

'*Powerco v. Commerce Commission*: Developing Trends of Proportionality in New Zealand Administrative Law' (2006) 4 NZJPIL 339

Von Hayek, F., *The Road to Serfdom* (University of Chicago Press, 1944)

Waddams, S.M., 'Judicial Discretion' (2001) 1 OUCLJ 59

Wade, W., 'The Twilight of Natural Justice?' (1951) 67 LQR 103

'Anglo-American Administrative Law: More Reflections' (1966) 82 LQR 226

'Constitutional and Administrative Aspects of the *Anisminic* Case' (1969) 85 LQR 211

Wade, W. and C. Forsyth, *Administrative Law* (11th edn, Oxford University Press, 2014)

Waldron, J., 'Why Law? – Efficacy, Freedom or Fidelity?' (1994) 13 Law & Phil 259

Walker, P., 'What's Wrong with Irrationality' [1995] PL 556

Walters, M.D., 'Jurisdiction, Functionalism, and Constitutionalism in Canadian Administrative Law' in C. Forsyth and others (eds.), *Effective Judicial Review: A Cornerstone of Good Governance* (Oxford University Press, 2010), 300

Waluchow, W.J., 'Legal Rules and Palm Tree Justice' (1985) 4 Law & Phil 41

Watson, A., *Legal Transplants* (University of Georgia Press, 1974)
   Comparative Law (2nd edn, Vandeplas, 2008)

Weaver, R.L. and L.D. Jellum, 'Neither Fish nor Fowl: Administrative Judges in the Modern Administrative State' (2010) 28 Windsor YB Access Just 243

Webber, G.C., *The Negotiable Constitution: On the Limitation of Fights* (Cambridge University Press, 2009)
   'Proportionality, Balancing, and the Cult of Constitutional Rights Scholarship' (2010) 23 CJLJ 179

Weber, M., *Economy and Society* (University of California Press, 1978)

Weinrib, E.J., 'The Jurisprudence of Legal Formalism' (1993) 16 Harv J L & Pub Pol'y 584

Wilberg, H., 'Administrative Law' [2010] NZ Law Rev 177
   'Substantive Grounds of Review' (Legal Research Foundation Conference, Auckland, April, 2011)

Wildeman, S., 'Pas de Deux: Deference and non-Deference in Action' in C. Flood and L. Sossin (eds.), *Administrative Law in Context* (2nd edn, Emond Montgomery, 2012), 323

Williams, D., 'Judicial Review of Administrative Action' (1974) 33 CLJ 324 (book review)
   'Justiciability and the Control of Discretionary Power' in M. Taggart (ed.), *Judicial Review of Administrative Action in the 1980s* (Oxford University Press, 1986), 103

Williams, R., 'When is an Error not an Error: Reform of Jurisdictional Review of Error of Law and Fact' [2007] PL 793

Willis, E., 'Judicial Review and Deference' [2011] NZLJ 283

Woolf, H., 'The Role of the English Judiciary in Developing Public Law' (1986) 27 Wm & Mary L Rev 669

Woolf, H. and J. Jowell, *Judicial Review of Administrative Action* (5th edn, Sweet & Maxwell, 1995)

Woolf, H., J. Jowell and A. Le Sueur, *De Smith's Judicial Review* (6th edn, Sweet & Maxwell, 2007)

Woolf, H. and others, *De Smith's Judicial Review* (7th edn, Sweet & Maxwell, 2013)

Woolley, A., 'The Metaphysical Court: *Dunsmuir v. New Brunswick* and the Standard of Review' (2008) 21 CJALP 259

Young, A.L., 'Professor SA de Smith' (1974) 33 CLJ 177 (obituary)
   'Professor SA de Smith' (1974) 37 MLR 241 (obituary)

'In Defence of Due Deference' (2009) 74 MLR 554

'Deference, Dialogue and the Search for Legitimacy' (2010) 30 OJLS 815

'Proportionality is Dead, Long Live Proportionality' in G. Huscroft, B.W. Miller and G. Webber (eds.), *Proportionality and the Rule of Law* (Cambridge University Press, 2014), 43

'Will You, Won't You, Will You Join in the Deference Dance' (2014) 34 OJLS 375.

INDEX

BOOKS IN THE SERIES